SOCIAL PROBLEMS

A Canadian Profile

SOCIAL PROBLEMS

A Canadian Profile

Edited by

RICHARD LASKIN, Ph.D.

*Assistant Professor
of Sociology*

*University of Alberta
Edmonton*

McGraw-Hill Company of Canada Limited
NEW YORK   TORONTO   LONDON

SOCIAL PROBLEMS
A Canadian Profile

Library of Congress Catalog
Card Number 64-24408

94574

Second Printing, 1965

Printed and Bound in Canada

PREFACE

We live in troubled times. This old cliché is often heard because it is always true. No problems are of more concern than *today's* problems. Happily, Canada is not now at war; nor are we foundering in a great economic depression or other national calamity. But Canada is part of a vastly complicated and rapidly changing social world, and she is not without troubles. This volume is an attempt to draw together, from a wealth of available literature, a profile of Canada's problems and, in doing so, to get to know our country better.

As we approach the centennial anniversary of our nation's confederation we find ourselves in an aura of self-examination and national stock-taking. A renewed interest in national unity (a flag, an anthem) and disunity (the separatist movement) are sufficient evidence of this. Let us take stock, then, of our major social problems, including separatism, and difficulties in various racial and ethnic group relations, work, population and immigration, family relations, health services, addictions, mental illness, sexual deviance, crime and delinquency. Information and opinions on various aspects of these subjects are presented, in this book, by almost seventy different authors. Their articles, mostly reprinted from a variety of sources (occasionally after careful revision by the author), with some written specially for this collection, have been organized and edited from the point of view of the discipline of sociology. The editor has never intentionally altered the meaning of the contributing authors, but he has, in every chapter, deleted sections from some articles, as well as most footnotes, in the belief that he has been improving the book by making space for a greater number of different articles.

The greatest disappointments, in assembling this volume, have come from the necessary decisions to omit many very worthwhile articles. Most of these have been included in the bibliographies which follow each chapter. The major criteria in the selection of material for inclusion have been that it be Canadian (or oriented toward Canada), that it be recent (although a few excellent older pieces are included), and that it be interesting. A general goal has been to achieve "balance", and, to the extent that it has been possible, each chapter following the introduction contains some factual material, some opinions; some "academic" material, some "lay"; some drawn from the professional literature, some from the popular.

The greatest joy, in preparing the book, has been evoked by the generous and encouraging responses to the letters sent to authors and publishers all over Canada (and in a few instances to the United States and England) requesting their permission to reproduce published material. To these people and organizations, all noted later in the book, I owe a great debt of gratitude. Special thanks are due to Dr. Hanns W. Lungstrass who undertook most of the editorial work for chapter six, and to Drs. Charles W. Hobart, Warren E. Kalbach, Arthur P. Jacoby, Robert J. Gibbins and James N. McCrorie, for the articles they wrote especially for this book. Gratitude must also be expressed to Dr. Robert L. James, formerly Head of the Department of Sociology at the University of Alberta, for permitting me a reduced teaching load so as to be able to work on this collection; to the University of Alberta General Research Committee for a grant to pay some of the expenses of preparation; to Douglas E. Smith, Dean of Arts at the University, for unlimited use of university photo-copying machinery; to Drs. Donald E. Wilmott and Henry Zentner for some very helpful comments on the first two articles; to Dr. Thomas L. Waugh of McGraw-Hill for the translation of one selection from its original French version; and to the following students who contributed in a variety of ways to make this book possible: Lorraine Bice, Linda Scharf, Serena L. Phillett, Cecile Baril and Ilse M. Laskin.

RICHARD LASKIN
University of Alberta
May 29, 1964

CONTENTS

v

chapter five

PROBLEMS OF ETHNIC GROUP RELATIONS · 163

vii

part one

INTRODUCTION

chapter one

THE NATURE OF SOCIAL PROBLEMS

1. *THE NATURE OF SOCIAL PROBLEMS: A CONCEPTUAL REVIEW*

Richard Laskin

This chapter attempts what may be called a brief review of the literature pertaining to an explanation of the phrase *social problems* as it is currently used by sociologists. So much has been written on the subject that it would be unreasonable to expect that we could cover it all. It shall be our purpose here to (1) introduce the subject, noting both divergencies in interpretation and degrees of concensus, and (2) explain the particular organization of this collection of readings.

In 1924 a text in sociology by Clarence Marsh Case offered the following definition of a social problem:

> . . . any social situation which attracts the attention of a considerable number of competent observers within a society, and appeals to them as calling for readjustment or remedy by social, *i.e.,* collective, action of some kind or other.[1]

He then proceeded to suggest the possibility of a classification of social problems on the basis of their "source" in the society. Included in this classification system would be those problems which are rooted in some

---

[1]In Lee, E.B. and Lee A.M., *Social Problems in America*, New York, Henry Holt and Company, 1958, pp. 7-8.

3

unfortunate aspect of the physical environment, those which are inherent in the nature or distribution of the population involved, some which result from "poor social organization" and those which evolve from a conflict of cultural values within the society. In Case's writing we find an attempt at definition and classification, plus a suggestion regarding causal theory. As such it is a good place to begin our survey.

Richard C. Fuller and Richard R. Myers, writing in an American sociological journal in 1941, contributed a "three-fold classification of social problems on the principle of different levels of relationship to the value-scheme."[2] The first problem level noted involves *physical* problems (floods, droughts, etc.). There should be common agreement regarding these conditions as problems to the society, but social values would not be involved in their causation. The second problem level involves *ameliorative* problems — situations about which there would again be concensus as to their undesirability but about which there would be some conflict of values regarding what might be the best solution. Illustrations would include crime and delinquency; the public agrees that criminality is a problem, but does not agree as to whether harsh punishment, more stringent laws, rehabilitative efforts, or something else would be the best corrective action. Finally Fuller and Myers consider the *moral* type of problem; for example, gambling, divorce or racial segregation. These are moral problems because there is not agreement or concensus as to the desirability or undesirability of these conditions.

The Fuller-Myers classification system does, of course, also act to define what is a social problem, and furthermore it suggests an agreement with Case that these problems (excepting the physical ones) are all basically functions of value conflicts in the culture. That is, if there were "complete homogeneity of social values" there would be no ameliorative or moral social problems.

With this background let us now proceed first to an examination of a number of other suggested definitions of social problems and then to a consideration of the major sociological approaches to the question of causation.

American publishing houses have produced literally dozens of books on the subject of social problems written by sociologists over the past several years. The definitions of social problems presented below have been selected from a few of these texts on the basis of brevity and clarity to show some of the variations in the criteria used in defining this concept. Some sociologists choose to discuss the meaning of social problems

---

[2]*Ibid.*, pp. 9-11.

but never get to a brief definitive statement. Others, it should be noted, simply go on to present data, illustrations and discussions of problem areas with little or no attempt to define their subject title at all.

In a text by Martin H. Neumeyer the following definition is offered:

> To state it briefly and simply, the concept 'social problems' involves at least three elements or considerations: (1) it implies an objective situation of social and personal disorganization; (2) a social value or system of values is believed by significant parts of the population to be endangered thereby; and (3) a realization that the situation requires appropriate social action.[3]

Note, in the above, the appearance of the following words or terms: *objective situation, social and personal disorganization, social values, significant parts of the population, danger,* and, *requires appropriate social action.* We shall look for these criteria in other definitions.

Paul B. Horton and Gerald R. Leslie offered, as a definition, the following: "A social problem is a condition affecting a significant number of people in ways considered undesirable, and about which it is felt something can be done through collective action."[4] They agree with Neumeyer with regard to the inclusion of such ideas as a significant number of people being affected, the realization or feeling that something could be done, and done through collective (hence social) action. In addition, we might be able to equate undesirable with dangerous. They do not make specific reference, as criteria, to objectivity of the situation or condition (there could perhaps be a subjective — that is, perceived — condition which is not objective in empirical terms), disorganization of society or persons, or involvement of social values. Perhaps they simply assume some of these, but do not include them in their list of identifying characteristics of a social problem. They do not add any items to Neumeyer's list.

In a text by Earl Raab and Gertrude Jaeger Selznick, a few years later, this brief definition is presented:

> A social problem exists (1) where prevailing relationships among people frustrate the important personal goals of a substantial number of people; or (2) where organized society appears to be seriously threatened by an inability to order relationships among people.[5]

In defining two different types of social problems, one "which seriously threatens society itself" and one which "impedes the *important* aspirations of *many* people", Raab and Selznick are, in effect, offering a system of

[3]Neumeyer, M.H., *Social Problems and the Changing Society,* New York, D. Van Nostrand Company, Inc., 1953, p. 21.

[4]Horton, P.B., and Leslie, G.R., *The Sociology of Social Problems,* New York, Appleton-Century-Crofts, Inc., 1955, p. 4.

[5]Raab, E. and Selznick, G.J., *Major Social Problems,* Evanston, Illinois, Row, Peterson and Company, 1959, p. 4.

classification as well. We note, in these definitions, some of the criteria which were included by other authors (*e.g.,* a substantial number of people affected, serious threat or danger) but also some ideas which the others had not included (*e.g.,* the idea of frustration of personal goals). Frustration, however, is a most important consideration in the definition of a social problem according to Harry C. Bredemeier and Jackson Toby. In their 1960 text they state that:

> A situation must fulfill *all three* of the following conditions in order for it to be considered a social problem in this book.
>
> 1. It involves people who are frustrated because they fail to meet the adequacy, security, worthiness, or gratification standards of their society — or who anticipate failing to meet these standards.
>
> 2. It involves their attempts to cope with this frustration and, in particular, the channeling of these attempts by the governing principles of . . . (their) society.
>
> 3. The form that this attempt to cope with frustration takes arouses widespread concern within the society.[6]

Finally, let us see what Robert A. Nisbet calls a social problem: " . . . breakdowns or deviations in social behavior, involving a considerable number of people, which are of serious concern to many members of the society in which the aberrations occur." Although he goes on to state that "At bottom social problems are problems of moral value",[7] the definition offered includes the seeds of two other theoretical approaches to the understanding of social problems; that is, *breakdowns in social behaviour* and *deviations in social behaviour*. We might interpret these as *social disorganization* and *deviant behaviour*, respectively, and note that the text in which this definition appears (a collection of essays, written by different people, on fourteen important social problem areas) is organized into two parts: one treats the problems of deviance; the other, the problems of disorganization. We shall have more to say on this particular arrangement of the various social problem areas presently.

Many more pages could be filled with differently phrased definitions of social problems found in various books, but this would surely add more to confusion than to clarification. It should be sufficiently obvious that, although there are a few criteria which are incorporated into almost every definition, there will probably never be a single, final, uniform definition of social problems. Why should this be so? Because, in the final analysis, social problems involve values, and values are at all times

---

[6]Bredemeier, H.C., and Toby, J., *Social Problems in America,* New York, John Wiley & Sons, Inc., 1960, pp. 145-146.

[7]Merton, R.K. and Nisbet, R.A., *Contemporary Social Problems,* New York, Harcourt, Brace & World, Inc., 1961, p. 11.

relative. *It is not the inherent nature of social problems,* per se, *which determines their definition, but the approach or frame of reference of the investigator.* Let us see, through the technique of hypothetical illustration, how this comes about. For simplicity the illustration shall be concerned with the idea of a personal problem instead of a social problem.

Let us suppose that Mr. X is standing in the middle of a road, looking downhill. A truck, of which he is not aware, was parked farther up the hill but had not been properly braked. It is now rolling rapidly and silently toward him. Does Mr. X have a problem?

Someone will immediately reply in the affirmative; anyone who is in danger of being run down by a truck most certainly has a problem. Another will argue that we are all in potential danger of being run down by a truck someday. In answer to this the first will suggest that the potential for Mr. X is particularly great, that he is in more serious trouble than is ordinarily the case, hence his problem. Now a third observer will rise with another objection. Mr. X does not *know* about the truck, is therefore not aware of the danger, and consequently *he* does not have a problem. Furthermore, if he did know about it, he could easily step aside and eliminate the danger.

Now we shall advance the situation slightly by allowing a few moments to pass. The truck is only inches from striking the unfortunate Mr. X. He would no longer be able to escape even if he were made aware of the danger. Now someone will argue that he does *not* have a problem for one of two reasons. The first is that he is still unaware of the situation, and awareness must be a characteristic of a problem. The second reason is that, if he were aware, there would be nothing that he could do about it, and another characteristic of a problem is the possibility of some ameliorative action. This, of course, fails to convince all of us, for some feel that surely if a man is about to be struck down by a truck he has a problem — that is, the objective situation is the essential characteristic. Apparently, it all depends upon how you look at it.

But we are not through yet. Let us introduce Mr. Y into the picture. He is now standing nearby on the sidewalk and observing Mr. X's predicament. If we arrange for Mr. Y. to shout a warning while the truck is still some distance away, some will argue that now Mr. X surely has a problem because he has been made aware of the truck, others that he has no problem because now he can easily escape the danger. If we have Mr. Y shout the warning when it is already too late for Mr. X to save himself, some will say that Mr. X's awareness of his fate defines the existence of a problem, others that his inability to take corrective action eliminates his predicament from the problem category.

And, finally, let us further examine the significance of the criteria of awareness and objective situation. Now we shall have Mr. X in the roadway and Mr. Y shouting to him of an imminent danger. But this time we shall make Mr. Y into a crude practical joker. He shouts, "Look out!" when in reality there is no truck or other danger in sight. Does Mr. X now have a problem? Using the criterion of an objective situation one would argue no, there being no real danger there could be no problem. Using awareness of a situation (whether it is "real" or not becomes irrelevant) as a criterion, Mr. X does have a problem because he *thinks* a truck is bearing down on him. The situation may not be real, but the perception he has is. And he will certainly *behave* as if he has a problem. The cynic might suggest that now it is Mr. Y who has the problem; that is, Mr. X may want to take a poke at his nose!

There is no simple conclusion to the story of Mr. X and Mr. Y. A problem, be it personal or social in nature, can be defined in terms of more than one frame of reference, and what appears to be a problem according to one is not that according to another. Consider divorce as an example. Many would argue that divorce is a serious problem in our society, and they would relate the serious consequences of our increasing divorce rate. Others, however, would maintain that divorce is not a problem, but indeed a solution; a solution to the personal problems of a marital mis-match, and a solution to the difficulties ensuing from the conflict between our traditional monogomous familial system, and our hectic, depersonalized, rapidly changing society.

It appears, therefore, that we might consider any of a number of stated definitions of a social problem, as long as we are willing to agree to the relative merit of the assumptions which underlie that particular frame of reference. But one point should be made quite clear. A good definition must be one which seeks to identify phenomena which are alike in that they are functions of the same causal factor or factors. It is for this reason that a definition which also serves to classify appears to have merit.

In addition to these formal definitions, another criterion has been used in the selection of materials for inclusion in this book. In a sense it serves the functions of a definition, but although it is operationally useful it is not necessarily sociological. In combing the Canadian literature of the last decade or so, many hundreds of articles, books and other pieces of literature were collected or noted. These were sorted into what appear to be the traditional problem areas: crime, race relations, family problems, mental disorders, drug addiction, and so forth. In some areas there accumulated a very large number of pieces, in others relatively few. The development of this book has necessarily been, to some extent, a function of the availability of material in print. Operationally, then, for the purposes of the book, we can suggest that the existence of material in the literature of the country, including books, pamphlets, periodicals and all other sources, constitutes a rough indicant of what are actually Canada's social problems. The problem could not be too severe if not much is written on it; it is likely to be severe if a great deal is written on it. This operational approach involves, however, at least two important weaknesses or limitations of which the author is fully aware. The first is that our method of research was limited by the particular collections in the available libraries and by the somewhat arbitrary decisions which were made as to where to search and what potential sources might be passed over in terms of the limitations of time. The second weakness is that some types of aberrant behaviour have a greater appeal to the general reader (*e.g.,* drug addiction or sex offences) and are likely to get more treatment in the literature for this reason. The selection of materials for inclusion in this volume has been done in such a way as to try to correct for these factors at least to some extent.

There are probably as many rationals for organizing the chapters of a book in social problems as there are authors or editors interested in attempting the task. The one which appeals most to this writer is essentially similar to that used by Merton and Nisbet in their previously cited text. It is based upon the acceptance of the fact that all social problems necessarily involve values (we omit strictly physical problems from consideration here) and that, beyond this, they can properly be divided into two categories in terms of whether they are basically a function of societal disorganization or of individual deviance. The latter might include deviance due to personality disorganization (*e.g.,* mental illness) or due to individual reactions to given social situations (*e.g.,* delinquency).

Some social problems texts attempt to explain just about every kind of problem in terms of a series of theoretical approaches; for example, Horton and Leslie apply the approaches of social disorganization, personal deviation *and* value conflict to more than a dozen different problem areas.[8] Others commit themselves to one theoretical frame of reference and analyze only those social problems to which they believe it applies. Prominent examples of books committed to the social disorganization

---

[8]*op. cit.*

approach are ones by Robert E. L. Faris[9] and by Mabel A. Elliott and Francis E. Merrill.[10]

A word about the social disorganization theory or approach. The concept was first presented in 1927 by two important pioneers in sociology, William I. Thomas and Florian Znaniecki. They defined social disorganization briefly as "a decrease of the influence of existing social rules of behavior upon individual members of the group." Individual disorganization was defined as "a decrease of the individual's ability to organize his whole life for the efficient, progressive and continuous realization of his fundamental interests."[11] The two concepts were presented as entirely distinct and not as dependent upon or coextensive with one another. These definitions have been refined and altered to some extent by subsequent writers, but the basic meaning of disorganization theory has not changed significantly. It remains one of the more important theoretical explanations of social problems.[12]

Finally, there is at least one important American sociologist who takes exception to the theory of social disorganization and presents his treatment of social problems in a book which is committed to a theory of deviant behaviour. Deviant behaviour, as Marshall B. Clinard uses the term, does not refer to "deviations from norms which are tolerated or which provoke only mild disapproval" but only to "those situations in which behavior is in a disapproved direction, and of sufficient degree to exceed the tolerance limit of the community."[13] In focusing on patterns of social deviation Clinard eschews the concept of disorganization entirely. In stating his objections he argues that social disorganization is too vague and subjective a concept, that it assumes the pre-existence of a state of organization which cannot be proven, that it carries the connotation of badness, which is often an unreasonable value judgment, that emphasis should not be put on the relatively small degree of so-called disorganization when the society is, essentially, a highly organized entity

---

[9]Faris, R.E.L., *Social Disorganization*, New York, The Ronald Press Co., 1955.

[10]Elliott, M.A. and Merrill, F.E., *Social Disorganization*, New York, Harper & Brothers, 1950.

[11]Lee and Lee, *op. cit.*, p. 17.

[12]If the reader feels that an understanding of the concept of *social organization* is desirable at this point he is referred to an excellent little book by Scott A. Greer on that subject. At the conclusion of a discussion of its definition that runs for over three pages he states that: "Organizations . . . set limits on individual behavior and direct it into channels designed for the functioning of the total group; and the individual's behavior is frequently highly predictable on these grounds alone." (Greer, S.A., *Social Organization*, New York, Random House, 1955, p. 9.)

[13]Clinard, M.B., *Sociology of Deviant Behavior*, New York, Holt, Rinehart and Winston, Inc., rev. ed., 1963, p. 22.

accomplishing many of its major goals, that what appears to be disorganization may only be the competition of highly organized but different norm systems, and, finally, that variations in the society may tend to strengthen rather than weaken (disorganize) it. These points, taken one by one and argued from both points of view, would greatly facilitate understanding of these divergent frames of reference.

The present writer would simply like to conclude that (1) he feels that a book such as this one should probably be organized in terms of pertinent sociological theory rather than some other criterion such as degree of severity of the problem, (2) he finds confusing and unsatisfactory the so-called eclectic approach which submits each problem area to a number of alternative theoretical positions, and (3) he finds considerable merit in both the social disorganization and the deviant behaviour approaches, *when each is focused only upon those problems which seem to derive from it.* Therefore the organization of this book follows, with some modifications, the lead set by Merton and Nisbet[14] and collects into Part Two and Part Three respectively those social problems which might be best understood through the social disorganization approach and those which might be best understood in terms of personal disorganization and individual deviance.

SELECTED BIBLIOGRAPHY

Bernard, J., *Social Problems at Midcentury,* New York, The Dryden Press, 1957.

Bloch, H. A., *Disorganization: Personal and Social,* New York, Alfred A. Knopf, Inc., 1952.

Bredemeier, H. C. and Toby, J., *Social Problems in America,* New York, John Wiley & Sons, Inc., 1960.

Clinard, M. B., *Sociology of Deviant Behavior,* New York, Holt, Rinehart and Winston, Inc., rev. ed., 1963.

Faris, R. E. L., *Social Disorganization,* New York, The Ronald Press Company, 1955.

Horton, P. B., and Leslie, G. R. *The Sociology of Social Problems,* New York, Appleton-Century-Crofts, Inc., 1955.

Lee, E. B., and Lee, A. M., (Editors), *Social Problems in America,* New York, Henry Holt and Company, 1955. (Especially Part I.)

---

[14]*op. cit.*

Merton, R. K., and Nisbet, R. A., (Editors), *Contemporary Social Problems,* New York, Harcourt, Brace, and World, Inc., 1961.

Neumeyer, M. H. *Social Problems and the Changing Society,* New York, D. Van Nostrand Company, Inc., 1953.

Raab, E., and Selznick, G. J., *Major Social Problems,* Evanston, Illinois, Row, Peterson and Company, 1959.

chapter two

CANADA AS A SOCIETY:
ITS IDENTITY AND INTERNAL UNITY

Having discussed the nature of social problems, we now turn to a consideration of Canada as a society. In the first article in this chapter some considerations of an academic nature (for example, the definition of the term "society")
are followed by some observations on the nature of the Canadian nation
state in relation to its fellow nations. Canadian nationalism is seen as being
of a unique character, and some similarities and differences between the
Canadian and American nations are explored.

The concluding pages of W. L. Morton's book, *The Canadian Identity*,
make up the next article, under the title of "The Character of Canadian
Nationality." It is Dr. Morton's contention that the relevance of Canadian
history and the significance of its search for identity and survival lie in the
fact that it has successfully "preserved and confirmed the essentials of the
greatest of civilizations in the grimmest of environments."

Dennis Wrong contributes a "background for understanding" the differences and similarities of American and Canadian cultures. After glancing
over some of the geographic, economic, historical and other highlights of
both countries, a later portion from his book, *American and Canadian Viewpoints*, discusses attitudes toward ethnic minority groups in both countries.
In this section Wrong treats, for example, differing attitudes of French- and
English-speaking Canadians toward new immigrants and their assimilation
problems. The French-English differential in Canada is then examined from
the anthropological point of view in an article by A. G. Bailey. Here Bailey

13

contributes to the development of the following chapter on separatism by pointing out that there is no significant "racial" basis for the observed cultural differences. In doing so he clears the air for an examination of this important Canadian social problem on purely social, cultural, historical and political grounds, where it rightly belongs.

2. CANADA AS A SOCIETY: SOME OBSERVATIONS

Richard Laskin

To the sociologist the term "society" is a most important one. Although it is variously defined by different writers, there remains a general agreement on its meaning and a concensus that it is one of the basic units of sociological analysis. It represents one end-point on a continuum of social organization. On the other end of the continuum is the individual. In between there are a great many different organizational entities like the family, the voluntary group, the local community and the bureaucratic organization. One sociology text defines society as "a relatively self-sufficient unit that consists at any one time of a number of persons carrying on a common, interdependent life that has continuity through successive generations."[1] Another devotes a few pages to a discussion of four basic "characteristics of societies," including "(1) definite territory, (2) sexual reproduction, (3) comprehensive culture, and (4) independence."[2] For the most part sociology, or at least what might be called descriptive sociology, involves a study of the operations of that independent social system referred to as the society, or of any of the dependent sub-systems within a society, and almost always the society in question is the one in which the sociologist lives.

Because of the way in which the peoples of the world are grouped and organized, it might be suggested that the term society can roughly

---

[1]Lundberg, G.A., Schrag, C.C. and Larsen, O.N., *Sociology,* New York, Harper & Row, 1963, p. 766.

[2]Johnson, H.M., *Sociology: A Systematic Introduction,* New York, Harcourt, Brace and Company, 1960, pp. 9-13.

be equated to the modern nation state. That is, these states are essentially independent, culturally whole and territorially defined entities. So we often refer to the American society, the Russian society, and so forth. Of course, we sometimes group more broadly and speak of Western society as compared to Eastern society. At the other extreme, we might not feel correct in referring to one of the very small nations of the world as a society *per se,* although the residents of that land might think it quite fitting. The fact of their political independence, even if it is only relative independence, establishes them as nations and therefore, perhaps, societies.

Canadians, because of their proximity and cultural similarity to their more powerful neighbour to the south are understandably very concerned with their societal and national status and identity. Is this a society, or a part of the larger "American" society? The general feeling in Canada seems to be that the latter condition would be most unfortunate. The very subject of this book implies acceptance of the idea of Canada as a society.

On the one hand it might be argued that the sociologist is, or at least should be, essentially interested in the nature of social systems generally and that his data may be drawn from the workings of any society. Certainly modern sociologists do take a considerable interest in research materials and other literature from foreign sources. On the other hand, a strong case can be made to the effect that the analysis of his own society is the first task of the social scientist and that his theories and hypotheses should first be tested at home. He should *then,* perhaps, seek to compare his conclusions with those of researchers in other lands. Accordingly, let us consider first what is the nature of this Canadian society.

In a recent collection of readings entitled *Canadian Society,* Kaspar D. Naegele, one of the editors and a well-known Canadian sociologist, presents a lengthy introductory essay called "Canadian Society: Some Reflections." This essay proceeds from two points of departure: one is "some immediately known and visible facts that lie, as it were, in the foreground"[3]; the other is the sociological approach developed by the German sociologist, Max Weber. It is worth noting, here, the following lines from Naegele's concluding paragraph:

> To conclude this essay, this might be said: nothing is more absurd than nationalism in science, but the comprehension of national societies

---

[3] Blishen, B.R., Jones, F.E., Naegele, K.D. and Porter, J., (Eds.), *Canadian Society,* Toronto, The Macmillan Company of Canada Limited, 1961, p. 1.

is not absurd — though it may be difficult. In a measure the discovery of Canadian society, or at least its systematic disclosure through the cumulative reciprocities of distributed and individual work, will, in the first place, have to be the burden and promise of Canadian sociologists themselves. Such an enterprise is not the same as the effort to build a Canadian, as distinct from a British, German, or American, sociology. Surely the most promising start for an articulate and reliable account of Canadian society is to see it at once as yet another modern industrial society and yet as unique.[4]

In the remainder of this article I shall endeavour to discuss Canada, as a society, from a different point in view. My purpose shall be a defend or justify a collection of readings on Canadian social problems *per se*. Although this would seem to require the maximization of evidence of Canada as a distinct society, nevertheless the essential conclusion that will be drawn will not emphasize this point. First, the degree to which Canadian society overlaps with others will be noted. Second, evidence of Canada's existence as a "multi-society" itself (politically combining more than one societal entity) will be given.

Let us consider some of the characteristics of Canadian society which mark it as a more or less distinct societal system. Geographically Canada is clearly defined by international boundaries. Although this would seem to satisfy the "definition" of a society there are some qualifications to be noted. To the extent that these boundaries have been determined by significant physical considerations (oceans, lakes, the arctic zone), its societal status is reinforced. But to the extent that the boundaries are "artificially" drawn, international culture sharing and societal blending are ecologically encouraged.[5] Furthermore, there exist a number of geographic conditions within Canada's boundaries (mountain ranges, bush country) which tend to inhibit the flow of social and cultural communication. Finally, some areas of the country (British Columbia, Quebec, the Maritimes) have been populated by quite different migration flows, coming from different sources, or occurring at different times, or both. Hence the traditions from which the modern culture has derived vary, and this suggests at least sub-societal variations within the nation. The most obvious illustration, of course, is what we refer to as French Canada. The issue of separatism, reflecting the views of some French-Canadians, illustrates one current Canadian social problem which is the concern of the third chapter of this book. Other illustrations are found in the

---

[4]*Ibid.*, p. 53.
[5]Human ecology is "primarily concerned with the interrelations between culture and its physical habitat." Lundberg, *op. cit.*, p. 762.

problems which inhere in Canada's unique geographical distribution of population, strung out mainly along a thin strip of land some 4,000 miles long but only a few hundred miles wide.

Some of the other characteristics which are notably Canadian include its avowed system of official bilingualism and its peculiar political perplexity which includes some provinces which strongly back one party locally, then turn to another for their federal representatives. But what would perhaps be rated highest on this list is the amazingly ambivalent attitude which Canadians seem to have regarding their American neighbour. Canadians seem to both love and hate, admire yet disparage, criticize but still follow the lead of the American society. Elaboration of this important point will be presented below.

The more important characteristics which Canada shares with other Western nations are quite obvious, and we need only offer a few examples here. These would include the overwhelming Christian majority in population, an essentially democratic tradition and design, an urban and industrial trend, and the competitive, materialistic, semi-capitalism which is overlayed (or perhaps underlayed) with a broad social welfare orientation.

That the development of Canada owes much to the country's place in the Commonwealth and to its British heritage goes without saying. Equally obvious is the influence of the French culture, on one segment of the population at least, and to a lesser extent the contributions of other ethnic groups. Yet the suggestion that Canada still exists as a part of any European society is no longer acceptable. Canada exists, both geographically and culturally, in North America. The question now is its place on this continent.

Let us first argue that Canada and the United States are of the same society; that all of the trappings of independent nationhood are merely part of a facade or international masquerade. We might list as evidence the generally common use of the English language, the similarity of the religious distributions and, without going into all of the details, the generally common cultural content which is sufficiently obvious to anyone who has travelled extensively in both countries. But the alternative argument — that Canada and the United States are different and distinct societies — is supportable by an equal number of good points, including Canada's closer relationship to both its British and French origins, political structures which differ significantly both in terms of the party systems and in terms of the official organization of government, and so forth. Most important here, perhaps, are the facts that *Canadians want to feel inde-*

pendent and that Americans don't consider Canada to be a part of their milieu.

Although we have decided to treat Canada as a society (for the purposes of this book) on the basis of our operational equation of the society and the nation state, we find it very difficult to satisfy ourselves that this is the most meaningful decision to make, or that its alternative is, in fact, any better. Perhaps the problem lies in the phrasing of the question; perhaps it is not legitimate to postulate Canada and the United States as whole and inclusive cultural entities, and to inquire into their generalized relationship to one another. Perhaps it is misleading to represent *either* as simply "a society" when, in fact, each nation is a complex of some quite different sub-cultural or sub-societal parts. Then let us consider each nation *regionally*, and let us consider the varied relationships of regions, one to another. Do we see within Canada's boundaries or between different areas of the United States cultural variations as great as or greater than those we see across the international border?

Our data will be subjective — the impressions of the observer and of the traveller — yet not without significance. It seems that we can locate a number of illustrations where there appears to be greater cultural similarity in the north-south direction across the border than in the east-west direction across each country. Does not the industrially developed urban area of Southern Ontario bear more cultural resemblance to the industrial Eastern United States (New York, Pennsylvania, Ohio) than to much of the rest of Canada? Does not a city like Winnipeg compare better with the cities of the North Central states than with the Maritime or French-Canadian cities? Is not the affinity between the American and Canadian prairie regions also striking, as is the degree of cultural sharing that occurs on the West Coast (admittedly amid some apparent local differentiations)?

It appears that in Canada we could hypothesize the existence of at least six somewhat distinct "regions" or "sub-societal areas": the Maritime Provinces, Quebec (especially French-Quebec), Ontario, the Prairie Provinces, British Columbia, and the Territories. A larger number can be postulated for the United States including, for example, the New England States, the industrial North-East, the "deep" South, the Middle-West, the South-West, the Prairie States, the Pacific Coast, and so forth. We need not agree as to the specific regional divisions — I have not stated any criteria but one's impressions — but the general conclusion remains obvious. Both nations are regionally segmented in such a way that they include some more or less distinct sub-cultural areas. There are some regions in each country which are very like regions (usually directly north and south of one another) in the other country. And each country includes some areas which are like no other on the continent (e.g. the deep South, French Canada). On the one hand, then, we have the basis to conclude that there exists on this continent, north of the Rio Grande, a large, heterogeneous, generally English-speaking, Christian-based, democratically oriented, industrial social system; a society politically organized into a large number of different states, provinces and territories. On the other hand, should we choose to consider as salient a somewhat arbitrary international border bisecting the continent in an east-west direction, roughly in the area of the Great Lakes, then we can conceive of two separable entities, *each bearing all of those characteristics noted above,* but organized into relatively autonomous social structures.

Considering what has been said, the outside observer might be quite surprised at all of the concern with "independence" and the Canadian national identity. There *is* a great concern with the Canadian identity, however, but the concern is almost entirely one-sided. Canadians discuss and argue the possibility of "merger" with the United States and the question of *de facto* identity without official political merger, but the idea rarely occurs to Americans. *Canada rarely occurs to Americans,* but the United States is very often in the minds of Canadians. Now, perhaps, we have come to the heart of the problem. Canadians probably know almost as much as Americans do about the United States — its history, its geography, its foreign policy, its current events. They follow American sporting events, cheer American heroes, read American books and magazines, and follow American trends, fads and fashions. But most Americans are abominably ignorant of Canada; they are startled when they "discover" it, startled at its great modern cities, its very American character — and only amused at the small differences like differently coloured (colored?) money and those funny electric plugs hanging from the grills of cars.

One further observation: Americans are generally secure in the belief that they live in "the greatest country in the world". They display, as do the Russians, French, Italians and many others, a fierce positive ethnocentric pride. We call this nationalism. Canadians have a strong nationalism as well. But the important difference is, it seems to me, that Canadian nationalism is not based upon what Canadians *are* but upon what they *are not.* They are not Americans! And they are not British either! In a 1957 McGill University student theatrical production entitled *My Fur Lady* this point was made quite clear. A fictional foreign princess was in Canada seeking to learn what Canadian society was like. The following is the text of an exchange between herself and her Canadian guide.

Princess (*singing*): " . . . Look, you claim to be a national entity. . . . I want to see your Canadian identity. . . . I want to be shocked by the national morality and come to grips with Canadian mentality."

Guide (*speaking*): "But don't you see: the trouble with Canadians is they spend half their time convincing the Americans they're not British, the other half convincing the British they're not Americans, which leaves them no time to be themselves."[9]

Canadians enjoy what may be called a "negative nationalism". Whereas other nationals talk about what they are, Canadians pride themselves in what they are not. And then, of course, there is a great difference between precept and practice.

It is this negative nationalism which is, I think, the moving force behind the demand for a "real" Canadians identity — a flag, a national anthem, an independent foreign policy and so forth. This force is felt in government, in politics, in the economic system, and in most other facets of Canadian life. It is, perhaps, the most striking and differentiating aspect of the "Canadian society"!

The matter is not, of course, quite so simple as may be implied by this brief presentation. In the first place this impressionistic hypothesis has been presented forcefully, as a challenge to the reader. It is now open for discussion and for objective research. In the second place no attempt has been made here to deal with the intriguing development of the modern Canadian national situation. That chore is left to the historians. But make no mistake about the fact that we are dealing here with a unique social phenomenon, a condition which is not quite like any other in the world. While some of the problems Canadian society faces are very similar to those experienced in other countries, others are peculiar to Canada. Through the examination of a wide range of these problems we can perhaps gain a greater insight into the nation and its people.

---

[9]Excerpts taken from recording number MRS-LPM-5 produced by the McGill Recording Service, 3851 University Street, Montreal, for the Graduates' Society of McGill University and Quince Productions, June 12, 1957.

3. THE CHARACTER OF CANADIAN NATIONALITY*

W. L. Morton†

Canada has never been a country royalist in sentiment any more than Canadian society has remained formally hierarchical in structure. Canadian manners have always tended to be simple, and Canadian society has steadily become a society of social equals. But for many reasons it has been a monarchical country, and not a country of the social compact like its great neighbour. The reasons for this have been historic rather than sentimental. Allegiance means that the law and the state have an objective reality embodied in the succession of persons designated by Parliament and hereditary right. They do not rest on contemporary assent, although the policies and acts of government do. In Canada therefore government possesses an objective life of its own. It moves in all its parts at popular impulse, but if there were no impulse, it would still move. In the United States government is subjective. It is designed to move on popular impulse, and if there is no impulse, the movement soon flags and falters. The republican government, massive as are its institutions, historic as is its momentum, in a very real sense rests upon assent periodically renewed. Such a government requires as basis a society of great intrinsic unity and conformity in which a consensus works to a common end. In Canada, a country of economic hazard, external dependence, and plural culture, only the objective reality of a monarchy and the permanent force of monarchical institutions could form the centre and pivot of unity. Allegiance was a social and political necessity of national existence and prevailed over the manifest and insistent attraction of republican institutions and republican liberty.

Not life, liberty, and the pursuit of happiness, but peace, order, and good government are what the national government of Canada guarantees. Under these, it is assumed, life, liberty, and happiness may be achieved, but by each according to his taste. For the society of allegiance admits of a diversity the society of compact does not, and one of the blessings of Canadian life is that there is no Canadian way of life, much less two, but a unity under the Crown admitting of a thousand diversities.

*From "The Relevance of Canadian History," *Report of the Canadian Historical Association*, Ottawa, 1960. Later reprinted in *The Canadian Identity*, Toronto, University of Toronto Press, 1961.

†Dr. Morton is Professor of Canadian History and Head of the Department of History at the University of Manitoba, Winnipeg.

For this reason it is not a matter of political concern that Canada has two major cultures and many smaller ones. It would be foolish to deny that the dual culture is one of history's many harsh gifts to Canada, that the duality arose from the ordeal of conquest and suppression and that it has given rise to friction and to weakness. But it is manifest that it is a gift which admits of transmutation into something rich and strange, into a political order as liberal as those which Lord Acton, by way of example, thought approached nearest the ideal. The transmutation can be wrought when the two cultures are seen as variations on a common experience of the land and history of Canada, and of the common allegiance in law and spirit of the traditions and the Crown of that land.

That common experience has created a common psychology, the psychology of endurance and survival. Canadian experience teaches two clear lessons. One is that the only real victories are the victories over defeat. We have been beaten many times, defeat has been our national portion in America, but we survive and we go on in strength. And our experience teaches also that what is important is not to have triumphed, but to have endured. The pride of victory passes, but a people may survive and have its way if it abides by the traditions which have fostered its growth and clarified its purpose.

The common experience extends also to the Canadian achievement of the secret of Commonwealth, that free association in self-government is a bond of union which may yet outlast the controls and authority of empires, however strong. That achievement was the work of Canadians of both the major stocks, it is the outward expression of our domestic institutions, and its spirit informs Canadians of all other origins with an equal pride in free institutions elaborated by the Canadian political genius. We must bring to the working out of the American alliance the same persistence in freedom and the same stubborn ingenuity, recognizing always that this special relationship with the United States is different in kind from the historic associations of Canada and can in no sense take their place.

In the end, that common experience extends to a common affirmation of moral purpose, the purpose which makes Canadian history relevant to universal history. Canadians, if one may judge by their history, believe that society cannot live by the state alone. Society has its own autonomous life, which is sustained by sources which may enrich the life of the state, but over which the state has neither authority nor control. These sources are religious or moral, and flow into society only through persons. The personality of the individual citizen, then, is the object of the justice the state exists to provide and of the welfare society exists to ensure. The individual thus possesses the ultimate autonomy, since he is the end to which both state and society are means. But that autonomy carries with it a sovereign obligation to respect and safeguard the autonomy of his fellows, primarily by manners, which are the dealings of man with man, and secondarily through the social and political order. So reciprocal and delicate a complex of justice, welfare, and good manners may function only in an organic unity of state, society, and individual. It was such a unity of king, church, and people Canadians, both French and English, inherited from their remoter past and have elaborated in their history as a monarchical and democratic nation.

The preservation of such a national society is not the unique mission of Canada, but it is the central fact of Canadian history that it has been preserved and elaborated by Canadians in one of the largest, harshest, and most intimidating countries on earth. Canada, that is, has preserved and confirmed the essentials of the greatest of civilizations in the grimmest of environments. It is an accomplishment worthy of a better end than absorption in another and an alien society, however friendly and however strong in its own ideals. In that accomplishment and its continuance lies the relevance of Canadian history.

4. BACKGROUND FOR UNDERSTANDING*

Dennis Wrong†

The bulk of the North American Continent is divided into two sovereign nations of continental expanse — the United States of America and Canada. Both were originally colonies of European nations and both ultimately gained complete political independence from their mother countries. The slow and gradual evolution of Canada from the status of first a French and then a British colony to full-fledged nationhood — a process that has been completed only in the present century — is often

*From *American and Canadian Viewpoints,* Washington, D.C., American Council on Education, 1955.
†Dr. Wrong, a Canadian now resident in the U.S.A., is Professor of Sociology at New York University and Editor of the journal *Social Research.*

overlooked by Americans, who won their political independence in the eighteenth century by a far more abrupt and violent rupture with the mother country. The United States is a republic and Canada a democratic monarchy retaining a formal tie to the British Crown, but both are self-governing nations.

The histories of Canada and the United States have other outstanding features in common. Each expanded its borders to include the western part of the continent and eventually incorporated its western territories into a federal government structure. The resourcefulness and mobility demanded by life on the frontier have left their mark on the institutions of both countries. The westward expansion of the United States precipitated a conflict between the Southern states and the Northern states over the status of chattel slavery in the new Western territories, which eventually led to the Civil War of 1861-65. Canada has been spared the experience of civil war, though her national institutions have had to be accommodated to the presence within her borders of two ethnic groups differing in language, religion, and culture, and a talent for compromise has often been required to prevent conflict between them.

Both nations possess complex, highly diversified social structures, containing the internal occupational and socioeconomic class divisions typical of mature industrial economies. Both rank among the most urbanized nations of the world with more than half of their populations living in cities and towns. Mass immigration from Europe in the late nineteenth and early twentieth centuries increased the diversity of their populations and created the problem of assimilating the immigrants. Since World War II there has been a renewed influx of European immigrants into Canada.

French-speaking Canadians have a higher birth rate than any other ethnic group of comparable size on the North American Continent, thus raising the general level of Canadian fertility. Both Canada and the United States, however, are presently in the same broad stage of population growth: their birth rates and death rates have declined rapidly since the beginning of the century, although in the past decade the decline has been reversed by a surprising resurgence of fertility in both countries. The pattern of internal group differences in fertility and mortality is also much the same in the two countries. From the standpoint of economic and demographic analysis the continent can virtually be treated as a unit, ignoring the existence of the boundary line along the forty-second parallel. Although the geographic, economic, and historical similarities between the United States and Canada have been generally recognized and the differences in their systems of government and of legal administration have been thoroughly analyzed by many scholars, few attempts have been made to discuss systematically the similarities and differences in the major values, ideals, and attitudes of Americans and Canadians. Very often these subjective dimensions of conduct have been dealt with only on the level of superficial generalizations about "national character." Americans, including even many professional scholars, are frequently far from well informed about Canadians and tend to regard them either as radically different from themselves, resembling in most particulars the English, or as altogether American in all but name. Canadians, on the other hand, are apt to take for granted many of the similarities between themselves and Americans, and anxious to assert their own national distinctiveness, they often overemphasize and exaggerate the respects in which they differ from citizens of the United States.

The purpose of this essay is to outline in a brief and tentative manner the similarities and differences in the outlooks of Canadians and Americans with respect to the major areas of social life. Because of the uniqueness of the way of life of French-speaking Canadians, it is necessary to treat them separately, viewing them as a homogeneous nationality group with a culture of their own. Thus, in effect, the ideals and attitudes of three distinct nationality groups — Americans, English-speaking Canadians, and French-speaking Canadians — are compared and contrasted. Canada is a binational state similar to such European countries as Belgium and Czechoslovakia. Roughly one-third of the Canadian population is French-speaking.

French-speaking Canadians are not, as many Americans believe, a "minority group" faced with the prospect of being "assimilated" by the majority like immigrant groups of European origin, but are equal partners with English-speaking Canadians in the Canadian confederation. The Canadian Constitution provides French-speaking Canadians with guarantees that their language shall share official status with English and gives them the right to maintain a state-supported Roman Catholic school system. These rights were first guaranteed to the French in Canada by the Quebec Act of 1774 following the British conquest, and thus antedate the formation of the Canadian nation in 1867 by nearly a century. In conjunction with French-speaking Canadian determination to preserve their cultural distinctiveness, they present formidable barriers to assimilation, which, indeed, has not been a real possibility at any time in Canadian history.

French-speaking Canadians are a good deal more culturally homogeneous than either Americans or English-speaking Canadians. In fact, to speak of an outlook common to all Americans or all English-speaking Canadians appears to deny the very considerable diversity — religious, ethnic, regional, educational, socio-economic, and even linguistic — which exists *within* each of these groups, quite apart from the differences *between* them. How much do a Negro sharecropper in Alabama and a Wall Street banker have in common, or a Newfoundland fisherman in an outport village and a university professor in Toronto or Montreal? Even in French-speaking Canada, where the bond of ethnic solidarity created by a shared language and religion is a strong one, there are great differences in the ways of life of, say, an urban upper-class Montrealer and a Gaspé farmer or lumberjack. And when one recalls the Mexican-Americans of the Southwest, or the continuing immigration of Spanish-speaking Puerto Ricans to eastern American cities, and the Doukhobor and Hutterite communities in western Canada, the diversity of cultures existing within the borders of each country is even more striking.

There are groups on opposite sides of the border resembling one another more closely in cultural outlook than they resemble compatriots on the same side of the border. The several million French-speaking Canadian immigrants who now reside in the United States — the majority in the New England area — are a particularly striking instance of this. Catholics on both sides of the border obviously share many attitudes stemming from their common religious affiliation which differentiate them from their Protestant and Jewish neighbors to whom the same applies. Some of the attitudes attributed in this study to French-speaking Canadians are not peculiar to them but are shared by English- or Spanish-speaking Catholics in Canada and the United States, although other features of the French-speaking Canadian outlook reflect the unique nuances of their particular variant of Catholic culture.

Yet in spite of the great differences within each of the three nationality groups, one can still discern some values that are shared by the great majority in each group — certain ideals and attitudes which appear to constitute the "core values" on which group solidarity is based.

Most of the values enumerated below are especially characteristic of the urban middle class in both countries, with the exception of those attributed to French-speaking Canada where the traditional outlook of an earlier, less urbanized social order continues to have vitality. The justification for selecting urban middle-class values to represent the national norm is that, although they are far from dominant in the lives of many rural, working-class, and ethnic minority groups, they nevertheless represent a way of life that is usually aspired to by these groups in both the United States and English-speaking Canada. A common level of aspiration shared by the vast majority of citizens is, indeed, one of the main features distinguishing the North American democracies from European countries where class and rural-urban divisions are more sharply drawn and reflect clear-cut differences in modes of life. It is noteworthy that the prevailing images of American and Canadian life presented by the mass media reflect urban middle-class values and styles of living.

In considering both the *similarities* and the *differences* between Americans and Canadians, too much attention perhaps has been given in this essay to the differences, while the similarities have not been sufficiently stressed. North American civilization, however novel many of its contributions to world history may have been, is simply a variant of the civilization of the West now dispersed over much of the earth. Many of the common elements in the cultures of the three North American nationalities are therefore shared with other Western peoples in the British Isles, Europe, and the territories overseas that have been settled by Europeans. To mention a few of these shared values: Americans and English-speaking and French-speaking Canadians believe, like other Western peoples, in a monogamous family system, a monotheistic religion, and in an ethic of human brotherhood derived from the Judaeo-Christian religious tradition. Since these ideals — shared as they have been by all Western peoples past and present — are assumed by the present study, certain of the more basic though less salient resemblances between Americans and English-speaking and French-speaking Canadians are obscured.

As the very organization of the text which follows may appear to do the thing we do not wish to do — that is, emphasize differences more than similarities — perhaps a brief explanation of the organization might be helpful. In each of the areas of social life that are considered, the ideals and attitudes of Americans are described first. When these are attributable also to English-speaking Canadians, this is indicated briefly and then variations in their emphasis and phrasing in Canada are discussed at greater length, often perhaps leaving the impression that the differences, however slight, are in some way of greater significance than the underlying similarities. The French-speaking Canadians, many of whose dominant values are essentially those of Europe before the Reformation, the Enlightenment, and the industrial revolution, represent a unique cultural strain within Western civilization. So there is a strong inclination to draw a sharp contrast between their culture and that of the civilization surrounding them — as, in fact, many French Canadians themselves are inclined to do. The procedure followed here is to characterize at the outset their distinctive values and then to note the social changes that are transforming their traditional way of life into something more closely resembling that of the rest of North America.

• • •

ATTITUDES TOWARD ETHNIC MINORITY GROUPS

One of the most popular images of the United States has been that of the melting pot, an image concisely expressing American attitudes toward the many immigrant groups who have brought with them to the New World the diverse cultural heritages of their countries of origin. The melting-pot concept symbolizes the democratic conviction that no one should be disqualified from full participation in American life on grounds of ethnic status or origin. But it implies also the necessity of "melting," of becoming Americanized, and this carries the suggestion that ethnic differences are undesirable and efforts to maintain them un-American.

The absence of a fully developed sense of Canadian nationality has retarded the application of the melting-pot concept to the Canadian scene. As A. R. M. Lower has noted, " 'New Canadians' in Canada have had little chance of becoming 'Canadians' in the same sense that they would become American in the United States. In that country distinctions of origin are, in theory at least, kept to a minimum; in Canada they are practically and in certain ways legally maintained."

In public discussions of New Canadians the emphasis tends to be on the contributions which the diverse cultural heritages they bring with them will make to Canadian life rather than, as is commonly the case in the United States, on their expectations of life in the New World. New Canadians have been encouraged to maintain many of their distinctive folk traditions, and their songs, dress, and folklore are often publicized as indications of the richness and diversity of Canadian life — an approach to ethnic differences that is much less common in the United States where retaining Old World habits has often been stigmatized as refusal to become good Americans or to appreciate adequately the superiority of the "American way of life."

Other reasons in addition to the lack of a clear-cut Canadian nationality explain the greater acceptance in Canada of a "cultural pluralist" approach to ethnic minority groups: Canada is a binational state uniting two culturally divergent peoples under a single system of government, a circumstance which obviously makes it impossible to advance a single uniform conception of the "Canadian way of life" for immigrants to emulate; also, in western Canada some ethnic communities have remained geographically and sometimes occupationally segregated from the native-born population, reproducing in this respect the pattern of settlement and of consequent ethnic particularism of many of the major groups making up the "old immigration" to the United States before the First World War.

In addition to appreciation of cultural diversity, however, there also appears to be a marked sense of social distance between those of British origin and the foreign-born or even second- and third-generation immigrants. Many forms of social discrimination have persisted in Canada which in the United States, although they survive there too, have increasingly been condemned as undemocratic. In the United States highly vocal campaigns against prejudice and discrimination have tended to drive expressions of prejudice underground or into extremist "lunatic fringe" forms of political protest, whereas in Canada genteel expressions of prejudice and the practice of social discrimination appear to be more widely accepted as a matter of course, at least tacitly if not openly. A good many observers, for example, have reported their impression that anti-Semitism is both more widespread and more open in Canadian than in American life. Yet, as in the United States, even the mildest forms of prejudice have increasingly come under attack. In political campaigns in both countries (with the exception of the American South) a covert appeal to prejudice is likely to bring down such a storm of criticism on the head of the candidate who makes it that he risks losing more votes than he might gain from the support of the prejudiced.

French-speaking Canadians are not a minority group in the sense that recent overseas immigrants are in view of the constitutional guarantees maintaining the use of their language and the practice of their religion, but statistically they are an ethnic and religious minority in the population of Canada. There is a sense in which French Canadians may be described as more successful practitioners of cultural pluralism than any of the other ethnic groups in North America who, when in the minority have usually experienced considerable tension between their ethnic and national loyalties, and, when in the majority have practiced discrimination against those who differed from themselves in ethnic origin. The French Canadian's desire to preserve their language, religion, and traditional customs has only rarely conflicted with their allegiance to the Canadian nation. Ethnic loyalty to their group and political allegiance to Canada have existed side by side. While they have occasionally been at odds in the past over such issues as the Manitoba schools question and military conscription in the two world wars, their continued coexistence is becoming more and more natural to French Canadians with the decline of separatist senti-ment in recent years.

In their attitude to immigrant groups from overseas, French Canadians have not been particularly receptive to the possibility of assimilating them into French-Canadian culture. Most non-English speaking immigrants to Canada have settled in areas where English is the main language and have absorbed the culture of English-speaking rather than of French-speaking Canada. This has usually been true even of Catholic immigrants. There is some evidence that Italians settling in Montreal have learned French as their second language, but very little information is available concerning the extent to which immigrants settling in predominantly French-Cana-dian towns and cities have tended to assimilate into the French-Canadian culture, or of the attitudes toward them of the French Canadians. In Montreal there has been conflict and antagonism between French Cana-dians and Jews in areas where the two groups have been economic com-petitors and anti-Semitism has been common throughout French Canada. On the whole, however, the French Canadian has adopted a "live and let live" attitude toward minority ethnic groups in Canada as long as the newcomers have not interfered with or challenged the French-Canadian way of life.

5. ON THE NATURE OF THE DISTINCTION BETWEEN THE FRENCH AND THE ENGLISH IN CANADA: AN ANTHROPOLOGICAL INQUIRY*

A. G. Bailey†

Anthropological investigations have long since revealed the frequency with which the names used by primitive tribes to designate themselves are, on being translated, found to mean "the people" in the sense that the users

*From the Canadian Historical Association *Annual Report*, 1947.
†Dr. Bailey is Dean of Arts and Head of the Department of History and Anthro-pology at the University of New Brunswick, Fredericton.

are the only "true" or "real" people and that their neighbours are scarcely to be regarded as fully qualified members of the human species. Although divine authority has not always been claimed in support of this view, the virtual universality of the conception of the chosen people, in some form or other, is generally recognized. Readers of Green and Freeman will recall the inherent virtues which they attributed to the so-called "Anglo-Saxon" element in the British population, wherever that element may be. Although the distressing history of the spurious ideas of race and racial superiority, from Gobineau through Houston Stuart Chamberlain to Hitler, has long been recognized for what it is worth, and has within the last few years been exposed in widely circulated books and pamphlets, it is astonishing how much confusion reigns and how doggedly popular misconceptions of the subject persist. Barring catastrophes, shocking to think of, it is always easier to go on thinking in the habitual wrong-headed way. It conserves energy, and perhaps a general recognition of the truth would be repugnant to those self-regarding emotions that give collective coherence to large masses of men.

These misconceptions concerning the nature of race and nationality, and of the relationship between them, are not merely of academic interest. They underlie persistent mass attitudes and serve as either the springs of action, or the verbal ammunition directed against some group which is primarily an object of attack for economic or ideological reasons, far removed from that group's alleged inherent inferiority or undesirability. If these misconceptions underlie semitism, they also underlie anti-semitism. They serve to fortify the suspicions and hatred of one group for another. They nourish and add flesh to the delusions of the more virulent "racists" of Ontario and Quebec.

That the average citizen who has not made a special study of the subject often confuses the effects of nature and nurture in attributing certain mental endowment and temperament to particular racial stocks is perhaps not surprising in view of the fact that even scholars of eminence appear to have done so. Professor Trevelyan suggests that the sources of Shakespeare's poetic genius may be sought in the fact that he sprang from an area that was near an old borderland of Welsh and Saxon conflict. How "wild Celtic fancy" could be regarded as a cultural endowment as late as the sixteenth century, and in England at that, is hard to conceive. It is evident however that this is not how Professor Trevelyan thinks of the influence as having been handed down, for he speculates on the possible influence of the inheritance of Celtic "blood" upon the English temper. We know well enough that blood is not inherited, and that even if it were,

there would be no reason to suppose that it bore any relationship whatsoever to either intelligence or temperament. The statement is all the more
inadmissible when it is remembered that there is not and never has been
any such thing as Celtic blood.

Professor Toynbee does not appear to have taken same view in his
search for the origins of Egyptian civilization. Having exposed the fallacy
of concomitant variations in physical and psychical characteristics with
masterful irony directed against modern western racists, in what must
stand as one of the finest pieces of writing on the subject, he goes on to
observe that the creative contributions of more than one racial stock are
necessary to the geneses of civilizations. The unwary reader might suppose
that what Professor Toynbee is asserting is that the mental and emotional
endowment required for cultural advancement must derive from a
mingling of racial stocks through miscegenation and the consequent
production of a superior biological type. A closer reading, however, surely
will reveal that what he intends is that there must be a mingling, not
necessarily of races, but of the cultural features that they bear with them
in migration, and that these cultures become creative in the moment of
contact through interaction and mutual stimulation. Although the fusion
of cultural strains into a richer and more vital amalgam would no doubt
be hastened by the greater intimacy resulting from intermarriage between
members of the converging peoples, yet the production of a hybrid physical
type is incidental and irrelevant, since the association of a particular racial
structure with a particular mentality is fortuitous and does not stand in
the relation of cause and effect. For, as Dr. Jenness argued so convincingly
some years ago, the degree of cultural advancement of any given people,
and the style and content of their culture, are not in any way related to
their physique by virtue of its relative purity or as the product of racial
mixture.

The foregoing observations may serve as a sketch of the larger setting
within which the question of the nature of the distinction between the
French and the English in Canada may be considered. We have been
speaking of culture in the sense in which it was defined by Tylor, as "that
complex whole which includes knowledge, belief, art, morals, law, custom
and other capabilities and habits acquired by man as a member of society."
We have employed the term "race" in its biological sense as a hereditary
subdivision of the species homo sapiens, corresponding to a breed in
domestic animals, or, in Professor Ginsberg's words as "a group of individuals who, within given limits of variation, possess in common a combination of hereditary traits sufficient to mark them off from other groups."

He adds that if they are to be used as criteria of race, traits must be hereditary and remain relatively constant despite changes in the environment, and that they must be common to a fairly large group. It is to be inferred that he is referring to physical and not to mental traits.

We are now in a position to apply our criteria to the problem in hand, as to the terms in which the two major Canadian peoples are to be distinguished from each other. Our submission is simply that the differences between them as French and as English are not differences of racial inheritance but of cultural acquisition, have not arisen as a result of a biological diversity, are not in any way a reflection of unlike blood, but on the contrary are no more and no less than very limited differences between the cultural traits and configurations that they have acquired through the social interaction of mind and mind, and through which their common psychic endowment as human beings finds a degree of expression and fulfilment. This means that the terms French and English denote acquired mental variations and do not denote, either significant or relevant variations in physique, or inherited differences in mentality. One man is not born to think in a certain way because his headshape is dolichocephalic, and another man differently because he is brachycephalic. No man is born to think in a particular way at all, or if he is, that way may not be labelled either French or English; and no man ever had or ever will have dolichocephalic thoughts. A man may think in a way that can be described as English; but if he does he has learned to think that way through his social contacts with persons of English culture in some of its various manifestations. His doing so is thus a cultural and not a biological phenomenon.

If there are any racial differences as between the English-speaking and the French-speaking populations they are very slight. It may be that certain physical types are more commonly found in the area where English is spoken than where French is the prevailing language, or that the average tendencies towards certain types of physique are not exactly the same in the two populations. They are not exactly alike in any two selected populations. They are not alike as between Rivière du Loup and Chicoutimi, or as between Moose Jaw and Regina. And yet these facts, even if recognized by the people themselves, would not make the people of Rivière du Loup regard themselves as any more or any less truly French than the people of Chicoutimi, nor would they develop a sense of distinctive nationality on the bases of such recognition. If it were claimed that the English exhibited a stronger tendency towards blondness than the French, the same might conceivably be said of Hamilton as compared with Toronto, but we could only add that the difference, if such exists, would be totally lacking in significance. If all other marks of identification were lacking how could a pathologist decide from the physical characteristics alone whether a body recovered from the St. Lawrence River at Montreal were that of an English or a French person? What, one might well ask, does an English Canadian look like? We cannot answer that question. Many varieties are found among English Canadians, and much the same varieties are found in French Canada. If there were a general notion among the English that the French Canadians were overwhelmingly brunette, how would they account for the frequency with which blue-eyed and flaxen-haired children may be observed on the roadways of Les Escoumins, Baie Milles Vaches, and the Saguenay villages, to mention only a remote and isolated part of the Province of Quebec. We may conclude therefore that much the same range of variation is found among both peoples, that it is impossible to identify an individual with absolute certainty from his racial features alone as belonging to either one or the other group, while admitting at the same time that certain physical types may be found more frequently among the English than among the French, or that the tendency towards certain physical characteristics may be found more pronounced and more widely diffused in the one than in the other.

But when we have said this we have said very little, for we cannot claim that any very slight differences in average tendency that there may be are of any greater significance as a basis for distinction between French and English than are the slight racial differences between any two English-Canadian communities, which means that they are no real bases at all. Such differences as there are between the French and the English are national, not racial, cultural and acquired, not inherited. It is conceivable that there might be a people possessing a high degree of racial uniformity, as among themselves, and a considerable divergence in appearance between themselves and their neighbours, the recognition of which might form an ingredient of their sense of distinctive nationality. But no such uniformity within, nor marked divergence between, the French and the English may be said to exist. Such differences as exist are popularly exaggerated and are generally misconstrued as meaning an inherited difference in mentality as between the two. There is no predisposition of a child born to English-speaking parents to speak English also. The child could as easily acquire any other language as English, in the way that all languages are acquired. That child could be taken at birth and reared in a French-Canadian household, and it would be just as truly a French Canadian as any other child, because it would acquire from its social environment those traits which would make it a French Canadian in the way in which all French Canadians come to be what they are. The reverse procedure would be exactly the same.

The complete lack of significance of the racial factor as a mark of distinctiveness between the French-Canadian and English-Canadian nationalities may be accepted more readily than the view that these groups are not to be divided from each other on the basis of hereditary temperamental differences. The question of the nature and method of transmission of temperament is an important but vexing one, since much scientific investigation remains to be carried out before positive statements can be made.

The disentanglement and clarification of the basic human categories of race, language, and culture is one of the major contributions of the science of anthropology. There was a time when it was thought that there was an organic relationship between the shape of a man's skull and the language he spoke, instead, as is now clearly realized, of an association which is really fortuitous. It was like saying that a green apple tastes green when there is no such thing as a green taste. Although language is replete with such metaphors it is essentially the language of poetry, not the language of science. As Confucius said, only social confusion and disorder can be expected to result from not calling things by their right names. To speak of an English race is to employ a cultural adjective to describe a physical noun. The effect is almost as meaningless as to reverse the order and use a physical adjective to qualify a cultural noun. The absurdity of speaking of a blue-eyed language or of a dolichocephalic religion is evident enough. As Professor Kroeber wrote a quarter of a century ago, it represents a confusion between the organic and the superorganic, between inherited and acquired characteristics. Nor is it a harmless confusion, for it attributes to nature what is in reality a product of society. The widespread belief that the French and the English in Canada are distinguished from each other as are two breeds of domestic animals imposes a barrier where none in reality exists. From attributing to nature the distinction between the two peoples, it is only a step to the belief that intimacy between them is contrary to divine ordinance. The eradication of such notions should lead to an improvement of the mutual relations of the French and the English in Canada. It would represent a victory of science and rational inference from ascertained facts over the prejudice to which selfishness and ignorance give rise. One could go further than the Spanish ambassador to the court of Louis XIV, and say that, as far as a barrier in nature is concerned, the Pyrenees never did exist.

SELECTED BIBLIOGRAPHY

Blishen, B. R., Jones, F. E., Naegele, K. D., and Porter, J., (Editors), *Canadian Society*, Toronto, The Macmillan Company of Canada, Ltd., 1961. (Especially Part I; other parts relevant to other chapters of this book.)

Clark, S. D., *The Developing Canadian Community*, Toronto, University of Toronto Press, 1962.

Forsey, E. A., "Canada: Two Nations or One?," *The Canadian Journal of Economics and Political Science*, Vol. XXVIII, No. 4, November, 1962.

MacPherson, C. B., *The Culture of Contemporary Canada*, Ithaca, New York, Cornell University Press, 1956.

McGeachy, J. B., "Is Canada Cracking Up Under Stress After 95 Years as a Federal Union?," *The Financial Post*, June 30, 1962.

Morton, W. L., *The Canadian Identity*, Madison, Wisconsin, The University of Wisconsin Press, 1961.

Wrong, D. H., *American and Canadian Viewpoints*, Washington, D.C., American Council on Education, 1955.

part two

PROBLEMS
OF
SOCIETAL
DISORGANIZATION

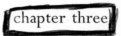

chapter three

THE SOCIAL MOVEMENT KNOWN
AS SEPARATISM

In the last chapter the subjects of Canadian identity and Canadian unity were examined. The logical development of this latter subject is a consideration, in some detail, of the separatist movement in Quebec. In the past few years a great deal has been written and said, especially in the French language, on this topic. What follows is just a small portion of that very interesting literature.

The first selection is a translation of a speech entitled "The Origin and Character of the Nationalism of Growth," by Professor Leon Dion. This speech, delivered at the Third Congress on Canadian Affairs at Laval University in November, 1963, is a true elaboration of its title and it provides a great deal of insightful information about the origins and character of "Quebec nationalism".

The next two selections are both taken from recent books, originally entitled *Pourquoi Je Suis Séparatiste* and *Pourquoi Je Suis Antiséparatiste* respectively. The first was written by Dr. Marcel Chaput, well known as the leader of the separatist movement, and is a direct and emotional appeal to Quebec's French-speaking population to strike out for independence. Reprinted here is almost all of the last two chapters of the book which first consider the two alternatives for the French-Canadians (to "remain a minority in a large country" or to "become a majority in a smaller country") and then argue that, after all is said and done, there is only one reason for the cause — "dignity".

The selection taken from the second book (by Jean-Charles Harvey) was put together from parts of almost every chapter, and argues, among other things, that French-Canadians are already free, that being part of Canada and the North American community in general is a tremendous advantage which has barely been exploited thus far, that human freedom is far more valuable than national freedom, and that "the great victory of the French in America will be in knowing how to absorb and assimilate the good and salutary offered to us by the English-speaking portion of this continent." His book was written a year after Chaput's, and attempts to be a rebuttal of it.

The final selection in the chapter is again taken from a book, and again involves a give-and-take between authors. French-Canadian Solange Chaput Rolland and English-Canadian Gwethalyn Graham have published, in *Dear Enemies*, correspondence between themselves which "reveals the angry feelings now driving Quebec towards separatism, and the English to a crisis of conscience" (according to the cover statement). A few paragraphs from here and there have been put together to make up the abbreviated correspondence reprinted below.

THE ORIGIN AND CHARACTER OF THE NATIONALISM OF GROWTH*

Leon Dion†

For three or four years, it is generally affirmed, we have been experiencing a re-awakening of French-Canadian nationalism in Quebec. What is it all about?

At first one might be tempted to question this affirmation. Indeed today's nationalists borrow their language from earlier generations. The slogans, the key formulae, the motifs themselves, put forward by nationalists of all tendencies have not changed. To reconstruct the geneology of such an expression as "Etat du Québec", for example, it would be neces-

*From *The Canadian Forum*, Vol. XLIII, No. 516, January 1964. This is a translation of a speech delivered on November 6, 1963, at the Third Congress on Canadian Affairs held at Laval University.
†Dr. Dion is Head of the Department of Political Science at Laval University, Quebec.

sary to reconstruct an entire century of the history of our social and political thought.

In 1963, the young people, in their journals and newspapers, resume without knowing it, the ideas and arguments enunciated in the youthful work of a man born in 1878, Abbé Groulx. Such permanence of themes, such continuity in the definitions of the situation, are in themselves significant. They confirm the survival, beyond the generations, of the soul of a people. "Nothing has changed, nothing will ever change in Quebec." Although it is no longer fashionable to cite this judgment of half a century ago, in a certain sense it still remains valid today. Men have passed on, the mind is released by the spread of literacy; industry and the town have pushed back the forest; books, the press, movies, radio, television, have imposed new ways of living and have opened wider horizons. And yet the extraordinary permanence of the same language at the level of collective definitions seems to indicate that the French Canadians, through the evolutions they have passed in all areas of thought and activity, have not known how or have not been able to resolve the problems of their infancy as a people.

But if we pass from the level of signs to that of significance we note the singular variations in the times according to the different conjunctures in which French Canadians have found themselves placed. It is thus that the general tone of nationalist ideology has been modified in each of the last four decades. We have had successively a depression nationalism, a wartime nationalism, a nationalism of prosperity and finally, in the present decade, a nationalism of growth. It is thus to the style of nationalism rather than to the content of the ideology that one refers when one speaks of the "re-awakening of nationalism" during the last three or four years.

This nationalist renewal animates and sustains the great ambition of development which is manifested in all areas and in all sectors of the population. What is the origin of this nationalism of growth? What are its characteristics? It is these two questions which I will attempt to answer.

THE ORIGIN OF THE NATIONALISM OF GROWTH

The emergence, in the course of recent years, of a nationalism which I have just qualified with "growth," has been made possible by a conjuncture of which the principal elements are well known: on the federal scene the defeat of the Liberal party and the departure of Mr. St. Laurent, the victory of the Conservative party and the accession to power of Mr. Diefenbaker; on the provincial scene, the disappearance of Mr. Duplessis, "the most important death in the political history of Canada," the unexpected death of Mr. Paul Sauvé, the victory of the Liberal party and the accession to power of Mr. Jean Lesage after the election of June 22,

1960; on the international scene, finally, the gaining of independence of a large number of Afro-Asian peoples.

The first consequence of the development of this conjuncture was to solve the dilemma of the nationalism of prosperity. The postwar years marked, in effect, in all areas for Quebec, at the same time the apogee of the federal government and the decline, which was accelerated after 1956, of the provincial government. The most ardent nationalists recognized that the rapid progress of the province resulted especially from the initiatives of the federal government while the provincial government remained inactive or even applied retrograde measures in response to the problems of the hour. On the one hand the federal government was accused of usurping the functions reserved to the provinces but, on the other hand, the corruption and inefficiency which engulfed more and more the Duplessis regime was deplored. It is perhaps in the realm of education that the dilemma of the nationalism of prosperity was most acutely felt. Thus, it is incontestable that federal aid to universities came in response to a pressing need, in Quebec as in the other provinces. But nevertheless to accept this assistance was to agree to give up the direct and exclusive control which Quebec until then had exercised in an area judged essential to the survival and development of French culture. After having finally prevented the Universities from benefitting from the federal assistance, the Duplessis government accorded to them, at least in appearance, equivalent grants by establishing a provincial income tax.

At the same time the presence of a French Canadian prime minister at Ottawa further accentuated the dilemma of the nationalism of prosperity. Because of this situation Canadianism, which had found its definitive ideological expression in the Massey Report, knew a certain popularity among intellectuals and politicians. In its extreme formulations, Canadianism affirmed that, for all practical purposes, the development of the French culture would be assured not by Quebec, but by Ottawa. This nationalism in reverse, was only, it is true to say, the reflection of a profound state of political crisis into which the French Canadians of Quebec then found themselves plunged. To "Canadianists" who supported their cause with facts and precise plans the nationalists countered chiefly with defensive arguments which found faithful echoes in the purely negative use that the Duplessis regime made of the concept of provincial autonomy.

With the accession to power at Ottawa of the Diefenbaker regime the eclipse of the prestige of the federal power began. Fiscal deficits accumulated, unemployment increased, immigration decreased, administrative difficulties emerged, grave political mistakes were committed by the Prime

Minister himself and his principal lieutenants, the French Canadian ministers made themselves the reputation of being ineffective and colorless. The development of these conditions released, by the reverse process, the most impressive movement of withdrawal towards the province since Confederation. The Duplessis regime submitted to increasingly violent attacks which shook it to its own foundations. The death of "Le Chef" opened the way to progressive forces. Mr. Lesage and his team gathered up the ideas which had germinated in intellectual circles during the long period of opposition and, not without difficulty, not without hesitations or compromises sometimes, went on henceforth to make every effort to spread the new message among the people. In short, the dilemma of the nationalism of prosperity found its solution.

The second consequence of the development of this conjuncture was the affirmation of a strong Quebec and the giving of form to the nationalism of growth which we are witnessing today. The new men, or the renewed men, have everywhere taken the positions of command and they have converted into positive formulae of collective action nationalism which, until these last years, had been intellectually entertained by a conservative, clerical, paternalistic class, in short, much more semi-feudal than typically bourgeois. Pressed by the feverish impatience of a rising generation which had not felt the inhibiting experiences of the depression, the war, and of Duplessism, these new men must ceaselessly march forward without being able to explore previously, in order to know the terrain, the unknown regions in which they have committed themselves. For those who have known politics chiefly as misdeeds and ineptitude and who, in default of being able to live democracy had to content themselves with dreaming and speaking of it, it was necessary, without a period of transition, to be converted to the idea that the state is a sort of friendly demiurge or in any case the principal instrument put at the disposition of the people to produce the marvellous works that are hoped for in every area.

No government of Quebec has ever before tied together so closely politics and nationalism. The liaison has become, in effect, so firm that an eventual political set-back could strike French Canadian culture at the very heart of its vitality. I think that our best political men inside the two principal parties have the feeling of the risk that this close liaison involves. Such a feeling would explain both their ardor to recommend reform measures and the development of their ambiguous attitude toward the federal power as well as to separatism. I sense increasingly that they are putting themselves in the position of being able to place on the federal authorities the responsibility for an eventual political set-back while rendering possible recourse to the alternative political formula that separatism recommends. If I understand correctly what is going on in the minds of our politicians, they are seeking, consciously or not, to protect the mental structure of French Canadians that a long nationalist tradition has fashioned and impregnated step by step against the risks inherent in the present conjuncture.

From this point of view separatism, in the same way as the diverse independentist tendencies, fulfils a useful function. It presents itself not only as a logical development of the conjuncture but even as a possible solution to the problems which have issued from the conjuncture itself. Separatist sentiment runs like a thread, sometimes impressive sometimes tenuous but never broken, through the entire woof of more than a century of French Canadian nationalism. The example, before our eyes, of several ex-colonial peoples, who have won independence and of whom a great number speak French, brings a dramatic confirmation of the possible vitality for Quebec of the separatist formula.

But looking closer perhaps, we find among the independentists, who are not strict separatists, the same hesitation as to the route to choose as that which I think I have detected among our public men. These also, it seems to me, often hesitate to destroy all the bridges with the rest of the country for fear perhaps of seeing their own backs smashed by the present difficult conjuncture. Between the federalist *status quo* and strict separatism a whole series of intermediate positions spread out which leave the door open to negotiations with the federal government. Among these positions there is one which during the last six or eight months has attracted a great number of militant independentists and several public men. It is a question, according to this intermediate formula, of reorganizing the Canadian federal system so that "two nations" could become, as such, equally sovereign at Ottawa. This is very attractive theoretically, at least for French Canadians in Québec, but it appears to me to involve considerable difficulties in practical application: the physical character of Canada, the enormous regional differences, the geographic division of the ethnic groups, the absence of a common wave length in the sense of a national identity among French Canadians, English Canadians, and those of the third group, and so on, pose for the supporters of the "two nations" thesis serious problems when they set themselves concretely to the task of installing a confederal regime. Nevertheless, it may be that the application of the theory of "concurrent majorities" in the very precise areas of activity where cultural contacts are considerable would permit the reabsorption of the major sources of tension and conflict between the two principal ethnic groups of the country.

It could be that the thesis of "two nations" constitutes only a step on the way to strict separatism or even that it expresses the beginning of a return to the more familiar horizons of federalism. If seems, in effect, that the major part of the population of Quebec nourishes the hope that in order that the French Canadians may live in conformity with their new aspirations it would be sufficient to re-shape, more or less radically, the existing federal system. What form should this re-shaping take? No one to my knowledge has yet concretely envisaged this question other than under the form of suggestions about detail and it seems to me that the imaginations of the partisans of federalism have been taken unawares. Some estimate that the existing Canadian constitution, amended in some of its more outdated features, will remain for a long time yet the fundamental law of the country, and that the political instruments at the disposition of Quebec during the phase of the nationalism of growth remain, on the legal level, noticeably the same as in the past.

But we must recognize that far from having exhausted in Canada the resources of federalism as a system of political organization, we have not yet taken seriously the task of marking an inventory of the theoretical possibilities that it includes in the context of a country like ours.

At this time, consequently, none of the options that the nationalism of growth renders theoretically possible finds itself excluded. And no one can predict how Quebec will react finally to the conjuncture which confronts it. One knows only this, and it is a capital fact: Quebec ought to be very conscious of the risks that the present conjuncture holds for the future of the French Canadians. What are the difficult problems which are inherent in the present conjuncture?

THE CHARACTERISTIC OF THE NATIONALISM OF GROWTH

The nationalism of growth is characterized essentially by the conviction that Quebec finds itself on the threshold of a gigantic development in all areas of thought and activity. The leaders of my generation spoke to us of "our master, the past." We say to the young people of today "our hope, the future." But to construct the future to which we aspire it is necessary to know how to put to work the possibilities of the present time. The nationalism of growth, in essence and vocation, is pragmatic rather than doctrinaire. In effect, its destination is to permit energies and talents to emerge in action.

The exceptionally aggressive and singularly attractive characteristics of the nationalism of growth makes one conscious of the difficulty as well as the grandeur of the work to be done. In the interview that he gave to M.

Jean-Marc Leger (*Le Devoir,* 5 July 1963) M. Réne Lévesque exposed, in the picturesque language which is his habit, the dimensions and demands of the nationalism of growth. It is a question of making collective energies converge on precise, concrete objectives and of appealing to all the proper means to permit, as soon as possible, the realization of these objectives. Here rise up like a nightmare, the great ambitions of the past which were frustrated by inertia or the betrayal of men. It is a question of becoming convinced that hereafter it is no longer possible to act simply for the survival of French Canada, and then to act so that it will no longer be possible to return to the point of departure. Moreover, whatever the international economic conditions are, which unfortunately will probably be rather unfavorable in the course of the next years, the future which opens for French Canadians must mark for them a move forward or else they will disappear as a people. When the most dynamic men have made such a wager, and they are sincere, they cannot fail to demand of themselves, and of the people, efforts which would appear extravagant to those who remain strangers to the solicitations of the nationalism of growth.

Whence an extreme and perhaps excessive consciousness of our collective weaknesses on every level from the economy to the spoken and written language, and the search for solutions by the most diverse means and which contain sometimes much more of magical incantation than cold and realistic analysis of our true possibilities. Whence also the intense propagation of symbols and nationalist formulae in order to galvanise the people or even, perhaps, to maintain for the longest possible time the illusion of grandeur.

It could be that the nationalism of growth, in certain of its manifestations, artificially creates an impression of a general unity of viewpoint by obscuring the consciousness of diversity and ideological opposition which cannot fail to be engendered when the deaf resistance of historical anchorages fuses with the pluralist society in which we have arrived. It is thus that the separatist movements, in making all efforts converge on a single direction, prevent themselves from taking an active part in the perhaps more decisive debates which are unfolding at the present time in the consciousness of individuals, inside of parties and groups on the clerical question, education, the development of political maturity, the evaluation of the civil service, the role of the state, economic philosophy, the betterment of underprivileged groups, rural and regional development, unemployment, dominion-provincial relations themselves, and so forth. Bill 60 would have been necessary to make us aware of the size of the crisis which presently crosses Quebec, caught with the necessity of putting in the waste basket worn-out, yet still dear, traditions and giving ourselves a soul rejuvenated and adapted to present conditions. It has been said and repeated that the separatist formula presented a response to a condition of collective alienation issued from the conquest, affirmed by subsequent history, and recently aggravated by the rapid breakdown of traditional institutions and protective values. That is possible. But, in failing to analyse the ideologies that make the social structures themselves emerge and which divide French Canadians, in attempting rather to conceal these ideological divisions in order to facilitate the eventual triumph of their cause, separatism threatens to place us on the road to fatal mystifications. At the present time not only does separatism, in my view, offer no solution to our most real problems, but it even tends to distract us from the patient search for real solutions. Moreover, the internal divisions which appear in spite of everything inside of the separatist movements confirm in striking fashion the great ideological diversity that social pluralism engenders.

I do not discard, however, the separatist formula since it imposes itself immediately as a theoretically possible option to the period of the nationalism of growth. But I do not judge that this formula has not been sufficiently acclimatized to local conditions to permit it to penetrate, without breaking, both the consciousness and the social structure. In order to be usable it needs to be previously filtered and domesticated by a great brain and a great heart that is typically French Canadian, it needs to be fused to our dominant idiosyncracies, and to take shape within the values and norms which inspire and sanction our daily acts, in short, to root itself deeply among the people. Someone asks: does this man exist? That is not the question. The problem is to know if the conjuncture will evolve in such a way that the separatist idea can incarnate itself in a party capable of drawing to it the best men in all sectors of society and of uniting with the people. Among them it would doubtless find someone enjoying a great authority and a great prestige who would lead the party and make it a powerful movement.

Even the familiar forms of the nationalism of growth at present meet here and there an opinionated resistance. This resistance expresses itself even inside the government and in the ranks of our two principal political parties and from there among institutions, and groups and individuals, and that in regard to reform projects however concrete and well defined. When our best politicians have affirmed that it is necessary for us to become "masters in our own house," "to take the economy into our own hands," "to create a great educational system," and so forth, they are seeking to stimulate, under an attractive and inspiring form of action, in individuals and in groups, the proper motivation to produce the enormous amount of energy made necessary by the very dimensions of the tasks undertaken. Likewise when M. René Lévesque has said and repeated that "the state is one of us, the best among us," he has wished to underline the fact that in the specific conditions of Quebec, the state must be exceptionally dynamic in order to direct the canalization of individual initiatives as well as supplement their evident deficiencies. But our public men run up against individuals and groups paralysed by fear of the state, fear arising from a long tradition of unbridled liberalism and bad government. And when they have wished to check quickly this very understandable fear and when, in addition, they begin to convert their political formulae into electoral slogans, perhaps they have excited among certain categories of intellectuals and young people, aspirations altogether out of proportion to our real possibilities, even supposing that we should have a government ten times better and more efficient than it actually is, and that the latter could count on the total support of the people.

One tends consequently to pass silently over the presence of objective factors which, regardless of formula and political regimes, have always conditioned, still condition today, and will always condition our existence as a people. One tends to forget that even the relative grandeur to which we are allowed to pretend can only be achieved by laborious and persevering efforts. One tends to lose sight of the necessary co-operation from outside that we must look for and maintain in order precisely to arrive at and participate fully in the complex interrelations and multiple financial, commercial and industrial networks which intersect in every sense, and which, whether we wish it or not, for better or for worse, condition our development and enclose our daily lives. One tends to misunderstand the true nature of our ethnic temperament. We are perhaps, to borrow a very old phrase from Abbé Groulx, the most European of all the American peoples, but we carry in our minds and in our bodies the indelible mark of the irresistible attraction that the new world has exercised on all those it has drawn during four centuries into its immense spaces to the always provisional frontiers. We, the descendants of a handful of the millions of immigrants of all races and all cultures, have humanized in the French fashion a corner of this immense North American continent which is otherwise entirely Anglo-Saxon. This environment, in its turn, has acted on our original temperament in making us, to pursue Abbé Groulx's idea, the most American of Europeans. Until now we have been, as a people, prevented from succumbing to the charm of the continent for fear of losing our identity. But we have done it at the price of a costly loss of energy. The production of the Manicougan dam brings us the very tangible proof, in an era of the nationalism of growth, that it is not in protecting ourselves but in taking up the challenge that this continent poses to men that we will establish firmly on the banks of the St. Lawrence the seat of another great French civilization.

Unless we take care and return to a language and to attitudes more in proportion with our situation and our collective possibilities, we will soon become incapable of warding off the risks inherent in the nationalism of growth. The tasks we must at any price undertake, the problems that we absolutely must resolve are already sufficiently complex and will demand from us sufficient efforts that we should not take to dreaming of illusory chateaux, somewhere other than on the North American continent.

We can and we certainly must improve our written and spoken language, our system of education. We can and we must increase our participation in economic life. We can and we must create contacts with French speaking countries. But the real questions to pose today are as follows: It this what we really want? Are we prepared to make the necessary efforts? Are we not inclined to take the pretext of a supposed lack of the present means at our disposal as a group to hide our lack of adaptation to the conditions of a technical society and to excuse our lack of dynamism? Do we always use these means themselves thoroughly and purposely? And in so far as we have proved that they are insufficient, do we really look for the proper methods to make up their deficiency?

It is the responsibility of public men, of intellectuals, of leaders of groups, first to pose these questions to themselves, and then to address them to all the people.

The French Canadians of Quebec have always had a tendency to lay on the federal government the responsibility for problems and set-backs which often had their source and their cause in their own governments. In the period of the nationalism of prosperity this fault led us to apathy and to the edge of dictatorship. But in the period of the nationalism of growth, this fault could be fatal to our existence as a people. For do not forget that in order to deploy a degree of dynamism comparable to that of the people who, for better or for worse, surround us, it will be necessary for us first to have learned to give ourselves and to conserve for ourselves, good governments in Quebec. The present government intends precisely to be a good government. Our first task consists in creating a climate of opinion which will permit it to become a truly good government without which it runs the risk of being rejected by the electorate at the next turn in the road.

When we have had over a long enough period of time a good government in Quebec, the relative position of this province in the whole country and at Ottawa will undoubtedly be sufficiently reinforced so that we can draw all the advantages inherent in a large country.

But the future does not belong to us yet even if our acts today contribute toward fashioning it. In the period of the nationalism of growth federal-provincial relations are going to raise thorny problems of all types. In order to realize our projects in all sectors of activity, Quebec will need enormous revenues and the question of tax sharing is going to be posed with growing acuteness. But we delude ourselves greatly if we believe thereby to ensure the financial stability of the government of Quebec which has been engaged for three years in several programmes of great scope from which the direct income is small or even will only be forthcoming in several years time. Moreover, to catch up lost steps in several areas and to engage resolutely in developmental policies, Quebec must manifest a degree of dynamism which will give its government a much more progressive allure than the federal government. Contrary to what happened during the period of the nationalism of prosperity, it is no longer the federal government which will precede Quebec in the preparation and putting into effect of political programmes, but rather the reverse. We see already indications of this reversal of roles. There can result from this sources of new conflict in dominion-provincial relations. In my opinion, only the establishment of a dominion-provincial pre-legislative organization which would integrate and share out respective functions can put an end to the annoying, precipitate counter measures to which the two levels of government have begun to have recourse. Finally, so that Quebec in the period of the nationalism of growth will agree to adhere firmly to the federal formula, it is necessary that there be the possibility of allowing the French fact to spread out to the measure of its aspirations and of its capability across the country, inside the federal administration, in crown corporations and in private enterprise. It could not be a question of arriving at a kind of generalized bilingualism nor a "biculturalism of the cocktail party type." By bilingualism it is necessary to understand not the knowledge of the two principal languages of the country by all Canadians, which would be an absurdity, but rather the practical acceptance by all Canadians of the equality of the two languages as well as the rigorous practise of bilingualism inside the major institutions of the country. By biculturalism it is necessary to understand, in the first place, the coexistence of two different ethnic groups which, for the preservation and development of their respective cultures, support themselves, up to a certain point, on the same political, social and economic institutions, and, in the second place, the complex of inter-relations that they have been led to establish, as a consequence of their association and necessary co-operation for the accomplishment of their common responsibility with regard to the whole community. It is, I think, to the examination of the dimensions of bilingualism and biculturalism understood in this sense that the Laurendeau-Dunton commission is going to turn its attention.

If we succeed in resolving the difficulties that I have just mentioned, and in the measure that we become more conscious of the strategic position of Quebec in the country, our very understandable distrust of the federal government will gradually be replaced by an ambition to play a role of the first order on that level. There is no reason that Quebec, which, according to some, is called in the course of the next decades to catch up to and perhaps pass Ontario, should not have the ambition to dispute with its neighbouring province the place which she presently occupies in the government of the country. The nationalism of growth, in my opinion, will not be able, as preceding nationalisms, to be purely enthnocentric. Whatever happens elsewhere, Quebec will need allies and clients among the English Canadians. The allies and the clients will be now the industrial interests of the Niagara peninsula, now the interests of the Western farmer, now the forestry interests of British Columbia, now finally, the farming and fishing interests of the Maritimes. One day Quebec will understand that it is only in profiting from all the possibilities of democracy that it will cease to be a permanent minority in order to become a minority which, in association with other minorities, will be able on particular questions to become a majority. On that day one can be assured that the ordeal of the nationalism of growth will have been overcome successfully. In the long run Quebec will obtain more and better results by the conciliation of differences with the other provinces and the federal government than by blackmail, menaces and especially terrorism. Those who among us foresee or employ such tactics either do not understand the Anglo Saxon mentality or seek to discourage the manifestations of extreme good will which have been expressed in very tangible fashion by some of our Anglo-Canadian compatriots for some time.

I have attempted to show at length in my exposition that whatever may be, after all, the political option that we wish for the Quebec of Tomorrow, it is desirable, even necessary, to assure the success of our choice that we work together today for the realisation of the great possibilities that the pre-

onjuncture offers. We are all, at bottom, in one fashion or another, ialists of the period of growth. And we ought to feel ourselves jointly liable for the risks as well as the very grandeur of the future which opens to us. The nationalism of growth is fundamentally sane in itself, and in its possible consequences. It ought to permit Quebec to place itself resolutely on the road of development, provided that doctrinaire attitudes and conflicts do not sterilize it along the way, and provided that we know how to be patient.

7. WHY I AM A SEPARATIST*

Marcel Chaput†

I

THE TWO CHOICES FOR THE FRENCH-CANADIAN NATION

REMAIN A MINORITY IN A LARGE COUNTRY

What we lack most

I have never claimed to have made a thorough study of French-Canadian nationalism. My knowledge of Canadian history is that of a man who went through school and who has continued to read but, especially, one who has kept his eyes open. Since I have been drawn by nature to join all sorts of so-called nationalist societies, I have come to understand after twenty years of adult life that my French-Canadian people lacks one element. Not that this deficiency is a natural defect—on the contrary, it is the effect of our history, a result of the Conquest, the consequence of long domination. The French-Canadians are a people in search of itself, a nation unaware of itself, and the element that is most lacking is not will, capability or maturity. What is lacking is orientation.

I begin with the postulate that the French-Canadians form a nation

*From *Why I Am a Separatist,* by Marcel Chaput (translated by Robert A. Taylor), Toronto, The Ryerson Press, 1962.
†Dr. Chaput identifies himself as follows: "Ph.D. in Biochemistry. Born in Hull (Quebec) 14 October, 1918. Resigned from Federal Government December, 1961. Since, battles for independence of Quebec."

like any other. And like all other nations, the French-Canadian nation has it good and bad points, a soul capable of love and reaction, aspirations to grandeur, a need for dignity and self-expression, the capacity for joy and tears, a feeling of solidarity. In short, the French-Canadian needs a national identity, within the framework of concrete political structures and incarnated in universally accepted symbols.

Instead, what is he offered? With the best of intentions, his leaders recommend the life of a minority with its continual stream of unsatisfied demands — for bilingual cheques when the money belongs to others, for a historical name for a hotel when everything is carried on in English within the hotel, a bronze plaque with three words in French to remind him that *he* must be bilingual, translations in order to soak up better the thoughts of others, more English in the schools to emphasize the useless-ness of his native language.

And all this simply to give them the privilege of making more demands tomorrow.

Battling for crumbs. There you have two hundred years of French-Canadian history in three words. What we win on one side we lose on the other; and our heritage is being dissipated. Tired of battling for crumbs, our people has been reduced to one platoon of resistance fighters among an army in full flight.

EPITAPH

Here lies a people which died on the way
For want of knowing where it was going.

Defeatism?

I can already hear the thunder of protest from all sides. That is defeatist talk, sacrilegious thought, iconoclasm.

No, I am not destroying anything. French resistance in America has been too glorious to consign it to the flames now. But let us think while there is still time. It is not normal for a people to spend its life on the ramparts battling for a ghost. You are right, life is a perpetual battle — but against the normal adversities of history, not those that you stupidly set up for yourself.

The warrior who refuses battle is a coward. The man who lets himself be robbed is a poltroon. A people which allows itself to be invaded is servile. But the hero who battles for an illusion is a fool.

Where is the illusion?

In the name of French reason, I ask you where is the illusion? In the achievement of one great bilingual Canada where at best we can run a close second, or in the formation of a sovereign, French Quebec in which we would be able the sole masters?

In the name of French valor, I ask you which is defeatism? The stubborn battle for crumbs, trinkets and trifles, or the enlightened march toward the free country our ancestors wanted?

The French-Canadians, like any proud people, are ready to fight as much as necessary to ensure their liberation and to fulfil the most legitimate and natural of aspirations — to build a nation of their own. But it is absolutely certain that they won't show the same courage in fighting for the illusion that is destroying them — the illusion of a bilingual Canada.

The hour of decision

French Canada has arrived at its hour of decision. Its real problem is to decide now, once and for all, what it wants to be — an eternal minority, in eternal retreat in an immense country — which doesn't belong to it, or a living and progressive majority, in a country which is smaller but all its own.

To those who choose to be a minority

The experience of ninety-four years of Confederation is enough to convince us that minority status in a two-nation country can lead only to mediocrity. To hope that by some sort of miracle the French-Canadian people should suddenly reform, demand with one voice that it be respected, become anxious to speak correctly, desire culture and great works, without the inspiration of an animating ideal—that is a dangerous case of delirium.

Let us suppose that the miracle should happen, and that our people should acquire the desired virtues of resistance—we would still remain a numerical minority, whose democratic responsibility would still and forever be to bow to the wishes, legitimate or not, just or not, generous or not, of a majority which is foreign to us in language and spirit.

The urgent need for orientation

Through the fault of its élite groups, the French-Canadian are a people which doesn't know where it is going or what it wants. It is the victim of an immense confusion, torn between proposals that are as fantastic as they are contradictory.

Faced with this tangled mass of choices, it is absolutely necessary to choose one, once and for all; we must answer the one question we are allowed to ask—which of the choices, a bilingual Canada or an independent Quebec, will ensure the French-Canadian nation its greatest development? Personally, I have chosen independence.

BECOME A MAJORITY IN A SMALLER COUNTRY

The present movement of independence for Quebec is essentially an expression of this free choice between two possibilities. And the Separatists, Independentists or whatever name you give them have chosen to be a minority no longer.

After a man has been in an unfavourable position for many years, he winds up believing that this position is inevitable. He reaches the point where he no longer entertains the notion of being in any other position. I imagine that in a people that has lived in subjection for a long time, there must likewise be many men and women who would assert the futility of speaking about liberty. History has so ordained; their people was irrevocably destined to live under the domination of another.

The same holds true of the French-Canadian nation which has endured two hundred years of bondage. Certainly Confederation in 1867 or the Statute of Westminster in 1931 have done nothing to change their attitude. For two hundred years the French-Canadians have been suffering under political bondage, economic bondage, cultural bondage, social bondage and, above all, psychological bondage.

I say "above all," because all other types of bondage are temporary, as long as the spirit has not been infected. But when you reach the point where you no longer see your chains, or even deny their existence, where you tell yourself that the situation is normal, that your people cannot be other than a people in bondage, an eternal minority, then this people is in danger of disappearing forever.

We no longer want to be a minority

No, the French-Canadian people is not obliged to remain a minority against its will and against its interests. Nothing forces us to wilt away in an unfavourable environment, to twiddle our thumbs with a few sterile demands and useless reports while waiting for the end to come. I refuse to believe that Providence wants us to destroy ourselves in the interests of English culture in America.

Perhaps you are one of the people who say, "What a cry-baby! There will always be French-Canadians!"

You are probably right; there will always be, or at least for a long time yet, French-Canadians in Canada, even in spite of adverse conditions. But will there always be a French-Canadian *nation*? Just as one flower does not mean spring, the presence of a few diehards does not make a nation. If present conditions continue, and everything points to just that, it is not certain that there will be a French-Canadian nation in America in another century—unless the French-Canadians make up their minds to demand independence for Quebec.

We must choose between Balkanization or Louisianization

I have in mind the argument that comes up so often in high circles— Quebec's independence would mean the Balkanization of Canada, which Ottawa and Washington would not accept.

We are therefore faced with the dilemma of Balkanization for Canada or Louisianization for Quebec.

Can you claim that Louisiana gained by entering the Federation of the U.S.A.? Economically, yes. Demographically perhaps. And Quebec would likewise gain by such annexation—at least economically for a time. There is only one aspect in which Louisiana lost by the transaction—it is no longer French, but American. The French language is gone.

Let's turn the tables

Let's turn the tables for a moment. Suppose that Quebec is a unilingual French country, independent, situated beside an English-speaking Canada made up of nine provinces. One fine day, Ottawa, the capital of this English Canada, comes to propose that Quebec enter a federation. Quebec would say *perhaps*—but what kind of federation?

Don't you see, the mission of the French race is too great to confine it to Quebec alone. Become a province in our federation. You will be bilingual, French will be official in the Federal parliament, we'll print you up some money and stamps with a picture of our Queen. Cheques? We can discuss them later.

And so on, spreading out all the beauties of Canadian Confederation before your eyes.

What will *your* answer be? What would be the answer of an independent Quebec?

All Quebec would answer in chorus—No thanks! We like you well enough as a neighbour, but we prefer to govern ourselves. We have no desire to become a minority.

II
THE ONE REASON FOR OUR CAUSE
Dignity

DIGNITY

History decreed that we were to be the losers in the battle for a continent. We have no quarrel with history. No one needs to be told that the English are solidly established in America. But we too, a people of six million, or perhaps eight or nine if you include all the territory from the Yukon to the Gulf of Mexico, we too have settled down to stay on the continent which our fathers were the first to colonize.

However, if we are going to stay, we want to play our part. Not the part of a people dragging out a shadowy French existence made up of demands and reports which are nothing but a perpetual inventory of our continuous retreat, but instead a life worthy of our own genius, the French genius.

Do you consider this an insult to those who have preceeded us, to those who have made it possible for us to survive this long? If you or your fathers were among those brave men who knew how to put up resistance, then I understand your protests. But what else are we to do? Are we to refuse forever the normal life of free peoples because we are a minority? By what sort of logic or decree is the French-Canadian nation able to do without something which is essential for other nations? It is a marvellous thing that our people were able to survive under the difficult conditions they had to face. But survival is not an end in itself. It only has a meaning insofar as it leads to *Life*.

No, the independence movement in Quebec is not a condemnation of history. We refuses to judge our fathers, since we are entirely devoted to the future of our people. They did what they could under the circumstances.

It is true that you can't change past history. But we can write our own future history—and greatness belongs to the peoples with a great ideal.

An ideal that crops up every twenty years

Perhaps you have said in a sceptical tone of voice, as so many others have: "Oh, this Separatism is nothing new; it crops up every twenty years!"

It is true that Separatism is not new, that it comes back periodically. But that only proves that it is a feeling deeply embedded in the French-Canadian soul. Twenty years make up one generation. And each new generation says to itself: "What sort of people are we French-Canadians? The other peoples of the world are independent, free, their own masters —and we aren't."

Then this new generation puts up a fight until the day when, caught up in the rounds of self-interest, comfort and human respect, it finally imitates its predecessors by throwing off with a derisive smile "this folly of youth."

If only the older generation would keep quiet instead of making a spectacle of itself before French-Canadian youth which is trying to be noble, instead of trying to justify itself in public for no longer being what it once was. It would not then be obstructing the liberation of its people as it is now doing. Because in these twentieth-century surroundings, the Golden Age of independence in the world, the French-Canadian nation will have sealed its own doom if it misses this last chance.

There is no more pact between two nations

A people does not live on never-ending demands, but on Dignity.

A people which wants to live must do much more than keep itself from dying.

Do you think you can find this intense life that is so desirable for French-Canada in the pact between two nations?

You are telling yourself stories. There is no more pact between two nations. There was a winner and a loser. There were four provinces, now ten, of which one happened to be French. It is true that this one is not a province like the others—Quebec is the national State of the French-Canadians—but Confederation relegated it to the rank of a province like the others.

Do you think you can find this intense life that is so desirable for French Canada in the rectification of injustices?

You are being unjust yourself. There is no injustice in this so-called Confederation. There is only an English majority, unchanging, which by virtue of the Conquest, or of Democracy, is in undisputed control of a government; and a French minority, unchanging, which by virtue of the same Conquest or the same Democracy, is living in bondage.

Democracy and human nature will always require that the French-Canadian people submit to the will of the majority, whether they like it or not.

If the French-Canadians are not satisfied with this so-called confederation, it is up to them to get out.

And the Dignity of the French-Canadian nation requires that it get out, in order to do justice to the French-Canadian as a man and to the French nations of the world.

Independence is a matter of character

Whether we get out or not is, in the last analysis, a matter of character. It is true of peoples as well as of men—some have a feeling for Dignity, Nobility and Liberty; some haven't.

The logic of independence is open to discussion and I have tried to present my ideas on the subject. But there can be no discussion about the character of people who desire independence.

The whole problem may be summed up in one question—does the French-Canadian nation possess this character, this sense of Dignity, the stuff of which free nations are made?

I believe it does.

Independence is a matter of civilization

In view of the extraordinary awakening of the French-Canadian nation, the time has come to clear up some misconceptions about Separatism.

• No, Independence for Quebec is not the uncertain and hazardous separation of a province from its metropolis, but the liberation of a people.

• No, Independence for Quebec is not the explosion of revenge toward the Conquerors of 1760, but the quest for Dignity which is every people's right.

• No, Independence for Quebec is not the isolation of a fearful group behind a protective wall, but the expression of a national individuality, before the eyes of the world.

• No, Independence for Quebec is not the regression of the French-Canadian community to a tribal status in the Quebec reservation, but the elevation of a French-speaking people to the rank of a free nation.

• No, Independence for Quebec is not the last resort of cowards who are tired of fighting, but the battle of lucid minds for the triumph of a Cause consistent with material and human reality.

• No, Independence for Quebec is not a Damocles sword held over Ottawa's head in order to hurry along the granting of a distinctive flag or bilingual cheques, but *the unconditional and irrevocable rejection of minority status.*

The present time will mark the end of an epoch in world history—that of empires. The present time will mark the beginning of an epoch for French-Canada—that of its entry into the brotherhood of free nations.

French-Canadians who believe in yourself and in your brothers,

French-Canadians who have maintained the Dignity of your heritage,

French-Canadians who desire the liberation of man and French Grandeur in America,

French-Canadians who acknowledge a spiritual bond with the twenty-five nations and one hundred and fifty million French-speaking people of the world,

Cry out your thirst for Liberty and Independence. You owe it to yourselves; you owe it to your people; you owe it to Civilization.

8. WHY I AM AN ANTI-SEPARATIST*

Jean-Charles Harvey†

Why am I an anti-separatist? Mostly because I love freedom — mine and that of others.

The liberty of man comes well before the liberty of a nation.

That is why, throughout history, millions of men have fled national independence which stifled them, in order to breath the air of personal liberty, without which life is not worth living.

This explains the endless series of human migrations by which civilization has been able to survive and the mind able to triumph over brute force.

I could see that freedom aborted if it depended upon the foolish fancy of a few hundred fanatics who deny almost all the data of history and philosophy, who never have a profound thought, who never take the essential needs of the human being into account, and who seek to persuade French-Canadians that a few pen scratches at the bottom of a paper will bring happiness to a humanity of which they understand nothing at all.

This is why I believe it my duty to make an appeal to the traditional good sense of my French-speaking compatriots and ask them this vital question:

"Are you ready to renounce the great advantages you already have, the almost unlimited freedoms you already enjoy under the democratic institutions which rule you, merely to yield to the illusory hopes of a handful of visionaries or jokers more interested in establishing a French-Canadian dictatorship—their dictatorship—than in working for the happiness of the people?"

The leaders of separatism have nothing to offer us. I have read their writings; I have followed their campaigns; I have analyzed their speeches: we already have what they would give us — and more.

Such an uproar, so much recrimination, so many appeals to prejudice and hate — for nothing!

---

*From *Pourquoi Je Suis Antiséparatiste,* Montreal, Les Editions de L'homme, 1962. Translated by Thomas L. Waugh.
†Mr. Harvey, author of a number of books and articles in both French and English, is Managing Editor of *Le Petit Journal,* Montreal.

From what are we to be freed?

Is there really a desire to increase the total freedoms already actually exercised by each citizen of Quebec? Let us go into detail, if you like.

Are we free, yes or no, to learn and to speak French? Who is there to prevent it? Who would dream of preventing it? Did the "damned English-speakers" teach us our dialect?

We have not even succeeded—as was desirable, even necessary—in propagating the use and knowledge of the two native languages of our country throughout the ordinary people.

After almost two centuries of common citizenship with the elements of British stock and our neighbours in America (a nation of extreme dynamism), we French-Canadians, descendants of France, still know and speak only one language in most cases: French—perhaps to our misfortune.

One can state without fear of contradiction that in our rural areas more than 95% of our people scarcely know "yes" and "no" in English.

In most of our cities, it is the minority which is bilingual. In old Quebec, capital of our province, seat of our government, out of more than 300,000 inhabitants, are there more than 10,000 who can speak English fluently?

The fallacy of Anglicization

Even in Montreal, a metropolis which our sniveling patriots call Anglicized and Americanized, take a walk east of Main, to the edge of Pointe-aux-Trembles, and even to the tip of the island. How many bilingual people will you find? Less than 30%, perhaps 20%. Or less!

Yet Montreal is the most Anglicized of French-Canadian cities. It would be more correct to say that it is in Quebec City that the most English-speakers abound—Canadians of British stock, Jews, Poles, Scandinavians, Germans, Italians, and many French families from France.

Therefore, in the province of Quebec the vast majority of people speak only French. *And the minority which occasionally, for social or economic reasons, use English, are usually those very ones who speak and write the best French.*

This is how it stands after almost two centuries of English presence and one century of confederation.

One wonders then what "unilingualism" could add to the political system envisioned by our independents. Instead, being realistic, one is tempted to think that an independent French-Canada would be obliged to foster the knowledge of English. In America, north from Mexico to the Pole, a state like ours will either be bilingual or not exist at all.

Our freedom is protected

The federal covenant is the protector of our freedom — I am speaking of personal freedom, which is worth more than so-called national freedom.

Is there anything in this covenant which impedes our writers, our journalists, or our thinkers?

The condemnations or censures which fall on French books, newspapers, or speeches—are they federal and from outside French-Canada? Do the obstacles erected in this domain come from those whom our separatists wrongly call foreigners, or from our own compatriots?

Do not the freedoms of speech and of the press, which are actually protected by essentially democratic institutions, risk perishing the day certain elements of a dictatorial or arbitrary nature (in the shadow of the Citadel of Quebec) exercise an absolute and sovereign power?

Alas! How numerous are the men who, giving in to the cajoling of bad shepherds and false prophets, leave their prey for the shadows, and fall into an abyss!

Finally let's mention the freedom to travel, to choose employment or a home, to possess, to spend, to save, to contract marriage, to raise children according to belief, to sell or to buy, to use or abuse property, to criticize or praise anything—in short, the complete range of democratic prerogatives to which a separate state can add nothing, but which it can restrict or abolish.

Here, then, the contribution of separatism is reduced to nothing.

We are promised what we already have

The independence of Quebec cannot give us institutions which we already have. Also, it cannot bring us closer to France and her culture; it cannot bring about free distribution of French books in our bookstores, libraries, and homes; it cannot speed up the free circulation, in French-Canada, of many Parisian publications which have already taken hold there. And as for French textbooks, two colleges in the metropolis— Stanislaus and Marie de France—use them exclusively, and it is up to the others to do as much. It is not the federal covenant which stops them from doing so.

At school it is doubtless necessary to restrict the press, radio and television because of their educational value.

Today Montreal has, in proportion to its population, more daily newspapers than any other large North American city. Four of these dailies are in French. There are also influential weeklies which certainly do their part for the French-Canadian word.

In the field of information, radio and television play a large role. Without counting private radio stations which reach all our homes, let us emphasize the fact that the federal government has provided Quebec and various French groups scattered throughout the rest of Canada with an incomparable radio network and television channels of inestimable importance.

What can a separate state add to these advantages? Once again, nothing.

Will secession make us more the masters of our fate?

In order to justify themselves for offering us independence like a national resurrection, our separatists are forced to destroy history *by showing Quebec as a sort of Canadian colony.* It is not infrequently that one hears them use this expression: "Let us throw off the colonial yoke!" It is in making simple and credulous people swallow this drivel that they have been able to construct their peculiar theory of independence. Quebec and Canada are one and the same thing. Ignoring this essential fact, our independents do not hestitate to compare us with Negroes recently liberated from a colonial status and encourage us to seek liberty too. This is an outrageous, ridiculous comparison.

These childish and deceitful arguments will not stand up one instant under examination. Quebec fully possesses that independence they demand for us. Why? Because—let's say it again—it is an integral and unreserved part of Canada, a sovereign country and known as such throughout the world. French-Canadians all participate fully in this sovereignty.

The sacred cow

This means that our independents are obliged to lie, to deceive themselves and the whole world in trying to sell us a bill of goods we already own. They make me think of a man who would take his neighbour's cow and try to sell it back to him with the honourable title of Sacred Cow, Independence Cow.

How far can we go with this confusion of ideas, production of brains unbalanced or bewildered by passion? One can even state, for example, that the condition of ethnic *minority* is synonymous with subjugation and incompatible with the idea of sovereignty. It is a gratuitous statement because we know well that there always have existed, that there still exist, and that there will never cease being minorities to which majorities will be subject materially, culturally, socially, and morally.

In fact, in looking over a map of the world, I do not see any country more independent than the Province of Quebec. Therefore, let no one have the audacity to come and sell us a cow he has stolen from us!

The human element transcends the national

As for myself, attempting to be simple and realistic, I have for some time committed the crime of thinking that it is more important to be a man than to be of a race; more important to be a Canadian than a Frenchman, Englishman, or American; more important to speak two languages than to speak only one; more important to assure each person of drink, food, shelter, and necessary knowledge than to feed us on wind and intoxicate us with hollow words.

The national element is not part of the nature of man. Woe to him who exaggerates its sense and meaning! For him it means to turn his back on life. Concerning the recent vain effort of the government of this country to make acceptable the fact that "Canadian origin" must be a reality, it has been said and written that it is necessary that French-Canadians be able to count themselves across the ten provinces of the confederation. And we pass the time counting ourselves. For people weak in counting, this is strange. Never mind. Here can be seen one of our great defects; namely, that we have lost our sense of value, and it is time for us to recover it.

Do you know who, in the future, will be the most respected in our country? It will be he who made Canada loved by the men and women who live here.

On the other hand, there are those today who are insulted at being called Canadian. One of my dearest friends says this offends his dignity as an independent.

A well-placed pride

Poor dignity! Poor pride! What's to become of you? Here we have the unique privilege of living in one of the most beautiful and happiest countries on the globe, and yet we blush at the mention of some embryonic racism.

I have travelled my country from Halifax to Vancouver. Three times I have crossed the western plains and the Rockies and gone through our cities on the Pacific coast. To the beauties of the banks of the St. Lawrence, of Cape Diamond, of the superb cliffs at Charlevoix and the Gaspé Peninsula, of the granite peaks of the Saguenay and the Laurentian Chain, dotted with lakes, I add, as though it were my own patrimony, an incredible sunset on Lake Superior, waves on the oceans of wheat as far as the eye can see in Manitoba, Saskatchewan and Alberta; the slow march of herds of cattle on the plains; the thunder of a stampede in Calgary; the incomparable green of the Bow and Spray rivers in the splendour of Banff; the flashing glacier which dominates Lake Louise; the wild animals, deer and bear, which come to eat out of our hands at Jasper; the white rocky mountain sheep hanging on the side of rocks; the rich valley of the Okanagan with its fruits, vineyards, wine, silky pheasants; then, the port of Vancouver, so blue, so clear, so well divided into water and rock that one would say that it was sculptured by a giant out of *A Thousand and One Nights*; next, Victoria, a garden city all in flowers with enormous trees, so high and strong, between Nanaimo, Port Alberni, and Qualicum Beach; and above this marvelous ocean coast, the haughty peaks of the distant mountains under their eternal cap of ice and snow.

I returned, my head ringing with images, and I said to myself that if Canadians only knew how to see, notice, and appreciate, there would be, to them, no question of breaking the Canadian unity because they would be ashamed to disfigure a country so worthy of the grandeur and honour of their whole love. That is what I call a feeling of national dignity. The separatists, in distorting this picture, become the agents of national depreciation.

Willful misleading, or foolishness?

The Assembly for National Independence seeks to integrate, to put into the same basket, French-Canadians living in various provinces of Canada (that is to say, at home here), and the French-Canadians who have *emigrated* to the United States and become *naturalized*; i.e., have become foreigners to Quebec. The distinction is important. And if the independents do not make this distinction, it is either because they are of bad faith or very ignorant.

Any Canadian from Quebec, no matter what his language or ethnic origin, can go to live in Alberta or British Columbia without leaving *his country*, that is to say, *his home*. His national status remains absolutely the same. There he will participate in the election of his representative, his city councillors, or his mayor. He will occasionally achieve public responsibilities in his city or his region. In short, he will be a 100% citizen because the *Canadian nation* is *his nation*. Such is the fact legally, constitutionally, and historically.

The situation is different for a French-Canadian who leaves his native land and goes to the United States with the intention of making that his country. He is nothing more than an immigrant. None of the advantages mentioned above regarding a move inside our borders are due him before he gets his certificate of naturalization. But then he ceases being a Canadian and becomes an American. He does not belong to us any more. The rights he has are American rights. He no longer has any rights specifically Canadian. On our side, if we were to follow him on foreign soil and an official offer were tendered to re-enfranchise him, the American authorities would be justified in sending us home and telling us to mind our own business.

A theory founded on an ignorance of history and nature

Separatist sovereignty is based on a belief which has no foundation in reality, history or nature.

Its point of departure is that a nation is the product of a community of language, tradition, beliefs, habits, culture, and hopes of any given corner of the earth.

This is a false premise.

No important nation is so founded. The ancient Roman Empire would never have existed if it had depended upon the manifestation of such conditions. The same is true for France, Great Britain, Germany, the United States, and Russia. All of these countries have become organized out of an unbelievable diversity of languages, customs, and even races.

From the points of view of race, character, moral and social attitudes, physique, methods of thought and expression, there is as much difference between a Breton and someone from Provence in France as there is between someone from Alberta and a Québecois in Canada. Don't tell a Scot that he is English or he will be insulted; further, there are three Switzerlands in one: French, German, and Italian. There are two Belgiums in one: French and Flemish. There are 17 Russias, divided by several languages and all types of races.

Race, language, origin, and tradition are not facts of nature. In other words, they are not part of the *essence* of man. Man can live without them; whereas he cannot live without bread. They are, then, *accidents.* Very important accidents, certainly, but accidents just the same.

One doesn't get fir trees from apples

From an apple seed, one can get only apple trees, not fir trees; with grains of wheat you don't get oats; from the seed of man you get only men, not races. Let's suppose, for example, that some Canadians (let's call them Chaput or Barbeau) were born in Sweden. After having lost their father and mother while young, they were raised in a Swedish family to speak Swedish, to go to Swedish schools, and to participate in Swedish society. What would be the result? A Swedish Chaput or a Swedish Barbeau.

This explains why millions of North Americans in Canada and the United States, coming from all the countries of the world, have forgotten the past of their families and have become wholly Canadian or wholly American.

If I insist on this point, where others see only the truth of La Palice, it is because one of the leaders of the separatist movement has stated, more than once in different ways, that the formation of a French-Canadian nation is a *natural right*. They even give it an air of Divine Will, with great words about an elect people and a mission of Providence. One must remember, however, that Germany rushed upon Europe in 1914 and that she burned and killed with the cry, "God is with us!"

The mystique of folly

I noticed the fanaticism which underlies such an illusion one day when crossing Western Canada by train. I talked with a young French-Canadian officer on the question of race. For him the greatest misfortune which could strike one of our compatriots emigrating to the United States or British Columbia was to condemn his descendents to a loss of identity. I wanted to find out just how deeply rooted this feeling was in him.

I said, "Let's suppose that a baby was born in a hovel in Montreal, of French-speaking parents, and that he lost his parents shortly after birth. He is adopted by a rich Catholic family in California, and there he enjoys all comfort imaginable. He receives excellent training in the best schools and universities, and when he becomes an adult, he is one of the most eminent and useful citizens of his adopted country. Do you believe that this child lost in the exchange?

"I do," the young officer replied.

From then on, all discussion became useless. In the silence which followed, I wondered how a particular education could, to such an extent, destroy reason and human compassion in a young man who was intelligent, educated, and well brought up. Certainly the good sense of the French-Canadian people is foreign to such mentality. But we find this, unfortunately, in a certain number of the lower middle class from which the separatist element gathers almost all its strength.

But this is also its weakness. Because it puts forward nothing serious in the light of *nature*, because its theory of racial independence is based on a historical heresy and not on the human factor, it can periodically come to life in spurts, but it wears itself out quickly like something artificial and without substance.

A North American culture

More than a year ago I realized that the Canadian anxiety vis-a-vis the devouring dynamism of its neighbouring republic, is of a social and cultural order rather than political and economic. It seems proper that this aspect of the danger of Americanization should be discussed.

In this regard, I have the courage to state that we would show ourselves as simply intelligent and honest if, instead of hiding our weaknesses under continued campaigns of casting aspersions, we would have the integrity to concede certain levels of superiority in our neighbours and friends. In a way we might draw upon this as a practical inspiration — that is, an aspiration to raise ourselves to the same height.

Without giving up anything of our French language, our Latin heritage, or our identity, what wrong is there in being able to read in the original an impressive number of essays, novels, short stories, and plays which are among the best of the modern and contemporary world and which, let's admit it, surpass anything that Canada (including Quebec) has produced in this genre?

We have nothing here which even approaches the works of Edgar Allan Poe, Ruskin, Eugene O'Neill, Mark Twain, Mencken, Steinbeck, Hemingway, Faulkner, Caldwell, Tennessee Williams, and at least a hundred others too numerous to mention.

Without underestimating the effort actually expended by some of our writers in the French language, let's concede without shame that the Americans, those barbarians, have long given us lessons in literary art, in thought, and in philosophy, from which we could gain inspiration even if we never wanted to achieve the universality which they themselves have.

Let's take the good, reject the bad

Instead of exhausting ourselves — perhaps in vain — in wanting to repel all influence which could modify what we are, would it not be wiser to know how to distinguish between good and bad influences in order to modestly choose the former, which would make us better, and repudiate the others which would ruin us? Shall I give examples?

The Americans have music which has gone into all the countries of the world. We have nothing like it. We could well be proud if we had been able to produce only half of Gershwin.

Not one of our composers could come up to the ankles of Stephen Foster. And each year in the United States there are songs on the "hit parade", several of which surpass our best local efforts by far.

For several years New York theatre has had the edge on that of Paris in both art and vitality.

There, too, are seen musical comedies which have no equal anywhere.

Must one insist that the Americans have: the most worthwhile and, on the whole, the best staged and liveliest films in the world; better newspapers than ours; magazines superior to ours; enchanting shows in which feminine talent is combined with physical perfection; a goodly number of television shows obviously better than ours; thinkers, philosophers, scientists, and technicians such as are unknown here; several universities quite superior to those of Montreal and Laval?

And why shouldn't we admire the gigantic effort being expended in the southern United States to prepare for the great human adventure of conquering space and exploring the planets?

And, once again, why not appreciate the American power which saved Western civilization and human liberty by covering, with billions of dollars, a Europe devastated by war and incapable of helping itself?

But in order to fully appreciate all these things, it is necessary to know, besides French, the English language—sole vehicle of communication with the humanity which surrounds us.

I insist on this so much because socially, economically, politically, geographically, and (from certain points of view) culturally, we are North Americans rather than French or English.

One cannot repeat this too much: we are North Americans.

Certainly Europe, led by France, is still the fount of Occidental culture. The best in North America is of European derivation, a European development. The North American population is almost totally of European origin.

Hence it is not extreme to say that North America is the best thing Europe has created outside itself. We can be justly proud. The great experiment of the fusion of races and peoples in our land will probably never ever be duplicated. It is one of the greatest human adventures in history.

Nevertheless, there are those Canadians, English-speaking as well as French-speaking, who want, contrary to reality, to remain in the European context instead of placing themselves, as they really are, in the North American context.

Hence a bizarre, abnormal sentiment on the part of a certain number of our compatriots: *they despise North American success*—that is to say, their own success — for the sole reason that they refuse to be what they are. Perhaps this explains why it is so difficult to consolidate the Canadian nation.

THE AWAKENING OF A PEOPLE

There is salvation. It is certainly not in a separatism which brings us absolutely no important advantages, but which might just *isolate us by a stupid denial of America*. Our people and their leaders finally understand this. More than ever they speak of culture and instruction in French-Canada. Who speaks of it? Everyone. Under the pressure of thawing opinion, the government of Quebec has put all its available millions of dollars at the service of schools.

An intense campaign is now being waged in all areas to convince the people of the extreme importance of human knowledge in our century. And public opinion is moved. Free education as well as compulsory attendance until an older age has been decreed; people with private fortunes are asked to help in order to enrich the minds of children and the young, as happens in more advanced countries. Why? Because we must go full-speed ahead.

We find ourselves in this dilemma: either submit to the influence of our stronger neighbours, who are better equipped and more practical than we, to the point of being assimilated by them for the good reason that we find theirs a better way of life; or show to the outside world, as well as to ourselves, that we contribute positively to the progress of science, art, and letters; that our men and women, in all fields of endeavour, are equal to (if not teachers of) the most learned persons in the New World, that our growth allows us to live as well as and sometimes better than others—in short, that we are recognized by other peoples as an indispensible leaven of civilization.

IS IT ENOUGH TO STAY WHAT WE ARE?

For us, strength is to form superior abilities in all spheres and scatter them across the continent. It seems to me that for a minority like ours, there is no other way, no other hope of lasting. The naive or simpleminded will try to persuade us to flee from contact with foreigners and withdraw into the great Laurentian wigwam. They are the ones who urge us to keep what we have and stay what we are. That's all right; it's even more. But it's not enough. It is the way of life to ceaselessly change and acquire perfection. Those who do not, die. Also it is not enough that a Minister of Culture be a defense AGAINST this or that; he must be FOR something worthy. Prime Minister Lesage has said that he wants to make Quebec a "source of radiation". That's the way he should speak.

Bravo! Because "to radiate" does not mean to turn in on oneself. The great victory of the French in America will be in knowing how to absorb and assimilate the good and salutary offered to us by the English-speaking portion of this continent. For us it would be defeat and cowardice to be happy to stay what we are.

FADED FLOWERS AND NEW FLOWERS

Therefore, our first duty is not to place faded flowers on the feet of cadavers, nor to sow madness, hate or division in a great country which has everything necessary to be powerful and happy, but to prepare a highly cultured new generation — based on French, if you wish — which will give to America and to the world superior writers, superior artists, superior manufacturers (not only honest), superior techniques—in a word, remarkable people and not an amorphous and servile collection, men capable of showing that their existence is useful to their age. Otherwise we would seem to be part of useless existence.

It is with this condition alone that the French-speaking group of the *Canadian nation* will escape total disintegration. The rest is only derision and raving, if not a downright betrayal — the betrayal of the country of our children.

Some try to create a mystique of independence — a false independence — by giving this cry aimed at a collective hysteria: LET'S SEPARATE OURSELVES FROM CANADA!

To this slogan, answer the following: LET'S STAY WITH CANADA! Not by blood and tears but by eternal weapons, the force of our thought and the excellence of our work.

9. *DEAR ENEMIES**

Solange Chaput Rolland and Gwethalyn Graham†

Dear Gwen:

At the moment relations between English and French Canada are nervous and strained; it wouldn't take much to provoke a serious incident between our two groups. A sluggish, rumbling hatred sets Separatists against Federalists. Scarcely two years ago, some English newspapers in Quebec, the *Star* and the *Gazette*, for example, were still systematically ignoring the reality of French Canada. Reading them, one could have sworn that Quebec was an English province! Today they are making a real effort to pay some attention to us, but we haven't the slightest illusion about this sudden interest in our problems. What makes us suddenly attractive to your compatriots is our nationalization of electricity, our almost miraculous industrial development, and our astonishing possibility of becoming in less than ten years one of the most prosperous provinces in Canada. We are no longer the poor relations of Confederation; we are no longer employees to be exploited or poverty-stricken citizens to be tolerated; we have become a force to be reckoned with. So 'Bravo, French Canada; you are suddenly wonderful and we love you.' And what I say to you is . . . zut. I listen to your politicians extolling our merits, recognizing our vital role in the history of our national identity. Your businessmen suddenly discover ours and are astonished by their industrial intelligence. All this is good, fine, but it reeks of political capital — this anxiety, which is a little too recent, not to lose a promising market in the future by committing more blunders. Yes, Gwen, zut it is!

What *is* a Canadian? Please enlighten me. Guy Sylvestre has said of us that a French Canadian is an American of French language living under British domination. Quite a cocktail, isn't it? This mixture, however, does explain us. What is an English Canadian then? A gentleman

---

**Selections from correspondence between a French-Canadian and an English-Canadian, published as *Dear Enemies,* Toronto, The Macmillan Company of Canada Limited, 1963. Although appearing as if they were whole letters, the selections reprinted here are actually paragraphs drawn from different letters, some written weeks apart. This accounts for occasional lack of continuity.*
†Mlle Rolland is a French-Canadian journalist, editor and book critic, and a frequent contributor to French and English CBC radio and television programs. Mrs. Graham, a free-lance journalist, is author of two novels which won the Governor-General's Award.

who is very polite, who has a son, a daughter, and a dog; who reads the Bible and *The Financial Post*, plays golf and goes curling, glances through *Time* magazine, drinks sherry with his soup and tea at five o'clock, and never makes passes at his secretary? Obviously I am joking, but this series of clichés is typical of what we think of one another, or rather of what we do not make an effort *not* to think of one another. If only we could talk perhaps we would understand each other better. But this joy is withheld from us. In the matter of bilingualism, will you admit the complete failure of our Confederative understanding? The two cultures vegetate side by side; they grow poorer on a diet of French and English imitations and American buffoonery because they have not yet discovered the richness of their own thinking. We are a people without understanding, without communication, without love. And this voluntary misunderstanding can be summed up in one question: When are we going to have the courage to accept one another?

Because I live in a democracy, I want above all a freedom of being. But if, in order to live in freedom in a Canada entirely dominated by English thinking and an English way of life, I must constantly do battle to keep my language and its spirit intact, then both what I have to say and my happiness in being alive will always be clouded. I shall shut myself up again in my French solitude, and my bitterness will snuff out the dynamism that is indispensible to creative work and to economic or social success. We Canadians don't recognize the love which is within us; this country of snow and desolation, this icy tundra, this people closed in on themselves and their problems, creates in our souls a hunger for love from which will flow one day, perhaps, a stream of moral richness. But life demands love, and we don't know how to live with it.

I believe in the future of Quebec — if our people can go on being patient and if they resist the skilful persuasion of the separatists who are holding up before them a shining independence as derisive as it is economically impossible to realize. If we have a redrafting of the Act of Confederation, we shall march side by side with you and with our heads up. From now until then, we shall be patient in the face of reality, but impatient to demonstrate it.

I am still suffering under the conviction that English Canada has absolutely no interest in the awakening of French Canada or in our struggles, our history, or our reality. Between you and us there is a gap of cordial misunderstanding, free of any animosity but also lacking any real will to make even a gesture of friendship, one towards the other. Beyond Winnipeg, for example, the very existence of Quebec becomes a sort of myth, a folklore of trappers and traders. Please don't think I am exaggerating; between one city and the next I was constantly obliged to rewrite my lectures, to change my speeches so as to talk not about a revolution in Quebec, but literally about the fact that Quebec is *there*. As an example of nothing very significant: one day I was invited to appear on television in one of the cities on the Prairies. A young journalist, curious about Quebec, asked, 'Do your children speak French at home?' When I said yes, he said something that temporarily stopped me in my tracks: 'How clever of them!' Later, in order to prove how interested he was, he asked if French Canadians understand the Queen when she speaks French.

Such ignorance isn't too serious in itself, but when it is repeated almost every day one has to fight down a sense of resentment and bitterness, and I didn't always succeed.

If we could only laugh a bit more in Canada, life would be easier. I remember one day I was present at a national convention. We were ten from Quebec among hundreds of delegates from all over Canada. At some point during the adoption of resolutions, a strange and very ridiculous proposal came before the assembly. It had to do with the learning of Esperanto as a means 'of reducing the difficulties in language between French and English Canada'. At this point, many friends in the room thought that we of Quebec might be a little shocked by this strange request. We were — but instead of getting angry we roared with laughter at the joyful prospect of visiting France and England, happily conversing in Esperanto. I must say that our laughter was contagious and, with spontaneous good humour, the whole assembly ruled out this starting resolution.

I would like to make one point clear before ending this letter. Please tell your compatriots that, although we recognize the authenticity of their efforts to understand us better, they must do it themselves and not come to us trying too hard to please, too hard to apologize for their lack of French. So let us both do our parts, but let's not bend over backwards in doing them.

● ● ●

Dear Solange:

As for that boring and worn-out word 'Anglo-Saxon', let us try to establish a few facts, if possible, once and for all. The population of Canada is divided into three roughly equal groups of which one is of French origin, one of British origin, and the third of diverse origin. It should be emphasized that the last group is larger than either of the other two, outnumbering each of them by more than half a million, and that they are beginning, in their turn, to wish that French Canada would stop ignoring their existence.

Canadians of British origin are divided into four groups — English, Scots, Irish, and Welsh. I like French Canadians and I must warn you that if you are invited to make a speech in Edinburgh, Cardiff, Belfast, or Dublin and you refer to your audience as Anglo-Saxons, you'll be killed on the spot. It isn't that anyone wants to bait the English any more — that is out of date too — but, in general, people simply don't like being called what they're not. I doubt if a Chinese would be particularly enchanted to find himself described as an Italian, or that an Egyptian would like it much if you called him a Pole.

We whose ancestry is Scots, Irish or Welsh are a different race from the English, although it seems to me to be rather ridiculous to be talking about 'race' in 1963. But, as French Canadians, has it ever occurred to you that, as Jean-Jacques Le François has pointed out, if your ancestors came from Normandy or Brittany you're a lot more 'Anglo-Saxon' than Hugh MacLennan, Powys Thomas, Morley Callaghan, or — oh horror — Mr. Donald Gordon himself?

To toss thirteen million English-speaking Canadians into one basket labelled 'Anglo-Saxon' creates an impression of English Canada just as distorted as that of my portrait above. The persistent abuse of this word in French Canada does nothing but falsify the image of English-speaking Canada and only serves to make French-English relations still worse, because the word is almost always used in a pejorative sense although in fact it doesn't mean anything at all but 'English'; most often it is used as a description of England before the Norman Conquest in 1066 — its people, its architecture, its writings (the Anglo-Saxon chronicles, Beowulf, etc.). At the present time, 'Anglo-Saxon' means simply English or of English tradition or origin.

And nothing else.

I feel very ill at ease with this rising tide of French Canadians who demand bilingualism from English-speaking Canadians while at the same time regarding the necessity to learn English as a burden. This argument is a two-edged sword which seems to me to be thoroughly contradictory. The moment when English Canada, or at least the young people of English Canada are beginning to wake up (and this awakening is genuine, even though it comes so late) is not the moment for French Canadians, imitating the separatists, to go to sleep.

Such gratuitous statements as those which I've quoted here find their way into the French press every day. It is time to put a stop to them, because we are headed toward a state of things which threatens Quebec and all of Canada. Responsible people should not fall into the trap against which students of philosophy are put on guard during their first year — that of drawing conclusions from special cases, and of presenting affirmations as facts. Such prejudices, allusions, and insinuations are not *facts*; they are only words. The usage of the word-turned-into-fact in the present climate of opinion raises the spectre of fascism, and fascism is a state of mind that leads nowhere.

• • •

Dear Gwen:

I'll try now to talk about separatism, not in the historical sense (for that, all our readers have to do is read Marcel Chaput and Raymond Barbeau) but so that you will understand my ideas on the subject. First, I accept the judgment of those who might think my views are short-sighted.

Let us begin with this problem. The economic 'facts' of some of the self-styled experts graduated too recently from the School of Advanced Economic Studies don't convince me in the least that a province suddenly cut off from federal aid on every level has a possibility of existing, much less of thriving. Certainly, if our 'Made-in-Quebec' products are good, there will perhaps be no reason not to sell them, to export them to foreign countries (like Ontario), but there is equally no reason why your compatriots, who in the last analysis will have been politely shown the door, should feel much like encouraging our local industries. It isn't difficult for me to imagine that English Canadians, justifiably hurt by our attitude, would doubtless turn toward those 'Made-in-U.S.A.' products in order to satisfy their everyday needs — and, incidentally, at a lower price. Let us be realistic; the economy of a country is dependent on the markets available to its products. If we were to weave the most beautiful *ceintures fléchées* in the world, who would wear them? And I have no confidence in the possibility of our constructing modern or ultra-modern factories if we voluntarily isolate ourselves from what we *already* lack in Canada as a whole. There are undoubtedly economists who can elaborate on the economics of foreign capital, competition, non-convertible currency, investments, and taxes recoverable from the federal government

— all those factors exist, but what we have lacked fundamentally so far is the desire to go on coping, to deprive ourselves in order to continue as the proprietors of our own private enterprises. And I don't believe that the day we become independent — *therefore* impoverished, *therefore* obliged to tighten our belts, *therefore* obliged to undergo considerable sacrifices in physical comforts, in sports, and in actual luxuries — we are suddenly going to find ourselves captains of industry. Between calculations on paper and the intelligent and practical use of the capital at our own disposition there is, unfortunately, a gap which we are still a long way from having bridged.

I don't get much fun out of writing these things. I may lack detailed knowledge of the economics of my own province, but, having been brought up in an environment in which one talked more about 'business' than about 'ideas', I do know, I think, something about the mentality of the industrialist. As much as I admire his courage and willingness to take a risk on occasion, I am just as disturbed by his willingness to hand over to someone else his entire firm, which has often been built up over generations.

Some of your people are in part responsible for our sudden appetite for wealth, power, and *la dolce vita.* For more than a hundred years we have carried the burden of defeat, the post-conquest ruin of our businessmen. In less than twenty years we have gone from cultivating turnips to the construction of the giant Manicouagan Dam. Such a revolution explains both our potentialities for success, which seem to contradict my dim view of our industrial future as an independent state, and our lack of experience in the world of industry, which explains my fears for a separate Quebec. To the 'too little and too late' of André Laurendeau about bilingual federal cheques, which seem to me so comically futile, I would like to counter with 'too much and too soon' to our believers in an independence resting on a false concept of a viable Quebec economy.

But on the emotional plane, or the cultural one, to put it more explicitly, how can you expect French Canadians not to be separatists? One can't live on two levels at once. I, too, would like to believe in a genuinely binational and bicultural nation, but I think my own people and yours are too selfish to achieve a future that will be based not on the unity of our thinking but on its diversity. Yet in writing the words 'diversity of thought' I am already foreseeing the difficulties to come. It is perfectly obvious that only the province of Quebec has paid heed to this divergency of view up to now, and that only those of your compatriots who live in Quebec are beginning to understand it.

•　　　•　　　o

Dear Solange:

Any English-speaking Canadian writing on the subject of separatism is likely to be told, at least by the separatists themselves, to go and mind her own business. Since few if any of us, however, want to see our country split into three sections, with the Maritimes and Newfoundland on the one hand, and Ontario, The Prairie Provinces, and British Columbia on the other, looking more like a North American version of East and West Pakistan than anything else, presumably we are at least entitled to express our opinions even if the final decision is up to Quebec.

First of all, you have considerable backing for your belief that an independent Quebec would be poorer and not richer. Some noted French-Canadian economists who have studied the question have come to the conclusion that a Quebec separated from the rest of Canada would not be economically viable. None of them, so far as I know, believes that the province could even maintain its present standard of living, let alone raise it as the separatists claim. Nor would the rest of Canada, which would probably end up being directly absorbed by the United States with Quebec existing as a French-speaking American satellite, technically independent but actually controlled by Washington and Wall Street.

One of the aspects of separatism which I find particularly baffling and illogical is the argument about sovereignty. Quebec is only just beginning, under the Lesage government, to exercise the sovereignity it has always possessed but of which it has taken little advantage until now. A case in point is the recent nationalization of electricity. Ontario has had publicly-owned power for forty years; there is nothing in the B.N.A. Act that obliged Quebec to wait so long before making this and other changes and reforms which are urgently needed and long overdue. From such a standpoint, the separatists seem to me to be in the position of someone who owns a house with fifteen rooms of which he has never occupied more than one, proclaiming to the world that he requires a thirty-room house before he can be comfortable. Possibly he may require it in the end, but the end is a long way off, and surely, in the meantime, he might try to make use of what he already has before declaring that it is inadequate. The separatist position on sovereignty would be absurd, at the present time, if it were not so worrying, because separatist propaganda and the publicity given to it by the press is a diversionary tactic at a period of crisis when Quebec cannot afford diversions of such a nature. There is too much to be done and too much talent, skill, energy, and determination needed to do it for young people in Quebec to be frittering away their time ignoring the realities of the present in order to construct a mythical future.

In addition to their failure to answer the detailed and closely reasoned objections of the economists and their essentially defeatist all-or-nothing attitude toward sovereignty, have they yet even tried to show us how an independent Quebec will produce a better artist or scientist or engineer?

Even if none of these grounds for being anti-separatist existed, there would still remain one crucial fact which ought to be enough to damn the movement outright: *it is fundamentally racist.* The separatist thesis rests on an ethnic foundation and, whatever its present political orientation, there is a danger that it will veer further and further to the Right, because racist political parties usually do, until they are captured by ultra-nationalists and turn into overt fascism. I cannot see the separatist position evolving into anything else because the separatists themselves have made it abundantly clear that they put ethnic before economic and social values. One has only to read a little history to hear the echoes from the twenties when Hitler and Mussolini were still sounding like innocent nationalists, concerned only with the advancement of their own people.

•　　•　　•

Dear Gwen:

Now I have come to the end of our dialogue and yet how many things remain to be said! But, because it is necessary to write period to this exchange of ideas, let me sum up my hopes as a French Canadian. They are definite and precise.

I no longer want to be considered a second-class citizen in my own country.

I no longer want to think of my compatriots living outside Quebec struggling heroically for a right to speak and pray in French.

I no longer want to think of the unjust sacrifices to which parents in an English area are forced to agree in order to give their children a French education, when, in fact, their numbers justify the construction of French and Catholic schools. I am particularly concerned with the question of separate schools in all the provinces of Canada (except Quebec) which sets French and English Canadians in opposition to one another.

I can no longer accept the fact that my son, for example, should occupy a lesser position in the service of his country simply because his companion in the civil service or the armed forces possesses, over him, the sole advantage of being unable to speak one word of French.

I no longer want to believe that in 1967 there will still be places where it will be unacceptable to speak French.

I no longer want to have to prove in a book, an argument, a conversation, or a newspaper article that Quebec is not still living, in the words of Goldwin Smith, 'like an antediluvian animal preseved in Siberian ice'.

I refuse to look forward to a future time when one of my children will come home hurt — devastated — because he in his turn has been ordered to 'speak white'.

I will no longer accept bad service anywhere in Canada because I am French-speaking. I do not ask to be understood, but I shall not tolerate contempt, bad manners, or sarcasm if I am overheard expressing myself in my own language by your compatriots.

• • •

Dear Solange:

At the base of the whole problem described by that one word 'bilingualism' are the elementary and high schools of English Canada. The French language should be regarded as a compulsory subject from Grade 1, and I would hope that the Tan-Gau method would be adopted across the country, because it is at once the easiest and most effective way of teaching small children another language yet devised, so far as I know —they simply learn by listening, the way they learned English as babies.

Across English Canada, then, French should be a compulsory subject through university. If English Canadians want to lapse back into unilingualism after that, it will be their affair, but if they are intending to go into business, federal politics, or the federal civil service, they will be making a serious mistake in the first instance and a fatal one in the second and third. A bilingual federal government will have no use for employees, and the Canadian people no use for politicians, who can't speak French. As for the future businessmen, French is one of the languages of the Common Market and a sister language to the Spanish and Portuguese of all Latin America. It would seem a great pity for them deliberately to abandon their inherent advantage of having been born in an Anglo-French nation.

And the French departments of the schools and universities of English Canada must be staffed by French Canadians. This, if you like, is the price your people are going to have to pay as their *due* share in the continuance of the pact of Confederation.

I do not think there is any other solution.

SELECTED BIBLIOGRAPHY

Burghardt, A. F., "If Quebec Secedes From Canada," *Saturday Night*, June-July, 1963.

Chaput, M., *Why I Am a Separatist*, Toronto, The Ryerson Press, 1961.

Dion, L., "Reflections on the FLQ," *The Canadian Forum*, August, 1963.

Fox, P., "Separatism and Quebec," in *Politics: Canada* (Fox, P., Editor), Toronto, McGraw-Hill Company of Canada Ltd., 1962.

Graham, G., and Rolland, S. C., *Dear Enemies,* Toronto, The Macmillan Company of Canada, Ltd., 1963.

Harvey, J.-C., *Pourquoi Je Suis Antiséparatiste,* Montréal, Les Editions de L'homme, 1962.

Johnson, D., "We Want a Quebec that is Strong and Free," *Canada Month*, January, 1964.

Keate, S., and Lemelin, R., "What the Hell is Going on in Quebec?," *Saturday Night*, February, 1964.

Keyfitz, N., "Canadians and Canadiens," *Queen's Quarterly,* Vol. LXX, No. 2, Summer, 1963.

LaPierre, L. L., "Le Séparatisme and French Canadians," *The Canadian Forum,* January, 1962.

McGeachy, J. B., "Quebec Minority Hasn't a Hope of Breaking Up Confederation, *The Financial Post*, July 13, 1963.

Trudeau, P. E., "The Multi-National State in Canada," *The Canadian Forum,* June, 1962.

Wade, M. (Editor), *Canadian Dualism*, Toronto, University of Toronto Press, 1960.

chapter four

PROBLEMS OF RACE RELATIONS

This chapter, the longest in the book, deals with some of the problems of disorganization in Canadian society as a function of its heterogeneous racial composition. An earlier selection has adequately demonstrated, on anthropological grounds, the fallacy of treating French-English relations as a racial issue (except insofar as the participants themselves *perceive* one another as different racial entities). However, in this chapter, which discusses the difficulties of our Indian, Métis, Eskimo and Negro minorities, the idea of race is pertinent.

To introduce and give direction to the chapter, Dr. Charles Hobart, sociologist at the University of Alberta in Edmonton and a specialist in minority group relations, has written an article entitled "Non-Whites in Canada: Indians, Eskimos, Negroes" especially for this book. This article, which raises a number of vital issues and questions regarding these groups in Canada, is followed by a short piece by Richard D. Jones, National Executive Director of the Canadian Council of Christians and Jews, which discusses the basic problem of "The Economics of Discrimination." Writing for an audience of businessmen in Canada, Jones clearly outlines the costs, both human and financial, of prejudice and consequent discrimination and, suggesting that we can ill afford this luxury, places the final responsibility for eradication of the problem on the individual, "you and me".

The next several selections deal specifically with the "Indian problem." First, a chart graphically demonstrates the growing importance of this problem by indicating the growth in Indian population since 1949. Diamond Jenness carefully describes prejudice against the Indian, and what he calls an "apartheid" situation during the 1920's and asks, in terms of the misfortunes of these past conditions, "What of Today?" William Morris, writing in 1959, partially answers the question in "The Plight of the Indian in Canada". His concern is with making citizenship a meaningful status for the Indian, and he suggests seven points which must be considered to make desirable changes possible. These include increased government cooperation on all levels, secularization of the Indian schools under regular provincial departments of education, provincial handling of matters of public health and welfare, realistic economic development, a complete program of social science research, the removal of "paternalistic legislation", and dignity instead of despair as the "new face" of Indian-white relations. While Morris clearly places the onus upon the government once again to *do something*, John T. Schmidt feels that much *has* been done for the Indian, and that there have been "colossal sums set aside by the Ottawa government for him and his family," but that although he has been "given a chance . . . he can't or won't pull himself into an improved status." The fault, says Schmidt, is his own.

More and more have social scientists come into the field and, with or without government sponsorship, conducted studies which are designed to shed light on the factors underlying Canada's minority group problems. Two illustrations are presented in this chapter. Henry Zentner, a sociologist, studied "Cultural Assimilation Between Indians and Non-Indians in Southern Alberta" through an analysis of questionnaires administered to over 400 Indian and non-Indian high school students. In concluding he asserts that "the rate of Indian assimilation is quickening remarkably" and that the young Indian wants to secure the full benefits of "his potential as a citizen and as a person." Public policy, he suggests, should be brought into line with this situation.

A report on "Some Problems of the Métis of Northern Saskatchewan" by V. F. Valentine, in 1954, represents the social anthropologist at work. Valentine's challenging article reviews the unfortunate effects of what was doubtless well-meaning provincial legislation to help the Métis in Saskatchewan's northern areas, and concludes by questioning our administrators concerning their role in solving these social problems.

Our attention is next turned to Canada's Eskimo population. Writing in the publication *North*, A. F. Flucke advises that the development of the Arctic will provide enough future jobs and prosperity for even the growing Eskimo population, but wonders whether the Eskimo will be able to change sufficiently to take advantage of these opportunities. An Eskimo, Abraham Okpik, offers a very different view of the situation, worrying not whether the Eskimo will be able to change enough, but that he might change at all. He pleads that the whites are as numerous as "mosquitoes" the Eskimo as rare as the "snow geese", and that it would be a great tragedy for this small group to give up their special heritage just to join the ranks of the mosquitoes!

The next article on the Eskimo problem is, appropriately, the work of another social scientist, Frank G. Vallee of McMaster University. An edited version of the concluding chapter of his report, *Kabloona and Eskimo in the Central Keewatin*, presents the essence of the results and conclusions drawn from extensive research in the arctic community. The author envisions, for example, "not the assimilation, or swallowing up, of the Eskimos in Canadian society, but rather their integration as an ethnic group in that society."

Finally the Negro in Canada comes under our spotlight. Harold H. Potter of Sir George Williams University in Montreal presents many aspects of the situation of "Negroes in Canada" in a much abridged version of an article from the British publication *Race*. This academic discussion is followed by Austin C. Clarke's provocative article expressing his claims of anti-Negro prejudice in Canada. The concluding selection is, again, of an academic nature and treats the rather depressed "Socio-Economic Condition of Negroes in Halifax".

The review presented in this chapter might well lead us to conclude that, while Canada does not suffer from the severity of anything like South Africa's apartheid policy, nor the extensiveness of America's "Negro problem", it is not without some serious social problems with regard to race relations, problems which are evidence of certain degrees of disorganization in the general society.

10. NON-WHITES IN CANADA: INDIANS, ESKIMOS, NEGROES*

Charles W. Hobart†

Against such important internal problems facing Canada today as separatism, economic balance, and the integration of immigrant peoples, the integration of coloured minorities would seem to be the least significant. Throughout the twentieth century no more than 3 per cent of the population have been members of coloured minorities, and the current proportion is less than 1.5 per cent. In comparison to the massiveness of similar problems in the United States where more than ten per cent are Negro second class citizens, and where the history of Indian-white relations has been described in one book title as *A Century of Dishonor,* the Canadian picture looks relatively serene. In Canada there has been no slavery (since 1793), no sit-in's, no Black Muslims. Here there is no history of great Indian wars, of reservations ravaged, of Indian policy changing capriciously with changing Presidential administrations.

Nevertheless, although the people involved are not so numerous, and the history and the incidents not so spectacular, "race relations" in Canada, that is, relations between Caucasoid, Negroid and Mongoloid (which includes Indians and Eskimos), do pose some serious and complex problems. They are problems whose resolution will take decades and generations to work out; *constructive* solution of them will depend upon the understanding and patience and to some degree the personal involvement of many Canadians.

A rather basic question is: Can we identify a *Canadian* pattern of race relations? As in many other areas of Canadian life, the answer appears to be both yes and no. The answer is clearly yes in the sense that the Canadian pattern is not merely an extension of ways found south of the border. Here there are no race riots. Instead one encounters cases of Negro doctors accepted and respected by white patients. There was no sentiment that "the only good Injun is a dead Injun"; indeed during the 19th century American Indian bands, harried and hounded by American troops, on occasion sought and were granted asylum in Canada. But there are also incidents which have a distressingly familiar American

---

*Published here for the first time.

†Dr. Hobart, a specialist in minority group relations, is Associate Professor of Sociology at the University of Alberta, Edmonton.

ring. A Métis family moves into a comfortable middle class residential district in Calgary — and finds garbage dumped in their front yard as a protest. A rather well-known Negro professional football player joins the Edmonton team and has difficulty finding a house to live in. An Indian girl performs creditably as a file clerk — but has to be fired because other girls in the office refuse to share the same washroom with her.

These sound rather like transplanted American patterns and perhaps in part they are. Canada is swamped with American mass media: American magazines, American television and radio material, American motion pictures, American books. These materials are loaded with American values, stereotypes, prejudices and myths. Thus Canadians often "know" that Negroes damage residential property values for the same reason that Americans "know"; both have learned this falsehood from the same source. The origins of Canadian stereotypes about Indians and Métis cannot be so clearly sorted out, but the same process of American contamination is immediately apparent. The structure of cross-racial interaction is often very similar north and south of the border: Indians on relatively isolated rural reserves; Negroes herded together in the slums of large cities. The cultural heritage of the one tends to become the culture of both.

What is the background of problems of race relations in Canada? How have they come into existence? We have already noted that there are three different problems which have drawn public attention, those involving Indians, Eskimos and Negroes. The circumstances which have culminated in the current problems of each group are different in each case.

I

The Indians of Canada, in a series of treaties negotiated with the federal government, gave up their rights to traditional hunting grounds in exchange for very much smaller band or tribal reserves and a variety of rights including continuous open season for hunting game on Crown lands and small annual cash payments, usually between five and seven dollars per year. Under the impact of the changed circumstances of their lives and the ravages of the diseases which the whites introduced, the numbers of Indians declined as they did all over North America, from an estimated high of 220,000[1] to a low of about 95,000 in 1911. Since that time their numbers have been increasing, slowly at first, but more recently with increasing rapidity. In 1941 they numbered about 115,000,

---

[1] Mooney, J., *Aboriginal Population of America*, Smith Misc. Coll., Vol. 80, No. 7, p. 33., Washington, 1928.

in 1951 they had increased to over 155,000 and in the following decade their numbers increased by over 50,000 so that the 1961 census reported 207,500 Indians in Canada.

The "Indian problem" has three main facets: one is cultural-ethical, another is biological, and the third is motivational. The cultural-ethical issue is found in the question: Should the Indian be permitted, and indeed encouraged, to live his life and to continue to evolve his culture along traditional lines, or should a break with the past be accomplished so that he can be transformed into an "ordinary", contemporary Canadian? A variety of policy issues affecting the Indian depend upon how this issue is decided; for example, the amount, type and location of educational facilities which will crucially affect the future of the next Indian generation. Many groups feel that they have vested interests at stake here, including the Church, farmers, certain commercial interests, and various branches of government. The federal policy in general has been not to take any really decisive action, either to try to protect reserves from white influences or to speed the assimilation of Indians into the dominant Canadian way of life. There is evidence that the lack of a clearly formulated policy has been a source of confusion for Indians themselves, leaving them bewildered as to the goals toward which they should be moving.

The biological facet of the "Indian problem" involves the rapid growth of the Indian population. The increase in numbers began during the decade from 1911 to 1921, but it was rather slow and gradual at first. During each of the last two decades, however, the Indian population has increased by over 30 per cent. This is, of course, the expected consequence of the death control which has been the result of curative and preventative medical care provisions in Indian communities, while there has been no simultaneous influence tending toward birth control. The point of difficulty in this development lies in the fact that although Canada may be spacious and underpopulated, the Indian reserves are not. Thus some Indians are beginning to find themselves forced off the reserves for lack of adequate subsistence on them, and more and more will inevitably find themselves in this situation.

When Indians leave the reserve they are usually drawn to the city by the bright lights and excitement, the promise of jobs, perhaps by the example of relatives or friends who have gone earlier. They arrive, often enough, to settle in the slum district, with its rundown crowded quarters, its dingy restaurants and bars, its lonely, drifting crowds of men and its cheap prostitution. They face the condescending pity, the contemptuous disdain, or the disinterested apathy of many whites.

Perhaps that facet of the Indian problem where solution is the most difficult to foresee is the motivational one, seen in the sullen air of shame and apathy of so many Indians. The origins of this attitude are easily traced: (1) the collapse of the traditional tribal culture with the unique values, symbols of achievement, socialization stages, and structuring of motivation, meaning, and life that it involved; (2) the introduction of the white man's religion and education which either condemned the past as diabolical and pagan or ignored it as apparently unworthy of official acknowledgement; and (3) the encounter with wages and jobs involving new skills and work disciplines which, being initially difficult to master, earned for Indians the stigma — lazy, stupid, good-for-nothing. The reserves themselves have become, for many, doomed havens — sanctuaries where subsistence may be had, and relief rations perhaps shamefully but stolidly received — from the loneliness and contempt and failures of life in the white man's world.

II

The "Eskimo problem" is remarkable because numerically it is so small, and yet as a subject of public concern, it is both recent and sizable. The 1961 Department of Northern Affairs tabulation listed only 12,526 "Eskimos" in all Canada; though a brief excursion into any Arctic coastal community — Inuvik or Tutoyaktuk in the West, Coppermine or Cambridge Bay in the Central Arctic, Sugluk or Frobisher Bay in the East — quickly reveals that many who have Eskimo disk number identification look more white than Eskimo.

But despite the small numbers of people involved and the vast expanses of arctic landscape over which they are scattered, the problem posed by the Eskimo today is a disturbing and complex one, dramatic because it has been discovered only yesterday, in the second half of the twentieth century. There is need to distinguish among a number of perspectives on the problem, and the various elements of it.

Perhaps the first person to call the attention of the Canadian public to the "Eskimo problem" was the writer Farley Mowat in his controversial and upsetting books *The People of the Deer* and *The Desperate People*. Canadians reading his books discovered that there were Eskimos, whole small communties of them, starving in 1956, and that often enough the preventative steps taken were "too little and too late." For this to be the fate of the smiling, ingenuous, admiration-inspiring Eskimo seemed tragic; for it to happen because of white-introduced changes — white diseases decimating his ranks, guns and trapping depleting the caribou — was worse yet. For whites to be inactive while Eskimos sickened, starved, and died was not to be tolerated. There was a public outcry, political response, and in consequence a series of crash programs dealing with education, health, vocational training, job placement, land resource survey and management.

Eskimos themselves are only slowly learning to define as problems some of the vagaries of the life they experience. Life has always been an uncertain proposition: accident, starvation and sudden death have always been imminent. If these had come more frequently and afflicted larger numbers of late, they were still inescapable and were to be borne with the traditional fortitude. Only recently have they learned from whites that there is a government in Ottawa whose responsibility it is to alleviate these circumstances as far as possible. Unfortunately, however, this new learning for many has preceded understanding of the duties of responsible citizenship. Dependency on Ottawa for disaster relief can become dependency on Ottawa at all times, and there is some growing concern on the part of both Eskimos and whites about this situation.

The major elements of the Eskimo problem resemble somewhat those of the Indian, but with some important differences. A crucial aspect is the depletion of the caribou, which traditionally fed, clothed, housed (in summer), and often armed the Eskimo. Another aspect is the depopulation of many traditional hunting grounds. Schooling, missions, trading posts, nursing and hospital access, occasional wage work, family allowance cheques, relief rations, and immunity to starvation, all serve to some extent to draw Eskimos closer into settlements, and away from many areas which are so rich in traditional subsistence resources.

A final aspect is the sudden and almost cataclysmic impact of southern Canadian influences, intended and unintended, during the latter half of the 1950's. The intended influences included the federal day schools, the nursing stations, the Northern Service, Projects, Training, and Placement Officers of the Department of Northern Affairs. The unintended influences include, perhaps most importantly, the building and maintenance of the DEW line. Ferguson[2] has estimated that the 24 DEW line sites which are located in the Western Arctic, between the Alaskan border and the Boothis Peninsula, have significantly affected the life of at least one quarter of the Eskimo inhabitants of that area. Similar have been the effects of D.O.T. and military bases, such as those at Coppermine, Baker Lake, Inuvik and Frobisher Bay.

---

[2] Ferguson, J. D., *A Study of the Effects of the Distant Early Warning Line Upon the Eskimo of the Western Arctic of Canada,* unpublished manuscript on file at Northern Research Co-ordination Centre, Department of Northern Affairs, Ottawa, April, 1957.

The question might be raised: Had not the Church, the Hudson's Bay Company, and the R.C.M.P. been on the scene in most cases for at least 50 years before the arrival of the influences cited above? The answer is of course, yes. But for a variety of reasons, including the factors of expense and difficulties of transportation and communication, the representatives of these organizations tended to adapt to the Arctic environment very largely in Eskimo terms. Thus their influence on the Eskimo was less dramatic. The latecomers, with bulldozer, airplane, radio, utiladore and electric generator, and a hundred other lesser importations from the south, have decisively changed the life of Eskimo groups.

The consequences of these changes are very similar to the pattern sketched as characteristic of the Indians. The traditional way of life has been shattered, the population is now expanding rapidly, education is eagerly sought, and in some areas disorganization and demoralization are increasing rapidly. The breakdown of motivation, and the increase in dependency is becoming rather general. "Education for what" is a pressing issue, both in terms of how people should be educated, and in terms of what kinds of work are available to those who have acquired perhaps four or six or eight grades of schooling.

III

Perhaps one of the most consistent sources of Canadian complacency on the subject of race relations is the contrast between Negro-white relations in the United States and in Canada. It has seemed to many that in the States there is a problem of sizable proportions, whereas in Canada there is no problem at all. Within the last few years, however, there have been a number of articles and discussions by Negro as well as by white authors which demonstrate that this is simply not true. Rather, the picture appears to be that although in many Canadian cities the Negro population is extremely small, much too small for there to be a significant problem, in other cities, where there is a sizable group of Negroes (*e.g.*, Halifax and Toronto), the pattern of Negro-white relationships is very similar to that in the Northern States, and there is too often segregation in housing and discrimination in employment, in use of accommodations, and in social relations.

11. *THE ECONOMICS OF DISCRIMINATION**

Richard D. Jones†

There is a legend that came out of Germany in the dark days of Jewish persecution. A Christian pastor, acting on the orders of Nazi storm troopers, said to his congregation: "I must ask all of you who had Jewish fathers to leave the church and never return." A few worshippers rose from their seats and quietly left the church.

"Now all of you who had Jewish mothers must leave and never return", said the pastor. Again a few of the congregation departed.

As the echoes of the footsteps of the worshippers leaving the sanctuary died down, a deathly silence descended, and those still in their seats turned pale. The figure on the crucifix above the altar had loosed itself and left the church.

Christianity and Judaism are based on the ideal of brotherhood.

As a social scientist, I draw attention to the personality injuries suffered by those who hold prejudices and practice acts of discrimination and those who suffer from these acts. I point out there are no differences in intelligence levels, in behavior patterns, in emotional reactions that are determined by skin color or ethnic origin.

As one who believes in Canada, I point to the harm that is done to our country internally and in its external affairs, by those who deny to others the same privileges and opportunities they demand for themselves. The cornerstone of democracy, of freedom under law, is the giving to every group the same rights the majority group expects for itself.

These approaches that I and thousands of others have made to the problem of human relations have had some effect, and I am convinced that in this nation today equal rights and equal privileges for all who live here are far more prevalent than they were two decades, or even a decade ago. Today in Canada those who insist on practicing discrimination are more unpopular than those who practice brotherhood. The public by and large rises up in indignation against hate-mongers, and even against the gentle people of prejudice. The newspapers give headlines to discriminatory acts, for they are sufficiently rare to be news. When such a story breaks, the public outcry is such that the guilty party quickly acts

---

*From *The MacLaren Advertiser*, Vol. II, No. 4, Winter 1960, The MacLaren Advertising Co. Ltd., Toronto.

†Mr. Jones is National Executive Director of the Canadian Council of Christians and Jews.

to make amends, or to dissociate himself from the organization involved. The Government in Ottawa and many of the provincial governments have made acts of discrimination in certain fields illegal, and pressure is constantly at work to increase the scope and effectiveness of these laws. Recently a Bill of Rights was enacted. However, human relations in Canada have not yet reached the level of perfection, and for our own country nothing less than this should be accepted. There is one fact about discrimination that is often overlooked — that is, its cost in dollars and cents.

Thus, in the remainder of this article I will forget the arguments of the clergyman and the social scientist for brotherhood, and I will concentrate on the fact that brotherhood is good business. Through its practice, money is saved and the standard of living for all people is raised.

Elmo Roper, an American, known for his analyses of public opinion, marketing research and employee attitudes, bluntly states: "The waste in manpower, morale and productivity, costs American industry $30 billion a year". If this gigantic sum is reduced to figures the average person can comprehend, it means ten dollars out of every $75.00 pay check is wasted on the phony luxury of indulging our prejudices".

Canada, of course, is far different from the United States. Our population is only one-tenth as large and our problems in human relations are vastly different. However, discrimination in Canada involves an economic loss to our people and our Government, just as it does in the United States and in every other country of the world where it is practiced. While the cost in Canada may be only a minute part of what it is in certain other countries, it is still too much.

Let us look at some of these costs. When a capable worker who has skills needed by a certain store, bank, insurance office, factory, is turned away from the employment manager's office because of color, religion, ethnic origin, an economic loss is suffered. In our country there are men and women not doing the work for which they are best fitted simply because they are Negroes, Indians, Jews, or so-called New Canadians. They are forced, by circumstances beyond their control, to accept positions or jobs in which they have little or no interest. Consequently, their morale is not good, and productivity is low.

When promotion is denied to a person for similar reasons, costs are again involved. Were society, including all employers and employees, free of prejudice, the best qualified personnel would be hired, and advancement to supervisory and executive positions would be determined by merit alone. Good leadership, improved morale, would certainly result in lower costs and increased productivity.

In Canada we are still far from the ideal situation. White men are reluctant to take orders from Negroes; native-born Canadians often react negatively to being told what to do by foreign-born bosses. Canadians by birth often feel they cannot reach the top in firms owned by American or European interests. On occasion I have heard such accusations as: "You have to be a Japanese, a German, an American, a Mason, an R.C., an English-speaking Canadian, a French-speaking Canadian, to get anywhere in that firm". Thus personalities clash, sniping and criticism of one's fellow employees or of management takes place, and the entire operation suffers.

Ambition is blunted in the victims of discrimination. In Metropolitan Toronto one out of every five residents has arrived from overseas in the last ten years. There are 300,000 men, women and children in this group. Many have come filled with ambition, the desire to get ahead, and to be truly a part of this great nation. However, once these people feel they are victims of discrimination in job opportunities, in wages received, in being accepted by those who preceded them to this country, their initiative is killed, their personalities are warped. Our native Indians, our Negro and Oriental residents have often suffered in the same way. Why strive for added education, for new and improved skills, when an opportunity will not be given to use this education and these skills? I wonder if this does not in part account for the fact that only 27 of more than 180,000 Indians are at present in Canadian universities.

Recently when the CBC televised a program dealing with the rise of a Nazi party in Canada, the Canadian Jewish Congress was deluged with calls from people new to this country who were terribly scared. Having suffered, as many of them had, in the Concentration Camps of Europe, they were in fear that similar evils would overtake them in Canada. In turn, immigrants from those European countries where the Nazi ideology once controlled the nation, had the finger of accusation and suspicion levelled against them. I am certain these feelings of fear, hostility, and hatred, affected business relationships, and cost would again be a factor.

Let us now turn from employment to housing. Here, too, financial losses are involved in discrimination. At the present time, in many parts of the country, apartments and homes are vacant. They are for rent or for sale. Surveys have shown that real estate agents, landlords, refuse to do business with certain potential tenants or buyers because of race, religion or ethnic origin. Their excuse is they would lose other tenants or prospective buyers. As I write this article, a deputation is being organized to present a brief to the Ontario Government, asking that the Fair Accommodation Practices Act be amended to cover apartment dwellings. Instances of discrimination are cited in the brief. One can readily see an unsold house or vacant apartment means a loss to the individual and to the government, and when the situation exists because of prejudice and discrimination, it is a needless loss.

I stated previously that the Federal Government and several of the provincial governments have Statutes outlawing certain types of discrimination. These Statutes must be enforced. The public must be made aware that they exist, and an educational job must be done. All this requires government employees, and costs are involved.

There are private agencies, such as the one of which I am the National Executive Director, the Canadian Council of Christians and Jews, that raise funds from corporations and individuals to improve by educational means human relations in our country. It is obvious the fight against prejudice and discrimination costs money, money that could well be spent in other ways.

I have touched on just a few of the many costs involved in discrimination. There are many others, both human and financial. You will agree with me there is a needless economic loss involved when a Canadian holds fast his prejudices and practices discrimination.

The ultimate eradication of this evil rests on the individual. Management and labor, churches and schools, service clubs and lodges, the Federal and provincial governments, can do their part, but the final responsibility rests with you and me.

12 *CANADA'S INDIANS YESTERDAY.*
*WHAT OF TODAY?**

Diamond Jenness†

Between the years 1920 and 1930 I visited many tribes and bands of Indians on different reserves throughout Canada — in the east, on the

*From *The Canadian Journal of Economics and Political Science*, Vol. XX, No. 1, February 1954.
†Mr. Jenness, who for many years served as Chief of the Division of Anthropology in the National Museum of Canada, is author of the well-known book *The Indians of Canada* (Ottawa, Queen's Printer, 6th ed., 1963).

prairies, in British Columbia, and on the upper waters of the Peace River. In every region I found a deep-rooted prejudice against them, a prejudice that was stronger in some places than in others, but one which was noticeable everywhere from the Atlantic to the Pacific. It was strongest in western frontier settlements where the Indian population outnumbered the white and the latter was struggling to uphold its prestige. And it was least apparent in Quebec — probably because the French-Canadians of that province had associated with the Indians longer than had the English-Canadians, and because their Latin tradition had made them more tolerant of other races than are we northerners who speak a Teutonic tongue.

CAUSES OF PREJUDICE

One major cause for prejudice was the reserve or *apartheid* system which separated the Indians from the whites and conferred on them a special status. It exempted them, for example, from the income and other taxes that their white neighbours paid, released them from any law-suits for debt, prohibited them from selling or renting any part of their reserves except through the government, and debarred them from the white man's privilege of purchasing alcoholic liquor. Their reserves therefore formed distinct enclaves, which had a life and individuality of their own different from that of the white communities around them. And this difference, this failure to conform to the prevailing pattern, aroused the prejudice of the surrounding majority, as non-conformity always does, whether it be in religion, in politics, or in social customs.

Still another ground for prejudice was the economic status of the Indians, which was generally considerably lower than that of their white neighbours. Their clothes were shabbier and of inferior quality, their houses smaller and more ramshackle, and their motor-cars, when they possessed any, Model-T Fords whose clatter was audible half a mile away.

Not merely was their living standard lower, but they lacked the education of their white neighbours. Only a minority spoke fluent English or French: a high percentage could neither read nor write. The average Canadian, himself but half educated, tolerated the immigrant Italian labourers and the Chinese market gardeners and laundrymen because he was vaguely conscious that these foreigners, despite their defective knowledge of English, possessed civilizations of their own comparable to his Canadian one. But the Indians, he thought, lacked any true cultural background: they were but half-regenerate savages. Accordingly, he treated them with hardly concealed contempt. He barred his house against them, associated with them no more than was absolutely necessary, and employed them only when he was unable to dispense with their services.

Geog discrim

Lest I be accused of exaggeration, let us run our eyes briefly from British Columbia to the Atlantic. On the Pacific coast during that period people frequently spoke of the native population as "Siwashes," and, for good measure, they occasionally added the epithet "dirty". As labourers, it was said, the Indians were shiftless and unreliable. They could be stevedores, fishermen, casual labourers; their women might work in canneries, or sometimes as domestics; but everywhere the white population preferred Chinese or Japanese. Chinese and Japanese children were freely accepted in the schools and colleges of the province; but for Indian children there had to be special schools financed by the federal government, even when, as at Duncan, their reserves lay right inside a white community. In the interior of British Columbia one or two villages actually enforced a Jim Crow law: thus at Hazelton (which in 1926 counted some 300 white inhabitants to perhaps 400 Indians), no Indian might walk beside a white man or woman, or sit on the same side in the village church. Still farther north, on the upper waters of the Peace River, white trappers by threats of violence sometimes expelled Indian families from their traditional trapping grounds; and the Indians had no protection or redress.

The prairie farmers during that same period shared the prejudices of their countrymen beyond the Rockies. In 1921 those around Calgary were paying $4 a day to immigrant harvesters of Polish and Ukrainian nationalities, but to Indians working in the same fields only $2.50.

The situation was somewhat different in the southern parts of Ontario and Quebec. There the Indians had practised agriculture for many centuries, and their economic condition approximated that of their rural white neighbours. Moreover, the primary schools on their reserves were little if at all inferior to those in the surrounding countryside. Nevertheless, any Indian who left the Six Nations Reserve at Brantford, or the Mohawk reserve at Caughnawaga, in order to attend high school or university in Toronto or Montreal encountered considerable prejudice which not every youth was fitted to withstand. An Ojibwa Indian of Parry Sound who had won the Military Medal with two bars and the French Croix de Guerre during World War I lived almost as an outcast: he was too modern, too disturbing, to find favour among his own people, and the local whites were unwilling to receive him into their homes because he was an Indian. In the lumbering districts farther north the Indians were rated indifferent teamsters, and their women considered fair prey for the lumberjacks. A similar attitude prevails even today, apparently, in parts of the Mackenzie

River basin, for in 1943 coloured employees of a firm that had contracted to build an oil pipeline in the region openly offered a prize of $500 to the first Indian woman who should give birth to a baby with black kinkly hair.

EFFECT OF APARTHEID ON THE INDIANS

Confined as they were to their reserves, the Indians had little opportunity to acquire any technical training or experience, little or no chance to diversify their activities and improve their economic position. Their main occupations were farming (or ranching) and, in some places, fishing, neither of which offered much more than a bare subsistence. Particularly precarious was the condition of the non-farming tribes of northern Canada, who derived most of their revenue from trapping the fur-bearing animals.

It was the difficulty of obtaining employment (itself, of course, the result of white prejudice) that prevented the Indians from leaving their reserves in considerable numbers. Each year did, indeed, witness a small seepage into the world of whites, a seepage mainly of young girls who married white men and followed their husbands into the white communities. A few young men also drifted away, principally in eastern Canada, where some Iroquois, for example, would cross the international boundary to work in the automobile plants of Detroit, which asked no questions about racial origin. At no time, however, did this seepage overtake the natural increase of the population; and already on more than one reserve the ugly problem of living space had begun to raise its head.

Can we wonder if under these circumstances the older Indians were thrown back upon their past? Their ancient religion had peopled the world with spiritual forces, and our white civilization with its materialistic outlook seemed to them hollow and empty. Knowing, however, that they lacked the strength to resist it, they resigned themselves to its current and ceased to care where it carried them. They could and did retain their ancient pride and dignity, but the upheaval was so drastic that they accepted with apathy whatever fate set in their path.

Totally different was *apartheid's* effect upon the younger Indians, or at least a considerable percentage of them. They developed what can be described as a "segregation camp" mentality, the mentality that characterized so many refugees and displaced persons during and after the last war. Fate, the irresistible, had subjected them to the white race, which had scornfully pushed them to one side. It had taken practically all their land, deprived them of their ancient freedom, and denied them political and social equality, or at least made that status almost unobtainable. The knowledge that they were no longer their own masters sapped their enterprise and destroyed their ambition. If their diet was deficient, their health poor, their housing unsatisfactory, it was the fault of the white man, they said, and the white man's government should set things right.

So it came about that an atmosphere of mingled apathy and discontent had settled on the reserves; and it was the apathy that dominated. Only at rare intervals did the underlying discontent send forth an audible murmur. Small delegations of Indians then travelled from British Columbia, from the Prairies, and from southern Ontario to lay their complaints before the government in Ottawa. But the results of these delegations were negligible.

OTTAWA ADMINISTRATION

The Indian administration of that period was a "holding" one, more concerned with preserving the *status quo* than with improving the economic and social status of the Indians or with raising their living standard. The head of the administration disliked them as a people, and gave a cool reception to the delegations that visited him in Ottawa. Parliament, for its part, contented itself with voting whatever amount of money seemed necessary to fulfil Canada's treaty obligations towards its aborigines and then promptly forgot them, because their number was small and exercised no influence at the ballot box.

What were the obligations of the Canadian Parliament and people? Briefly these: to protect the Indians from exploitation, to safeguard their health, to educate them, and to train them for eventual citizenship. No one ever asked how long the training should endure, how long the Indians should be kept as wards — whether for one century, two centuries, or a millenium. The Indian administration did not ask: its job was simply to administer, and, like many a custodian, it was so involved in the routine of its administration that it forgot the purpose of its custodianship, especially since the fulfilment of that purpose would sign its own death-warrant. Neither did Parliament nor the Canadian people ask how long: their attitude seemed to be that the less heard of the Indians the better. If the churches felt concerned for Indian welfare and wished to set up special schools and hospitals, the government should support their action and aid it with subsidies. In that way it could transfer some of its responsibilities, promote the spread of Christianity, and (*sotto voce*, be it confessed) silence any murmurs or complaints.

Now and again circumstances forced the administration to adopt a more active policy. In 1920, for example, when the number of the Sarcee Indians had declined from roughly 500 to 120 and the tribe was threatened with extinction, the government stationed a medical officer on the reserve to arrest the epidemic of tuberculosis that was carrying off three children out of every four before they reached the age of twenty. A few years later, under pressure from some missionairies, it passed the controversial potlatch law that prohibited certain Indian ceremonies on the Pacific Coast. Furthermore, it promoted an investigation of the reserves in eastern Canada in order to ascertain how many of their occupants were ready for full citizenship; and when the investigation revealed that all but a few old people could qualify, it drew up a law authorizing the administration to enfranchise any Indian who applied for that status. Down to 1930, however, the number of enfranchisements could be counted on the fingers of one hand. Ottawa placidly continued to devote most of its attention to the financial aspects of Indian administration — to the leasing of mining and timber rights, the payment of treaty and other charges; and it let the Indians themselves drift along as best they could within the boundaries of their reserves.

Parallel with this failure to promote the political and economic welfare of the Indians went negligence in providing them with adequate educational facilities. Although the primary schools on some of the reserves, especially in eastern Canada, were reasonably good, there was little or no encouragement for Indian children to go on to technical or high school, and never any thought of helping them find employment when their school-days ended. In many parts of Canada the Indians had no schools at all; in others only elementary mission schools in which the standard of teaching was exceedingly low. A few mission boarding-schools, subsidized by the government, accepted Indian children when they were very young, raised them to the age of 16, then sent them back to their people, well indoctrinated in the Christian faith, but totally unfitted for life in an Indian community and, of course, not acceptable in any white one. We should not blame the missions. They lacked the resources and the staffs to provide a proper education, or technical training that would develop special skills; and they were totally unfitted to serve as employment bureaux. It was not the missions that shirked their responsibility, but the federal government, and behind that government the people of Canada.

Nor did we neglect only the education of the Indians, but also their health. Among the hunting and fishing tribes of northern Canada malnutrition and its accompanying ailments (tuberculosis, pyorrhoea, etc.) were epidemic in almost every district, and the government paid very little attention to it. The condition of our Hudson Bay Eskimos shocked the

Danes of Knud Rasmussen's 1921-4 expedition, so infinitely worse was it than that of the Eskimos of Danish Greenland. Scabies, or some similar disease, was rife on the Upper Peace River, trachoma on the Nass and Skeena; while dental decay was so common everywhere, even in little children, that it seemed to be the rule rather than the exception.

CHANGES SINCE 1930

Such, in outline, was the condition of our Indians between 1920 and 1930. Much water has flowed over the dam since that period, and the Indian administration has undergone a very great change. No longer is it just a "holding" administration, but, under capable and far-sighted leadership, it has made notable efforts to improve the economic and social conditions among the Indians and to integrate them gradually into the life of the country.

That integration, however, is still far from complete. It would therefore appear timely for the administration to review what it has accomplished during the last quarter of a century, and, in particular, to set before the public clear and straightforward answers to the following questions:

1. What progress has been made in ameliorating home conditions among the Indians, in ending malnutrition and improving health?

2. What progress is being made towards abolishing special schools for Indian children and providing them (through scholarships etc.) with the same educational facilities as their white neighbours?

3. What measures are being taken to help the Indians find employment off the reserves and to absorb them into our industrial and commercial life?

4. What steps are being taken to liquidate the Indian reserves, and to end once and for all that *apartheid* system which was never intended to endure more than one or two generations, but which in eastern Canada has lasted more than 200 years?

13. CANADA'S GROWING INDIAN POPULATION*

The Financial Post

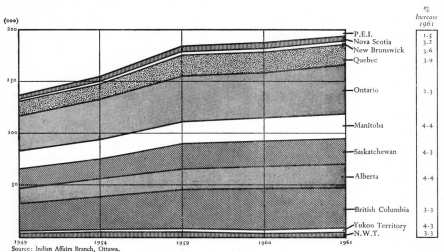

	% Increase 1961
P.E.I.	1.5
Nova Scotia	3.2
New Brunswick	3.6
Quebec	3.9
Ontario	2.3
Manitoba	4.4
Saskatchewan	4.3
Alberta	4.4
British Columbia	3.3
Yukon Territory	4.3
N.W.T.	3.3

Source: Indian Affairs Branch, Ottawa.

*From *The Financial Post,* February 9, 1963.

14. THE PLIGHT OF THE INDIAN IN CANADA*

William Morris†

I

From the Atlantic to the Pacific, the Indians of Canada constitute the most economically depressed segment of our population. No matter where one travels from the fishing villages of the maritimes to those of the northwest British Columbia coast one finds innumerable scattered Indian settlements in conditions of filth and squalor that are a shame to our national pride. And yet there are many Canadians who continue in blithe

*From *Canadian Commentator,* Vol. 3, June 1959 and July 1959.

†Mr. Morris is currently a Lecturer in the Department of Economics and Sociology at the University of Western Ontario, London.

unawareness of the problem, some hardly knowing there are Indians who are also citizens of Canada. We are heard to complain bitterly of the treatment native peoples receive in other parts of the world never looking into our own back yards at what is to all intents and purposes the sorest blight on our national conscience. We are heard to speak in altruistic tones of the nature of human dignity and the rights of man as a human being, and we have distinguished ourselves in the United Nations for the stand we have in the past as a nation adopted on these issues.

But in the midst of our concern for the welfare of those in other parts of the world we all too often neglect the problems on our own door step. Our ministers proclaim loudly of the sanctity of the human spirit and the worthwhileness of human endeavour, and yet how many of them receive the support of their congregation in alleviating the distress of Indians in their own communities. One often hears it said by educators that everyone deserves the right to an education and the fulfillment of his own capabilities, yet how many of them receive the support of their boards in attempting to secure complete attendance of Indian children living in their areas and away from the reserve. Indeed it could almost be assumed that many Canadians would prefer not to have Indians in their public schools by the neglect and apathy we have shown toward them.

Many of our most respected citizens speak of the necessity to help others and many are concerned regarding the welfare of those in hospital or in distant lands, but how many of them allow their children to associate with children of Indian ancestry?

Let us bear in mind that the Indian Canadian has had only a few short years in which to become adjusted to our way of life. Those of us who are employers expect of him a motivation and way of looking at wage employment quite beyond what we have any right to expect, and when he does not succeed we explain it all away by claiming he is really inferior. We often find that he is unwilling to work long hours for abstract gain such as money, and that the money he earns he all too unwillingly gives to those of his relatives and friends who are in need. We see his excesses in other areas, and think that he is incapable of handling himself in ordinary situations of our social life. In our larger cities, such as Winnipeg and Vancouver, we have grown accustomed to Indian slums, and in smaller centers we are used to his surrounding impoverished communities.

How long has the Indian really had, and how much have we really accomplished by way of fulfilling our obligations to him?

It was only one hundred and nine years ago last September 7th, that the first treaty was ever signed by any Indian band. The most recent one was made only thirty years ago next November 15th. It has only been eighty-five years since the then newly constituted R.C.M.P. set out on what has since come to be known as the "grand march". This was occasioned by the entry into Canada of the Sioux under Sitting Bull after their defeat of the American 7th Cavalry under Major General George A. Custer, and the threat of renewed violence now in the young Canadian west.

There is an apocryphal story dating from this period that Crowfoot, chief of the Blackfoot Confederacy, rising to make this speech of acceptance of the treaty on September 22, 1877 plucked from his eagle wing fan a downy feather, and giving it to Governor Laird said: "Keep us like this feather forever, keep us like a pampered child." What has been our record?

Well, to begin with we haven't done badly so far as the pampered children are concerned. We granted the Indian land, and we provided him with funds to build homes. We gave him schools and churches and we gave him special consideration so far as health facilities are concerned. We have even given him special protection under laws which were designed to assist him in his development.

To a great extent this legislation has been effective. Those living near more populated areas have by and large progressed to the point where it is quite clear to all concerned that they are able to take care of themselves — such as the Iroquois of the Six Nations reserve near Brantford, Ontario or the Stonies near the city of Calgary. Others have gone into our cities and while some have distinguished themselves others have not. Many have become fine members of our communities and we are often unaware of their Indian ancestry. In most cases this is as they desire it. Some have distinguished themselves too in the professions and in government. But for the most part there have been all too many of them who have been able only to secure labour of the most menial sort, and their prospects of advancement have been all too meagre. This does not imply that there has been any conscious policy on the part of Canadians to deny them labour, we simply haven't thought enough about them to have formed any clear idea of what our responsibilities were. In addition we have frequently tied the hands of those in the government service who have attempted to assist the Indian in his integration, but we are always quick to criticize government for what are in effect our omissions as a nation.

As a result the attempts that the Indian has made are usually unsuccessful and he has become filled with despair and frustration. Let us make no mistake about this. Even though he in many cases does not understand our ways or our point of view, he has attempted to a far greater degree than we often realize to adjust and change his way of doing things to what we expect of him. But in our classrooms and in our industrial positions we expect of him a level of achievement that we often do not expect of our own citizens, almost hoping it seems that he will not succeed.

It used to be said in England in the 18th century that to take the worker out of the slums would be to deprive him of his sense of security and his feeling of "belongingness". (Today we would probably use the word togetherness.) The history of trade union movement has shown what the workers thought of such ridiculous notions.

This is precisely what one all too often hears in Canada. It is said that we should leave the Indian on the reserve as this is the environment he best understands. Although his level of hygiene is much below that of our communities he has become so completely adjusted to it that it is of no harm to him. His children live under conditions usually far below what we would consider necessary for the maintenance of life of our own children, but they too have become adapted to it, and have developed a natural immunity from disease. Many see no contradiction between these views and singing lustily in church choirs!

We are today faced with an alternative, the implications of which will determine the course of Indian development for the next fifty years. Either we adopt a more humane policy as a nation toward the Indian and initiate a positive program of integration or we will doom him to a continuing life of hardship and misery, and a level of living barely above starvation. If this is to be the case we can expect a marked increase in the rate of crime and violence and disorder among Indians, as they cannot for much longer tolerate what is rapidly deteriorating into an impossible situation. We shall furthermore commit the government to continue a fruitless policy of handouts which can never alleviate real sources of hardship, and by our indifference tie the hands of those who are vitally concerned with Indian affairs. No democratic government can move more rapidly than its electors will allow. What then, of the Indian?

II

If Canadian citizenship, which the Indian now enjoys, is to mean anything we shall have to radically overhaul our way of handling him. We must put an end to self-defeating legislation and loose the hands of those Indians who are already in a position to become independent — if only the opportunity were adequately presented to them. We must get over the fiction that Indians prefer to live in isolation, like museum pieces on reserves, enjoying a level of living barely above starvation. In short, we must devise a new and more dynamic program of self-help which is sufficiently comprehensive to continue special privilege to those who still require it, but at the same time is sufficiently flexible to allow younger Indians the freedom they so desperately need.

Since the beginning of the historical period, the Crown has always recognized a special right of Indians. For many centuries the Indian was in great need of protection in order for his survival to have been possible at all. Much that has been enacted on his behalf has been done so on the highest motives possible, and we in Canada have a proud record of dedicated individuals who have spent their lives in the Indian services, clergymen, teachers, and Indian superintendents. Times have changed but our attitudes and our legislation have not. We still have some provisions in the Indian Act (1951) which are centuries old and just as out of date. How did this come about?

In the beginning the Indian was both an ally of the settler and one of his most forbidding foes. In recognition of this Charles II in 1670 instructed his colonial governor that protection and assistance should be given to any Indian if he requested it, in return for his support of the Imperial cause. A century later these sentiments were emphasized in the Royal Proclamation of 1763 establishing the right of the Indian in the soil and setting forth an assurance that this right could not be extinguished without his consent and that of the crown. Almost one hundred years later various agreements were made with Indians as the population of Canada increased, and some means had to be found for an adequate basis of settlement and the establishment of law and order.

Today these agreements go by the name of treaties, but their original purpose should not be lost sight of. This was merely the recognition of the necessity on the part of the European for land upon which he could settle and, at the same time, the protection of Indian interests in their traditional hunting and trapping territories.

For many years this agreement met with wide success in achieving its purpose, and many benefits were derived by the Indians as a result of their contact with the Europeans. The introduction of trade goods, and later the establishment of educational institutions and the extensions of medical care allowed a degree of freedom and security hitherto unknown to them.

It is commonly thought that it was the treaty which gave the Indian his most important rights. This is not true! The treaty gave him only the right of settlement on lands he used to inhabit, and it was never the intention of the treaty that even this right should be for all time. There is much loose talk about such phrases as "as long as the sun shines, the grass grows or rivers flow" as being part of the agreements indicating the duration of these grants of land. No phrase of this nature can be found in any treaty ever made. What is accurate about such words, however, is the measure of responsibility which was recognized by the crown so long as Indians were in need of special assistance. It was then by way of a moral obligation and so it remains to the present. Just as centuries ago, many Indians in Canada today require special legislation and special care, and programs designed for their particular problem situation. This is a responsibility which must be honoured!

Also in the treaties were certain secondary benefits, which have been so distorted in the public mind that it is often assumed they were the major provisions.

In general the crown undertook to provide such things as annual cash payments of about 4 dollars a year (in some instances it was as high as five). Furthermore, annual grants of potato seed, fishing equipment, ammunition were thrown into the bargain, and for chiefs and headmen a new suit of clothes each three years. Every year these agreements are carried out, and treaty day has become a major event on many reserves in Canada.

There was also provision made for the establishment of schools on reserves, if the Indians requested them. Most have by now. These were to be established by the churches, depending upon which of them could claim the allegiance of the majority of the members of the band. This has usually come to mean that the first church to enter an area has been able to claim this right!

It didn't take long for the inadequacies of these provisions to have made themselves clear. With confederation there grew up a large and copious body of Indian law which took for granted the provisions of the treaties, and then went far beyond them to provide for new emerging problems.

As more than half the Indians of Canada were never made subject of any treaty their rights had to be protected, and brought into line with those of other Indians elsewhere. It is not usually known that no treaties were made with Indians of British Columbia or with any Indian bands of Quebec or the maritimes. Within the province of Ontario, it should be pointed out, no treaties were made with the Iroquois of Brantford and the Tyendinaga or certain other groups who immigrated to Canada from what is now the United States and were given lands in Canada.

Most of the laws which were enacted were brought into force in light of the best information available at the time, taking into account the commitments which had been given to the churches by the treaties. Legislation here as elsewhere reflected the temper of Canadians and their expressed wishes to the government. By the mid-twentieth century however it had become obvious that existing legislation was out of touch with changed conditions. Accordingly a committee of the Senate and the House of Commons was established which reviewed recent developments and in cooperation with Indians and others interested in their welfare, made recommendations which have subsequently been embodied in the existing Indian Act of 1951. The government has recently announced its intention of establishing another committee, and it is to be hoped that it will take the lead from its predecessor and make recommendations of an even more positive and dynamic nature. For this to happen, some long standing traditions will have to be at least altered, if not scrapped entirely!

A start in this direction can be made by considering the following points. They are offered only as guides to thinking, as a basis for clearing the ground and viewing the problem more than superficially.

First: There must be increased cooperation of all levels of government. Until provincial and municipal governments are brought directly into the picture in some way they cannot be expected to be in a position to take a firm lead in solving problems existing in their own areas. It is high time that some wealthy provinces stopped talking such nonsense as to suggest they have no Indian problem. Provincial and municipal government will require assistance of the Federal Government in advice and in financial resources, but implementation of policy in so far as possible should be among the responsibilities of the provincial governments concerned.

Second: Indian schools should be made subject to regular provincial departments of education, as ordinary public schools. While the churches now have special obligations under law, is it either necessary or desirable that the education of Indian children should be left to religious groups exclusively? Is it sensible to continue a policy of paying for schools which must by law be staffed by members of the teaching profession who adhere to one of a half dozen denominations? Elsewhere in Canada we rejected this idea in 1867. Apart from religious conviction the teacher in an Indian school needs special training for his job in addition to the ordinary requirements of the profession. Religious enthusiasm is a poor substitute for training.

Third: Matters pertaining to welfare and public health should also be brought under existing provincial legislation so that voluntary organizations now in operation can assume some responsibility. Financial assistance and advice may or may not be necessary on the part of the Federal Government but the details can be worked out later after the principle has been established.

Fourth: Begin now a realistic program of economic development. In order to be effective this will have to take into account Indians off reserves as well as those on reserves. At the present time, the Federal Government is empowered by Parliament to act only on behalf of Indians on reserves. Responsibility for those off the reserve should not be made subject of Federal legislation but rather of provincial legislation. Economic development programs now in operation on reserves should be stepped up considerably but they must work in cooperation with those off reserves. Economic development on reserves will generally take the form of group orientation towards, and training into, the management of a new type of industry, or of a revitalized industry. Off reserves the problem is to develop the economic and occupational potential of individuals. To be effective, cooperation must be forthcoming from employers to ensure that Indians trained to assume responsibility and who desire it, will be able to find some rewards and satisfactions.

Fifth: A comprehensive and continuing program of social science research must accompany any new program. It is manifestly impossible to expect that development programs can be effective unless they are constructed on the basis of accurate information concerning the people they are designed to assist. Furthermore there must be a recognition in the planning stages of the diversity of the problem and attempts made to adapt the program to the needs of particular areas. Increased cooperation from psychologists, anthropologists, and sociologists and economists can aid immeasurably in the establishment and operation of the program. We must know more than we do now about the problems of adjustment off reserves together with the actual potential of human resources on reserves so that those who decide to remain can do so with greater success.

Sixth: Begin now planning ways and means of removing paternalistic legislation from those reserves where these measures are no longer required. If a group is in a position to take care of itself, and if its members desire greater freedom in the conduct of their own affairs, they must be given a responsibility to do so. Such measures must come from the Indians themselves when they are ready and willing to rest their claim on their Canadian citizenship with all the obligations it implies.

Seventh: There must be a new face put upon Indian-White relationships. This will come as a by-product, and it is crucial to its success. Dignity must replace despair among them, and all levels of leadership must be united in common cause.

I do not believe that the Indian Canadian wishes to live by charity. I believe he wants the guidance and help necessary to enable him to help himself. With a little understanding from his fellow Canadians he will achieve his goal which is to be as healthy and as competent in our ways as we are ourselves, and an active and contributing citizen. This will be the Indian as a Canadian.

15. *LO, THE POOR, IRRESPONSIBLE, LAZY INDIAN**

John T. Schmidt†

A few weeks ago the goose boss of a Hutterite colony in southern Alberta was showing me around the farm. I saw I was not the only visitor. A carload of Blood Indians was departing with a large package of freshly baked buns from the communal bakery.

"Our Indian friends have paid us a visit again," commented the wife of the goose boss. "They come around here to beg every time we bake. I can't understand them at all. They won't work — those big lazy fellows."

This remark of pity and scorn, coming as it did from a member of one of Canada's most oppressed minority groups, is a succinct comment on the status of the Canadian Indian in the west. It is a departure from comments made by his many champions who regard him as a downtrodden aristocrat — champions who disregard the fact that he is a dull, slow, untidy person and a careless workman.

Many who espouse his cause are merely sentimentalists whose know-

---

*From *Saturday Night*, November 21, 1959.
†Mr. Schmidt, a journalist, is Farm Editor of *The Calgary Herald*.

ledge of Indian affairs stems from having paid an occasional visit to a reserve or who have seen him dressed to the hilt in native costume — buckskin, beads, lipstick, feathers and dyed underwear — holding forth at the Ohsweken Indian fair, the Calgary Stampede or Banff's Indian Days. They do not realize that nine times out of ten to be present at these affairs, the Indians will have gone off and left crops and livestock unattended.

At a recent meeting of the Calgary Friends of Indians Society, a district agriculturalist cited instance after instance of local bands' poor records as farmers. When the urge comes upon them they up and leave their homes to spend a week or two with relatives. Dozens of times he has seen bright Indian 4H Club members raise top calves only to be dragged off by their parents to leave the calves to shift for themselves.

The Blackfoot reserve at Gleichen, Alberta, is 174,595 acres. Years ago the band used to lease 140,000 acres to the white man as grazing land for $300,000 annually. A few years ago they decided to cancel the grazing leases and put their own young people on the land to farm it. And what's happened to that farming venture? It's $330,000 in the red! They even had to hire outside help!

Because the Indian has a built-in sense of irresponsibility, many employers who demand good, steady, sober personnel, are adverse to Indian labor. I know one large farm employer who hires twice as many Indians as he needs on the assumption that half will have taken off by mid-season.

The Indian never worries. What tomorrow will bring is of no concern today. He won't put in a sustained effort at anything. He can do it, really, but just hasn't the inclination.

The history of minority ethnic groups in this country has shown that any who are willing to work and educate themselves attained a higher standard of living than that to which they were previously accustomed.

Unlike most minority groups, the Indian by and large stuck to reserves which are conducive to inbreeding and subsequent lowering of intelligence. The sooner the Indian forgets about the reserves and treaties written in the time of Queen Victoria the better. Both served their purpose in an agricultural economy; both are now obsolete in an industrial economy. Both offer an easy security and the temptation to remain living in untidy shacks surrounded by hulks of wrecked cars.

William Wuttunee, young Cree Indian lawyer in the employ of the Saskatchewan government, said at a recent Western Citizenship Seminar in Banff: "The treaties should be done away with. At the time they were signed they brought peace but they mean nothing now.

"'What is needed now is a radical approach with a real desire to attack the problem. I once thought that in 35 years there would be no more Indian problem. At the rate we are going now, we are going to have it with us 150 years."

It would not be thoughtless or unkind to say the average Indian has not the slightest understanding of the colossal sums set aside by the Ottawa government for him and his family. I suspect the government set up the joint Commons-Senate committee not so much to assist the Indian to raise his status as to devise ways of halting treasury giveaways, predicted on the fact the Indian firmly believes the government owes him a living. This belief has been inculcated into the young by the parents and in the Indian residential schools where education, clothing and food are provided "for free."

Although the standard of intelligence varies from band to band I was amazed to learn from a man who has been connected with Indian residential schools for 30 years that on Prairie reserves and even in some areas of British Columbia and Ontario children are admitted to school without knowing a word of English. It is a losing battle because Indian parents don't yet seem to realize turning a child loose from school merely able to read and write just isn't enough today. Many leave school at 16 and thereafter make little or no attempt to improve their knowledge of English. They shy away from speaking English on the reserves for fear of ridicule from their own people and off the reserve for fear of silent scorn of the white man.

They have no incentive to seek further training, academic or vocational. Some, such as the ones I saw in the Yukon, proved to be smart enough to hold a job and do enough work to become eligible for unemployment insurance.

The Indian has been given a chance. But it seems that he can't or won't pull himself into an improved status in today's Canada. The fault is no one's but his own.

16. CULTURAL ASSIMILATION BETWEEN INDIANS AND NON-INDIANS IN SOUTHERN ALBERTA*

Henry Zentner†

This paper compares attitudes and values respecting cultural assimilation between Indian and non-Indian high school students in Southern Alberta.

The high school students involved included both Indian and non-Indian students attending the partially integrated high school located in Cardston, Alberta, as well as Indian students attending a number of denominational residential schools on the Blood and Blackfoot reservations in Southern Alberta. A total of 115 Indian students and 335 non-Indian students were sampled in the survey. These totals represent the usable returns obtained from a questionnaire which was circulated in the classrooms among the high school populations in each of the several schools mentioned. In no case was the net response rate below 80 per cent.

DESCRIPTION OF SAMPLES

In terms of basic composition the two populations showed considerable difference in respect to age, sex, class standing in high school, rural-urban residence, and father's educational achievement.

Differences in sex composition were minimal, with males predominating slightly over females in either instance. With respect to age, the Indian population showed a considerably higher average age than did the non-Indian. In terms of class-standing, the Indian population again bulked larger in grades IX and X, with markedly smaller numbers in grades XI and XII, as compared with a much more uniform distribution over the four grades among non-Indian students.

In regard to rural-urban differences in residence, the relative proportion of Indian students residing on farms was approximately twice as large as that among non-Indians. Further, only a small proportion of the Indian students lived in either a town or city, as compared with more than half of the non-Indian students.

Respecting father's educational achievement there were again marked differences. The Indian population had a much larger proportion of students whose fathers had completed only elementary school or less than did the non-Indian population. Also, more Indian than non-Indian stu-

*From the Alberta Journal of Educational Research, Vol. IX, No. 2, June 1963.
†Dr. Zentner is Associate Professor of Sociology at the University of Alberta, Calgary.

dents gave a "don't know" response to the question pertaining to father's educational achievement.

STATEMENT OF THE PROBLEM

The issue of assimilation between two or more diverse racial or ethnic groups can fruitfully be analyzed by consideration of three major classes of variables: (1) prejudice, or a feeling of status inequality; (2) discrimination or the refusal to associate freely with members of a different racial or ethnic group; and (3) conflict, or feelings and acts of mutual repulsion which arise out of differences in standards of conduct. Accordingly, in an effort to determine the state of tension existing between Indian and non-Indian school students a series of statements bearing upon attitudes toward the issues of equality, association, and conduct were formulated for presentation to and evaluation by the respondents.

It will be apparent that in dealing with the general issue of cultural assimilation it is possible to approach the issue from the standpoint of implied endorsement of mutual assimilation, i.e., by giving it a positive sanction, or to come at it from the standpoint of implied rejection, i.e., by giving it a negative sanction. In the present survey it was decided to employ both alternatives. Thus, a series of three statements, bearing upon the issues of equality, association, and conduct, were formulated in a positive vein; alternatively, a reciprocal series of three statements bearing upon the same issues were formulated in a negative vein. By proceeding in this manner it became possible to compare the results of the two approaches and to make an assessment as to which of the two discriminates similarities and differences between the two populations most effectively.

The positively formulated statements were: (1) "There is no need for an Indian to feel inferior because most of them are already accepted as equals by Whites!"; (2) "Indians ought to leave the reservation and compete on equal terms with Whites!"; and (3) "Indians ought to stop thinking of themselves as Indians and try to behave like Whites!".

The negatively formulated statements were: (1) "Most Whites are so prejudiced that no matter how an Indian behaves he is not acceptable as an equal!"; (2) "It is better for an Indian person to stay on his reservation where people know and understand him personally!"; and (3) "Indians ought to take pride in their race and not try to behave like Whites!".

The pattern of responses to the two statements bearing upon equality between Indians and non-Indians suggests that the Indian population is split into fairly equal halves. One half of the Indian students endorsed the proposition that the Indian is already accepted as an equal, while the other half endorsed the proposition that no matter how the Indian behaves he is not acceptable as an equal. In the non-Indian population it would appear that approximately one-third of the students agree with the proposition that the Indian is already accepted as an equal, another one-third agree that no matter how he behaves the Indian is *not* acceptable as an equal, and the remaining one-third are undecided. Evidently, then, Indian students view their acceptance as equals more optimistically than do their non-Indian peers.

Regarding the contact issue, it is apparent from the findings that substantially less than one-half of the students in either population are in favor of the Indian leaving the reservation and competing on equal terms with Whites. It is noteworthy, however, that while the proportion of non-Indian students who agree that the Indian should stay on the reservation is about the same as that which agrees that the Indian should leave the reservation, among Indian students a significantly greater proportion agree that the Indian *should leave* than agree that he should remain on the reservation.

From the standpoint of progress toward assimilation this finding indicates that a clear majority of students in either population are not in favor of full and unrestricted contact between members of the two respective racial-ethnic communities. That a substantial minority of both populations are in favor of full and unrestricted contact, however, is a measure of change that has already been made in the direction of mutual cultural assimilation.

The finding that less advanced and younger Indian students were significantly more inclined to agree with the proposition that Indians ought to leave the reservation than were older and more advanced Indian students is not readily interpretable. Conceivably, however, less advanced and younger Indian students express a greater optimism about Indians leaving the reservation than their older confreres because they have many more older members of their community to look to as models. At the same time, the changes in transportation and communication, such as the auto and TV, which have been adopted on a large scale by Indians in recent years have probably had the effect of decreasing the attachment of the young to the Indian culture and likely, too, these same developments have served to build up in their minds a more favorable attitude toward the non-Indian culture and society.

Alternatively, the finding that non-Indian boys were more prone to endorse the proposition that Indians leave the reservation than were non-Indian girls is likewise problematic. Conceivably, however, the non-Indian boys responded to the statement from the perspective of such masculine qualities as initiative and aggressiveness which are more fully emphasized in the non-Indian culture. Similarly, the finding that less advanced non-Indian students were more inclined than their more advanced confreres to endorse the proposition that it is better for an Indian to stay on the reservation is again problematic. It is possible, however, that these less advanced members of the non-Indian population may have been projecting their own feelings of strangeness and confusion which they were experiencing in their adjustment to the new and unfamiliar high school situation. The nature of the data, however, is such as to preclude a firm conclusion in this respect.

Respecting the behavioral issue, the finding that the vast majority of students in either of the two populations are in favor of maintaining the *status quo* so far as Indian and non-Indian behavioral standards are concerned is noteworthy. It it noteworthy also, however, that approximately one-fourth of the students in either of the two populations are in favor of abandonment of Indian standards of behavior by Indians and the adoption by them of non-Indian behavioral standards. In a sense these data constitute a measure of the degree of assimilation which has already taken place and which may be viewed as a sound basis on which to build in the future.

The finding that more advanced and older non-Indian students were more frequently inclined to agree with the proposition that Indians ought to try to behave like Whites than were less advanced and younger non-Indian students is again not readily interpretable. Conceivably, however, the more advanced and older students responded to the question from the perspective of the advantages which the Indian would gain in the community at large if he adopted non-Indian standards of conduct. Younger and less advanced non-Indian students, on the other hand, may have been projecting their resistance to pressures for conformity to the adult world. The data do not, however, permit a firm conclusion respecting this issue.

In summary it is apparent from both the data here reported and that obtained through follow-up interviews with both Indian students and their parents that the rate of Indian assimilation is quickening remarkably. Indian parents of all socio-economic status levels recognize the necessity and desirability of adopting more of the non-Indian ways of behaving, albeit selectively. The Indian youth, however, goes further; not only does he believe that there are distinct advantages to more education and greater acceptance of non-Indian standards of behavior, but he believes also that the time has come for him to cease being an Indian in the traditional sense and simply be a citizen and a person. While he wants to retain the reservation as a refuge, he also wants to explore the challenge and excitement of the non-Indian world outside the reservation. Like his non-Indian peers, he wants to explore the full limits of his potential as a citizen and as a person. It remains only for public policy, and educational policy in particular, at all levels of government — federal, provincial, and local — to be brought into line with these developments and to overcome the non-Indian cultural lag which appears to characterize the situation at the present time.

17. SOME PROBLEMS OF THE METIS OF NORTHERN SASKATCHEWAN*

V. F. Valentine†

From the history of western Canada we learn of a group of people who have variously been referred to as half-breeds, *bois-brûlés,* or Métis. They were the offspring of unions — both casual and permanent — between Indian mothers and European fathers. Since their beginnings over 250 years ago only a few of them had shared the enthusiasm of the European for a sedentary life based on agriculture. The majority preferred the nomadic life of the hunt, as did their aboriginal ancestors. In northern Saskatchewan, where they number some 3,550, they experienced no major changes in this way of life until 1944 when the C.C.F. party came into power.

Prior to 1944, the Métis were dependent on wildlife for sustenance. Hunting, fishing, and trapping took up the bulk of the yearly work period and provided the main sources of food and income. Each man was more

*From *The Canadian Journal of Economics and Political Science*, Vol. XX, No. 1, February 1954.

†Mr. Valentine is Chief of the Northern Co-ordination and Research Centre, Department of Northern Affairs and Natural Resources, Ottawa.

or less in business for himself once he had acquired such necessary equipment as traps, nets, weapons, and food. Because these items took a lot of capital to acquire, a man "bought" them on credit from the Hudson's Bay Company or the private trader to whom he usually sold his catch. The amount of credit he was given was determined by his skill as a trapper or fisherman and by his honesty. There was no system of saving money from one season's catch to provide food for in-between seasons or, for that matter, to provide equipment for the next season; consequently, he simply had to have credit. Further, the yearly work cycle and the credit system were so interwoven that he was always in debt to the trader. It had come to be the accepted mode of living.

It was a semi-nomadic life in which every man was proudly a hunter. With no strong political focus, no complex division of labour, nor a clearly defined notion of owning this or that specific piece of land, there was no strong community life in the Euro-Canadian sense of the term. The only real social units were the self-sufficient families and the loosely knit bands. Each man provided for himself and his family in an isolated camp with the aid of simple tools. Stationary settlements as they are known today in the north were non-existent.

By 1944, it was no longer possible for the Métis to live in this fashion. A depletion of wildlife coupled with a disappearance of the demand for long-haired furs such as fox, and an increase in population through immigration from the south had combined to produce an economic situation which made outside help mandatory. In some regions the Métis had become almost totally dependent upon family allowance and provincial relief moneys.

In this connection it is to be noted that unlike the Treaty Indians, the Métis enjoy no special federal protection. They are considered to be citizens under the law, with all the rights and responsibilities inherent in that status. Thus their only source of special aid, such as unemployment relief and hospitalization, is the government of the province.

Before 1944, for one reason or another, the general populace of Saskatchewan was not particularly concerned with the conditions under which the Métis of the north dwelt, or with the development of northern natural resources. Hence there were no definite policies on the part of the government. But with the change in government a new attitude became accepted which can best be described as one favouring improvement of the general economic and social conditions of the Métis through their participation in whatever new developments took place. To achieve this the new administration developed, for the first time in the north, a series of systematic programmes dealing with the distribution of land and the conservation of wildlife, and in addition, further developed programmes in education, health, agriculture, and collective marketing. It was hoped by these means not only to raise the living standard of the Métis but at the same time to wean them from their nomadic hunting and collecting existence.

These programmes, though well meant, have been met with resistance from the outset, since the Métis have seen them as threats to their entire customary mode of living. This resistance is clearly evidenced in the results of the provincial elections held in June, 1952. The distribution of votes in the four settlements with which this paper is concerned are given in the accompanying table.

The programmes which were the focus of greatest resistance and which have created most problems for the Métis were those involving the conservation of wildlife and the distribution of land. These have been associated with two government undertakings: (1) the Saskatchewan Fur Marketing Service, a system of collective marketing; and (2) the Block Conservation System, a system of allocating land for trapping in the interest of wildlife conservation.

	Population		Vote	
	White	*Métis*	*C.C.F.*	*Liberal*
Portage La Loche	26	441	18	171
Buffalo Narrows	98	269	41	129
Ile-à-la-Crosse	81	516	6	163
Beauval	51	317		106
TOTAL			65	569

A similar pattern obtained in the other northern settlements.

The task of the remainder of this paper is to describe some of the more outstanding problems that have arisen in the life of the Métis as a result of these two programmes. In fairness to the present government, however, it should be clearly understood that these programmes were meant to assist the Métis rather than to hinder them in any way. If they have not done so, it has been owing to the erroneous but common assumption on the part of administrators that an economic logic which has been derived from a Euro-Canadian society can be imposed upon a people who have a totally different social background.

The Fur Marketing Service is a non-profit Crown Corporation, incorporated in 1945. Its purpose is twofold: (1) to bring greater profit to the trapper for muskrat and beaver fur by marketing these furs collectively without the aid of a middleman; and (2) to assist in the conservation of these two furs by placing tight controls on catches. In order to do this it compels the trapper by law to market his muskrat and beaver catches with the Service. This means that in the north where the common fur is muskrat, a trapper can no longer trade freely with the Hudson's Bay Company or private traders. His fur must be sold to the local government field officer.

Thus, a trapper gets more dollars for his fur, but he doesn't get the money all at once. There are two payments. The first is 50 per cent of the current market price for the particular fur when it is presented to the field officer. The second is the difference between the first payment and the actual amount realized on the final sale when the fur is sold by the Service to the wholesaler on a marketing day. This procedure enables the Service to protect itself from paying more initially than the fur might be worth when sold.

As it turns out, the fact that the Métis eventually get more dollars for their fur does not help them very much. Compulsory marketing has cut them off from the only type of wealth they really understand: credit. The Hudson's Bay Company and the private trader, since they can no longer buy these two staple furs, are reluctant to give a trapper credit. They claim they no longer have a guarantee that they will be paid. When the Métis dealt directly with them they made sure that the debt was first subtracted from the value of the fur before any other bartering took place. Only two people, the trapper and the trader, and two items, the raw fur and the trade goods, were involved. Now there are three of each: the trapper, the field officer, and the trader; the raw fur, dollars, and the trade goods. The trader is not sure he will get the dollars, especially in a settlement where there is more than one trader.

Before, a fairly good trapper could get from the Hudson's Bay Company or a private trader up to $400 credit for food and equipment to go on the trap-line. When he returned with his catch at the end of the season he first paid his debt, then bought flour, lard, tea, and tobacco to keep himself and his family for awhile, next he bought whatever hardware or equipment he might need, and finally took whatever value was left in cash. With the latter he invariably bought liquor and perhaps a few expensive new gadgets which he might use conspicuously for a time as a symbol of his great hunting abilities and then cast aside or sell unconcernedly at a fraction of their true worth. Seldom did he save a penny. As long as he could hunt effectively and had a good credit standing he felt no need to do so. There was no desire to accumulate any form of material wealth beyond his tent, canoe, toboggan, and simple tools. Since his life was nomadic, and since the bush and lakes had always supplied his wants, the idea of carting a wood-pile or an ice-box filled with food along the trail with him was completely foreign. Thus any cash on hand, once the immediate needs of the family had been supplied, was usually spent freely and rapidly on entertainment. More than anyone else in the north the traders are fully aware of this habit.

Today this way of life has become more difficult to follow. When the trapping season comes the Métis trapper may get no more than $15 or $20 credit from the Hudson's Bay Company or a private trader. This enables him to go on the trap-line with his family for about one week, rather than the whole season. After that time he must return, because of short supplies, with whatever fur he may have obtained, sell it to the Fur Marketing Service, get enough supplies to last another week or so, and then go back to the trap-line. This procedure is usually repeated throughout the season. When the season is over, those who do not live in the immediate vicinity of a post office are in a dilemma because their second payment cheques come from a central office by mail. If they go back to their homes, they will have to return later in order to collect the cheques, and if they stay and wait for them to come they waste much time which could be profitably spent in other activities. Neither the amount of the cheques nor the time they will arrive is known. In the majority of cases the trapper and his family simply pitch a tent in the vicinity of the post office or move in with friends who live close by, and wait for perhaps two months. During the waiting period most of the cash on hand received from the last sale of fur is spent in almost reckless abandon; while some food is bought, most of the cash is spent on liquor and gambling. Drinking and gambling parties with continual visiting of kith and kin go on most of the night and day until everyone is broke. When this happens whole families simply live on family allowance moneys or get credit from the traders by signing the incoming Fur Marketing Service cheques over to them. When the cheques do arrive they are usually for smaller amounts than had been anticipated and a man, therefore, very often finds himself, after his long wait, broke, without credit, without a food supply, and in debt. Those who are left destitute immediately demand financial assistance from the relief office, on the grounds that the government has taken away their livelihood by destroying their credit system and putting nothing in its place. Thus, although the fur crop has increased since the Service came into existence and more dollars have been paid to the Métis, the amount of money paid to them as relief has nearly doubled (the figures for only four settlements indicate a rise from approximately $7,000 in 1948 to $13,000 in 1951).

While the Fur Marketing Service is meant to bring higher profits to the Métis trapper and therefore help to increase the general standard of living, the Block Conservation System is meant to regulate, by means of a defined area surrounding a particular settlement, the conservation of fur-bearing animals, and at the same time to put an end to their nomadic life by confining them to a settlement. In operation, the System is a democratic one in which the trappers of each conservation block are encouraged to decide the number of muskrats and beaver which can and should be taken on a sustained yield basis. The fur in each block can be taken only by the Métis or white men who have the necessary residence requirements and who have purchased a trapping licence.

Now, until the Block System was introduced, the Métis were a nomadic people who hunted, fished, and trapped wherever the needed item was most prevalent. The settlements around which the Block System is built were previously composed simply of a mission and a trading-post. With the exception of those who worked for the mission, very few families had ever lived in them permanently. They were really little more than foci for widespread population distributions; people came to church or to trade and then returned to their isolated family camps.

Today these settlements have become a hodge-podge of overcrowded homesteads. There are no public services; each family still believes itself to be self-sufficient; and it has only been since the Block System was introduced, with subsequent efforts to survey the settlements into homestead lots, that ownership of land in our specific terms has entered the picture. The man who clears enough space behind his cabin for a garden is likely to wake up one morning and find someone building on it. Thus, in those settlements where fences have become necessary to keep the mission's cattle out of vegetable gardens, the fences seldom surround one home but take in many to create the impression of an enclosed compound.

The problem that arises is coupled with current health measures. The establishing of four new hospitals and of immediate air service for the more remote places, as well as the making available of pre- and postnatal care, have resulted in a considerable fall in the rate of infant mortality. In each of the past four years the population has increased naturally at the rate of 60 persons per 1000.[1] Yet the blocks with their rigid boundaries must provide for this increasing population while the

[1]Estimated by C. S. Brown in his 1951 Report of the Buffalo Region for the Department of Natural Resources of Saskatchewan. Large families are desired because of family allowance moneys. They are the main source of income at Portage la Loche where it is a very common practice for a man, whose wife is able to have many children, to give a child for adoption to a brother whose wife is unable to have any or can have only a few.

wildlife is steadily decreasing. What happens is that a large number of the young and middle-aged men leave the area to become migrant labourers on projects as distant as Alberta and the Northwest Territories. The effect of this on the family structure has been shattering: married men leave their wives and children for months, perhaps years. Sometimes they send money back to keep their families but more often than not the families live solely on what they can buy at the trading-post with family allowance moneys and what they can catch or collect by way of fish, rabbits, and edible berries. In some cases, as local postmasters have pointed out, these migrant labourers have written back demanding that the family allowance cheque be sent directly to them.

To alleviate the situation, the administration has been making every effort to instruct the Métis in the elements of agriculture. So far this has not been particularly successful. For one thing, neither the land nor the climate (54° N. Latitude) is suitable for anything more extensive than market gardening, and for another, the constellation of concepts so necessary for agricultural activity are either not understood or simply not desired. To encourage at least vegetable gardening, a series of prizes for the best garden is given, but it has been found that most of the people have been more interested in the prizes than in the produce. The main reason for this seems to be that few know what to do with the produce when it comes out of the ground. All of them are familiar with the potato as a food but few have yet acquired a taste for vegetables like carrots, turnips, and cabbages, which must be grown for the prize. Their diet had always been composed of wild fowl, fish, or meat, bannocks (made from flour and baking powder), berries, lard, potatoes, and tea. While, no doubt, there has been dietary indiscretion, the Métis have preferred this fare to anything the white man had to offer. Further, because they live in small makeshift homes, there is difficulty in storing produce over the winter and there is neither sufficient money for equipment nor knowledge available to attempt canning or preserving. More often than not the harvest simply rots in the ground.

As an illustration of some of the misconceptions that exist, one very enthusiastic middle-aged novice, not being content to grow just vegetables, planted peanuts, tobacco, and Solon berries, and although he has never had a crop he is very proud to have been the first Métis in the north to grow them.

The present rapid transition from a well-understood bartering economy to a complex one that involves liquid cash, complex cheque arrangements, fancy book-keeping, and mysterious market fluctuations, coupled with current restrictions on wildlife has forced the Métis to become dependent on store goods for sustenance — on a dollar basis. Yet there are no local industries except a little commercial fishing. The Métis no longer make their canoes, toboggans, nets and such; everything they use and most of what they eat must be bought in cash from the stores. In the north, where the average yearly income seldom exceeds $500, where food costs are high and credit is no longer available, it has become difficult to obtain an adequate living. But the problems are not only economic ones; the current hardship and confusion have penetrated every aspect of social life. With a growing number of men becoming migrant labourers, marriage has become unstable to the point that conflict and mistrust dominate the marital relationship. Promiscuity has become the rule rather than the exception, since wives whose husbands have left them without money usually take up with any man who can provide food enough to keep them and their children. An increase in the demand on the part of Métis women for white men as husbands or partners because of the advantage of a stable income has led to a loss of prestige on the part of the Métis men. This loss has been further aggravated by the current difficulty in obtaining credit, which had been the core of the prestige system.

With the concentration of population in settlements there has been an increase in undesirable habits but very little routine work. The little money that people do earn is soon dissipated in the continual round of visiting, drinking, and gambling. The children have little opportunity to maintain regular living habits. Yet they are expected every morning at 9 o'clock to fit into the routine of a local school.

Most children and adolescents are left with a minimum of parental control. They are no longer taught by their parents how to exploit forest and stream effectively and, as a result, a generation of inefficient trappers is arising.

It is true that the population is increasing, but it is by no means what we might call a healthy population. An increase in venereal disease, tuberculosis, crimes (especially drunkenness and theft), and illegitimate births typifies conditions among the modern Métis.

At present much confusion and misunderstanding exists between the Métis and the administration. The Métis feel that they are being robbed of their natural heritage and that the new programmes are rapidly bringing about the disintegration of their society. The resentment is such that to be called a "C.C.F.'er" is an anathema. The administration cannot understand why the well-meant schemes are not being accepted and are even sabotaged at times; it seems to them that the harder they try to do something the worse the situation becomes. This brings the discussion to a point from which it might well have started, to the two questions: (1) What are we, as administrators, really doing when we define other people's problems? and (2) What are we, as administrators, really trying to do when we say we are trying to help people?

18. *WHITHER THE ESKIMO?**

A. F. Flucke†

For those of us who are interested in the future of the Eskimo, an expansion of job opportunities in the Arctic could sound the death knell of under-privilege by offering employment to every available able-bodied adult. And possibly 20 thousand jobs will be created in the next 20 years. But for those who are concerned with Eskimo employment problems, there is a real question here. It is not whether the jobs will be ready for the Eskimo, but whether the Eskimo will be ready for the jobs. Will he be sufficiently educated and trained? Will he have the right attitude towards wage employment? Will he desire the living standards wage employment can bring him, enough to bear with its normal routine of labour? In other words, will he have become essentially an average Canadian capable of measuring up to the stiff requirements of job-holding in competitive Canadian enterprise?

Whether the Eskimo acquires these traits will depend upon a great deal more than simply knowing sixth or even eighth grade arithmetic, or on having acquired the ability to read a few school books. It will depend much more on the degree of acculturation he has reached; on the extent to which he has become aware of the qualities expected in a worker by Canadian employers; on his recognition of the attitudes and values he must acquire if he is to become a respected and welcome member of Canada's labour force.

Today, the Eskimo (in particular the Eastern Arctic Eskimo to whom

*From *North*, January-February, 1963.
†Mr. Flucke is Industrial Superintendent for the Arctic District, Department of Northern Affairs, Ottawa.

the writer's working experience is confined) is still not far removed in his thinking from his aboriginal stone-age forebears, despite nearly half a century of contact with traders, missionaries and government officials. He is still improvident to an extreme, lacking in foresight, tradition-bound and superstitious — primarily a gatherer of food, tied to the ways of his ancestors by economic habits and traditions of behaviour much stronger than the average southern Canadian would realize. If the Eskimo is to play an important role in the development of the Arctic — if, as an employee, he is to satisfy the requirements of his southern Canadian employer, and to become something more than a mere mover of oil barrels — then many of his old habits and customs must suffer drastic changes. Traditional ways must be discarded in favour of values and attitudes which will give him competitive equality with other Canadian workers wending their way north for adventure and profit.

It has been affirmed many times that the southern man must have the Eskimo to help him to survive in the Arctic climate, and in earlier days of Arctic travel this was no doubt true. Even today the inexperienced land traveller certainly needs an Eskimo to guide him from point to point, and to show him how to travel and how to shelter himself. But development of Arctic resources (and by these I do not mean art forms) could and would have taken place had there been no Eskimos in the Arctic at all. In fact, the Eskimo, rather than contributing to the solution of Arctic resources development, is himself a part of the problem requiring solution. That he provides, to some extent, a relatively stable unskilled labour pool for manual tasks cannot be denied, but whether in this respect he is an asset to Arctic development is open to question. As a worker on a project distant from his home settlement, his initial enthusiasm soon wanes, and after a few weeks he is anxious for home. Since his living standard shows no immediate appreciable rise, the advantages of employment are not obvious enough to him to offset his desire to be close to family and friends. When it becomes necessary to provide the Eskimo worker with housing, rations for his family, etc., at the job site, then the advantages of employing him become dubious. Conversations with Arctic development groups indicate that much of the present Eskimo employment is provided as an act of charity — perhaps of reluctant acquiesence in government suggestion. This situation will continue until such time as Eskimo labour can meet the competition of imported southern labour. Since the development of the Arctic will continue to be largely the result of efforts by southern commercial and industrial groups, Eskimo labour will reach a competitive vantage point only after massive absorption of southern language, southern values and southern ways of working and living. The Eskimo must reach the standard where his prospective employer need not consider the fact that he is an "Eskimo". But can the Eskimo discard many of the traditional attributes of his group, while retaining a basic and justifiable pride in language and origins? Can he transfer part of the unreasoning racial pride of accomplishment — seeing worth in his ability to raise himself from a primitive food gatherer to a position of equality with his southern associates, while still seeing value in many aspects of his aboriginal culture? In my opinion, this optimum out-look can come about only after a great measure of acculturation to Canadian standards has been achieved. Until the Eskimo is secure in his role as an equal participant in Canadian society, he will not be able to shake the feeling, however misguided it may be, that he comes from an inferior stock.

From his own keen observations as well as from repeated admonitions by various categories of "bosses", he realizes that *in relation to the non-Eskimo Arctic resident* he is improvident, that his living conditions are squalorous, and that his health habits leave much to be desired. No amount of encouraging words will truly convince him that there are aspects of his culture which we admire and from which we feel we can learn. The Eskimo is a materialist — a pragmatic one — unaccustomed to dealing with abstract ideals. He sees only the vast gulf separating his way of living from that of southern Canadians, and cannot but regard himself as an inferior being, even while showing his resentment and envy by acting as though the opposite were true.

Ethnic groups, in transition from a primitive to a technological way of life, do not attain cultural security merely by preserving their language. Cultural security is something which comes only with the group's ability to cope with its environment — to be able to see itself on a par with other groups in the same or similar environments. Only from the vantage point of confidence in their own ability can a people look back with pride on their primitive (or even colonial) past. Until that confidence is secure and soundly based, cultural security cannot exist.

The past is not too distant when the Eskimo coped with his environment, as ably as his primitive equipment allowed, even to the point of aiding the occasional intrepid visitor from the south. Since his only associates were other Eskimo groups who held no advantages, no comparisons were obvious to him. As his environment changed, he became progressively less sure of himself. He saw the southerners move in and cope with greater facility (because of the things they brought with them) than he had ever imagined possible, and Eskimo group-pride suffered.

Today this pride has degenerated to a simple negative reaction — a resentment against what appears to him to be the obviously superior capabilities and accomplishments of the invaders from the south. Such a reaction inhibits natural abilities and undermines any desires to achieve higher educational and cultural levels — abilities and desires which we are striving so painfully to nourish, through our educational and training programs.

To the Eskimo, nothing is worth the trouble unless it brings almost immediate rewards, or unless the goal and its rewards are obvious, clearly defined, and absolutely sure of realization. Eskimos are far from convinced of the usefulness of the educational and training programs offered by the government and other agencies. Many of them look upon these schemes as a great waste of time, worthwhile only because of the food and shelter they provide for the children, or the training allowances which accrue to the dependants of trainees. Motivation for learning is almost non-existent, because the goals, as explained by the white man, are too remote, and unlikely of realization.

Many Eskimos still regard the school and its curriculum of southern subjects as just another of the white man's peculiarities. "Why should my child go to school?" Kidlak asks. "So he will be able to work beside the white man," you answer. "How soon will he get a job?" Kidlak asks, and smiles as he speaks because he knows that his six-year old son cannot work yet. "Not soon", you reply, "perhaps when he is sixteen or so". And Kidlak smiles more broadly because you have said "perhaps" and obviously you are guessing and cannot see ten years into the future. And why should his child spend all those months and years in school instead of being out playing at hunting, or helping around the house, just to be able to work for the Kadlunait when he is a man. It is not reasonable. All the men work during the summer carrying supplies and none speaks English.

To provoke and sustain the Eskimo's continuing interest in our educational and training programs, we must provide an environment wherein the benefits and advantages to be obtained are tangible. The majority of Eskimos still lack an environment in which they can use their schooling, or in which they can see concrete results stemming from the inconveniences and cultural conflicts that arise from it. There is little opportunity or incentive for even the children to use the English they are taught, or to acquire experiences in southern ways of thinking and living. On leaving school at the end of the day, they revert to Eskimo language and Eskimo ways. They associate the English language, the lessons they learn, habits of diet and cleanliness, and all other aspects of the white man's culture which they observe, with the school and teacher, or the other "bosses". The "Eskimo camp" environment is not conducive to associating these traits with themselves and their own homes and families.

Even among the adults, there is little recognition of the association between learning and earning, between better jobs and higher living standards. They understand, in a hazy way, that the more education a white man has, the better living conditions he enjoys. But they fail to associate themselves with this phenomenon. The Eskimo is still an unwilling, and envious separatist. The gulf between his existence and ours will continue to exist as long as the Eskimo remains thinly scattered across the Arctic, isolated economically and socially.

What are the changes that must take place in the Eskimo way of life before the gulf can be bridged? For the most part, changes in the primitive Eskimo habits of thought and behaviour which impede improvement of his material circumstances. He must learn to want all the things which signify higher living standards, not only because his non-Eskimo neighbours have them, but also because of the improvements in health, comfort, and convenience which they bring. He must learn to value such things more than he values the primitive leisure of carrying out traditional actions in traditional ways within traditional time concepts. He must learn to dislike being without the things he sees his white associates enjoying, but he must learn also that to acquire them he must work as hard and as long as they do. He must learn to want better food, clothing and housing more than he wants the freedom of being able to sleep, eat and hunt as the spirit moves him. He must learn to dislike being without all the white man has, more than he dislikes the forty to fifty hour work-week. He must learn also to judge, assess, and place appropriate value on a host of new enticements offered to him. He must learn to want better household and sanitary facilities more than records and record players; better food and cooking facilities more than the easy laxity of allowing the children unlimited sweets, toys and useless trade goods. He must learn to value better health, better clothing, and more comfort, more than he values the primitive pleasure of purchasing every useless gadget he sees. If these changes in the Eskimo's approach to living do not take place, twenty years from now we still have, with the exception of the fortunate few, a race of oil-barrel movers — half-life Canadians, to whom the white man's world is still a distant utopia. To speed these changes, the whole gamut of southern Canadian culture — jobs, physical comforts, possessions, entertainment, social contacts — should be available to the Eskimos in as full measure as practical and in proportion to his desire to improve himself.

19. WHAT DOES IT MEAN TO BE AN ESKIMO?*

Abraham Okpik

We the Eskimo people, where do we come from and how did we get here? This is a big question to us all even in the white man's way of thinking or learning. We are still a mystery to them, but our ancestors are the ones to whom we give praise for all that they have achieved, to live, to feel, to survive for centuries before the white people came. Some of the kablonat[1] came with good intentions to teach us a better way to live, some came to destroy our livelihood and our culture. But this we must remember, what our ancestors have done to keep alive in the cold in scarcity of food; or are we forgetting?

Let us think back even fifty years ago and compare our people's living conditions then, with our present living environment. We have gained very little to add to what our forefathers have left us.

So now let us realize today we are living in the present times without observing what we are losing, and that is our own Eskimo Innuk culture, which our great-great-grandfathers have passed on to us generation after generation. Are we keeping our old traditions, or are we going to forget them for good? I am sorry to say we are forgetting it now, and if we don't start picking it up again, our race, our proud heritage will be extinct. All will never, never be heard or seen again. Our Eskimo songs that our fathers had, our old stories which we used to hear from our older people will be gone and we will never hear them again. All this will be lost, so let us wake up and restore our old methods and old culture while there is still time, because if we lose it, it will be a tragedy, after what our ancestors had shown us. We must remember this, where no other people could have survived, our ancestors did, with a hope that some day we would be known to the other parts of the world, not as the people of present new day, but as the people of old who had great determination to live, to survive, and to learn the daily needs. Today if we can think like our ancestors and put to use what they have achieved for us, and adopt the white man's way of learning, at the same time, and keep our own, we will be further ahead. We should learn as much as we can from this new culture, but we must not forget our own culture which is important to all of us.

---

*From *North*, March-April, 1962.

[1] "Kablonat" refers to non-Eskimos. (Ed.)

So let us wake up to a new day, with new thoughts, new gifts, new learning, from the new culture, but we must remember our ancestors who had to endure the cold with the help of their knowledge and ingenuity. We could put our learning with this new modern way of living, and only then we will have a bright future, with the white people's learning and our own culture.

To you older people I want to say this, you are the people who can still pass this culture to the younger generation. At the moment we the Eskimos seem to be in two different minds; first the older people know the old way of living, know the language because their forefathers have taught them this; and second the younger people are not interested to keep their own language. They are not being taught to keep their own language, how to keep it and preserve it. It is important to have our language. At least it will be something we have inherited from our fathers if we keep it.

To live happily, people need to feel they belong to something — a family, a group, a tribe, a nation, a race. The one thing which keeps people together is a common language.

When you learn to work and live the white man's way — you lose the Eskimo way. This can't be helped. We want progress and comfort and education and security. We can have these things — and still keep our language. We need our language to keep us happy together. If we lose our language, we lose our personality — we don't belong either to the Eskimo people or to the whites. An Eskimo who has lost his language is completely lost. He doesn't belong anywhere.

Keep our language alive, and keep the Eskimo people alive. Tell the old stories, sing the songs, dance the old dances, make jokes, enjoy this great power for thought developed from long ago by our ancestors.

The survival of the Eskimo people depends on the survival of the language. When people meet Eskimos, they are disappointed if they cannot show their knowledge of Eskimo ways. The Eskimo language is big. It could be used to give many great thoughts to the world. If the Eskimos themselves don't use their language more, it will be forgotten, and very soon the Eskimos too will be a forgotten people.

It is up to the Eskimos of today to use their Eskimo strength of word and thought. It is up to the young people. If they don't learn and use the language and the stories and songs, they will have nothing special to give to their children.

It's no good looking like an Eskimo if you can't speak like one.

There are only very few Eskimos, but millions of whites, just like mosquitoes. It is something very special and wonderful to be an Eskimo — they are like the snow geese. If an Eskimo forgets his language and Eskimo ways, he will be nothing but just another mosquito.

20. *KABLOONA AND ESKIMO IN THE CENTRAL KEEWATIN: TRENDS AND COMPARISONS**

Frank G. Vallee[†]

Things have been changing in the Arctic for many generations, but the pace of change has been greatly accelerated since World War II and particularly since the early 'fifties, creating an abrupt cultural discontinuity. Our general impression of the Eskimo response to the pitch and toss of change is that the great majority have rolled with it without falling overboard, a commentary on the flexibility and adaptability of their culture, social organization, and personality. There are some sharp discontinuities between the traditional and the new — for instance in making public what was private and private what was public, in the routinization and scheduling of life, in putting oneself in the paid employ of others, in modes of community organization, in conventional practices with respect to sanitation, secular and sacred ritual. These discontinuities are difficult to cope with, especially for those in settlements who are under front-line pressure from impatient Kabloona.[1]

On the other hand, there are many lines of continuity between the traditional way of life and the modern one: the general form and process of the family, the lack of profound attachment between a plot of land and a family name, the stress on achievement rather than on ascription, the link between worldly achievement and favour with the spirit world,

*From *Kabloona and Eskimo in the Central Keewatin*, Ottawa, Northern Co-ordination and Research Centre, Department of Northern Affairs and National Resources, May 1962.

†Dr. Vallee, a social anthropologist recently Associate Professor at McMaster University, Hamilton, is currently with the Department of Sociology at Carleton University, Ottawa.

[1]In this report we use Kabloona rather than White to designate non-Eskimo people. The term White has a biological connotation, whereas the most significant factors differentiating the Eskimo from the non-Eskimo are social and cultural.

the low esteem for the able-bodied person who is chronically poor and the high estimation of the successful entrepreneur. All of these and other features of traditional life are congenial to the new one.

Compared with many other indigenous groups which have been subjected to pressures of change from an overpowering industrial society, the Eskimos are remarkable for the absence among them of individuals and factions with profound material and emotional vested interests in the traditional *status quo*. The tradition-bearers, especially of the grandparental generation, have been edged into cultural backwaters. Most of the older people we encountered are resigned to the changes and do not actively combat them. As for the middle-aged adults, with few exceptions they are not passing on the distinctive traditions of their localities.

The most acute point of discontinuity and the one which is most likely to have disruptive consequences is between those who were brought up in a pre-1940 milieu — adults between about twenty-five and forty — and their children, especially among settlement dwellers. The children, raised in semi-urban surroundings, exposed to sustained contact with Kabloona teachers and other socializers, are eventually confronted with the fact that their own parents and grandparents are considered inferior 'role models' by representatives of the dominant society. It is too early to predict how they will come to terms with this realization, but some possible reactions are mentioned presently.

There is abroad in the Kabloona world a favourable image of the traditional Eskimo culture. Admiration has been expressed universally for the dauntless tenacity of generations of Eskimos in maintaining an edge in the struggle against a ferocious environment. Few ugly blotches mar the received historical image of the Eskimo compared with, say, the received historical images of those Indians who fought against white intrusion, dismembering a few martyrs and scalping a few Caucasoid skulls in the process. At least the descendants of the primitive Eskimos do not have to contend with this image of their ancestors in textbooks, popular literature, movies, and the like; the Eskimo abroad in the world does not have to live down the presumed animality of his remote ancestors.

On the other hand, although the Kabloona make a favourable, if romantic, judgment on the Eskimo past, this does not prevent them from showing contempt for the living Eskimos they meet, either openly or by implication. Consider what is implied where one learns that untidiness is sinful, and one's parents are untidy; that receiving handouts is a mark of inferior status while one's parents are forced to accept handouts to keep the household going; that self-respecting men are capable of protecting their womenfolk from human predators while one's sisters and mother have to be protected behind a social wall of non-fraternization, erected by the guardians of the predators. Under such conditions it is not unlikely that children will devalue their parents.

The devaluation of parents by offspring who accept, perhaps unconsciously, the Kabloona evaluations of what is desirable and what is reprehensible implies a weakening in the control which parents normally exercise over their offspring. Plausible explanations of the factors which pre-dispose the children of foreign-born in America to delinquency usually include the point that the children, accepting the dominant society's view that the immigrant parent is strange and perhaps uncouth, do not look up to the parents as role-models.

We have reported that there is no evidence of such a wedge between generations at the Baker Lake settlement, but information from larger and more urban Arctic centres, while not sufficiently reliable to permit the precise statement of statistical rates, points to a diminution of parental control and an increase of gang activity, vandalism, and petty theft. If this kind of deviance begets the punitive response so frequently manifested in the south by uncomprehending guardians of our conventions, there might emerge a vicious circle from which it could take many years to break out. Officials and other representatives of the dominant society in such places must be firm in defining what is lawful and unlawful, but must be mindful of the kinds of stresses under which the settlement Eskimos are living and conscious that their official actions will have rankling consequences long after their tenures have expired.

Turning from the matter of discontinuity of life-ways between generations, we consider the disruptive consequences on mature persons of being thrust into a new milieu. At Baker Lake the discontinuity between living on the land in the traditional style and living in the settlement is not remarkably acute. Living in the settlement, one may still hunt, fish, trap, contact relatives on the land and maintain at least the impression of living the old life without paying too high a price and without inviting drastic sanctions from the Kabloona. Moreover, if a person brought up on the land finds settlement living too stressful, it is relatively easy for him to withdraw and return to the land; the hinterland is at his doorstep. It is not as easy to disengage from commitment to settlement living in some of the other urbanized Arctic localities, such as Rankin Inlet, Frobisher Bay, and Inuvik. Reactions to the strains of settlement life in these places are less likely to be those of physical withdrawal, more likely to be those of what Kabloona regard as conventional deviance — drunkenness, aggression, theft, to mention a few.

Having earlier considered some of the reasons for the lower rates of deviant behaviour at Baker Lake, let us here comment on only one feature which has to do with community organization. A low rate of conventional deviance suggests an optimum degree of community cohesion so that the strains of settlement living are handled in such a way that deviance is prevented. One index of social cohesion is the extent to which individuals and groups in the community are detached or isolated from supportive and restraining relationships. Where such detachment and isolation are pronounced, one speaks of 'individuation' and 'anomie'! Studies from many parts of the world indicate that rates of conventional deviance are high under conditions of individuation and anomie. We suggest that at Baker Lake, the extended family and the congregations provide integrative or cohesive forces of a strength not matched by these groups in the larger, more urban settlements.

Kinship and congregational bonds in new Arctic settlements may be sufficient in themselves to ensure a high degree of communal cohesion and integration. We suggest that a requisite for the latter condition is the provision of some 'voice' or 'say' for all elements in the community. Voiceless people are not likely to have much of a stake in a community's record, and are more likely to have a purely self-interest approach. An effective voice is transmitted through social groups such as associations and is channelled through association spokesmen. One may have expected that the movement of large numbers of Eskimos into settlement would have resulted in the emergence of new forms of association in these settlements, association for purposes of mutual aid, the airing of grievances, the co-ordination of community activities, and so on.

The evidence at hand indicates that associations among the Eskimos are likely to thrive under the following conditions:

1. where the Eskimos command resources and facilities which are regarded as valuable and scarce;
2. where in the pre-settlement period leadership was channelled through one or two families of a strong band organization;
3. where there is no formal segregation between the Eskimos and Kabloona;
4. where no one Kabloona institution is overwhelmingly dominant in the community.

We have suggested that a sense of local citizenship, a sense that one has a role to play in local decision-making, is not likely to emerge among people who are living on the edge of subsistence and whose income depends not so much on the resources and skills which they command as on the good will and local policies of benefactors, governmental or private. What are the economic prospects in Arctic settlements?

In a few localities, for example in the Arctic Islands, along the Arctic Sea coast, and along the northern tip of the Ungava Peninsula, the wildlife resources continue to provide a substantial part of the livelihood for the Eskimos. In such locations, the pursuit of sea-mammal hunting with large boats is supplemented by other means of gaining a livelihood: stone carving, trapping, fishing for domestic consumption and for market sale, working for wages, and government relief. In at least a few places, like Tuktoyaktuk and Povungnituk, there are more families deriving income from entrepreneurial activities as independent producers of goods than from wage labour.

Baker Lake shares with many localities in the Arctic an economy in which hunting is secondary to other means of gaining a livelihood. Great Whale River, Rankin Inlet, Frobisher Bay, and many other regions have, like Baker Lake, a wildlife resource base which is insufficient to provide more than a bare subsistence to their populations, small as these are, and the only entrepreneurial endeavour worth notice is that of the trapper.

Even if the wildlife resource base in regions like Baker Lake could provide more than a bare subsistence without considerable supplementation in the form of wages and government aid, the resulting standard of living would not reach the level nowadays regarded as minimal by public opinion and by influential people like public health officials, teachers, journalists, and others with a hand in Eskimo affairs. We expect that criteria employed in judgments of adequacy about the Eskimo standard of living will grow increasingly like the criteria employed in the south, where it is felt that the family-household must have a distinct dwelling space, internally divided according to function, properly heated and not overcrowded, a stock of decent furnishings for the dwelling and of clothing and other accoutrements of daily life for each individual, besides a store of foods, medicines, cigarettes and other items regarded as indispensable in the south.

It is clear that such a standard of living will only be achieved with income derived from several sources. That part derived from wages and from entrepreneurial activity will have to expand greatly from its present amount, an expansion which can only come about when the Eskimos take over jobs now performed by Kabloona. There are, of course, certain imponderables which it is difficult to take into account in making such projections. For instance, the opening of a mine at Baker Lake would greatly increase the amount of wages flowing into households there. But even such an event is fraught with economic risk to the local population. The mine at Rankin Inlet provides the highest per capita income to the Eskimo population there, but the closing of that mine as a result of market pressures or of mineral exhaustion would have dire economic and social consequences locally, because the Eskimos have all their economic eggs in one basket.

As a response to the lack of economic opportunities in such localities as Baker Lake, can we expect large-scale migrations of families out of the Arctic altogether? In our opinion, this is not a realistic expectation. The author knows of a handful of individuals who have migrated to the south and who have come to terms with the environment there. However, we cannot point to one family group which has settled in the South, nor have we heard of one family group which even aspires to such a migration. It is possible that once the new educational system begins to produce young Eskimos with marketable skills, the rate of migration outside the Arctic will rise appreciably, but for at least the next few decades we cannot realistically expect spontaneous movement of significant numbers to the south in search of economic opportunity.

On the other hand, there have been numerous instances of family groups resettling in locations distant from their home territories but within the Arctic area and, usually, within the district of their birth and upbringing. Transfers of population within the Arctic, both of the spontaneous and administered or planned variety, should become increasingly common as a response to economic pressure.

Local economies in the future, then, will require an increasing flow of cash income from wages and entrepreneurial profits and, ideally, a larger measure of diversification than they possess now as protection against sudden collapses in any one area, whether this be mining, trapping, whaling, or whatever. Unfortunately, diversification at the local community level is an unlikely condition in most parts of the Arctic and particularly in the Barren Lands. This is one reason that economic thinking must be as much in terms of region as it is in terms of community, for a larger measure of diversification can be achieved at the regional than at the local level.

For communities in a region to form part of one diversified economy requires that they do not simply duplicate one another, but that they be interrelated in an organic way, so that the functions of one complement the functions of the others. Local specialization of function is common in the south, but if we look at the communities in the Keewatin District we find that most of them simply duplicate one another. Such settlements as Baker Lake, Eskimo Point, Chesterfield Inlet and Coral Harbour are linked in a network of radio communication in the national interest, exchanging and relaying messages about weather, flying conditions, flight programmes, and so on. Each is also a link to the others in an administrative chain. However, they are not linked in any kind of interdependent network as far as the local Eskimos are concerned. Each settlement is more oriented to the south than it is to other settlements in the same district. The people in any one settlement could die or be flown thousands of miles away from the Arctic without this altering the social organization and daily life of people in other settlements of the district.

The emergence of Rankin Inlet as a place where Eskimos can sell their labour has introduced an element of diversification in the district, but so far this has not led to a condition of interdependence between settlements, for the Rankin Inlet community is primarily dependent on the south for everything it needs, except unskilled labour. So far there is no sign of an emerging demand in Rankin Inlet for the products of other settlements in the Keewatin District, such as caribou meat and hides, fish, sea-mammal meat and skins, and so on. If such relations of mutual economic interdependence could be fostered and improvements in means of transportation between communities developed to handle the flow of goods and human traffic, the dependence of each community on the distant south would be much less acute.

The foregoing argument may be economically naive, but the author presses it because economic dependence usually implies social and psychological dependence, a condition deplored by Eskimo and Kabloona alike. Furthermore, we press it because we detect a trend towards the emergence of something which can be called an Eskimo social system in the Canadian Arctic, a social system which transcends local camps and communities and links widely separated people in a consciousness of kind. In traditional times this consciousness of kind transcending local groupings was absent and there existed instead a large number of small-scale, regional societies, having in common certain cultural characteristics in language, technology, and world-view. Although in the process of cultural assimilation the Eskimos have abandoned many of these cultural characteristics and are adopting Kabloona ones, they are not being assimilated socially into the Kabloona society. There is no evidence of significant numbers of Eskimos passing into Kabloona society: even the most acculturated Eskimos encountered by the author do not regard themselves as Kabloona. Economic interdependence among Eskimo communities would reinforce their social distinctiveness and ethnic solidarity.

To continue in this speculative vein, we envisage not the assimilation, or swallowing up, of the Eskimos in Canadian society, but rather their integration as an ethnic group into that society. By integration, we mean the joining together of parts into a whole, each part retaining an identity of its own which is distinct from the other parts. In this context, the parts are ethnic groups, not individuals. To illustrate: in Canada there is a French Canadian ethnic group, but all those born of French Canadian parents do not identify with this ethnic group. Persons may choose to identify with an ethnic group or think of themselves in non-ethnic terms. We believe that for a long time to come there will exist an Eskimo-Canadian ethnic group, although not all persons born of Eskimo parents will necessarily identify with it.

A requisite for the development of a strong Eskimo identity which cuts across settlement, rural-urban, social class, and sub-cultural distinctions, is some means of communication through which Eskimo points of view can be diffused. First steps in building such a communication network have already been taken: a publication entitled ESKIMO and printed in the Eskimo language has a wide readership in the Arctic, and radio broadcasts in Eskimo have been introduced, beamed through the transmitters at Frobisher, Inuvik and Churchill. Although the Kabloona have been the prime movers in these innovations and retain the ultimate right to censor the content, a large measure of control over the productions is vested in Eskimos. The fact that communications through these media are in the Eskimo language has important implications for the maintenance of a distinctive Eskimo ethnic group.

The trend towards a kind of pan-Eskimoism is given impetus by the emergence and growing influence of a class of persons committed to settlement living, the kind of persons we have called Kabloonamiut throughout this report. Data from recent reports on Port Harrison, Great Whale River, Rankin Inlet, and Eskimo Point indicate that the Baker Lake community is not unique in this respect.

In all Arctic communities for which we have information Kabloona and Eskimo groups form into sub-systems, and it is because of the barriers between these sub-systems that we are led to discount the early passing of Eskimos into the larger society in any substantial numbers. Articulate Eskimos are already claiming to speak for all Eskimos *vis-à-vis* all Kabloona. These articulate Eskimos are the products of either settlement living or lengthy stays in Kabloona institutions, such as hospitals and residential schools. In cultural terms they are closer to the Kabloona than to the traditional Eskimo. However, for many of them, identification with the Eskimo reference group is quite strong. Some control of the Arctic-wide communication system mentioned above is vested in people from this grouping. Their appearance is too recent to warrant prediction about their eventual role, but it is possible that they could inspire, or act as spokesmen for, protest movements as the Eskimos gain more insight into their predicaments. The assumption of such a role by the Eskimos who are most acculturated to Kabloona ways is likely to occur if they feel socially rebuffed by the Kabloona or if they view themselves as victims of discrimination.

21. NEGROES IN CANADA*

Harold H. Potter†

INTRODUCTION

Canadian literature on race relations deals first and foremost with the political aspirations of a 'race' of French Catholics *vis-à-vis* a 'race' of British Protestants. Of this larger picture Negroes form a minute and apparently unimportant part. J. M. Gibbon's *Canadian Mosaic,* published in 1938, contains no reference to Negroes, nor does *Canadian Society,* edited by Bernard Blishen and others and published in 1961. B. K. Sandwell's *The Canadian Peoples*, published in 1941 and 1947, mentions discrimination against Jews and Negroes in one line.

A little further investigation shows, however, that between 1920 and 1958 professional historians and students inclined to social work wrote at least thirty-four articles and theses for higher degrees on the subject of Canadian Negroes. In the media of broader mass communication, too — in wireless broadcast, telecasts, newspapers and magazines — coloured people have been the object of deep, sustained and well-intentioned interest for well over the past ten years. Through the same period they

*From *Race* (the journal of the Institute of Race Relations, London, England), Vol. III, No. 1, November 1961.
†Mr. Potter is Professor of Sociology at Sir George Williams University, Montreal.

have been included among those whose employment and civic rights have been discussed in literature published by the Department of Labour, the Canadian Jewish Congress, the United Church of Canada and labour unions.

NEGRO POPULATIONS

Canadian Negroes number much less than one-third of the estimated coloured population of London. The census of 1951 reported a few more than eighteen thousand scattered over almost three and a half million square miles of territory and forming a little more than one-tenth of one per cent of the entire population. An estimate of 23,500 was mentioned in 1957. They are not evenly distributed, but are concentrated in the rural and urban communities of four or five regions. In Sydney, Stellarton, Truro, Halifax, Yarmouth, Digby, and almost a dozen other Nova Scotian communities, they number from eight to thirteen thousand. There are a few hundreds in Saint John, Fredericton and Woodstock, New Brunswick; eight or ten thousand are divided between Montreal and Toronto; a few thousands more are in Dresden, Sandwich, Barrie, Chatham and Windsor, all in south-western Ontario; some are in Winnipeg, some in Edmonton, and several dozens in Vancouver, Victoria, and other Pacific places.

In the national census of 1941 slightly more than twenty-two thousand Negroes were reported. These statistics refer, of course, to avowed Negroes and do not include people who chose to report themselves in other ways to census enumerators. The decrease of more than four thousand Negroes between 1941 and 1951 meant that either more Negroes died and emigrated than arrived through birth and immigration in that period, or almost one-fifth of Canadian Negroes chose to report themselves under other labels after 1941. It must be said that official national statistics and unofficial local estimates of coloured populations differ and cannot be reconciled.

A coloured community may have a complex population structure. For example, the Negroes of Toronto, according to Daniel Hill, have four elements in their populations: 'old-line' native Canadians, British West Indians, American newcomers and, most recently, Nova Scotians. They are scattered and, in Hill's words, do not form a true community.

In Montreal there are no old-line Negroes. There were slaves in the late eighteenth century, but they seem to have left no traceable issue in the city. Americans formed the first significant nucleus of coloured population about the terminals of the railways that employed most of them around 1910 and 1920. They were joined later by West Indians who remained in Montreal because of their British connexion. Many of these latter lived away from the 'Negro district'. The Americans eventually disappeared; many returned to the United States with the advent there of the New Deal. A thin dribble of Nova Scotians westward to Montreal grew into a considerable migration during and after World War II, forming a new significant element in the local population.

Nowadays six classes of Negro can be distinguished in that city. First, there are avowed Negroes who dwell in a rundown area that is predominantly white in population but is widely known as the 'Negro district'. Outside this area, in various places on and off the islands comprising the city, other avowed Negroes live who have gained a relatively satisfactory economic place. Some have remained in the traditional low-status occupations of sleeping-car porter, station porter, washroom attendant, garage mechanic.

Scattered among the core category and the dispersed category are new arrivals from Caribbean islands. Some of these are virtually penniless strangers whose only friends or relatives in the city are poor coloured people like themselves. Some arrive with marketable skills, but many do not. Some are washed and some are not. Some are dressed outlandishly, others in perfect taste. To be thrown among the sharks and barracudas of a great central city shocks them.

There is a fourth class in the general picture: an undetermined number of non-confessing coloured people whose homes are scattered through various districts. They are in honoured occupations, and many of them marry white men and women.

Next are scores of students from different lands, many of whom have no connexion with coloured people here. Some find housing accommodation in the 'Negro community'; some live in the rooming-house areas surrounding the two English universities. Some live far from the centre of the city. Some are relatively well-to-do; some are poor. They are in Montreal for periods ranging from several months to eight or ten years. In spite of an immigration regulation requiring West Indians to return home after completion of their studies, some manage to stay north indefinitely, perhaps through the application of another regulation which permits immigration officers to recognise cases of 'exceptional merit' for admission to the country. Negroes from French territories are very few and are scattered.

Added to these five distinct categories of Montreal coloured people are professional and amateur players in football, baseball and basketball leagues, imported from the United States by entrepreneurs who supply sport to the general public. These seem to be located outside the Negro community, and at least one has become a Canadian citizen.

METROPOLITAN NEGROES IN 1941

Unpublished census data of 1941 show that families in the 'Negro district', comprising two-thirds of all Montreal Negroes who avowed themselves as such, reported incomes that averaged $400 per year in one neighbourhood, $500 per year in another, and $1,086 per year in a third, the variation directly agreeing with distance of the home from the ecological centre of the coloured population. These figures are hard to credit; but there is an impressive consistency in the amounts reported by wage-earners, especially when they are grouped by municipal wards of domicile. In 1948 I discussed this information with a professional engineer employed in a factory in the Negro district, and he assured me that the data fitted what he knew of the earnings of white workers recruited into his plant from that same part of the city. In fact, for the twelve months prior to the census date, 2 June 1941, 53.4 per cent of the city's 231,000 male wage-earners reported earnings of less than $950, while 67 per cent of its porters reported earnings of less than that amount.

In 1941 almost half the employed Negro males of Montreal were railway porters and four-fifths of the employed Negro females were domestic servants. Other Negroes were engaged in some eighty other gainful occupations ranging from menial to supervisory and professional employment. The general condition of the mass of coloured people is illustrated by the following excerpts from two interviews in 1948 with coloured women outside the Negro district:

> (1) The interviewer said that his information was that domestics in 1941 claimed to be earning anywhere from eight to twenty-five dollars per month.

Mrs. Chalmers replied:

> That's true. I knew any number of people doing housework for ten dollars a month before the war. And they did more than they do now. That was the standard wage. The employers tried to say that ten dollars plus meals and a room really worked out to forty dollars per month. Finns and Poles and Swedes and French girls — they were all getting the same.

(2) Elsewhere the interviewer dealt with the secretary to the top executive of a local industrial company. She came to Montreal from Quebec City in 1937, fully trained as a stenographer, able to take shorthand dictation in both English and French. Unable to find a stenographic job, she became a domestic servant. In the interview she said that ten

or fifteen dollars per month was the standard pre-war rate. Referring to former employers in Westmount City, she said: 'For fifteen or eighteen dollars a month they expected you to kiss their feet.'

> The interviewer said that according to his information girls in 1941 worked for wages ranging from two to six dollars per week.

Miss Munro answered:

> Yes; but you know what makes it hard for the coloured girls? It's these French girls coming from Gaspé and all those country places, and offering to work for six dollars a month! Coloured girls can't work for that; but they've got to stay here and take it. Of course those upper crust people don't care whether you have anything to wear or something for your grooming or whether you have time to look after your soul. My boss would say, 'Mrs. So-and-So has a French girl, and she only pays her six dollars a month.' I'd say, 'The girl must be a fool!' She'd say, 'Oh Cassie, don't say that.' I'd say, 'Well, she is.'

ASSIMILATION TODAY

Even for Negroes, times change. By 1951 the sleeping-car porter's role was no longer restricted to coloured men. Railway management acknowledged the right of porters to form unions independent of the companies, wages were greatly increased, and whites of various ethnic backgrounds began to earn their living in this way. It then became possible for a sleeping-car porter to rise within the industry to another position. The Canada Fair Employment Practices Act came into effect at the beginning of July 1953, and probably has worked to the advantage of the coloured porter. Of course, Negroes of various geographic origins pursued other occupations in other industries.

[The original article contains, at this point, a list of significant career successes of individual Negroes in Canada, but these have been omitted here, with the permission of the author, in order to conserve space.]

A NEW TREND

The dictum that Negroes form an unassimilable element in the Canadian population does not square with the facts. In very recent years that official position seems to have been abandoned. In fact, for almost a generation Negroes have benefited from enactments of municipalities, provinces and the federal Parliament, which do not refer to them in particular but are intended for the assurance and protection of Canadians in general. It is worth while to note some of this legislation specifically.

The Unemployment Insurance Acts of 1940 and 1955 as later amended give employees financial protection against involuntary unemployment. In Quebec province in 1943 a Compulsory Education Act abolished school fees and provided free textbooks to pupils. The Family Allowances Act of 1944 provides for monthly federal payments to the mothers of all children under the age of sixteen years, born in Canada or resident in Canada for at least one year, and attending school as required by the laws of the province in which they reside and are maintained by the parents. The National Housing Acts of 1944 and 1954 as later amended were designed to encourage the construction of dwellings for sale or rent, and recently they have been made to provide sanctions against builders who discriminate socially against prospective buyers. The Hospital Insurance and Diagnostic Services Act in April 1957 made federal grants-in-aid available to the provinces to assist them in operating publicly administered insurance plans for general hospital care. At this date of writing all ten provinces have entered the scheme.

In less than ten years seven provinces and the Government of Canada enacted laws that require employers to pay women the same wages they pay men for comparable work. Similarly, Acts prohibiting discrimination in gainful employment, in trade union membership and in public accommodation (such as hotels, restaurants, barber shops and theatres) on grounds of race, creed, colour, nationality, ancestry or place of origin have been put in effect by federal authorities and by six of the ten provincial governments. Ontario had a Racial Discrimination Act in 1944, and Saskatchewan had a Bill of Rights Act in 1947. These were followed in later years by more specific legislation concerning discrimination in employment and in public accommodation. Racial covenants in real estate transactions were outlawed in Ontario and Manitoba in 1950.

In 1948 the British Columbia franchise was extended to Canadians of East Indian and Chinese origins. (In fact, a Chinese Canadian war veteran now sits as Conservative Member of Parliament for Vancouver Centre.) Also, in 1948, clauses in the Federal Elections Act that discriminated against the same classes of Canadian in British Columbia were removed. In July 1960 Canadian Indians were granted the right to vote without having to surrender their various treaty rights. In August 1960 a Canadian Bill of Rights went into effect which lists certain 'human rights and fundamental freedoms' which 'shall continue to exist without discrimination by reason of race, national origin, colour, religion or sex'.

At the time of writing the Quebec Legislature had before it a Bill to provide to Quebec mothers ten dollars per month for ten months of each year, not taxable, for each student aged 16 or 17 years. This is to encourage parents to keep their children in school longer than they do at present.

Terms of the Fair Accommodation Practices Act of Ontario were extended in May 1961 to include the rental of premises in buildings with more than six apartment units.

This casual survey of welfare legislation brings us to the early spring of 1961. Legislation has not stopped there, but a reader may be convinced without further evidence that improvements in the position of the Canadian Negro can be properly understood only with reference to improvements in the well-being of the whole nation. The financial difficulties of raising children have been eased for him as well as for others, and the same is true of worries about involuntary unemployment and hospital care. These facts can be expected to produce a favourable result generally in the economic, educational and mental condition of future Canadian Negroes.

The wind of change has blown through business offices, banks and stores, as well as through parliamentary chambers. In Montreal, for instance, all five of the English department stores employ coloured men and women in a variety of occupations. One of them employs twenty or twenty-five Negroes in many categories of help, including that of sales clerk. Recently the director of personnel training in that store said to me, grinning, 'Remember that — (proper name) — I told you about? He starts with us next Monday. Everybody's excited.' He rubbed his hands gleefully and laughed. The Negro in question had worked for twenty years in a responsible post in another corporation before deciding to try his luck with this company.

In August 1960 a Montreal Negro applied to an industrial firm for employment and its chief accountant telephoned me for information about the applicant's background. He said: 'You know, integration, desegregation and all that sort of thing; we want to do our share.' The young man, of whom I knew nothing, was hired. The following month an executive of a very powerful corporation telephoned me to ask if I could recommend to him some coloured girls for employment. He explained that the coloured girls at present under his authority were 'eminently satisfactory' high school graduates, but not many of them were bilingual; the company's customers were seventy-five to eighty per cent French. The interesting thing about this request was that an officer of that same corporation was approached in 1941 by a white Y.M.C.A. secretary who asked that he should employ a coloured person. The officer's reply was that it was 'out of the question' to employ even one Negro.

It is worth mentioning that the improved position of Negroes, though substantial when compared with that of a generation ago, does not seem remarkable when compared with the social and economic gains of other ethnic groups through the same period. In the last twenty years the social advancement of Italians, Greeks, Armenians, Jews and French-Canadians — to mention only a few culture groups — has been spectacular.

CONCLUSION

This has been a short account of the efforts of a people to be law-abiding Canadian citizens since the middle of the nineteenth century. Many learned articles not touched on here describe their history. In metropolitan cities the social characteristics of Negroes have changed markedly in their favour through one or two generations but in some districts, notably in the Atlantic Provinces, coloured populations live even now in a backward state economically, educationally and culturally. In a number of communities many have made places for themselves in the middle ranks, though it is sad to note that a second World War was needed to speed the process. In recent years pictures of coloured newly-weds and of mixed couples have graced the society page of at least one metropolitan daily newspaper. This would have been unthinkable fifteen years ago, even although the record shows that Canadian popular opinion is divided on racial issues and always has been so.

Crime and dependency are brilliantly portrayed by Hill in his doctoral study of Toronto Negroes in the 1950's. In that work he devotes about ten thousand words to a discussion, with case histories, of the noticeable number of men and women who have married out of the coloured group in recent years. We note also that orphans of mixed racial origin are numerous and difficult to place in foster homes or in adoption, and that an *Open Door Society* has been formed in Montreal, composed of white couples who have legally adopted children of this kind.

A survey of occupational change among Montreal Negroes from 1941 to 1948 made it clear that a class of Jew played a significant part in providing opportunities for their upward mobility in employment. A generation or two earlier this intermediary role in Montreal seems to have been played more by Englishmen and Scots newly arrived in Canada and still governed by evangelical convictions concerning the brotherhood of man. (The Irish were Catholic and were still, on the whole, far down the social ladder.) In an ideal study, the attitudes of various classes of Jew would be compared with — let us say — the racial attitudes of corresponding classes of French-Canadian. Similarly, new Canadians' racial attitudes would be compared with those of more settled Canadians. In this way some light might be thrown on the process of Negro adjustment in Canada.

Studies are needed now which will focus on the types of coloured immigrant admitted since 1945 and the varieties of their adjustment to Canadian life. The occupational careers of longer-settled Negroes from the Atlantic Provinces west to British Columbia should be recorded, with some attention to details such as recruitment, membership in voluntary associations and occupational duties. One might ask: How great is the Negro's economic success? To what extent is economic success followed by assimilation into the ranks of cultivated people — by accumulations of books, attendance at symphony concerts, ballet performances, art exhibitions? How many make fortunes in the stock market? Also to be studied are the effects of scholastic and economic success on family solidarity.

The general tendency is for Negroes to be absorbed into white communities; but as poor and lonely foreign coloured students increase in universities across Canada their difficulties may becloud the adjustments between settled elements of the Negro and white populations.

22. *A BLACK MAN TALKS ABOUT RACE PREJUDICE IN WHITE CANADA**

Austin C. Clarke†

This year I became eligible for Canadian citizenship, but I do not intend to apply for it. Not because I undervalue this status which is so highly prized by so many immigrants from all over the world; rather, because I *do* value its privileges highly, but realize that I would be accepting in theory a status that Canada does not intend to give me in practice — because I am a black man.

In my eight years in Canada I have been treated with prejudice and discrimination by most white people, in large and small ways. In Canada

---

*From *Maclean's Magazine*, April 20, 1963.

†Mr. Clarke, a Torontonian originally from Barbados in the West Indies, is an author whose first novel, *Survivors of the Crossing*, will be published this fall, (1964).

the restaurants, buses, washrooms and other public facilities do not carry "white only" and "coloured only" signs; but every black man can read these signs in the attitude of white Canadians, and nothing will change if I become a citizen, except my own attitude — I will feel like a man who has just closed my last escape hatch.

There is actually a psychological advantage in remaining a black foreigner instead of becoming a black Canadian. I can find some comfort in rationalizing the prejudice amid which I live: "Canadians are intolerant of *all* foreigners because they look different, talk strangely, have unfamiliar customs and habits — in short, because they *are* foreigners. If I can no longer endure this atmosphere I can go back home to the West Indies, where at least I enjoyed the security of being a member of the majority race, and where poverty is the only penalty for being black."

But if I had taken Canadian citizenship I would have lost those defenses. I would not have had another country to return to, or think of returning to. I would have had to accept the fact that I am treated differently from other Canadians only because I am black. I would have had to tolerate being a highly visible citizen who can suddenly become invisible when he applies for a job, looks for living quarters or goes shopping.

White Canadians with whom I have discussed examples of discrimination have suggested that I and other black people living in Canada are hypersensitive, and too prone to see prejudice where it really doesn't exist. "How do you *know*," they have asked, "that you wouldn't have failed to get that job if you had been white? How do you know that the white woman who stood in the streetcar, when the only vacant seat was beside you, didn't simply *prefer* to stand?"

My answer is that as a black man I am *ipso facto* an expert on discrimination. I do not want to experience prejudice and I do not need to look for it — it is the very atmosphere in which a black man exists.

A black man knows there is discrimination even in overpoliteness and exaggerated solicitude from whites. I have gone into a restaurant and said to a waiter, "I'd like to use the washroom." He answered, "Certainly, sir, by all means sir, right this way sir." All I had wanted to know was the location of the washroom. His answer implied that I was asking *permission* to use the washroom and he was going to show me in no uncertain terms that *this* restaurant, believe it or not, did not discriminate against black customers.

No, I cannot agree that black West Indians in Canada are "prejudice prone." In any case many of the examples of discrimination are too obvious to be imaginary.

Discrimination against black West Indian immigrants starts before they ever get to Canada, with the practices (although not, in theory, the policies) of the federal department of immigration. Officials of the department have more than once publicly stated that there is no bar against black West Indians, that each case is considered on its merits.

If that is so, the immigration officials certainly do not consider there is much merit in black West Indians. The only black people freely admitted to Canada as landed immigrants are a limited number of women, who must accept the undignified classification of domestic servants, plus a few persons hand-picked by Canadian authorities because they have professions or special skills needed by Canada.

All foreign students, including white and black West Indians, are admitted to Canada on non-immigrant visas, generally called student visas. Those who want to remain must apply for "landed immigrant" status, which makes it legal for them to take a job and is the first step toward citizenship. White students, including white West Indians, seem to have no difficulty in acquiring landed-immigrant papers. I know several who did so.

But black West Indians who try to change student status for that of landed immigrant run into a labyrinth of delay, dissuasion and double-talk, even though their birthplace, background, culture and outlook are the same as that of their white compatriots, and their education and in-telligence are often higher. When I decided I would like to live and work in Toronto after I left the University of Toronto I applied for a landed-immigrant application form at the Bedford Road branch in Toronto. What happened there convinced me that the top immigration officials have not informed their clerks that there is no bar against black West Indian immigrants.

One clerk warned me that black people "found the going tough in Canada because of the bitterness of the winter." I know now that the bitter climate he was talking about was the bitterness of prejudice. Another clerk advised me not to apply for landed-immigrant status — that would cancel my status as a student, he said and since there was no guarantee that I would be accepted, I might be deported as a person with no status whatever. I decided not to run that risk, and did not apply.

BRITISH SUBJECTS? YES, BUT WHITE

But not long after that incident another member of the West Indian group at the university proudly showed us his passport, stamped "landed immigrant." We were surprised, because the successful applicant was, like us, Negro. The answer was that he was not as black as we were; he was what we call in Barbados "clear skinned" or "whitey white." In the southern U.S. he would be classified as a Negro at sight. The rest of us were glad for him, but sad at this evidence of the grim naïveté of Canadian discrimination based on a man's *degree* of blackness.

Of about twenty black West Indians who were friends of mine at the University of Toronto, only five attained landed-immigrant status — and none did so on individual merit. Four married Canadian girls, black or white. The fifth, married to a West Indian girl, had a child born in Canada who was therefore a Canadian citizen. Because of their child''s nationality, the authorities let the parents remain in Canada. My own present status as a landed immigrant, eligible for citizenship this year, resulted from my marriage.

I first encountered discrimination in Canada soon after I arrived. I put my name down to join the Canadian army through its university officers' training plan. The question of color did not arise during the preliminary tests and medical examination, but when I was interviewed by officers in charge of the plan, they told me that candidates must be British subjects. I pointed out that I was born in Barbados, British West Indies, my family had been born there for several generations, and I was consequently nothing if not a British subject. Without putting it in so many words, they left no doubt in my mind that to them "British subject" meant "white British subject."

In any case, my application was turned down. The interviewing officers did not have to write on my application "refused because of color," of course. Instead, they decided I was "rude and hard to get along with." Certainly I argued my case emphatically, and that may have made me seem "hard to get along with." Who wouldn't be, faced by presumably intelligent men who were denying the obvious truth that I was a British subject? I might well have been rude, though, if I had known at that time what I discovered soon afterward — that another West Indian student had been accepted for the officers' training course. His birthplace was the same as mine. But he was white.

The most serious effect of discrimination against the black man in Canada is his inability to get a job commensurate with his abilities. We soon learn that to get jobs at all we must aim far lower than white men of the same education and ability. And even then employers seem to imply that they are doing us a favor, that we're lucky to be taken on —

and that we must therefore work twice as hard as white workers to show our gratitude.

For example, a post-office foreman assigned me to drag heavy loads of Christmas cards across miles of floor in the sorting room during the Christmas rush, while white workers were "busy" lifting envelopes from one cage and putting them into another. Someone has to get the tough jobs, you say, and it just happened to be me? It's no use suggesting the law of chance to black workers — they know the chances are stacked against them.

A friend of mine — he happened to have a B.A. from the University of Toronto — failed to find a job that white university grads consider to be of "B.A. level" and applied for a job as teletype operator at the Canadian Press. He was told that he must have a minimum speed of sixty words a minute. After he had attained that speed he was taken on. Two weeks later he was assigned to teach the teletype routine to a white applicant — who had been taken on when he reached a speed of *fifty-five* words a minute. In neither of these cases would the employers have admitted that they were practising discrimination. Possibly they did not even realize it, so deeply was it lodged in their subconscious. Nor would we have openly accused them of it. To do so would not be behaving like a "nice black man."

Case after case of job discrimination comes up when black immigrants compare notes: A Toronto paper that editorialized indignantly against discrimination in Little Rock and at the University of Mississippi turned down the application of a black man who graduated at the top of his University of Western Ontario class, and hired a classmate who didn't even graduate. I knew both men, and I can testify that the only differences I could detect between them was that one was brilliant — and black, and the other was mediocre — and white.

Even if he survives the Canadian government's unwillingness to let him live in Canada, and Canadian employer's reluctance to give him a job (ably abetted by the government's own employment service) a black immigrant's problems are by no means solved. He must learn to live in a world which endlessly reminds him, in major and minor ways, that he is not only "different" but *undesirably* different. I have heard white Canadians call black men "lazy" and even "unclean" on the sole basis that their skin is black. It's not easy to be patient when a waitress or sales clerk bypasses you to serve white customers who arrived after you did.

It's not easy to shrug off the discrimination that makes it difficult to choose your living accommodation. The law requires that a landlord with more than six rental units in his building cannot discriminate against tenants because of race, color or creed. But when I knock at the door of a house which has a "rooms for rent" sign in the window, and the door is slammed in my face, how can I find out if it is because I am black, or because the landlord has fewer than seven units to rent? To this my reaction is "To hell with the landlord, and to hell with the Ontario regulation which does not have the guts to state that a landlord in the business of renting rooms must rent me one because I am in the business of renting a room." However, I'm not so lacking in personal pride as to want to live in a house where the landlord accepts me as a tenant only because the law says he must.

How do black immigrants react to the discrimination and prejudice that is part of their daily lives? Some live in terror of its icy fingers and avoid anything that might "give the white man a wrong impression of black people."

Others become hostile and take out their hostility in aggressive social and sexual behavior. Some marry white women and seek to drown their fears and complexes in their wives' environment. In my opinion they only create another problem — the problem of producing mulatto children who belong neither to the white world nor the black.

Many pretend that discrimination has never happened to them, like the B.A. employed by NES who has apparently forgotten that since he graduated in 1958 "nondiscrimination" has gained him the following jobs: night watchman, night-shift postal worker, short-order cook in a hospital, and assorted clerical jobs obtained through a part-time employment agency.

What can be done to improve the basic living conditions of the black immigrant in Canada? What, in short, would I want if I were to become a Canadian citizen?

In the first place, I do not expect that any law could be passed that would educate white Canadians in tolerance overnight — but I would expect to be protected against prejudiced landlords of any building that advertises vacancies for rent, not just those who have more than six rental units.

I do not expect to be given an executive job the day I become a citizen, but I would want and expect to find a job for which I am qualified — not a joe-job that no white Canadian with my qualifications would accept.

I would not want to be pampered, or invited to apply for membership in the Granite Club. But I would expect to be allowed to live in the degree of dignity which I earn and deserve: no more, no less.

23. SOCIO-ECONOMIC CONDITION OF NEGROES IN HALIFAX*

Institute of Public Affairs, Dalhousie University

Although the gathering of even such bland demographic data as age, sex, number of children, and so on is not without difficulty and possible confusion, the investigator faces a much more severe task when he seeks information about such items as occupation or income or education. Many people refuse to answer the question, or cannot understand it, or honestly do not know. Of those who do answer, some lie or misinterpret or embroider. People may, for example, understate their earnings if they fear tax (or wifely) reprisals, and they may overstate them in order to gain imagined prestige in the eyes of the interviewer — and there is no reason to believe that the distortions will be compensating. Almost certainly a survey yields more nearly accurate results than most "well informed guesses"; but even survey findings must be treated with some caution. Precise tabulations in particular must be taken as indicative rather than strictly enumerative.

With these limitations of our data in mind, we shall discuss first the employment of Halifax Negroes, and then the housing units that they occupy.

EMPLOYMENT

The depressed economic condition of Halifax Negroes derives of course in large part from the economic difficulties of the Maritime Provinces in general. The employment problems of Negroes go further, however, than this general condition would imply. They have employment opportunities even more unsatisfactory than the local average. A comparison of Halifax Negroes to the whole city population shows that they earn less than the mean income, that they are unemployed for many more weeks than the average, and that occupationally they are concentrated far more in manual or menial jobs and virtually are unrepresented in the profession. (See Tables 1-3.)

In part, of course, the explanation of this relatively poor employment showing may lie in racial prejudices. White employers may for personal reasons or in deference to the (real or supposed) wishes of others on the

---

*From *The Condition of the Negroes of Halifax, Nova Scotia*, Halifax, Institute of Public Affairs, Dalhousie University (Guy Henson, Director), No. 27, 1962.

staff, or of customers, decline to hire Negroes or else employ them only on less skilled jobs and away from the public view. Negroes themselves may anticipate rebuffs that they will meet if they try for a more desirable position — indeed, they may anticipate rebuffs where they might not exist — and so resign themselves to the bottom rungs of the employment ladder. Other matters associated at least partly with race (a larger proportion of young unmarried mothers who keep their babies and work only sporadically as household help, or young men who are part-time sleeping car porters in hopes of having a full-time position in a few years) also affect adversely the employment pattern of Negroes.

There are other reasons as well that are, at most, tenuously associated with race. Schooling, in particular, affects one's opportunities for higher level employment. To the extent that Negroes are poorly educated, they will experience difficulty in obtaining skilled work or even any work at all. Still, on this point there is room for a little optimism. In his thesis, *A Study of the Employment of the Coloured Man in Halifax,* George Matthews concluded his chapter "Work in Relation to Levels of Education", after a study of 158 Negro men in mid-city Halifax:

> "There is an increasing trend among the coloured men to remain in school longer than was evident in former years. The more education a coloured man has, the better chance he has of obtaining training in the professional, clerical and skilled trades . . . . From the data collected, it appeared to the writer that the more education a coloured man has the less discrimination he met when he applied for a job. It was found that those who had qualified themselves for a profession or one of the skilled or clerical trades met with less difficulty in obtaining employment."

This does not mean, of course, that Negroes have the same general opportunities as whites of equivalent education; it does mean that increased education usually does furnish by itself increased advantages to its holder. The opportunities of whites and Negroes may be arrayed along different scales, but in both cases the person with the more education tends to do better than others of his own race.

In making a closer examination of Negro employment, it will be useful, as before, to consider separately mid-city and Africville Negroes.[1]

A. Mid-City Negroes

Negro workers who live in the centre of Halifax have a smaller income than Halifax workers generally. Almost a third of these Negroes, in con-

---

[1]Mid-city and Africville refer, respectively, to two "Negro" districts in Halifax, the former in the downtown area, and the latter a "shack town" adjacent to the city where such amenities as water pipes, a sewage system and paved roads are non-existent. [Ed.]

trast to a fifth for the city as a whole, earn less than $1,000 a year, and only about two per cent (as against four per cent for the whole city) earn more than $4,000. In both cases men comprise more than two-thirds of the labour force, and there is a large discrepancy between the earnings of men and women.

Table 1

APPROXIMATE DISTRIBUTION OF ANNUAL INCOMES AMONG MALE AND
FEMALE MEMBERS OF THE LABOUR FORCE FOR MID-CITY NEGROES,
AFRICVILLE NEGROES, AND THE WHOLE CITY OF HALIFAX

Income	Mid-City Negroes			Africville			Whole City of Halifax		
	Male	Female	Total	Male	Female	Total	Male	Female	Total
Under $1000	13%	19%	32%	22%	13%	35%	7%	13%	20%
$1000-1999	19	12	31	21	15	36	26	13	39
$2000-2999	23	3	26	24	1	25	23	4	27
$3000-3999	8	1	9	3	0	3	8	1	9
$4,000 and over	2	0	2	1	0	1	5	0	5
Total	65%	35%	100%	71%	29%	100%	69%	31%	100%

Negro figures are from 1959 survey; city figures from 1951 census. Zeroes mean less than half of one per cent.

From data presented in Table 1 one may estimate the mean annual income of those in the Halifax labour force as about $2000, with that of men at about $2200 and of women about $1200. For mid-city Negroes the average is about $1700, with men at about $2000 and women about $1100.

Among mid-city Negroes, then, as among Halifax workers in general, men earn almost twice as much as women. This fact stems in part from women being employed in more menial occupations and in part from their working more sporadically than men. If, however, one compares men to men and women to women, it is clear that for both sexes Negroes earn considerably less on average than do their white counterparts.

Part of this difference between white and Negro incomes stems from the greater degree of unemployment experienced by Negroes. (See Table 2.) Four-fifths of all city workers were steadily employed (fifty weeks or more per year), whereas this was true of only one half of the Negro workers. Almost a quarter of the Negro workers were employed less than twenty weeks during the year, while only about a twentieth of those in the city as a whole had so few weeks of employment.

In addition, part of the difference lies in the fact that Negroes are largely unrepresented in the higher paying occupations. Of the approximately 250 Negro men from whom definite occupational information was available, only four were in the professions, a dozen in clerical work, and two dozen in skilled trades; and of the 130 Negro women, eight were in professions (teaching and nursing), thirteen in clerical positions, and two in skilled jobs. Most of the rest were in semiskilled jobs (96 males and 6 females), unskilled jobs (114 males and 33 females), or in such a service occupation as charwoman (67 females and 2 males).

Table 2

NUMBER OF WEEKS EMPLOYED ANNUALLY BY MALE AND FEMALE MEMBERS OF THE LABOUR FORCE FOR MID-CITY NEGROES, AFRICVILLE NEGROES, AND THE CITY OF HALIFAX

No. of Weeks Employed	Mid-City Negroes			Africville Negroes			Whole City of Halifax		
	Male	Female	Total	Male	Female	Total	Male	Female	Total
Under 10	9%	5%	14%	13%	1%	14%	1%	1%	2%
10-19	6	3	9	10	2	12	2	1	3
20-29	9	6	15	11	5	16	3	1	4
30-39	5	3	8	7	0	7	3	1	4
40-49	4	2	6	3	1	4	3	2	5
50 and over	32	18	50	29	18	47	58	24	82
Total	65%	35%	100%	73%	27%	100%	70%	30%	100%

Negro figures are from 1959 survey; city figures are from 1951 census. Zeroes mean less than half of one per cent.

Table 3

OCCUPATIONAL CLASSIFICATION OF MID-CITY NEGROES

	Male	Female
Professional	4	8
Clerical	11	13
Service	2	67
Skilled	25	2
Semiskilled	96	6
Unskilled	114	33
Armed Forces	3	1
Total	255	130

B. Africville Negroes

No matter what one uses as an index of a poor employment situation (low average income, large number of weeks unemployed, fewness of persons in the more skilled occupations), Africville Negroes rank worse than Halifax as a whole and in general worse even than the mid-city Negroes. More than a third of the Africville workers earn less than $1000 a year, and less than one per cent earn over $4000. (See Table 1 above.) Using the estimation procedure described earlier, one may put the mean Africville income at about $1500 a year, with men earning about $1650 and women about $1100. The low income of males is especially notable. Instead of earning twice as much as females, as is true for both the whole city and for mid-city Negroes, they earn only about fifty percent more. The reason for this discrepancy seems to lie in the fact that the same unskilled and service jobs are held by Negro women of both areas, but that the mid-city Negro men hold a greater proportion of skilled, semi-skilled, and clerical positions than do the males of Africville.

Unemployment in terms of weeks worked is about the same here as among the Negroes who live downtown. (See Table 2 above.) But in terms of underemployment the situation seems worse. Many jobs related to stevedoring and cartage during Halifax's winter shipping season may provide some work during a week and yet not a *full* week's work. While some in this area may occupy their idle days by fishing in the Bedford Basin or by foraging for salvageable materials on the nearby dump, such activities are of conceivable profit only for those who are living at a bare subsistence level.

HOUSING

A. Mid-City Negroes
The actual housing of Negroes, at least in the centre of Halifax, has changed considerably since this survey was conducted in January 1959. The demolition that has preceded the Jacob Street redevelopment, the tearing down of houses to provide large parking lots for the Gottingen Street shopping area, and the condemnation of some houses under Ordinance No. 50 (Respecting Minimum Standards for Housing Accommodation) of the City of Halifax, of January 1, 1958 — all these have changed markedly the precise residence pattern of mid-city Negroes. Their over-all location has changed much less, for most of those Negroes who have been forced to vacate dwellings live in the same general area, either doubling up with other families or occupying accommodations which in turn will soon be condemned. A number of families have been rehoused in the new Mulgrave Park project; and this marks the first major case in recent years of housing mobility for Halifax Negroes.

In view of these changes in much of the area, we shall limit our presentation of information on mid-city Negroes to a subsample of families, all resident on Maynard and Creighton Streets, where demolition and construction has been far less frequent than in other streets farther down the hill. Some 134 families were interviewed on these two streets. (See Table 4.) Slightly more than half lived in dwelling units that were in need of major repair; more than half the families had no bathing facilities, neither a private nor a shared bathroom; only a seventh of the families had private toilet facilities, while the rest shared them with one or more families; and only a little more than a quarter of the families had mechanically-produced hot water, with the rest depending on water heated on a stove. In addition, the researchers uncovered many examples of overcrowding: there were three cases of seven-member families and one of an eight-member family occupying only two rooms; and three cases of nine-member families and one of an eleven-member family occupying three rooms.

Table 4

CONDITION OF 134 NEGRO DWELLING UNITS ON
MAYNARD AND CREIGHTON STREETS

Condition	*Yes*	*No*	*Not Known*
No major repair needed	69	64	1
Bathroom	58	75	1
Private bathroom	17	116	1
Mechanical hot water	37	92	5
Owned by occupant	45	89	0
White neighbours adjacent or in same house	92	42	0
Family likes area	96	37	1

Clearly these dwelling units are indicative of slum or near-slum conditions. Certain other facts, however, should be added. First, many of these Negro families owned the housing units in which they lived: only two-thirds of the sample rented their accommodations. Second, the rents that Negroes paid were, especially in local terms, quite low, averaging less than $40 a month. This does not mean that the tenants got much for their money — residents in better neighbourhoods almost assuredly received more cubic feet, say, per dollar than did they — but just that they did not spend much money. Third, while Negroes in the mid-city area were pretty much restricted to this one neighbourhood, the area was not a segregated one. Two-thirds of the Negro families interviewed either had white neighbours living in an adjacent house or resided in a building that contained whites as well as Negroes. Finally, many Negroes appeared to have positive feelings towards the area in which they were living. More than two-thirds of those interviewed responded that they liked their neighbourhood, either because they "liked their neighbours; they had lived there all their lives; their friends were there and they knew the area," or because "the area was considered convenient to stores, work, school, church," or because the respondents felt that the area was quiet and clean.

This implies that physical slum clearance and reconstruction, without attention to the problems of adjustment and the long-term interests of the people to be relocated, may not solve the housing problem in anything like a satisfactory fashion for Negroes. One-third of the families of the Maynard-Creighton Street area owned their own homes in 1959. (See Table 4.) Public housing policies, however well designed for the city as a whole, may lead to loss of home ownership on the part of a considerable number of Negroes and to their being chronic tenants in public housing. The dangers of "resegregation" similar to that apparent in northern cities of the United States, are evident here. The refusal of housing in the better sections of the metropolitan area to Negroes willing and eager to pay the costs (as reported by local television and press) is a problem experienced by a segment of Negroes in Halifax. This refusal is indicative, however, of a *condition* faced by all Negroes in Halifax. At the same time, for many Halifax Negroes, dispersal to more attractive housing throughout the city might be an unsatisfactory way, from a social and psychological point of view, of alleviating present depressed housing conditions. Even persons who are free to move anywhere, sometimes prefer to live near friends and family. Clear progress in dealing with community problems in human relations is requisite for improvement of housing for Negroes.

B. Africville Negroes

Housing in Africville varies from fairly solid well-built houses to roughly patched one-room or two-room shacks built by amateurs. Nearly all houses are single-family dwelling units. Most have electricity and some have a number of electrical appliances. As mentioned already, however, there is no running water and no public sewage disposal, so that all families are dependent on wells and outside toilets.

Most families own their homes, only fifteen paying rent, but there is considerable uncertainty about land ownership. While a few families, perhaps twenty at most, appear to have deeds to their land, the majority of families seem uncertain of their true position. Many claim that Queen Victoria granted the land to their ancestors, a claim that may have more social significance than legal validity.

Despite the uncertainties of land ownership, there has been considerable stability in house tenure in Africville. Over forty families have lived in their present home over ten years; others have lived elsewhere in Africville that long or longer. In addition, almost two-thirds of those interviewed claimed that they liked living in Africville, citing as reasons the freedom of the place, the cleaner air, the view, the open spaces, the opportunities for fishing, and congenial neighbours. The sense of community that pervades Africville (stemming from kinship ties, long-term residence and, defensively it would seem, from the scorn felt from outsiders) might not survive the expropriation of this district for industrial purposes and the dispersal of the population elsewhere in the city. Indeed, the marginality of Africville's economy, with the low wages of its inhabitants compensated for in part by low housing costs and by the possibilities of foraging, fishing, and mutual self-help, might crumble entirely if transferred to any more competitively organized section of the city. So, once again, physical improvement of housing may involve problems of greater sensitivity than initially may be apparent to those desiring to improve conditions.

CONCLUSIONS

We have counted the Halifax Negroes, described their housing and occupational conditions, and discussed the capacity of Negro children for increased education. No part of this study affords reasons for satisfaction with the present or for optimism about the future. By itself the increase in the Halifax Negro population will make current problems only the more difficult. Redevelopment in downtown Halifax almost certainly will make housing conditions for Negroes worse before they get better; and will, for better or worse, disrupt severely the present social fabric of the Negro community. Unless far-sighted public policies are adopted, change may lead to "resegregation" or concentration of Negroes in public housing. Furthermore, while the extent of Negro education may be increasing, it is to be doubted seriously whether it is increasing as fast as that for the city's population as a whole, especially in post-high school education.

The members of a depressed social group cannot expect improvement of their position except through personal self-help and mutual help. The maintenance and even the intensification of present efforts of the Negroes themselves, as individuals and through their own formal and informal organizations, are essential to their advancement. Those in a minority group who are in the position indicated by this report may not, however, be able by their own unaided efforts to find remedies for their difficulties.

The severity of the problems facing the Negro population in Halifax cannot be lessened markedly by the Negro population itself. It does not have the financial resources to pay for the needed improvements, or the numbers necessary to exert pressure on the general community, or a well-developed leadership except within the specifically religious field.

Consequently, if the Negroes are to help themselves and improve their life, they must receive a good deal of help from outside their own numbers. They will need more private and public housing, more public welfare, more intensive social work, more effective ways of working with the larger political system of the city as a whole. All of this will go for nought unless much better employment opportunities, based on merit and not precluded by social barriers, are open to qualified Negro workers.

They will likely not receive these kinds of help effectively unless the community undertakes a rigorous self-examination of its existing employment and housing patterns, and of the practices or conditions which have led to these patterns of employment and of housing. Even then, they can receive enough help only through a great many helpful acts of persons in the majority group, stimulated by voluntary and official leadership and strengthened in their actions by such fair employment and accommodation legislation as has recently been adopted and by positive public policies. Organized effort to integrate help of the majority group and Negro self-help will be needed. To bring about substantial change these private acts of help must grow rapidly and be sustained in number and quality over a considerable period of years.

Giving help, to be sure, is more complicated in fact than an outsider might think. If done without insight and skill, it may meet with hostility. It cannot be expected to bring forth any explicit gratitude. Not to give such help will lead, eventually and inevitably, to even greater social and fiscal costs to the city and the province — to say nothing of the continued wastage of human and economic resources.

SELECTED BIBLIOGRAPHY

Card, B. Y., Hirabayashi, G. K., and French, C. L., *The Métis in Alberta Society,* Edmonton, University of Alberta Committee for Social Research, 1963.

Dallyn, F. J. G., and Earle, F. G., *A Study of Attitudes Towards Indians and People of Indian Descent,* Winnipeg, Canadian Council of Christians and Jews, 1958, 1959, 1961.

Eberlee, T. M., and Hill, D. G., "The Ontario Human Rights Code," *University of Toronto Law Journal,* Vol. XV, No. 2, 1964.

Edmonds, J. K., "Our Fast-Growing Indian Problem," *The Financial Post,* February 9, 1963.

Gordon, J., "Northern Indians: Their Economic Future," *North,* Vol. 9, September-October, 1962.

Hawthorne, H. B., Belshaw, C. S., and Jamieson, S. M., *The Indians of British Columbia,* Berkeley, California, University of California Press, 1958.

Lagasse, J. H., *A Study of the Population of Indian Ancestry Living in Manitoba,* (3 volumes), Winnipeg, Department of Agriculture and Immigration, 1959.

Leibow, E., and Trudeau, J., "Preliminary Study of Acculturation Among the Cree Indians of Winisk, Ontario, *Arctic,* Vol. 15, September, 1962.

Mowat, F. G., *Desperate People,* Boston, Mass., Little, Brown and Co., 1959.

Oliver, W. P., "Cultural Progress of the Negro in Nova Scotia," *Dalhousie Review,* Vol. 29, October, 1949.

Randle, M. C., "Educational Problems of Canadian Indians," *Food for Thought,* Vol. 13, March, 1953.

Stanley, G. F. G., "The Métis and the Conflict in Western Canada," *The Canadian Historical Review,* Vol. XXVIII, December, 1947.

Valentine, V. F., and Young, R. G., "The Situation of the Métis of Northern Saskatchewan in Relation to His Physical and Social Environment," *Canaian Geographer,* No. 4, 1954.

Yatsushiro, T., "Changing Eskimo," *Beaver,* Summer, 1962.

chapter five

PROBLEMS OF
ETHNIC GROUP RELATIONS

One of the most striking characteristics of Canadian society is the heterogeneity of its population. Some aspects of the major French-English ethnic
differentiation have already been examined in chapters two and three.
Various problems of race relations involving the Indian, Eskimo and Negro
minorities have been detailed in chapter four. Although these chapters convincingly demonstrate that the heterogeneity of her population is the source
of a number of Canada's social problems, they have by no means exhausted
the list of racial and minority group difficulties in the country. In this chapter
two of the more distinct of Canada's many ethnic and religious minority
groups, ones which have recently been very much in the news, become the
focus of attention. These are the Hutterites of Alberta and the Doukhobors of
British Columbia.

Two articles serve to present the Hutterite story. The first, by sociologist
John A. Hostetler, briefly describes some of the history of the Hutterite
colonies and the highlights of Hutterite social organization and culture. The
author goes on to explain the source and nature of "Hutterite Separatism",
and to show how the solution, if there is to be one, of this most complex
social problem may well depend upon the development and application of
much greater social science knowledge. Karl Peter, a graduate student in
sociology, contributes his well formed views on the subject in "The Hutterite
Problem in Alberta."

The Doukhobors of British Columbia present a problem of a unique sort
in Canada. As Economist Stuart Jamieson points out in his article "The
Doukhobors of B.C.," it is only a small "fanatical wing" of the Doukhobor

163

sect which, through a strong antagonism to the Canadian way of life (antagonism sometimes seasoned with violence), manages to create a social disturbance of considerable importance — important to the society generally, and important to the rest of the Doukhobor community, which is put into a rather bad light by the behaviour of this disruptive faction. Following this presentation, which sets out the nature of the problem in rather specific terms, is a selection by Professor Harry B. Hawthorn from a book entitled *The Doukhobors of British Columbia*. This selection offers "Some Background Information About the Doukhobors," including discussions of the development and nature of the Doukhobor communities in Canada, and religious and political values, the operation of these communities in Canada, and the relations which have existed between the Doukhobors and government.

24. *HUTTERITE SEPARATISM AND PUBLIC TOLERANCE**

John A. Hostetler†

The Hutterites, or Hutterian Brethern, who live on communally owned farms called *Bruderhofs* or colonies, are Christians whose historic Anabaptist faith requires them to own property and land in common. The group originated in Tyrol and Moravia in the sixteenth century, and after wandering from one country to another to flee persecution they came from the Ukraine to South Dakota in 1874-79. In 1918 they began to settle in the prairie provinces. Their agricultural colonies, each maintaining from 75 to 125 persons, total about 130 in North America. Sixty-two colonies are located in Alberta, with others in Saskatchewan, Manitoba, South and North Dakota, Montana, and Washington.

One of the most basic human rights — the right to the enjoyment of land — has virtually been taken from these 5,000 mostly native-born citizens of Alberta. An Alberta law known as the Communal Property Act,

*From *The Canadian Forum*, Vol. 41, April 1961, with slight revision.
†Dr. Hostetler, formerly of the University of Alberta, Edmonton, is currently Assistant Professor of Sociology at Pennsylvania State University, Ogontz Campus. He is an acknowledged authority on Hutterite, Amish and Mennonite life.

prohibits the group from acquiring new sites for colonies without a public hearing held by a Communal Property Board. The board in turn makes a recommendation to the Executive Council of the Legislature, which may approve or reject the sale of land to Hutterites. The Act provides that a person wishing to sell land to a colony must apply by written notice to the Communal Property Board. The board within thirty days fixes a time and place for the hearing of the application and must determine (a) whether or not the applicant has the right to dispose of the land to the colony and whether a colony has the right to acquire the land under the Act, and (b) whether or not it is in the public interest that the application be granted.

Much of what the public holds to be true of Hutterites is based upon erroneous information or prejudice. People have told me they are Marxists, that they do hostile acts like burning the farm buildings of neighbors, that they pay no taxes, that the government provides them with free land, that they have a high rate of mental illness — all of which are false. It is a sociological truism that wherever we find a minority that lives in relative isolation, we find more than the usual misconceptions. Groups that are "different" are regarded as a threat by other groups, especially when there is economic competition between them. Under such conditions, misconceptions, rumors, and scapegoating are often observed.

Unlike most Christians today, the Hutterites hold that communal ownership of property is essential to being Christian. This belief is based on the example of the early Christians who "had all things in common and parted them to all men as every man had need." While most Christians in the West have tended to equate Christianity with the "free enterprise system," the Hutterites have made "the community of goods" central to their religion. Their economic sharing requires that no wages be paid to an individual. Each member works according to his ability. In a common dining hall he eats his meals prepared by women in rotation. In case of sickness and death the individual has no financial worries or risks. The Hutterites abhor revolution and politics. Their faith requires them not to defend either self or country.

The motive for communal living is scarcely understood by the neighbors of the Hutterites. To them it is simply "brotherly love in action" or the idea of Christian sharing and togetherness. A certain intense brotherly love and mutual aid is often accepted by radical Christians, Mennonites, Pietists, Moravians, and even Unitarians. That is, if a brother is in need, the entire group will care for him and prevent his material suffering.

Hutterites go a decisive step further and insist that full communal living (of the monasterial type) is required as the absolute consequence of an inner Christian conversion and the "new life" in Christ, a sharing in both production and consumption whereby nothing is private anymore, neither house nor clothing. If a new person joins, he surrenders all that he owns; should he ever leave the group for any reason, he would receive nothing back of his former goods. That had been made clear to him from the very outset, and a period of novitiate makes it possible for the catechumen to re-think this condition. *Agape,* love, means a natural sharing and participating with the fellow brother. It means selflessness. "Private property is the greatest enemy of Christian love," Hutterites say. "Love is the tie of perfection — where she dwelleth she does not work partial but complete communion." Such a commandment of love is quite different from the common form of charity (welfare) as practised throughout Christendom. It is so-to-speak an institutionalized, almost routinized practice of brotherly love where nothing is mine and nothing is thine. One shares a common dining hall, shares the upbringing of children, and in general church and brotherhood fully coincide. Work and worship are not two separated activities as for most people, but one and the same. The medieval monastery would be the nearest comparison — were it not that marriage is affirmed among the brethren. Thus it is easily understood that when a child grows up in such a milieu, he eventually would not want anything else but this communal set-up. To him it is a God-sanctioned system, the lobby to paradise.

The law which restricts Hutterite land purchases reflects three fundamental dislikes of Hutterites: they are prolific, they are efficient, and they are different.

The fertility rate of Hutterite colonies is among the highest of all human groups. The average size of "completed" families is from seven to ten children. Women living in 1950 had on the average a probability of having twelve children if they were married during their eighteenth year and lived with their spouse through the end of the fertility period. In the year 1949 there were 38.6 Hutterite births per 1,000 population as compared to 22.1 among white rural people in the United States. The annual increase of the population is 4.1 per cent with the population doubling every sixteen years. Although the rate is high, it is no higher than the rate for some American Indians. Unlike the United States and Canadian population as a whole, the Hutterite men tend to outlive their wives. Hutterite population is predominantly youthful, as over 60 per cent of the population is under age 15.

The conditions for favorable population growth among Hutterites are attributed by experts to several factors. Hutterites take seriously the Biblical admonition to "Be fruitful and multiply." Methods of contraception are taboo. Hutterite parents have assurance of economic support for as many children as they can biologically conceive. Assistance in caring for children is never lacking in a communal colony. In spite of a rather high infant death rate, the Hutterites have an overall low mortality. The group has no taboos against securing proper medical care and treatment and is financially capable and willing to secure surgery or hospitalization services when needed. There is little separation of husband and wife during the fertility period. Few members desert the colony life, and many who "try the world" make amends and return.

A second factor is that Hutterites are among the most efficient producers of livestock and crops in Canada. Their land holdings average 58 acres per person while the Alberta farm population to land ratio is one person to 122 acres. Many who live near them envy their apparent prosperity. The Hutterites brought time-honored agricultural skills to the New World.

Hutterites today live about as frugally and with as few personal comforts as they did in the sixteenth century. But in the use of farm machines and agricultural tools they are modern and fully as advanced as their neighbors. The small, one-family farm cannot compete against a corporation with abundant cheap labor, using the most modern machinery to till the land. Production of goods in a colony is maintained on a high level. Grain raising, dairying, beef cattle, poultry, and hog raising provide a diversity of food for colony consumption and for cash sales. Honey, vegetables, fruits, smoked hams, and well-stocked larders provide the basic food supply. Power equipment including caterpillar tractors, trucks, combines and electrical machines are found in all colonies. Hutterites are adept at welding, repairing, or even making their own machines and tools.

Each colony manager (*Wirt* in German), authorized by the vote of the members, handles all the funds, holds the keys to the community storehouse, and arranges all the work of the members. Under him are departments with bosses in charge of special occupational phases: the farm boss for the work in the fields, the cattle boss, the hog boss, the poultryman, the blacksmith, the shoemaker, the carpenter, and the mechanic. Among the women there are kitchen and garden bosses. The only occasion for using money at all is for direct purchases from the outside world.

They purchase coffee, salt, dry goods, leather, and farm machinery at the most favorable prices and often from wholesale sources.

Hutterites are not tax free, as widespread rumour would have it. They pay all taxes required of them, including special taxes with respect to schools. But whether the Hutterites file as "religious or charitable" organizations, as corporations, or as persons, the amount they would have to pay is probably less than most people of any category. The reason is obvious. They live by a production rather than a cash economy. Hutterites make their own shoes, their own clothes, stockings, furniture. They spend no money for passenger cars and their upkeep, for weekend excursions, radios or TV sets, and little for personal travel and comfort, and indoor plumbing. Most of the colony income goes for capital expenditures and for the improvement of soil and property. Personal income or salaries are nonexistent.

The third factor that accounts for widespread attitudes supporting restrictive legislation is separatism. Hutterites have a demonstrated record of cultural survival surpassed by no other Reformation group. Of over sixty communal societies that have been tried in North America only the Hutterite system survives. They wish to exist peacefully within the larger society but do not want to become absorbed into it.

The social relations within the colonies reflect little exposure to outsiders. Infants are cared for in communal kindergartens where they learn Hutterite doctrine and scripture (all in Tyrolean-German) until they reach public school age. When the child enters the English school he need not leave the colony environment. The group builds its own school building adjacent to the colony and the teacher is appointed by the provincial school board. By the time the child reaches school age he is well fortified and "set" in his native mores and culture. Instruction in the German language continues throughout the elementary school period, and at the age of fifteen all Hutterite pupils discontinue schooling.

Separatism is perpetuated not only by the geographic isolation of the colony site from nearby towns and by the use of the German language and by a colony controlled educational experience, but also by the number of persons per colony. Decision-making in any human group is facilitated by a minimum of persons. The Hutterites have learned that colonies become unmanageable if they become too large, and so each colony forms a "daughter" colony when the total number reaches well over 100. In a colony of 100 persons, about sixty people are under fifteen years of age and twenty of the remaining are women, and women have no voting privileges. Colony decisions, as in the sixteenth century, are made by the voting male baptized membership, numbering probably from nine to twelve persons. It is easier to get consensus with a small number than with a large number, especially when the two most important positions, "Preacher" and "Financial Manager", articulate the wishes of the group. All financial transactions are made by the manager only upon the vote of the male membership. No tractor, combine, or equipment of any kind is acquired without the vote of the church body.

Social change within a colony is dealt with by deliberate voting decisions. Each colony is economically autonomous. Religious life is not governed by any outside hierarchy, although the colony maintains kinship and informal ties with others. When colony rules are violated widely, Hutterite leaders seek to change the colony rule before it produces too many law-breakers and weakens respect for colony life. In this way a certain amount of change has been incorporated into their social system without destroying the beliefs, sentiments, and goals of the colony. Thus the Hutterites have been able to avoid splintering into many factions as have the Amish and the Mennonites and other groups. Most persons within a colony do not aspire to become outsiders. Economic security has divine sanction and there are few intellectual problems that remain unsolved for the group members. Supernatural sanction tends to remove doubt and insure group security.

Are the Hutterites neighborly and are they good citizens? The experience of some farm people is that they are poor neighbors. The experience of others attests to years of purchasing expertly cleaned and superior quality products from them. Some colony leaders show more discretion and responsibility than others. The cleanliness, grooming, and general appearance of one colony may differ a great deal from another. Colony managers who take advantage of their position and who do an inadequate job of satisfying the personal needs of their members give rise to pilfering in nearby villages. It is perhaps unfair to generalize about Hutterites except to say that they, like other separatist groups, acknowledge that there are "black sheep" among them.

Those who advance legal reasons for restricting Hutterite expansion sometimes suggest that the Hutterites are aliens or not citizens of Canada because they do not take up arms and do not vote. The concept of citizenship differs widely among the population in any free country. The Hutterites have some qualities that fit most concepts of good citizenship. They obey all laws except those that conflict with their fundamental faith. They pay all taxes levied and have an excellent record as solvent tax payers. They improve the soil, and their wealth stays in the land.

They are quiet and orderly. They do not become public charges but care for their own aged and disabled. All can speak English in addition to German. They do not hoard wealth but invest it in land, equipment, and buildings. Their agricultural know-how can transform wastelands into very productive lands. The Hutterites possess a folk culture that is rich in primitive crafts, rhymes, proverbs, riddles, and common-sense knowledge. They have no foreign or nationalistic loyalties.

On the other hand, if conscripted for war, the Hutterites, like the Friends and Mennonites, would not enter the armed services for reasons of conscience and religion. They would go to work camps for conscientious objectors as they did in past wars. Their faith requires that they forego their possessions and their lives rather than kill or engage in acts of violence. In this regard, they are different from the society around them. But they donate blood to the Red Cross and make contributions to community drives for cancer and research.

What prospects lie ahead for a separatist group that is disliked for its population expansion, its economic and productive efficiency, and its cultural separatism?

It is ironical in a country with as much land-room as Canada that any people should be denied the right to own land, or that a people with a very high productive capacity in a country that encourages initiative cannot be economically tolerated. The solution perhaps most often advocated is to forcibly assimilate the Hutterites into the wider society. But this is no easy solution in a free society and perhaps a dubious goal if one takes the United Nations Convention on Genocide seriously. No nation has yet succeeded in assimilating the Hutterites by direct pressure. The opposite has generally been true. The greater the pressure and discrimination, the more intensified becomes the psychological distance between them and society.

All sects see reality in a black-white relationship. Conformity to the ingroup means security. In a truly sectarian society alternate choices do not exist. When the Hutterites are told by the school or government to integrate, the sect members see only black. If integration means giving up their fundamental community and faith, they see no alternative. If integration means to hear and see television, or to own land as families instead of communally, or to dance with others in the community, the Hutterites see only insecurity. Not many Hutterites covet the life of the outsider, and until they do the problem will remain with Canada.

The ultimate working solution will come by voluntary participation of group members in the wider society. A democratic country can do much to encourage these conditions. Increasing informal association between colonies and the wider society will provide alternatives for sect members. This is probably inevitable in the future with a steady growth of the Hutterite population. Although regulations may be essential, more discrimination and restrictive legislation would only postpone the process. There are some indications that the black-white reality is beginning to change to different shades of grey in some colonies.

Future provincial and national policy in respect to Hutterites would do well to utilize all the knowledge it can get from the social sciences. Law-makers are confronted with pressure groups, and the facts in the case just do not speak for themselves. Whether the Hutterites should be restricted to own less than 1 per cent of the arable land in Alberta (as they do at present) or be permitted to expand is a question of opinion, but this opinion deserves all the evidence it can get from the social sciences.

The practice of holding property communally is an old practice in many parts of the world. It may well be that there are other and more satisfactory legal methods to regulate and control communal utilization of the land. The practice of leasing land over long periods of time, even for more than a century, is common both in Europe and in the Anglo-American legal system. Satisfactory tenants rarely find it difficult to obtain renewal of shorter terms of leasing so that tenant farming over many generations is not an uncommon phenomenon. In this way high quality farming skills are utilized without affecting the ownership of the land, while the owner retains a secured income. A large number of religious communes were begun by Christians who were inspired by the example of the early apostles who "had all things in common and parted them to all men as every man had need." Communal farms were common among the early Christians; they are still common today in many countries, and are numerous among some Catholic religious orders.

Unfortunately for the Hutterites and the province of Alberta as a whole, much discrimination has resulted. The Brethren have become the scapegoat for the hard-pressed rural farmer who is faced with a serious problem in the business of agriculture. The disappearance of small villages is attributed to land-hungry Hutterite colonies.

While the public hearings held by the Alberta Communal Property Board provide an opportunity for all persons to present their views when the Hutterites make application for land, they also have the effect of intensifying attitudes against the colonies through demonstrations of public protests. Whether this is the best solution in the long run is a question government agencies must consider.

Both academic and administrative groups would benefit from further research. The antagonism between the majority and minority is a function of social distance. What factors will bring about less antagonism? What conditions will bring about desirable alternative choices in persons who no longer see reality as black or white? What is the cost in the depletion of natural resources for maintaining struggling, inefficient one-family farms? How can minority groups, including the Indian, Eskimo, Métis, and other ethnic groups, borrow that which is best from the surrounding culture without bringing debauchery and deterioration, as they put aside their traditional values? These are some of the problems which anthropologists, sociologists, and others can help solve if given research funds and opportunity.

25. *THE HUTTERITE PROBLEM IN ALBERTA**

Karl Peter†

I

During the last few years, the Alberta public has witnessed a continuous stream of comments, resolutions and reports on the so-called "Hutterite problem." A great many organizations took part in drawing them up.

Yet most of the people involved in these activities are ready to confess that they know little about Hutterites. These people begin by stating their own values in which they believe. And then they demand that Hutterites, who visibly seem to believe in different values, should be changed so that they believe in the same thing.

There are basically two groups who feel compelled to offer solutions to the so-called Hutterite problem. The first group is made up of parts of a patriotic-minded segment of the population with the Canadian Legion as its most powerful and most respected voice. The second group consists

*From *The Edmonton Journal*, originally published as a series of four articles, August 20 to September 10, 1963.

†Mr. Peter is currently a graduate student in sociology at the University of Alberta, Edmonton.

of various rural, governmental, educational or professional organizations which reflect the sentiments of certain parts of the Alberta farm population.

According to the groups involved, the Hutterite problem is defined in different terms. While the patriotic-minded section emphasizes the apparent lack of interest on the part of the Hutterities in Canadian patriotism (sometimes called citizenship), the other group is concerned with the spread of Hutterite colonies in Alberta. At least these are the issues they confess to be concerned with. Both groups make various suggestions to remedy the situation which is not compatible with their own sentiments.

It might be helpful to consider the most pronounced arguments brought forward by these groups in the light of the events as they occurred during the last 20 years.

In 1942, the Alberta Legislature passed the "Land Sales Prohibition Act" which prevented the purchase of land by Hutterites. Because the 1942 legislation referred to enemy aliens as well as to Hutterites, it was disallowed in 1944 and consequently re-enacted with reference to Hutterites only.

It is somewhat surprising to learn that the Alberta government at that time faced the threat of violence against Hutterites by enacting a bill designed to punish those who already were threatened, not to punish those which advocated violence. To prevent unlawful violence and to preserve unity, the government took it into its own hands to do violence to the Hutterites. A very strange way of legal reasoning indeed.

The reason to act against the Hutterites rested in the fact that they did not express the patriotic sentiments which at that time were commonly expected. The German origin of Hutterites and the use of the German language on colonies probably maintained an atmosphere of suspicion. There was also a feeling of deprivation on the part of those who thought that they were carrying the burden of war while others made profits from it.

To the extent that those war attitudes are re-interpreted in terms of citizenship attitudes, we are dealing with exactly the same arguments as they are expressed today by members of the patriotic-minded section.

There are two ways to pursue this matter further. One way would be to approach it with emotions, in which case we could stop right here because we know the answers already. The second way would consist of reasoning out this situation of conflicting values and the first step of reasoning might well begin with finding out the causes and underlying facts.

What determines the Hutterite behavior with respect to the government of this country? Their participation or non-participation in organized activities? Their mental involvement in feelings of loyalty toward this country?

For Hutterites the highest authority of human conduct is the Bible.

For 400 years they have labored to create a social setting exclusively designed to fulfil conditions as set out in various parts of the Bible. The result of this search is not only the unique set of human, religious and economic relations as observed in Hutterite colonies, but also the creation of definite attitudes toward the outside world.

Hutterites believe, and this belief is backed up by countless Bible quotations, that government is an instrument of God to punish the evil-doers among mankind.

As such, government is ordained by God and must be obeyed in all matters regarding human conduct not already laid down by God's word. The more diligent a person is to obey to the government the more pleasing it is to God. Only where the government gives commands and acts against God must one leave the government's command undone and obey God rather than man.

There are a number of areas in which the command of God must rather be obeyed than the command of the government. One of these areas is the conduct of war. Government is ordained by God as an instrument of punishment and war is a punishment of God.

A true believer can not claim to be a Christian and at the same time be involved in acting out punishment because God has reserved punishment for himself.

Therefore no Christian can go to war or be involved in patriotic sentiments leading to war. A true Hutterite therefore must flee from any situation which could get him involved in acts of strife and war unless he ceases to be a Christian. No Christian can be a ruler nor any ruler be a Christian. Those who are selected by God as an instrument of punishment can not be members of the kingdom of God, that is, the church in which all worldly warfare has come to an end.

These religious sentiments, of course, don't make sense in the minds of people who are members of the Canadian Legion, or otherwise patriotically inclined.

For Hutterites however, they are part of their mental reality just as real and important as the feeling of loyalty towards one's country is for other Canadians.

Furthermore, they have paid a terrible price for these sentiments. Thousands of Hutterites have been burned at the stakes, drowned, killed by the sword, put to death in the torture chambers in almost all countries of Europe. The women have been raped, abused and sold into slavery because they upheld the commands of God as they understand them, rather than obey those men who acted against the will of God.

And there is no question that the majority of Alberta Hutterites today would endure all kinds of hardship including physical punishment rather than yield on this point.

This leads us to the question, "What right do they have to subscribe to those ideas in the middle of Canadian society?" (which not in the least was and is maintained by people who have dedicated and will dedicate their lives in order that this society may survive).

The answer is very simple — none, except that by their own free will, Canadians have accepted Hutterites into this country and allowed them to live according to the sentiments of their religion.

Hutterites never made it a secret of what they are and what they believe in. When during the First World War Hutterites experienced similar situations of social conflict in the United States, all the difficulties resulting from a conflict of values were visible — open for everyone who bothered to see.

The eleven colonies which migrated to Canada in 1918 did so after they were given assurances that the specific guarantees of freedom from military and governmental service, given to a colony by order-in-council (1876, August 12, 1899) applied to them also.

Hutterites live in this country and are granted these exemptions because the Canadian government entered into a contract with them.

They did not come here to be assimilated or converted to our way of life.

They came here to exercise their faith, to work, and to pray. They made it clear to everyone who wanted to listen to them, that they willingly wanted to obey the government where it was the business of the government to give the commands, and that they intended to obey the commands of God wherever he has reserved those commands for himself.

II

The Hutterite situation is, understandably, not very satisfying to people who think in terms of duties and rights of Canadian citizenship. The trouble with the concept of citizenship is that people don't agree on what it means.

If it means to participate in elections, 80 to 90 per cent would not act as citizens because this is about the percentage that does not vote in municipal elections.

Does it mean the readiness to fight for the country?

A large part of the Canadian population actively resisted compulsory military service and if it wasn't for our commitments, Canada could just as well forget about its military contributions because it is of no use anyway. At least there are enough people in this country to hold this view to make themselves heard. Are they citizens or not?

Or does citizenship mean to work for the vague concept of the public good whatever that could be? What then about the farm representatives of the three prairie provinces who threatened the Canadian government in August, 1951, to refuse to co-operate in case of war unless their demands are met?

There is the Canadian judge who defined a citizen as a person who obeys the laws of the land. According to this, the Hutterites would be exceptionally good citizens.

Or is a citizen a person that yields to the pressure of conformity, drives a car, struggles to keep up with the payments, spends money he hopes to earn eventually and suffers from chronic unemployment?

If all this would happen to Hutterites, chances are we wouldn't notice any Hutterite problem. If they lived like many Indians do, we wouldn't even be concerned with their kind of citizenship just as much as the Canadian Legion is not concerned whether Indians do vote or not.

Only last spring the standard suggestion to force Hutterites into higher education once more was molded into a resolution.

The call for higher education for Hutterites is hardly an honest suggestion. Nobody who calls out so loudly is interested in a higher education for Hutterites. The real interest is reflected in the hope that higher education will cause a breakdown of Hutterite culture causing Hutterites to accept our way of life.

This is about as far as those people who suggest this scheme are willing to think.

Enough sociological knowledge in all parts of the world has been accumulated to predict that a breakdown of Hutterite culture will result in an increase of deviants who cannot adjust to the strange norms of the dominant society.

Canadian experiences with the breakdown of Indian cultures and the following creation of a normless shifting section of a population that tends to occupy the slum areas of our large cities should point out the dangers of this concept of assimilation. Yet it seems that slum areas, welfare services, crime and vice are more easily tolerated by society than the existence of a hard-working efficient Christian community whose isolation from this dominant society is a thorn in the side of almost everyone.

Furthermore, Hutterites know about the changes a higher education for their children is about to produce. They realize that the demands for education spell the doom of their existence. They resist these demands not because they are against education in general, but because education is used as a disguise to destroy their culture.

The peculiar group life of Hutterites produced a way of thinking, where the individual does not see the world so much in terms of his own person but in terms of his group. With Hutterites, this group includes the forefathers who founded their movement and maintained it during times of disaster and persecution.

All Hutterites today have a strong feeling of obligation to their forefathers, much stronger than the average North American's obligation to the founders of the United States or Canada, which to be sure, play an important part in our lives.

In addition Hutterites feel an obligation for generations as yet to come. Their religious sentiments are not exhausted by taking one's own salvation into consideration but also to assure the salvation of the coming generations.

It is only natural that Hutterites feel threatened. They are fighting the most vital fight of any society, the fight for survival of their culture.

They fight under the eyes of their forefathers for the salvation of their own souls and the souls of the generations to come. They fight the only way they know, by being passive and resisting change.

We began this discussion by looking into the aspects of patriotic behavior and what it means to Hutterites. To be a Canadian patriot of any shape or make-up means to a Hutterite to forsake his God, break with his church, leave his people and wander into a world he does not understand. For the Hutterite people as a whole it means to lose everything that is of any value to them.

Are we as a Christian nation really so naive as to expect that Hutterites would co-operate in their own destruction?

And do we have the nerve to demand that they make all those sacrifices just to become a conforming part of our society and gain the same or even higher crime, divorce or juvenile delinquent rate as we have?

III

The "Land Sales Prohibition Act" which prevented the purchase of land by Hutterites was made to expire about one year after the end of the Second World War.

By 1947 the emphasis of the Hutterite problem had shifted from the patriotic aspect to the aspect of controlling the spread of colonies. Consequently, "The Communal Property Act," which prevented the formation of any colony within 40 miles of an already existing colony and which limited the size of any colony to 6,400 acres, was passed by the Alberta Legislature.

We are now dealing with socio-economic problems involving both Hutterites and certain sections of the Alberta farm population. Again it might be helpful to uncover the underlying reality in order to get a picture about the nature of this problem.

The most important aspect of Hutterite culture in this context is the organization of labor.

Each Hutterite colony consists on the average of about 20 to 25 male members with an equal number of adult females. This actual labor force of around 40 to 50 people is rationally organized to achieve a maximum efficiency in the agricultural operation of the colony. Most of the men are specialized in one or the other job and all have an all-round capacity to do all jobs in a more or less accepted fashion.

The labor force of the women is equally organized between doing their private housework, or working for the good of the community, by cooking for the colony, taking care of the garden, milking the cows, grading eggs, and so on.

What are the results of this organization of labor?

For one thing, Hutterites are all-round farmers who spread their activities over the whole range of possible activities from bee-raising to sheep, chicken, hogs, to a variety of fruits. In doing so, they opened up many sources of income while at the same time they reduced the effect of any one crop failure.

The high degree of specialization which colony members underwent gave the insurance that all-operations are conducted with the utmost efficiency. Furthermore the pool of manpower available allows Hutterites to take care of necessary farm operations by concentrating this manpower for a short period of time on any one operation and therefore taking advantage of otherwise uncontrollable factors like rain, frost or a short season. Hutterites for example move into the fields at seeding time like a well-organized army.

While the average farmer tries to take advantage of favorable weather conditions by perhaps working 18 hours a day, Hutterites work 24 hours a day in three eight-hour shifts. Unlike the exhausted farmer, they are able to keep their pace indefinitely without reaching the point of physical breakdown.

By working less, they finish their work quicker, take more advantage of their machinery and don't need to neglect other work because they are able to draw on female labor temporarily for some lighter jobs usually done by men around the farm.

The next feature of the organization of labor is the existence of elaborate repair and even construction facilities on the colonies. Hutterites accepted modern farm machinery like all other farmers. But at the same time they trained their men and build up facilities to repair and maintain this machinery.

It is this capacity of repair and minor construction that helped them to escape in part from the burden of the cost-price squeeze of the average farmer.

What are the arguments against this agricultural set-up?

For one thing, Hutterites are not supposed to contribute to the economy of the country.

Such an argument is nothing but silly. Hutterites produce and consume.

If they save any money, they put it back into operation or they save it in the bank where it is available for investment in Canadian enterprises.

Next, Hutterites disrupt community development.

How a well-organized agricultural unit can disrupt community development is hard to visualize.

Hutterites need for their efficiency electric power as well as roads and telephones. To obtain these facilities they neither ask nor are given preferential treatment. Where they are to benefit from any community enterprise they consider the advantages and disadvantages just as every other farmer would do and make a decision according to their findings.

Some people are terribly annoyed that Hutterites' decisions contain an element of self-interest that otherwise is taken for granted among farmers.

They don't patronize local business.

Hutterites spend in their city. Inasfar as Hutterites buy products which satisfy their standards of quality, price and quantity, it is a well known fact that many of the local enterprises do not live up to these demands of their business.

Where a businessman bothered to look into these facts which apply to any business, he usually found Hutterites to be good customers.

The question is not whether local businessmen get the business. The question is who is flexible enough to realize that Hutterites form a potential market which can be served by meeting their different demands.

Another argument is that Hutterites buy up the land and eventually will squeeze out all other farmers.

There are about 63 colonies in this province. If all these colonies would possess their legitimate 6,400 acres per colony, which as far as I know is not the case, the total holdings of Hutterites would amount to about a little more than 400,000 acres. According to sources available to me, this amounts to about one-half of one per cent of the acreage suitable for cultivation in this province.

This argument, however, uncovers some other interesting facts.

It is hardly a secret that certain sections of the farm population in Alberta live in a state of constant frustration. The business of farming includes a great deal of risk inasmuch as weather conditions can eliminate the best of human efforts in a few hours. Frost, hail and drought in Alberta form an unholy trinity and have left a deep feeling of anxiety among many farmers.

In addition there are the unstable market conditions for Western Canadian products. Each farmer had to make a decision on how much to spend on increasing his farm efficiency and how much to keep up with the desired standard of living. Quite clearly, the farm income during the last 20 years has not been sufficient to satisfy both demands.

A further complication is caused by the fact that changing conditions in Western Canada seem to demand a change in the organization of farming. However, the farm population in Western Canada is deeply devoted to the family farm organization. The constitution for the Farmers Union of Alberta is dedicated to the family farm. And it seems that this is a common feeling among farmers.

These problems, caused by factors which have worldwide implications and cannot be controlled in any way, were met by the farm population in a certain way. Because the family system of farming is sacred, nobody is allowed to question it.

Instead, farmers tried to manipulate the outside world to make them fit their system. The countless resolutions passed on the yearly conventions of the Farmers Union of Alberta and ranging from the nationalization of the farm implement industry to various deficiency payments, producer controlled market boards to the declaration of Farmers Day as a legal holiday for the country, uncover the frustration and anxiety which many farmers acquired during the last 30 years.

What could be said about Hutterites in another context also holds for the family farm in Western Canada — the family farmer is fighting for survival.

There are dangers everywhere. The prices for equipment are rising constantly. The market conditions are as unstable as they ever were. The weather cannot be controlled despite some attempts to get the government involved into a hail control scheme. And yet the Hutterites seem to thrive despite all these adverse conditions.

Of all these frustration-causing factors, the Hutterite problem is the one that is the most visible and can be dealt with without much trouble.

It is somewhat hard to protest against rising prices when the manufacturers live in the East.

It is much easier to protest against Hutterites who live a few miles away.

IV

If I had to make a value judgment, it would be one of sympathy for the Alberta farmer and his difficulties.

I do not want to imply that all farmers in Alberta affected by what is customarily called the cost-price squeeze show symptoms of frustration or anxiety. It seems that the larger part has been able to adapt to changing conditions and establish an equilibrium which is an admirable product of flexibility and hard work.

What I want to say, however, is that fear and hostility against Hutterites is expressed most often by those who haven't found yet the security of operation and outlook into the future which is necessary to meet the competition of another culture.

Even these people don't hate Hutterites; they just fear their efficient impersonal operation which manages successfully under conditions under which they themselves might be forced to forsake their identity and give up farming.

What is the conclusion?

Certain segments of the Alberta farm population as well as Hutterites are fear-orientated. They face each other like people whose very existence is in danger and who are ready to rally their resources in order to fight off any encroachment on the part of the other party.

Because both sides consciously or unconsciously are involved in this antagonistic activity, they don't find any basis of discussion or compromise. They don't even make any attempt to understand each other.

The behavior of both groups is determined by more imaginary dangers than real ones. And both act on the basis of what they imagine, not on the basis of a factual inventory of the problem and an informed evaluation of possible consequences.

The depressing point of the Hutterite problem is not that it exists or that it touches a tremendous range of human values and activities. It is the fact that we don't like to come to grips with the problem at all.

We talk as if the other group does not exist. We demand things and we only know what those demands mean in terms of our own culture. We care little or not at all how it might effect the others.

Our government walks the tightrope. It operates the "Communal Property Act" as if it was a legal act but knows it has been questioned. It prefers to rule by legal doubt instead of established right.

As far as the social problem is concerned, it refuses to accept the responsibility and points to the federal government which created the mess in the first place by letting the Hutterites into the country.

We indulge in emotions and refuse to use our power of reason in order to accommodate our differences with the Hutterites, not to assimilate them.

We are breaking all kinds of porcelain because we haven't matured enough to look beyond our own desires and values.

We aren't bad. We are just a little young and a little too much pre-occupied with ourselves. But we also know that we will at some time have to find a common basis to live with Hutterites and I am convinced we will.

Whatever the peculiarities of Hutterite religion and way of life, they know that they live a life of interdependence with us and they have developed strong emotional ties toward this country and its people. Once the threat of assimilation is removed from them, there is a strong possibility that these ties will become dominant and create an atmosphere of co-operation and understanding rather than fear and hostility.

Whatever the frustrations on our part that cause us to act irrationally, there is our power of reasoning, our ability to see things in their real proportions, our understanding that enables us to create a social situation tolerable for both sides.

We might never be able to make Hutterites good soldiers. But we might live with them as they live with us.

And we might even be proud of the contribution they make toward our common concern.

26. THE DOUKHOBORS OF B.C.*

Stuart Jamieson†

Few immigrant groups have presented so difficult, and in some ways spectacular, a problem in Canada as have the Doukhobors, a unique religious sect of Russian origin. Numerically they are insignificant. Some 7,000 to 8,000 in Saskatchewan and Alberta seem now to have become adjusted more or less successfully to their environment. It is the main group of 10,000 to 12,000 in the West Kootenay region of British Columbia that presents the main problems.

The Doukhobors in B.C. today comprise three main groups. First, there is the *Orthodox* element, numbering some 5,000 to 6,000 people, the majority of whom belong to an organization known as the Union of Spiritual Communities of Christ. They live mainly in rural villages and small towns, in what were once communal enterprises. They represent the core of the Doukhobor movement, a group of people who seek to retain their traditional language, culture, and system of religious beliefs while making a peaceful adjustment to the Canadian way of life.

Secondly, there is the *Independent* element, numbering some 3,000 to 4,000 people. They comprise individual Doukhobors who have become partially or almost entirely assimilated. That is to say, while they still pay lip-service to the Doukhobor religious philosophy, they have severed most formal ties with exclusively Doukhobor organizations and left the distinct Doukhobor communities to live in their own separate residences on farms or in cities.

And finally, there is the group known as the *Sons of Freedom,* a fanatical wing numbering possibly 3,000 people. They are uncompromising fundamentalists who tend to react violently against forces in the Canadian environment which they feel threaten fundamental Doukhobor values.

The so-called "Doukhobor problem" tends to be identified in the public mind almost entirely with the activities of the Sons of Freedom — their refusal to register for vital statistics, to pay taxes, or send their children to school; their nude parades, their bombings and burnings of their own and other people's property; and so on. Such behavior, however, is only one symptom of broader underlying problems of maladjustment that

*From *The Canadian Forum,* Vol. 31, April 1951.
†Dr. Jamieson is Professor of Economics (specializing in Labour Relations) at the University of British Columbia, Vancouver.

seem to apply in greater or less degree to all Doukhobors. Where the reactions of the Sons of Freedom to these problems tend to be sensational and violent, the reactions of the Orthodox and Independent elements tend to be those of apathy, bewilderment, and general demoralization.

At first glance the main problems of the Doukhobors might appear to be primarily economic in character. Like a number of other Russian and German religious sects in this country, they uphold the principle of a communal way of life based on a self-sufficient farm economy. In this regard they have faced several discouraging setbacks in Canada. Their first communal undertaking, which was begun in northern Saskatchewan shortly after their arrival in Canada in 1899, failed in 1904 when they lost title to their land through refusing to register it in individual quarter-sections as required under the Homestead Act. A more ambitious communal enterprise subsequently undertaken in the West Kootenay region of B.C. was plagued with factionalism and conflict. It finally went bankrupt in 1937, through inability to handle the large mortgage indebtedness which had been incurred. To prevent foreclosure and dispossession of thousands of Doukhobors, the provincial government paid the balance owing on the mortgages and thereby assumed title to their land and improvements. The occupants were allowed to remain.

Most Orthodox Doukhobors today are thus tenants on government-owned land, for which they pay small annual rentals. The Sons of Freedom, who refuse to pay rent or taxes, are technically *squatters*. Because they no longer have an ownership interest in the property, and their tenure is insecure, the Doukhobors have allowed the land, buildings, and other facilities to deteriorate. The majority today are only part-time farmers operating poorly maintained and uneconomically small tracts of land.

The majority of Doukhobors consequently have come to depend upon outside employment for the main part of their livelihood. Here too their position is in many ways unsatisfactory. At first glance they present the all-too-familiar picture of an economically insecure ethnic minority whose position in the community is rendered precarious by widespread prejudice and discrimination. They are practically all manual workers, concentrated to an extreme degree in a few highly seasonal trades and industries, namely, carpentering and general construction labor, logging and saw-milling. Only a handful are in the more highly-paid or secure proprietary, managerial, professional, sales, clerical, or other salaried white-collar jobs. Very few likewise are to be found in other major industries of the region, such as mining and smelting; in other skilled trades like those of plumbers, electricians, and mechanics; or in local transportation and service industries. And finally, only a few dozen Doukhobors all told are members of trade unions, business and professional organizations, or service clubs in the industries and communities in which they are employed.

In comparison with other wage-earners in the West Kootenay region, on the other hand, the Doukhobors on the whole seem to enjoy certain definite advantages. They are not concentrated in the lowest paid, most unskilled or menial tasks by any means. The industries and trades in which they specialize, as listed above, are generally skilled or semi-skilled and have relatively high rates of pay. Their concentration in seasonal industries is not only a matter of discrimination. It is also partly a matter of choice. For in such fields as logging, sawmilling and construction, where employment is unstable and intermittent, the Doukhobors are able to carry on their part-time farming activities. In this regard they enjoy lower costs of living and greater security of livelihood than do other seasonal workers. And unlike many other immigrant groups, as well as native-born wage-earners, the Doukhobors have not been crowded into the tenements and slums of large towns and industrial cities. They have retained their connection to the land and to village life.

By our standards, or those of the typical Canadian wage-earner, the Doukhobors would seem to be doing pretty well. What then, are their problems? What are they protesting about? What accounts for the growing demoralization among some of them, and the periodically violent outbreaks on the part of others?

The answer does not seem to lie primarily in the Canadian or British Columbian environment as such. It lies, rather, within the Doukhobors themselves, in their past history, their present culture, their system of religious beliefs, values, and motivations, and the dissatisfaction and unrest which these generate in the present environment.

The circumstances of their origin, to begin with, were such as to create a peculiar social structure among the Doukhobors. Their sect began as a protest movement against the established Church and State of Russia some three hundred years ago. Its main following was drawn from people in the peasant or *serf class* — a people who, in the feudal system of Russia, had been conditioned for centuries to a state of servitude. In breaking away from the established system they carried over much of their attitude of submissiveness and dependence upon authority *without* at the same time carrying over the feudal structure of authority that went with it. The Doukhobor social and political system thus became a confusing mixture of democratic and dictatorial principles, of servile dependence upon, and at the same time hostility to, authority. *In principle* it was a classless society in which all men were considered equal. There was no established bureaucracy, no priesthood, and no hierarchy of classes. *In fact* it developed into a system of highly centralized theocracy. Divine powers were attributed to such leaders as Peter (the Lordly) Veregin. They could command a fanatically obedient following, yet at the same time they were constantly faced with internecine strife and opposition.

The Doukhobor social structure was, and is, poorly integrated and peculiarly subject to breakdown. It held together, and the movement survived for some three centuries, only under special circumstances. Persecution by Church and State was one of these, as it forced the Doukhobors together into a cohesive group. Another was geographic isolation, which required a self-sufficient farm economy. At one period in their history they were exiled to a remote and thinly populated region of the Caucasus. When they did in time come into extensive contact with other peoples, their leaders could hold them together only by defining their beliefs and customs more rigidly, to differentiate the Doukhobors more sharply from other groups and thus achieve social, if not geographic, isolation.

Under such pressures the Doukhobor philosophy and way of life came to involve a steadily more elaborate set of beliefs and taboos that brought the movement into increasing conflict with its environment, Canadian as well as Russian. The first and major tenet of the Doukhobor creed has been, throughout, the refusal to bear arms and take life. Insofar as the use of force was identified with the State, the pacifism of the Doukhobors developed into opposition toward virtually every phase of activity identified with the State: education, registration and licensing, collection and payment of taxes, and so on. From there, the Doukhobor creed came to condemn the institution of private property and the accumulation of wealth (and thus offered a rationalization to the extremists to destroy government and private property by fire). For wealth excites greed and envy in others, and thus serves to justify the need for governments and armed forces to protect property. This doctrine in turn gradually evolved into a puritanical code of passiveness and humility, that frowned upon virtually all personal expressions of competitiveness or self-assertion and all forms of enjoyment for its own sake (such as indulgence in liquor, tobacco, sex, games and dances). The weapon which the Doukhobors devised to protect themselves against attack from others was the one later made famous by Gandhi — namely, *passive resistance.* (Nudism is a relatively new and supplementary weapon of passive resistance devised by the Sons of Freedom in Canada. Its main explanation lies in its devastating effectiveness in Anglo-Saxon communities.)

The result of these trends has been to develop an impoverished culture and a peculiarly helpless type of people, in the sense of being unable *as a group,* on their own initiative, to devise rational means to organize and grapple with the problems that face them in a more complex society. Their culture and beliefs, and the various social pressures that enforce them, seem to suppress most outlets for individual energy and self-expression. These, in turn, have created attitudes of deep frustration and latent hostility that break out periodically, among the extremists, in acts of aggression against their environment. Their history has been one of extreme dependence upon land as a secure source of livelihood, and upon strong leadership to guide them and hold them together. Today they are a virtually landless and leaderless people. They have lost title to the land they occupy, and it is now owned by the government. Their leadership system, based upon hereditary succession, has broken down. While there are today a number of able leaders among the Doukhobors, no one of them has wide enough acceptance to prevent continued factionalism and disintegration. The Doukhobors thus tend to feel that they are operating in a vacuum, a prey to forces that they cannot interpret and understand, let alone control. Among the more orthodox this gives rise to a feeling of helplessness and drift, of passive resistance to they know not what. To the more fanatical and militant it creates a compulsion to strike out blindly — with the now traditional weapons of nudism and fire — against forces personified in government, that they feel threaten their survival.

27. SOME BACKGROUND INFORMATION ABOUT THE DOUKHOBORS*

Harry B. Hawthorn†

EMERGENCE AND PERSISTENCE OF THE COMMUNITIES

There is a clear continuity in Doukhobor belief going back to the seventeenth or eighteenth century in Russia, where it emerged from peasant attitudes towards authority, ritual and communal life. In similar fashion, the high value now placed on communal life by the Sons of Freedom in particular has its ultimate roots in the village life of the peasant before, during and after serfdom, with the intimate direction of work, family life, property, religion, and recreation by the *mir* or village group. At that time, communal life was merely the traditional way; it is only in recent decades that it has been elevated to the status of a holy aim.

Around the time of their origin, the Doukhobors were far from being unique. Dissension and schism were made possible by the partial independence of the village in rural Russia, and by intertwined illiteracy and self-reliance in philosophy and religion. Here, in their history as many Doukhobors see it, there appears a continuity which is in large part fictional. The Sons of Freedom see their opposition to authority as identical with that of the peasant against the despot of his time; they view the dream of a revived communal life as a bulwark against all threats, and see the Canadian Government as operating like the czars, hand in hand with corrupt officials and clergy. Most clearly they see their partial illiteracy and isolation as a protection against these threats.

The strength of the village society, self-reliance in religious matters, and opposition to authority led to the formation of many peasant reformist sects, the Doukhobors becoming noteworthy because of the effective simplicity of their religious and philosophical system, and because of the steadfastness with which they stood by it. Their own conflict with the Russian Orthodox Church becomes nearly lost to view in the many conflicts of the sort from the seventeenth century on, and the relative ineffectiveness of that body in impressing its doctrine on the large number and variety of dissenters in spite of persecution, which at times was harshly oppressive. The conflict with government came into greater prominence

---

*From Hawthorn, Harry B. (ed.), *The Doukhobors of British Columbia,* Vancouver, University of British Columbia and J. M. Dent & Sons (Canada) Ltd., 1955.
†Professor Hawthorn is Head of the Department of Anthropology and Sociology at the University of British Columbia, Vancouver, and Director, Project of Research on Integration of Indians, Government of Canada.

through the Doukhobor denial of the right of government to rule. Governments naturally objected to this doctrine and took repressive measures in reprisal, measures which still live in Doukhobor oral history, hymn and thought. Imprisonment, flogging, death, exile and military service were used as punishments for failure to recant. The last measure furnished an ineffective addition to the armed forces of the nation, as the Doukhobor soldier is said to have thrown down his arms at the last moment, before going into action, and to have persuaded others to adopt his refusal to kill.

This is a thumb-nail sketch of the background of exile. Doukhobor colonies were dispersed to various parts of Russia, from the Ukraine to settlements near the Sea of Azof, from there to Transcaucasia. In dispersion, they continued to offend in the old ways and developed new ones. The Russian Government complied with their emigration request at the end of the nineteenth century.

In exile, under real and imagined threats to existence, life was organized in various closely knit units, to which the individual was tied with bonds of belief and custom. Almost as firmly as before, these beliefs and customs reflected their suspicion of the outer world. Yet that the bonds were not permanent nor the life in the communities completely satisfactory has been demonstrated in startling fashion by continued schisms and defections.

Within the Doukhobor community seventy years ago the individual found his friends, his work and subsistence, his family life, the answers to all questions of justice, meaning and value, and direction for even the details of his existence. Hostility against outsiders had been acquired, though the ability to be assertive in dealings with them had been checked; the community gave protection in the ensuing condition of helplessness. It further made up for these inadequacies and for difficulties in its internal operations by endowing its members with a strong belief in moral superiority. Illiteracy also safeguarded against change, as did the development of a protective shell of evasion in dealing with the queries and conversation of non-Doukhobors. The development of sectarian education divided members and outsiders. In addition, in this earlier period when the *mir* supplied all needs, there was no satisfactory life for an individual leaving the sect, no role or occupation, no niche for a displaced individual.

Yet the historical fact is that the communities have disintegrated. In Russia they split several times on issues of principle as well as on disputes over leadership. In Canada they have dwindled by the defection of individuals until no communities in the former sense remain. Among the causes of this disintegration are the inducements offered by life in Canada. Added to these are the pressures of arbitrary personal leadership, of social suffocation by neighbours who feel called on to pry and control as well as aid — pressures tolerated when the alternative is fearful but unbearable when there is no threat from the outside. The inducements to leave community life include the picture of relative economic independence, life under generally impartial and temperate law, the greater comforts and more varied achievements that could be aspired to, the wide range of recreations, the choice of occupations, plus the possibility of maintaining most Doukhobor beliefs. It is small wonder that the extreme die-hards of the Sons of Freedom paint this as a blacker threat than any of the past. The effectiveness of such inducements was shown in the first years in Canada, with the splitting-off of independents, and is now shown in the fact that of all the Doukhobors in Canada only some two or three thousand are insistent on a return to communal life, which none are actually living. It was also shown through the years in the formation of the many new groupings, The Christian Community of Universal Brotherhood, the Named Doukhobors, the Society of Independent Doukhobors, the Union of Spiritual Communities of Christ, the Sons of Freedom, the Union of Doukhobors of Canada, and now the Christian Community and Brotherhood of Reformed Doukhobors, groups which retain in common only the essential points of principle related to pacifism, a few attitudes to be specified later and some problems in relation to their neighbours.

The search for an understanding of Doukhobor action leads to an examination of the beliefs which underlie it. These show differing characteristics of persistence, adaptability and intensity, and in a general way may be ranked in the degree to which they have been amenable to change or compromise. Of course these beliefs do not operate alone in guiding action or in giving rise to it. There are many other guides and motivations, some of them hidden and others more obvious.

The belief in individual guidance by divine revelation, and the belief that external authority lacks the necessary religious sanction or wisdom to direct anyone's life, seem to have been the first to arise. Today these remain within the central core of beliefs, the ones which are most resistant to change, which are most widely held and carry out a fundamental role in sanctioning action. Also within this central core are some which appeared later in the development of Doukhobor philosophy: the attitude toward war and killing, attitudes revolving around dependence on the group as a source of strength and a centre of action, and hostility to competition and the use of physical force.

Some of these beliefs have correlates, which are almost equally important. The rejection of the out-group, the non-Doukhobors, is linked to the dependence placed by the Doukhobor on his community. The rejection of ritual, of the written word and the sacraments, follows the denial of the authority of an organized church. The contradiction between rejecting human authority on the one hand and dependency and need of authority on the other has been partially resolved by crediting Doukhobor leadership with an extra endowment of the divine inspiration which is each man's possession.

These are the beliefs which seem least amenable to alteration or compromise. They have been embedded in tradition, are linked in childhood from endless repetition and illustration and are linked with action in every group enterprise.

Related to this core of beliefs are many which seem to be more peripheral. They have arisen as responses to specific situations; repetition of the situation has given them some persistence, but they do not possess the lasting qualities of the above. Of this sort are the beliefs related to protests, demonstrations, arson. These are maintained by the fear and frustration present in Doukhobor lives and would lose their main reason for existence if the emotional states could be altered. In like manner, the paranoid quality of Doukhobor attitudes toward outsiders could not be maintained indefinitely if it were given little to feed on. A decade of official policy and action which avoided giving cause for suspicion and fear and which consistently showed goodwill would work wonders.

Other beliefs of a peripheral and relatively changeable nature are those which centre around self-enhancement through education, development of the arts, acquisition of individual forms of self-expression. These appear to Doukhobors as leading to competitiveness and self-assertiveness, in contrast to which self-denial is sought. In like manner, those concerning schools, statistics and registration are extensions of some more central ones. Together with beliefs concerning communal property, return to a Garden of Eden existence, vegetarianism, refusal to exploit animals, prohibition of intoxicating liquors and tobacco, they have at one time or another been followed or advocated by part of the group.

In spite of its disjointed appearance when presented in this fashion, there is a very great degree of consistency within this system of belief. It does possess contradictions, but these are few and minor compared to the contradictions which obtain within the framework of beliefs in most human societies. Indeed its very consistency and logicality constitute much of the basis for conflict between the Doukhobors and the society which is their host. To be effectively linked to action and reality, beliefs must be adaptable to a greater degree than holds within the Doukhobor system. The process of adjustment almost always involves inconsistency, which most people and systems accept without being aware of contradiction. When the constant scrutiny of their own belief by the Doukhobors reveals contradictions, being unable to admit change or accept some inconsistency on a commonsense basis, they engage instead in frantic attempts to hold back the tide. The difference between the various Doukhobor sects lies to a large extent in this. The devouter ones among the Sons of Freedom grow anxious at any perceived contradiction in their beliefs and lead the movement of opposition to the change which they hold to have caused it.

Historically, the growth of the Doukhobor system of belief commenced with the anti-authoritarianism of the peasant, opposed to direction by officials of church and state, and assuming the common divinity of man and direction of Christ within. The rejection of the ritual of the church and of literacy and the written word, the opposition to war and force, the separation of the sect from others were protective devices whereby the fundamental beliefs were safe-guarded. Then in their turn the peripheral beliefs developed, as groups and individuals pondered over their life and religion and strove for consistency and progress.

There seems to be a loose correlation between the length of time Doukhobor beliefs have existed and the depth to which they are held to-day. The beliefs and attitudes of one of the reformist sects of the seventeenth century, preceding and perhaps influencing the emergence of the Doukhobors, included anti-authoritarianism, puritanism, a desire for ritual freedom and aims for reorganization of family life. Doukhobor belief itself was not recorded in detail until 1832 and then mainly in terms of the core of religion and opposition to government. Because of the techniques of evasion which were necessary for survival and already developed at that time, it is likely that other values relating to other parts of the culture were also elaborated but not revealed to outsiders. It was not until the time of the contributions made by Tolstoy, Tchertkoff, Bodiansky, and others that some of these came to light. From the time of migration to Canada, there sprang the full growth of the ideas of natural goodness and simplicity, of detailed opposition to the requirements of government departments, and rejection of material advance and science.

Tolstoy would have been more than human had he not tried to influence these protagonists of ideas something like his own. The close and able observer Maude wrote that similar personal reasons motivated Bodiansky to crystallize their ideas on the iniquity of private ownership of land. To the present day the Doukhobors have a fateful attraction for individuals with a social idea or a belief or a system to sell. To the extent that the proffered article seems to fit in the Doukhobor belief system, it is heeded, and may have effect.

The developments listed have been ones which tended to increase the distance between Doukhobor beliefs and those held by other Canadians. Yet not all the changes have been of this nature. Some have been adjustments toward increased compatibility. Even in Russia the Doukhobor culture was adaptive to outer circumstances, particularly in regard to the values belonging in the peripheral stratum. The most readily noticed changes occurred within the group of puritanical beliefs, which at various times relaxed to allow meat-eating, drinking and so on; and which now allow the great majority of Doukhobors in Canada to work for wages, be proprietors, save money, accumulate possessions, and partake of ordinary amusements of the life around them.

More important from the point of view of peaceful adjustment to this country, however, are the widespread alterations of attitudes toward government. While most Doukhobors still follow the doctrine that they cannot vote and hence share responsibility for a government, yet they also show an increasing acceptance of the idea that a government is an organization made for and responsive to the general welfare. This change in belief underlies the willingness of the majority of Doukhobors to register, send children to school and pay taxes. The continuing divergence in outlook on this point between the Doukhobors of the Prairie Provinces and those of British Columbia is due to the sense of grievance felt by even the Independents in this Province over the land for which they feel they worked so long and concerning which they still distrust the intention of the Government.

This very adaptability of the majority has been one of the motivating forces in the rise of the Sons of Freedom. Their mission, they have felt, has been to recall the majority to the path of true doctrine. In human fashion, they have continued to overlook the fact that they themselves are not fully consistent, and have also changed; in so far as this is felt, the resulting guilt spurs on their missionary work. They clamour for government aid, as do others; they demand the aid of medical science; and those in prison for arson and related disturbances complained about the housing condition of their families, crowded into the remaining unburned dwellings. It is, of course, possible to call this hypocrisy, but it is more helpful when thinking of corrective measures to recognize its universality. Compromise and inconsistency have existed in Doukhobor life from the time it became history, when the anti-authoritarians submitted to a strict theocratic rule. These qualities will no doubt continue to exist, making for some future philosophic turmoil but giving the possibility of change even among the Sons of Freedom. The contradictions in belief should be allowed to continue and wear slowly against facts and against one another. Misapplied force and tenacious argument will not accomplish helpful changes; they will most certainly delay them.

In spite of the attempt made by many Sons of Freedom to fit the practice of nudity in with the striving for natural simplicity, and that of arson with the opposition to materialism and with the pacifism of the historical burning of the arms on St. Peter's Day, 1895, nudity and arson are motivated primarily by hostility, to the non-Doukhobors or to the other Doukhobors who have been the chief losers of property.

OPERATION OF THE COMMUNITIES IN CANADA

Influenced both by the communal background of life for the Russian peasant with the *mir* organization, and by his Tolstoyan ideas which erected this once-customary state of affairs into a virtue, the exiled leader, Peter Vasilivich Verigin, advocated a communal basis for life in Canada. A complex variety of reasons led to early partial failure, and out of the resulting frustrations and differences the forerunners of the Sons of Freedom appeared, first in 1902. The allegations heard until recent years, that the Sons of Freedom have been used at times as a stalking-horse to distract the Government's attention, probably have a partial truth. The Sons of Freedom have obvious value as a threat, implying: That is what all Doukhobors will become if not treated right; and as an explanation, that these are the incredible difficulties with which the good Doukhobors have to contend. Moreover, in contrast with the extreme opposition of the Sons of Freedom to the law, the moderate opposition of the others might on many occasions have seemed reasonable or have escaped notice altogether. Yet this does not contradict the destructive influence of the Sons of Freedom on the communities themselves. From the beginning the integrity of the communities was threatened by the attacks of the Sons of Freedom within the ranks and by the strains produced by the success of the Independents; the new environment contributed to these threats by its hardships and the opportunities of individual success. Already by 1900 Bonch-Bruevich stated that there were

2,000 people living on individual farms and 5,000 in communities, two-thirds of whom wanted to become individual farmers.

In Canada the social structure of the communities and the motivations of individuals proved unequal to the stress of continued sharing. This is in part explained by the absence of any external threats such as existed in Russia and which might have held them together. Suspicion, echoes of which can still be heard, was directed against those who were in a position to avoid a full contribution of work or earnings or to claim a greater reward. Men were sent to work outside the community, and were assessed dues amounting in the early years of stress to the full sum of their earnings. Later the difference between their earnings and those of men who worked within the community and received only a small net return for such labour gave rise to feelings of prejudice, which have now risen again to trouble the settlement of the affairs of the bankrupt Christian Community of Universal Brotherhood.

This roughening of human relations in field, mill and orchard, and in business, was accomplished by dissension in community houses, by bad neighbourly relations and by a large amount of gossip and backbiting. These tensions are observable today, probably heightened by the absence of effective leadership. As noted earlier, single families live under very unsatisfactory conditions in the few community houses which remain. Internal discord can be seen externally in the patchwork repair on the roofs of some of these houses; a new patch is sometimes put on by the occupant directly underneath it, to shelter only his rooms.

The basic personality type — those attributes of Doukhobor personality which arise from the general conditioning given by the culture and which are held by the majority — may be searched for explanations of this lack of ability to run community affairs. It is remarked that few can assert themselves to the point of grasping a complex social situation clearly enough to take appropriate action. The resultant helplessness and misunderstanding foster suspicion and hostility, two qualities which stand out in their community life. Among the Sons of Freedom, in place of rationally directed action there is a tendency to substitute a practice like nudity.

Yet these attributes, which in varying degrees are common human ones, find meaning only in a certain social setting; their full results are realized where the social setting fosters uncertainty and confusion. The internal government of the communities has had an insufficiently clear structure; it has lacked any clear specification of functions and responsibilities. In contrast, indeed, there has been a long-fostered denial that a governmental structure exists. Thus the autocratic leaders in Russia and in Canada denied their role at times of conflict with the outside world, and Hooper records that the children of the parents imprisoned on Piers Island, themselves in the Industrial School, maintained their own autocratic direction but never admitted to its existence. The denial and the dissembling were brought about in an earlier century by needs of survival, but the resulting inner uncertainty in the workings of the community organization, has produced confusion, hostility and suspicion.

Another troublesome legacy has been inherited, this time from the self-government of the *mir*: a pattern of self-government in which unanimous consent had to be sought and which in its ideal form could not countenance the suppression of a dissident minority. It is obvious that such a pattern would be fully operative only with the existence of a great degree of rationality and self-confidence and flexibility. Yet the task was made harder by the inheritance of still another tradition from the same organization, that no permanent laws exist, that conscience is the guide.

Such a structure was the one least likely to maintain integration in Doukhobor communities. Coupled with the specifically Doukhobor belief in the existence of divinity in each man and the power of individual revelation, it ensured that every man could be a one-man minority, potentially a hold-out minority on whom no effective control could be brought to bear. Moreover, each man had strong antagonism to rank, authority, and direct orders and yet could not express that opposition openly. From all this, and from the mystical nature of Doukhobor political thought arises the incredible confusion in the interpretation of command and of other communication.

In the midst of the mystical thought surrounding government, special qualities of leadership and the means of conducting it did nevertheless develop a partial effectiveness. If commands were going to be interpreted by each man as his inner voice guided, a command could be successful if it employed the cues and symbols of his mainsprings of action. A career for a semanticist lies in perusing and interpreting the letters and other communications which have been taken as messages of command. The first reaction to the message from a leader had to be. What does it really mean? But the exegesis was carried out separately by every individual and every group, with no way of arriving at a consensus when the differing conclusions were reached.

Divine sanction was attributed to the most successful of the leaders in the belief that he possessed, usually by inheritance, a greater endowment of the Christ within, though the careful hiding from outsiders of the theocratic reality hindered it from its fullest operation within the community. Factors of striking personal endowment stand out in the accounts of the direction of community affairs by Peter Vasilivich and Peter Petrovich Verigin. Great dramatic ability, many-sided personalities, supported their positions; in addition, in the periods of inevitable breakdown of operations, they could and did use physical violence to get things going again.

GOVERNMENT AND THE DOUKHOBORS

The hand of the past lies heavily over the Governments of Canada and British Columbia in their relations with the Doukhobors in this Province.

Peasant hostility to government found expression in a doctrine denying the right of governments to exist. Their sole purpose, it was held, is to dominate for the purpose of exploitation, their sole basis of operation is brute force. The only authority recognized by the Doukhobor peasant in Russia stemmed from divine revelation within each man, the collective wisdom or revelation of the group of believers, or, occasionally, from an individual in their midst who had a greater share of divinity. Later elaborations equated the source of revelation with the "unspoiled impulses of natural man."

This doctrinal denial has been supplemented in early and recent times by an impressive battery of techniques for thwarting government. Relatively ineffective have been the outright refusals to render government its due; the resulting exile, imprisonment or comparable punishment also disrupted the operation of the community. More effective have been the techniques of peaceful non-cooperation and non-compliance, of concealing the community leadership, the operation of its treasury and other essentials, and of evading taxes by omission and excuse.

Some adjustment in the attitudes toward government has taken place by now, though there is still much ambivalence. Even the Sons of Freedom demand all sorts of welfare and governmental care while denying that government can serve any useful purpose and refusing the registration that could enable welfare to be given equitably. (It might be pointed out that they avoid recognizing this contradiction by the claim that they have been cheated of the results of their toil by the Government.) The communities have long sought state protection from arsonists even while failing, until recently, to produce information against them that must have been available. On the whole, however it seems that most Doukhobors, certainly all the USCC and Independents, will now accept the welfare, protective and liberating functions of state agencies, and will increasingly cooperate in their support. The possibility of a more complete change of this nature hinges largely on the spirit and form of administrative action.

Of key importance is the requirement that overall policy and the details of administration, as well as the officials involved, accept the right of the Doukhobors to hold to the non-destructive portion of their values. Moreover the policy must be unequivocal, giving no grounds for the easily-aroused suspicions of these long-time foes of government. It must be just and, at the present time, in order to help heal the past, generous a little beyond what may be their mere due.

Force should not be overestimated as a way of securing compliance with law in this situation; indeed, it would take a wilful denial of the facts of recent history to justify it as the main recourse. The effectiveness of force depends on the existence of a wish to avoid suffering, and it is ineffective if there is a strong drive to martyrdom and a strong belief in the virtue of resistence and in the ennobling effect of punishment. Many Sons of Freedom and a few others now regard prison as a place for the virtuous. Instead of bringing social condemnation down on the head of the convict, punishment meted out by the Government now brings social approval in its train. This does not suggest, however, the abnegation of the use of the judicial process along with the constraints of prison or corrective institutions. There is a necessity for the understanding and calculated use of legal restraint, with perhaps the devising of a specially suited system of detention for those whose inner compulsion will force them to continue on the violent path they have been following.

SELECTED BIBLIOGRAPHY

Allen, R., "The Hidden Kingdom of B. C.'s Holy Terrorists," *Maclean's Magazine*, March 10, 1962.

Francis, E. K., *In Search of Utopia: The Mennonites in Manitoba,* Glencoe, Illinois, The Free Press, 1955.

Friedmann, R., *Hutterite Studies* (Bender, H. S., Editor), Goshen, Indiana, Mennonite Historical Society, 1961.

Hawthorne, H. B., "A Test of Simmel on the Secret Society: The Doukhobors of British Columbia," *American Journal of Sociology*, Vol. LXII, No. 1, July, 1956.

Hawthorne, H. B. (Editor), *The Doukhobors of British Columbia*, Vancouver,

The University of British Columbia Press and J. M. Dent & Sons (Canada), Ltd., 1955.

Hughes, E. C., and Hughes, H. M., *Where Peoples Meet*, Glencoe, Illinois, The Free Press, 1952.

Just, L. R., "A Study of Mennonite Social Distance Reactions," *Mennonite Quarterly Review*, Vol. XXVIII, No. 3, July, 1954.

Lobb, H. O., and Agnew, N. M., *The Hutterites and Saskatchewan: A Study of Inter-group Relations*, Regina, The Canadian Mental Health Association, 1963.

Potter, H. H., "The Ethnic Sturcture of the Canadian Community," Montreal, Canadian Jewish Congress, No. 18, June, 1956.

Willms, A. M., "The Brethren Known As Hutterians," *The Canadian Journal of Economics and Political Science*, Vol. XXIV, No. 3, August, 1958.

chapter six

PROBLEMS IN THE WORLD OF WORK*

Most of us expend a very large portion of the energies of our lives preparing for and participating in the world of work in our society. If business, industry, agriculture, public service, the professions and, in general, the search for and use of the dollar are not the most important concerns of our lives, they are very nearly so. Naturally, then, many of the problems of our society and its people are involved in, or related to, this enormous world of work. The seven articles which follow, selected and edited by Dr. Hanns W. Lungstrass, represent some parts of that world in Canada, and indicate some of the problems which we face in these areas.

In his outline of "The Power Structure in Canadian Society" John Porter sets the stage for the subsequent selections by highlighting the fact that in Canadian society, more than in many other societies, the *corporate leaders* have a "pre-eminent place in the structure of power". In perceiving the relative distribution of "power" between these leaders and other important segments of the system (labour, government, etc.), we are better prepared to understand the causes and the consequences of disorganization in the general world of work.

Another salient background factor concerns the rapid changes which are occurring in our means of production, and the implications of adjustment and failure to adjust to these changes. In a selection from a much longer article

---

*This chapter was compiled and edited by a specialist in this area, Dr. Hanns W. Lungstrass of the Department of Sociology at the University of Alberta, Edmonton. Ultimate responsibility for format and selections, however, rests with the editor.

(actually originally a speech) by Eugene Forsey we have an introduction to some of the problems which may be inherent with the advent of technological change, especially as it relates to labour. A specific problem representing a *lag* in technological change and adjustment in the world of work is illustrated in a recent newspaper report of "sweatshop" conditions in a Toronto ethnic community. Long hours, low wages and a dearth of modern employment benefits and amenities still characterize the current "sweatshop" just as they did throughout much of the industrial world around the turn of the century.

The next three articles are concerned with various aspects of organized labour, first showing how its traditional "ultimate weapon" — the strike — is losing much of its potency in the modern world. An article from *The Financial Post* describes the sometimes strong but generally limited effects of a long strike occurring in a small community. A *Saturday Night* editorial follows with a discussion of the strike as "A Failing Weapon".

"Are Canadian Unions Dominated By Americans?" Norman DePoe assesses the situation as of 1959, considering arguments on both sides of the question and, in doing so, raising some of the more important issues which face organized labour on the one hand (the unions), and "business" on the other.

The final selection in this chapter is a sociological analysis of "The Place of the Professions in the Urban Community", by Oswald Hall. The section which Professor Lungstrass has chosen for inclusion here deals specifically with the "troubles" which professionals have in our society and implies a variety of related problems which our society now faces, and will face increasingly, as we become more and more an urbanized nation.

28. THE POWER STRUCTURE IN
CANADIAN SOCIETY*

John Porter†

We should at the outset make clear what we are talking about when we discuss the structure of power in Canadian society. Power is decision-making. Of course everyone makes decisions between alternative choices of action and therefore has power. The decisions that some people make however, are socially important and far-reaching. These socially far-reaching decisions are not all made through self-interest, and even when they are there is a social necessity that some people be put to work at the controlling centre of our complex social machinery.

In an advanced industrial society there is a division of labour between institutions. There is both independence and interdependence between economic, political, military, bureaucratic and ideological institutions. Each of these has specific social functions and each has its own leadership. Those who head these institutions can be designated as institutional elites. It is these institutional elites who are the major decision-makers, the holders of power. In some institutional systems there is a measure of responsibility of elites to a membership base, for example, directors to shareholders, union leaders to rank and file, political leaders to the electorate. From such responsibility it does not follow that the membership participates in the major decision-making process. There are various mechanisms, secrecy for example, to keep the membership out and only very seldom are efforts made to elicit the opinion, needs and desires of the membership. The check to the power of one elite group comes from other elites, not from its membership.

The decisions that institutional elites make determine the kind of society we have. Even more important is their control over the future. The analysis of power requires the identification of institutional elites, an analysis of their social composition, the career systems which govern their recruitment, their inter-relations and the values and philosophies which support the existing structure of power.

The term power has a conspiratorial flavour about it, and tends therefore to contradict our social values. Democratic political theory suggests that power is diffused through all members of society and where demo-

*From *Canadian Public Administration*, Vol. VI, No. 2, June 1963.
†Mr. Porter is Professor of Sociology at Carleton University, Ottawa.

cratic political systems exist the problems of power are solved. Because of a distaste for conspiracy we shy away from the subject of power. Because we sometimes think that a state of affairs is brought about simply by asserting that it exists, we very rarely put our democratic society up for critical examination.

The conspiratorial aspect of power can be set aside quite easily. People in positions of power do not have to conspire. The power roles which they occupy are part of a system of power which is viewed as legitimate by most members of the society. Directors and managers of large corporations make decisions about the major productive resources of our society because the members of that society view it as legitimate that they do so. It would be quite wrong for example to assign a conspiratorial role to the directors of Argus Corporation. This great industrial complex has been built up through procedures which the society views as quite acceptable and, even in the one instance where a charge of conspiracy was made, the case of Canadian Breweries, the courts, the final arbiters of what is legitimate, held that the behaviour of this Argus-controlled corporation was not against the public interest. Not only do we view the behaviour of these corporate officials as legitimate, we award them particular social honours. We make them governors of our institutions of higher learning, we make them the directors of almost all our associations devoted to cultural activities. The success of organized philanthropy is in their hands. If they own racehorses, they border on the celebrity world and entertain royalty. As we have seen recently, they even step into the political directorate, although the example of Senator McCutcheon was a reversal of the normal flow from cabinet office to corporation directorships. The corporate elite to whom the society accords such a high status could scarcely be considered conspirators against it.

Where does this sense of legitimacy come from? In a large measure it comes from the logic of the capitalist economy. The appeal of capitalism is not what it produces, for surely it never produces to capacity, but rather the appeal is in the logic of capitalist behaviour, or free-enterprise if that is a preferred term, as the behaviour has become systematized in economic and social theory. As with all social theories, we must ask whether the theory is no more than a rationalization of a particular kind of behaviour, or whether it is an objective theory independent of the phenomenon which it accounts for and against which behaviour can be judged. I do not propose to deal with this problem, but one can point out for example the failure of anti-combine legislation to prevent the increasing concentration of economic power. Anti-combines legislation has its roots in the liberal doctrines of laissez-faire. As industrial capitalism has become transformed into highly concentrated activity with centralized control, anti-combines legislation becomes suspect because it is thought to prevent the benefits of large scale production. The pressure is now mounting for what is called a "rationalization" of the Canadian economy, that is, a setting aside of some provisions of the anti-combines legislation to permit firms to merge their activities even more than they have during the last ten years of spectacular mergers and take-overs. I am not competent to judge the economic benefits which are thought to accrue as a result of these changes — I am somewhat skeptical of them — but I am concerned about the problems of power which they raise. On the question of social power, economics has little to say.

In addition to the logic of the capitalist economy other elements of social thought contribute to the legitimacy of the power of the corporate elite. One is the idea of property and ownership. There was a time when psychologists thought that the desire to own or to acquire was an inherited instinct, a proposition which, all too frequently, they inferred from watching squirrels collect nuts. More recently, the opposite view has been held, that the traits which human beings exhibit are acquired from the particular cultures in which they live. There are acquisitive societies and not so acquisitive ones. There is no doubt that property ownership in the United States is equated with the good life, indeed placed in the American constitution along with life and liberty. The ownership of personal belongings and, to a lesser extent, houses and cars is about the only experience of ownership that the vast majority of Canadians have had. However, the fact that ownership of at least something has been experienced by everybody makes it psychologically acceptable to vest the ownership of a society's major productive instruments in private hands. Private or corporate ownership of productive instruments is supported with almost the same arguments as is private ownership of houses and cars.

It is curious that in Canada where such a small minority of individuals or families have ownership rights in the major productive instruments of the society the legitimacy of corporate power should rest in part on this evaluation of property. Foreign ownership is only one aspect of this problem. Canada has such a small middle level investing class that corporate ownership has never become diffused. "People's capitalism" is now one of the image-labels attached to the American economy. The image may fit the facts there but in Canada it does not.

There are other ways in which the relationship between ownership and social structure can be shown. That is by examining the controlling interest in Canada's major corporations which are responsible for a very impressive proportion of all business activity in the country. A large number of these are wholly- or majority-owned subsidiaries of foreign parent corporations. There is little or no Canadian ownership participation in them. Large corporations in which there is Canadian participation can be arranged in categories according to whether or not the stock is closely held. Some are privately owned with no important stockholding by the Canadian public; some are controlled by majority ownership with small Canadian participation; some are minority controlled through an important minority block of stock.

Certain social benefits are said to result from the diffusion of stockholding. There may be some substance in these claims although of some of them I am dubious. One of these benefits lies in the fiduciary role of directors and managers. Their behaviour and decision-making is supposedly tempered by the existence of a large membership base of shareholders. In some discussions this fiduciary role is extended beyond the membership to the entire society. They are the custodians of the society's productive instruments and as such are restrained by the society's norms and values. This fiduciary role contrasts sharply with the identification of ownership and power during the period of the great tycoons or the robber barons. Along with widespread ownership goes a critical financial journalism and a much more extensive disclosure of corporate actions to the public. I doubt that these restraints operate effectively in Canada. The point is illustrated I think by the ease with which take-overs and mergers are accomplished. In none of them, except perhaps the St. Lawrence Corporation, has there been a proxy battle worthy of the name. When stock is closely held, decisions about take-over bids are made by a very small number of shareholders. There is little point in dissident shareholders mounting a proxy battle. The recent offer of Shell to the shareholders of Canadian Oil Co. had to wait until the largest shareholder, the Power Corporation of Canada, made up its mind. Relatively few people participate in the decision-making in the major productive industries of the society. Moreover the corporate elite is national with the growth of the nationwide corporations. Its smallness facilitates communication and its homogeneity in terms of the social background of its members provides for common outlook, attitudes and values.

I would then give a pre-eminent place in the structure of power in Canadian society to Canada's corporate leaders. Yet this does not mean that they have it all to themselves. Their power is challenged and in some measure circumscribed by the power of other elites. Within the economic system there is the power of organized labour, although I do not think that in Canada that power is nearly as great as some would make out. Of all institutional elites, labour leaders have the greatest difficulty in legitimating their power roles. They come closest to being looked upon as criminal conspirators, and the reason I think is that their historic role has been to interfere with the sanctity of property. Perhaps they are suspected of conspiracy because the popular press deals only with the breakdowns in industrial relations and says little about the peaceful nature of the collective bargaining process. No one would dispute that labour leaders have power in establishing wage rates and conditions of work in those industries in which they are strong. But what of their social power, their ability, that is, to give shape and sub-stance to our social order? We do not give labour leaders honorary degrees, nor do they govern philanthropy and culture, or slip through the Senate into the political directorate. Nor do they take part in deci-sions to abandon one community and invest in another. They have not, like Sidney Hillman and Walter Reuther, had an influence on the political leaders of their day. Canada has never produced through the union movement a political leader of any stature.

It is fairly easy to find explanations for this limited power role of the labour elite. Market or business unionism has been the dominant theme of the internationals rather than social movement unionism which sees the goals of working class organization to lie beyond the market place and to apply to a much wider social context. Some structural features of the government of the internationals have placed the Cana-dian leadership out of the control of the Canadian membership. There are some important exceptions among the internationals, particularly the industrial unions. It is these, formerly associated with the old Canadian Congress of Labour, which have some social movement philosophy about them. These are the unions with a high degree of Canadian auto-nomy and with the major national union, the C.B.R.T., they form a formidable *avant-garde* within the Canadian Labour Congress. Old traditions and prejudices, however, are not so easily jettisoned. In any case the present posture of the C.L.C. towards political action may have come too late. It seems likely that the apogee of labour organization has been reached at about one-third of the non-agricultural labour force. Basic changes in Canadian occupational structure have created two new classes of underprivileged workers, the lower white collar clerical worker, and the unskilled off-farm migrant. Neither of these groups has any marketable skills to protect through market or business unionism. The political education of the C.L.C. is unlikely to reach these two large groups. One of the splits that runs through organized labour is the separation of a large number of French-Canadian workers from the main body. There has been a long-standing hostility to international unionism in Quebec. The present C.S.N. unions are led in the main by intellectuals and they have brought a social movement concept into their operations. In many respects they are several steps ahead of the membership and on election night go to bed stunned by Quebec support for Social Credit. I would say then that organized labour has too many structural faults to be an effective system of power to counter the power of other elites in the society.

29. TECHNOLOGICAL CHANGE — A PROBLEM FOR LABOUR*

Eugene Forsey†

From my long past academic days, I know that the proper way to begin discussing this subject is to define my terms. I shall conform to the proprieties so far as to say that by "technological change" I mean all kinds of technological change, including automation; and by "Labour" I mean organized Labour. If I really tried to define technological change, I should find myself in the position of Dr. Johnson's straw man who defined a cow as "animal quadrupes ruminans," "Sir, 'cow' is clearer!" As for unorganized labour, I have no doubt technological change is a problem for it as well as for us; indeed, I have no doubt it is a far worse problem; but the only solution I can offer them is to get organized.

Technological change is a problem for Labour for three main reasons: it destroys jobs which workers have; creates jobs which they may not be able to take; and may not create enough new jobs.

Technological change can destroy jobs by destroying a whole industry.

*From *Labour Gazette*, Vol. 57, 1957.
†Dr. Forsey is Director of Research for the Canadian Labour Congress, Ottawa.

It destroyed the carriage and wagon industry, the coal oil lamp industry, the horseshoeing industry, the harness industry and the wooden ship-building industry. It is destroying the circus industry.

It can also destroy an industry, or part of an industry, in a particular region or country. It appears to be destroying a good deal of the Canadian coal industry. It may, if automation gets thoroughly launched in some big American industries, destroy more than one Canadian industry, because production in the United States will become so fantastically cheap that it simply will not be worth while for an American firm to run a branch plant in Canada, and no Canadian firm will be able to compete without a tarriff higher than the customers will stand.

But even without destroying a whole industry or part of an industry, technological change can destroy jobs by destroying occupations within an industry. It can destroy the skilled worker's job by making his skill obsolete. It can destroy the unskilled worker's job by simply handing it over to a machine which will do it faster, cheaper and better.

Fortunately technological change also creates jobs by creating new industries. It created the automobile industry, and so enormously enlarged the rubber industry, the oil industry, the steel industry, the road construction industry and a dozen other tributaries. It created the electric power and electrical apparatus industries, the movie industry, the radio and television industries, the steel shipbuilding industry, and the aeroplane industry. It is creating the atomic energy industry, as well as new chemical industries.

It can also create jobs without creating a new industry. It can create jobs for skilled workers by creating needs for new skills. It can create jobs for unskilled workers by creating machine-minding work.

Even assuming that enough new jobs are created to replace those destroyed, and to allow for the normal additions to the labour force, all jobs are not the same. The ones created may be considerably or totally different from those destroyed, and may be in different parts of the country. Matching the available jobs and the available workers may be no small task with technological change proceeding at its present pace. I think I can go further, and say that it will be no small task. Its size will not be reduced by the fact that a firm which contemplates introducing automation may well find that it is cheaper to build a completely new plant in a new place than to try to automate the old one, or to build the new one nearby. The old plant may have been where it was chiefly because there were plenty of workers available there. But the new plant may need very few workers; the skilled ones may all have to be trained or retrained from scratch; and the firm may feel that it is a golden opportunity to get away from traffic problems and perhaps from unions, to where beyond these voices there is peace.

The location of new jobs is particularly important in a country like Canada. In Britain, if an old job disappears in Manchester and a new one appears in London, the worker's actual costs of transportation are not very heavy; and after his move, he finds himself in an environment that is, on the whole, familiar. The law, the school system, the municipal institutions, most other institutions, and the written language are the same, and the spoken language near enough to be intelligible with a little practice. But in Canada, if an old job disappears in Three Rivers and a new one appears in Kitimat, it is nearly impossible for the worker to move. Just getting there costs him a small fortune; and when he does get there, almost the whole environment is unfamiliar. The civil law, the school system, the municipal institutions, most other social institutions, and the language are different.

This problem of the location of new jobs may be especially difficult for Quebec, for several reasons. The first is that even now Quebec is not providing enough jobs for its people. Its percentage of unemployment is chronically higher than the national average, and much higher than Ontario's, and the spread has on the whole been getting wider since the end of the war.

Second, technological change probably means less need, proportionately at any rate, for unskilled workers, and more need for workers who either have the necessary skills or can acquire them quickly because they have the knowledge of elementary science and mathematics. This is likely to work against Quebec since there is even less science and mathematics taught in the schools of Quebec than in those of other provinces. This is changing but for the time being, and for a while ahead, the new automated plants are more likely to be set up elsewhere.

Third, Quebec workers get less pay than workers in Ontario or the West, so the cost of moving is a bigger problem for them.

Fourth, Quebec workers' families are larger, so unless the worker is single this makes it harder for him to move.

Technological change means higher productivity. We can, and probably will, choose to take part of the gain in the form of shorter hours. But we may choose to take much, or most, of it in the form of extra goods and services, especially services. There are still a great many people even in Canada, with the second highest standard of living in the world, who are going short of things we like to think of as commonplace: decent housing, modern household facilities. We could do with a lot more schools, more hospitals, more roads, more parks. Most of us, even in Canada, are a very long way from having even all the modern conveniences that already exist, let alone the new ones technological change is making possible. We are a long way from being as healthy as we could be, or as well educated; a long way from having all the literature and art and music and travel we could enjoy. We are a long way from having all the fun we could. And even if we arrive fairly soon at the point where we feel we have enough of everything we can think of wanting, there are people in the hungry two-thirds of the world who are not going to run out of wants in a hurry.

30. SWEATSHOPS STILL PART
OF CANADIAN INDUSTRY*

Frank Drea†

The ghost of the sweatshop still hangs over Toronto's Little Italy, casting its shadow over thousands of women.

Hundreds of teen-age girls, wives, mothers, and widows will bring home as little as $55 for two weeks' work in small garment shops, knit goods firms, textile producers and cleaning plants.

Most of them have never had a paid holiday. Sickness is a disaster because only those who work are paid. Most know they are "cheap labor" but are almost reconciled to this as a way of life for Italian immigrants.

"These things don't happen to Canadians," shrugged a young wife whose last two weeks at work (80 hours) brought her $60.08.

Nobody but an Italian would be made to work for so little. But there is no alternative for women whose husbands often bring home less than $50 for a week's work in a factory. Tax receipts showing an immigrant factory hand earned as little as $2,138 for 52 weeks' labor are not uncommon.

---

*From the Toronto Telegram News Service, July 1963.
†Mr. Drea is Assistant Public Relations Director of the United Steelworkers of America (Canada).

Low pay and the language barrier compress them into an almost ghetto-like existence where three or four families squeeze into houses intended for a single family. Houses are generally clean and well cared for but there is an atmosphere of oppression, misery and constant fear — of sickness, old age, or loss of job.

There is also the fear that any stranger is someone sent by employers to ferret out the discontented. One family even drew the blinds for fear someone would see them talking about their jobs.

"I worked a whole year for $700 but last year was better because I made $1,100," said a young woman who emigrated from Sicily to work in a small textile plant.

"If the Government wanted to protect us, it could," said a factory worker, who has been unable to work for three weeks.

"I worked in one plant for three years at 90 cents an hour but I told them I had to get more money because I had to support a wife. The foreman went out into the street and hired another Italian for 75 cents. How can you fight that?"

The Department of Labor said the new minimum wage of 85 cents an hour for women and $1 for men is "a start against exploitation" of immigrants. It said its safety laws are being rewritten.

"There is no law in the world that says a person has to be paid for a holiday," a department spokesman said. "There is no legislation governing how hard a person must work."

31. *WHEN BIG STRIKE HITS SMALL TOWN**

The Financial Post

What happens in a town of 4,000 population when the main industry is closed by a long strike?

Who wins? Who loses? Who's caught in the middle?

How long does it take small business to get back to normal?

On Oct. 31, 1957, the plant of Canadian Gypsum Ltd., in Windsor,

---

*From *The Financial Post*, March 19, 1960.

Nova Scotia, went out on strike. The strike ended 14 months later, on Nov. 20, 1958.

Now 16 months after the end of the strike, most retailers agree that it took at least another year for Windsor to get back on its business feet. The strike also affected trade patterns — a change that some business-men still feel now.

Besides Canadian Gypsum, the town has two other big employers: Nova Scotia Textiles Ltd., and Gypsum, Lime & Alabastine Canada Ltd. They both worked steadily during the strike.

Most businesses contacted reported at least a 20% loss during the strike period — and it was growing progressively worse when the strike ended. Affected most were jewelry stores, service stations and automobile dealers. Some auto agencies had a 40% drop in new and used car sales. The buying slowdowns spread slowly from strikers to non-striking workers. Even families with steady pay cheques started to curtail spending.

"A sort of creeping paralysis," one businessman called it.

Strangely enough, two businesses had a noticeable increase during the strike, but it dropped to normal when the strike ended. Imperial Theatre of the B & L chain had a 10% increase in patrons. "Probably because people had more spare time," says management. The Windsor Diner, a small lunch counter in the business district, did a big extra business. Says the manager: "We sold more T-bones than in a long time. Mostly to Mounties, visiting union men and reporters."

Almost every customer is a friend in a small town. This makes for a different kind of business relationship. In strike-bound Windsor, there were few repossessions of cars, furniture or appliances, although in most cases payments were slow or stopped entirely. Most firms had the same attitude: "We'll be doing business with the same people later."

Some dealers continued time payments themselves and made arrange-ments with finance companies to extend terms. In most cases, customers have paid off debts — and bought new cars and appliances. J. Reigh Barnes, insurance and real estate agent, says:

"I paid car insurance premiums myself when customers fell behind. I didn't lose a nickel, and it actually helped me, because some other agents cancelled policies. After the strike it took some of my customers about eight months to get squared away."

The local office of a mail order firm reported no noticeable drop in sales. "Perhaps because people were shopping more carefully." Town officials told *The Financial Post* that, in the strike year, more than 95%

of taxes had been collected. A taxi driver found that business declined about 15%, and it never has come back.

Lowell Getson, Canadian Tire dealer, took over management of his store in the middle of the strike. He says: "Sales showed an increase over the previous year. I just worked that much harder to make up for any possible loss.

Clay Church, owner of Church Electrics Ltd., an appliance and furniture store says: "We didn't repossess a thing. We even repaired appliances, although sometimes there wasn't much chance of payment for a long time. With a dead TV screen, people would have been less inclined than ever to pay for the set. We were also thinking of future good will."

In credit, the smaller grocery stores felt the strain most, but most have been paid back in full. Hants Wholesalers Ltd. extended credit to retail customers caught in the squeeze. The wholesale grocery firm says volume during the strike period was normal, and that its customers have paid all strike debts.

The strike balance sheet:

Before the strike, the average wage at Canadian Gypsum was $1.34 an hour. Now it's $1.60.

Payroll loss of 125 workers: About $1¼ million.

Small businessmen suffered just about as badly as the strikers themselves.

"No one gained anything," was the way one Windsor man put it.

32. *A FAILING WEAPON**

Saturday Night

From its earliest beginnings, organized labor has held to the strike as its ultimate weapon. With this weapon, labor has won impressive victories and obtained, both for itself and for others, remarkable gains. It is no more than fair to say that the gains won by the militancy of labor have spread across the whole of Canadian society. Much of the higher incomes,

*From *Saturday Night*, (Editorial), April 28, 1962.

self-respect and human decency which Canadians enjoy is the direct result of the willingness of a relative few to walk a picket line.

But while a strike is still the ultimate weapon, it no longer is necessarily either an appropriate or an effective one. Two recent events provide illustration. For almost a year, the Hotel and Club Employees' Union struck the Royal York Hotel in Toronto. Final settlement gave the union, in effect, nothing more than the CPR had first offered. The only gain for the union was the essentially negative one of having most of its striking members rehired after the company had said it would rehire no more than half the strikers if a settlement should be agreed upon.

Here, the strike was an ineffective weapon. It did not prevent the Royal York from operating — indeed it caused only a short interruption in regular service. It did, however, create a great deal of embarrassment and considerable ill-will, particularly when the hotel fired the strikers, and it resulted in some loss of business. But because the union was small and the company big, the strike was not a success.

The second event was the strike threatened by employees of the Ontario Hydro Electric Power Commission. The union set a strike deadline, management announced it would run the service without the employees and, at the last minute, the provincial government said it wouldn't permit a strike.

It was bluff and counter-bluff, the Government having no choice but to save face for everyone. No one thought for an instant that the workers would strike or that management actually could run the system without the workers or that the Government could permit a strike. Here, the strike was an inappropriate weapon; it never could have been used.

There is a further complication, one which will become increasingly important. To continue as effective units, unions must reach white-collar workers — those persons who have traditionally associated themselves with management privileges. To these people the notion of "going on strike" is abhorrent. As David Archer, president of the Ontario Federation of Labor, observed recently, these workers might be more interested in unionism if they were certain there would be no strikes.

Even where strikes have been most effective — big, powerful unions fighting equally big, powerful companies — the realization is growing that they are losing their value. William Mahoney, Canadian director of the United Steelworkers of America, said recently that strikes have become more difficult to conduct and the cost to the workers and union treasury is high.

The fact is, of course, that the strike is as out of place in today's society as the 60-hour week it eliminated. It is economically wasteful, it invariably costs strikers more than they gain if it lasts more than a few weeks and the general benefits it now produces are minimal. The strike is an anachronism. Like the lockout, it symbolizes the belief that labor and management are enemies; it is the very symbol of anachronistic thinking.

Not that strikes should be illegal. But it is obvious that they are not the answer to an increasing number of labor disputes. That they are held out as weapons in every dispute, shows a distressing ossification of labor's thinking. The danger to unions is that Canadians, seeing the inability of labor to adapt to changing conditions, will accede to the demands of anti-labor groups and impose solutions damaging to the legitimate interests of organized labor.

33. *ARE CANADIAN UNIONS DOMINATED BY AMERICANS?**

Norman DePoe†

With 1958 and victory over "hold the line" just behind it, organized labor — particularly big international labor — faces a new kind of struggle in 1959.

The recent curbs on union activity imposed by the Newfoundland and British Columbia legislatures are backed up by a measurable swing both in the climate of public opinion and in the tone and temper of many public statements.

Opinion — as evinced by the kind of random sampling available to a travelling reporter — is less favorable to unions than it has been for at least a decade. Entirely apart from the criticism that businessmen have been making for years, one now encounters forthright satements from both white and blue-collar workers to the effect that "the unions have gone too far."

---

*From *Saturday Night*, June 6, 1959.
†Mr. DePoe is National Affairs Reporter for the Canadian Broadcasting Corporation and is well known for his radio and television presentations.

Particularly in the Maritimes and parts of the Prairies, comment of this kind is volunteered freely. And while most of it comes from men and women in non-union jobs, some of it stems from hitherto silent rank-and-file members of the unions themselves.

"The unions did a lot of good in the beginning," one middle-aged member said last month. "But now all they want is domination. They're trying to take over management."

Such individual expressions of feeling are coupled with new moves aimed at rewriting our present labor legislation. Oscar R. Olson, president of the B.C. division of the Canadian Manufacturers' Association, praises what he called the "courageous action" of the provincial legislature in limiting picketing and making unions legal entities able to prosecute or be prosecuted. He urged Premier Bennett to consider other moves that would "create an atmosphere which will attract industrial investors." And in Toronto, Frank Burnett, industrial relations manager for Canadian Industries Ltd., has predicted that management might seek to abolish the dues checkoff if unions contribute to a new political party.

Labor leaders have recognized the swing in opinion — but they question how wide it really is. President Claude Jodoin of the Canadian Labor Congress admits that there has been a noticeable increase both in the sharpness and volume of criticism. He ascribes this to a "Madison Avenue type PR campaign," which he says has seized on such elements as the United States Senate investigation of James R. Hoffa and recent price increases to build a "distorted" picture.

Both the CLC and its member unions will continue to answer individual charges which they feel are specifically harmful. But they plan no general campaign to alter public opinion in their favor. Besides expressing considerable doubt as to how many people are actually behind the criticism, Mr. Jodoin says: "We're like the politician who has given good government and wants to continue in office. We stand on our record."

The fact is that, despite the critics, the membership of both purely Canadian and internationally-affiliated unions continues to increase. Even the embattled Teamsters' Brotherhood, according to the records of the Ontario Labor Relations Board, picked up more than 1000 members last year in that province. This, of course, was exactly the period when public excoriation of International President James Hoffa was at its height.

A still bigger increase was registered by District 50 of the United Mine Workers — a sort of labor counterpart of the modern tendency of big business to diversify. District 50 includes no mine workers. Instead, it organizes construction workers, bakeries, shoe factories, or any other group of unorganized employees. Just as a skilled management team may buy up or start new industries, District 50 is in the business of supplying skilled negotiators, legal advice, and so on.

It has, in fact, been so successful that western Canada — once part of its jurisdiction — has been split off to form a new district of UMW.

While the unions continue to expand, their critics are concentrating on several main aspects of labor activity or organization. Many of the animadversions levelled at the unions have been dismissed long ago as pure mythology by labor leaders. Mythology or no, they appear to persist — the strongest group at the moment are accusations that international unionism means American control. The adjective "undesirable" is usually implied.

Perhaps the commonest of the charges is that international labor executives may force Canadian workers to adopt policies or make wage demands unsuitable in Canada generally, or against the Canadian member's own best interest.

The just-concluded dispute between the major railways and the Brotherhood of Locomotive Firemen and Enginemen is a case in point. Here, both sides professed to see outside influence in a struggle which would clearly affect similar negotiations in the United States at a later date.

There were unofficial, but darkly suspicious, suggestions from pro-labor groups that the big railroads in the U.S. had somehow persuaded Canada's railways — one of them publicly-owned — to fight a sort of advance skirmish on their behalf. On the other side, pro-management speakers and writers continually read some sinister import into the visits of the international president of the firemen to Canada for conferences with W. E. Gamble, the Canadian head of the brotherhood.

Railway officials simply point out one fact: the Canadian contracts covering the use of firemen on freight and yard diesels expired before the American ones; from their point of view it was merely sound management to negotiate for the elimination of jobs they felt had become superfluous. And the union feels that criticism would be far more justified if an international president had *not* come to Canada to look into a situation threatening the jobs of many of the rank and file. The anti-management charges, which were never elevated to the level of public statements, are now dying; but one still occasionally hears aggrieved comment on the international conferences among the firemen.

A still more self-contradictory situation has arisen within a single union: the much-publicized teamsters. Members of Local 514 in Alberta actually supported their employers in a decertification action. Their reason: the local, under a Hoffa-appointed trustee at the time of the hearing, had refused to accept a contract which the rank and file found acceptable, and was holding out for too much.

Almost simultaneously, there was another rank-and-file rebellion in Ontario's big Local 938. The reason: the executive, headed by a Hoffa-endorsed president, had settled with the Automotive Transport Association of Ontario for what the rebels said was too little!

Labor's principal answer to charges of American domination — aside from pointing to the constitution of their unions, which stipulate considerable local control in most cases — is to suggest that they are merely fighting fire with fire. Many of their negotiations are with United States companies. Arthur Williams, regional director of District 50 of UMW, says he has initialled scores of contracts on which the other signature was that of an industrial relations expert from the other side of the border.

"Why," he asks, "shouldn't we belong to an outfit just as big, which can supply us with negotiators as skilled and broad in views as the men on the company side of the table?"

Nowadays, in fact, this works both ways. During 1958, at least a dozen skilled Canadian negotiators found themselves dealing with disputes in the United States, much as an executive of a Canadian subsidiary may be promoted to head office.

Another firmly-rooted suspicion is that Canadian dues are drained off into a U.S. treasury for the benefit of the American section of the union. In the case of the Teamsters, Canadian director I. M. (Casey) Dodds denies this categorically. Per capita tax to the international, he says, goes out monthly in the form of a cheque drawn on the Canadian Bank of Commerce. It is endorsed in Washington, and mailed right back to the same bank in Toronto, for Canadian use.

The U.A.W. also defends the over-the-border payment. In this case, the extra money goes to Detroit to build up the international strike fund to a total of $25,000,000. Approximately 54,000 Canadians will have contributed almost $450,000 by the time the goal is reached.

Past history, the union says, shows an ultimate balance which is, if anything, in favor of Canadian members. In 1955, for instance, Canadian members paid $1,200,000 into the strike fund, while the international paid out $2,610,000 in Canada in support of a lengthy strike. This of course leads to an opposite charge: that international unions may use their financial power to support strikes in Canada for objectives the union could not reach if it depended on Canadian funds only.

This round-robin of criticism is almost exactly paralleled by a similar set of mutually-contradictory charges against international business: First, that profits are drained off from Canada into the pockets of U.S. shareholders. To which the company reply is that these are only a small fraction of sometimes massive investment; that profits are often put back into further expansion in Canada, and that in any case, the company creates far more wealth in this country than it takes out. And to which the anti-business opposite charge is raised that big American firms can use their financial power to compete unfairly with Canadian enterprise.

Stripped of the words "Business" and "labor," these grievances become, in many views, almost indistinguishable facets of another, and more general, phenomenon: rising Canadian nationalism and its uglier corollary, anti-Americanism.

While the arguments — even in some of their newer aspects — are familiar ones, it is evident that the balance of opinion about them has swung, and may still be swinging. Both labor leaders and observers of the labor-management scene look for further attempts to curb what business has long regarded as excessive union power. The main targets appear to be featherbedding, picketing, secondary boycotts, and perhaps "pattern" bargaining for master contracts. Labor leaders are girding themselves to deal with any specific attempts to pass legislation which they regard as unduly restrictive or undemocratic. There may be a test in B.C. of the new clause prohibiting "unfair" lists. But on the whole, the attitude is that of CLC President Jodoin: to stand on the record, and to go on signing up new members. For so long as the ranks of unions swell, a vague public opinion will not deter their leaders. What counts, as Hoffa and his like know, is money in the bank and action in the locals. But the fight, if there is a fight, will involve the public in a big way.

34. *THE PLACE OF THE PROFESSIONS IN THE URBAN COMMUNITY**

Oswald Hall†

The growth and spread of the professions is a salient feature of modern urban life. Urban living centres in work, in specialized occupations. Professions are specialized occupations, but specialized in a distinctive way. They provide services that in the normal pattern of events are used only on highly infrequent occasions by the majority of their clients. (Perhaps only once in a whole lifetime does a client require a surgeon to remove an appendix, a minister to marry him, or a lawyer to draw up a will.)

Historically the most respected professions have been medicine, law, and the priesthood. (The army, also with long-established claims, is excluded for the purposes of this discussion of urban life.) Over recent decades these have been supplemented by others: by a range of newer professions, by some premature professions, by some pseudo-professions, and by some lowly occupations eager to lift themselves so as to share in the prestige that the professions enjoy. This expansion of the professions in the urban environment is a complicated affair, involving three main currents of growth. There has been an expansion of the older professions and a consequent splintering into more specialized forms; new professions have arisen through the provision of services based on previously unused knowledge; and there has been a great deal of activity among occupations aroused by an admiration of the ancient professions and attempting to model themselves upon them with greater or lesser success.

If one proceeds to study this growth with reference to census data, it is clear that the growth has been an uneven affair. For the city of Toronto as a whole the professions, *in toto*, as listed in the census, have been growing faster than has the total working force of the community. Between the years 1931 and 1951, the total working force in the metropolitan area grew by approximately 80 per cent; for the professions listed the growth has been approximately 95 per cent. However, this growth has not been evenly distributed among the older and newer types of professions. The census includes nursing and school teaching (which have been largely the

*From Clark, S. D. (ed.), *Urbanism and the Changing Canadian Society*, Toronto, University of Toronto Press, 1961.
†Dr. Hall is Professor of Sociology at the University of Toronto.

preserve of women) among the professions and shows these to have grown over the two decades at approximately the same rate as has the total working force. The same pattern of growth appears for the classical masculine professions, law and medicine. (For the priesthood, there has been negligible growth, much less than for the working force at large.) Hence among both men and women there is a pattern of modest growth for the older professions, roughly the same as the growth for the working force in general.

On the other hand, there is a much more pronounced rate of growth for the professions on the newer fringes. Thus for men in the category of "draughtsmen and designers" the numbers have increased from approximately 800 to 2,800 in the two decades, an increase of 250 per cent; for women, the category of "authors, editors and journalists" has climbed from 120 to 360, an increase of 200 per cent. For both men and women the modest average changes in all professions conceal much larger changes in a few professions.

From the above discussion it should be clear the professions represent a very lively part of the occupational world. Among them several kinds of competitive struggles are occurring simultaneously. There is a struggle going on at the borders between professions; within specific professions, there are struggles between different kinds of people striving to gain a foothold therein or to maintain a foothold there. New professions are challenging old ones, some of which, indeed, may be shuffling off the scene.

This lively character of the professions poses numerous serious problems for the various kinds of people who try to record the numerical changes occurring among occupations. Within relatively short periods of time completely new species may arise. It is not surprising, therefore, that the occupations which the census lists under the heading of "professions" should differ somewhat from those which a sociologist would so classify. The census excludes some occupations which come close to the fringe of being professional in nature and includes some of doubtful credentials. It includes doctors and nurses in the health field; it also makes a place for chiropractors and osteopaths, even though the latter two practitioners may be considered non-professional by the doctors and nurses. On the other hand, it does not include undertakers, whose trade begins precisely at the point where that of the doctor ends; and similarly it excludes pharmacists who not only are recognized by doctors as having an important role in the healing process, but are taught (as are undertakers) in universities, and on occasion by doctors themselves. Along with priests and clergymen, representing the most ancient of professions, the census finds a place for nuns and lay brothers, yet neither group necessarily is engaged in work that can be called professional. Similarly, on the fringe of law, one finds that judges and magistrates are included; however, even though these may at one time in their careers have been lawyers, they belong, for the moment, in the category of dignitaries who preside over special institutions rather than in the class of people who render some sort of professional service.

PROFESSIONALS AND THEIR TROUBLES

It is the highly visible prestige accorded to the established professions that makes them so attractive to many occupations in our society which are, by contrast, relatively formless and in many cases somewhat unsatisfying to the practitioners thereof. On the other hand, there is an anomaly here. Precisely at the time when a large number of occupations are attempting to ape the model of the established professions, the latter find themselves in deep trouble. Many of them find themselves diverging far from their historic model, while others find it progressively difficult to approach that model.

By way of illustration, census data indicate that the old independent professions are giving up fee practice and are turning to salaried practice. The census for 1951 indicates that of the 1,632 physicians and surgeons in the Toronto area more than one-third are listed as "wage earners." Among notaries and lawyers the proportion working for salary or wages is somewhat higher. This means that in these old historic professions a considerable proportion are not adhering to the ancient model of an independent practice by which, for a fee, they provide services for clients; rather they are providing services for a single powerful client, or for an outright employer. The model of their work lives has become less that of a profession and more that of a modern bureaucracy. (Some observers claim that the same process can be traced out with respect to the priesthood, which likewise has become enmeshed in its own bureaucratic machinery.) It is especially noteworthy that, in the case of the medical profession, this development has occurred contrary to the express wishes of the members, and in large part in spite of their active opposition.

Among Toronto architects even fewer can make a livelihood as independent practitioners dealing directly with a body of clients. Thus among them, in 1951, over 70 per cent were classified as salaried workers. It is clear that, as one of the newer crop of professionals, they are far removed from the model of independent practice. Their troubles, however, have another root. Only a small proportion of the people who build houses sense a need for the services of an architect. Builders can manage without their services entirely, or may substitute the services of a draughts-man for those of an architect. Moreover, there is not much that architects can do to establish a durable demand for their services. Hence they are seriously limited in their efforts to develop a clientele to support them financially. Architects to date have achieved very little of the success of doctors and lawyers in establishing a wide and unchallenged demand for their distinctive services.

If the architect has extraordinary difficulty in creating a demand for his services, the pharmacist has suffered from the opposite condition. Although his self-image is that of a fellow-worker of the doctor, giving specialized attention to compounding medicine for the doctor too busy to do so, fate has decided against that image. He has many people demand-ing his services, but these people require him to be the salesman of a great variety of non-medical goods, rather than a clever compounder of esoteric drugs. They view him as merely another retail merchant or salesman. Moreover, they tend to act towards him as customers rather than as clients. What is more, the genuinely professional component in his services is continually being whittled away by the transfer of the main job of compounding remedies from the pharmacist's shop to the large pharma-ceutical house. As a result, the part played in the drama of medical care by the pharmacist seems slated for a progressive decline. The road to survival requires him to become more retail merchant and less professional man. It would seem, however, that success as a retail merchant fails to compensate for the loss of prestige involved in this loss of a professional function.

When one turns attention to the position of the engineer in present-day society the model of a professional man serving a set of clients is almost totally inapplicable. Of the electrical engineers (who are the most dependent of all engineers on salaried employment in the city), the proportion in independent practice is approximately 1 per cent. The re-maining 99 per cent are strictly employees. This state of affairs has become abundantly apparent to many of the members of this occupational group. They realize not only that they are salaried workers, who are hired in large numbers by a few powerful employers, but also that collective bargaining is their appropriate relationship to their employers. However, this realization does not necessarily diminish their desire for professional status and for the prestige accorded to professional work.

For the engineer, as for the architect, the claim to professional status hinges largely on the fact the training goes on within the university setting. As noted above, this is one of the obvious attributes of the doctor and of the lawyer, whose training schools have been traditionally associated with great universities. However, the mere fact of being trained in a university setting can do little to modify the basic character of the work of an occupation. Moreover, in many cases the climate of university training may be more apparent than real. The bond between the engineering student and the university seems very tenuous when compared with that of medical and law students. There is very little of a pre-professional or extra-professional component in their training. Few engineering students follow through on their professional training by turning to graduate studies or specializing in the intellectual components of their training. The very fact that engineers in many parts of the world are trained in technical institutes rather than in universities emphasizes the incidental nature of the bond between engineering students and the university *per se*. This realization is a matter of concern to many engineers who have developed an anxiety about their professional status, and the basis on which they may legitimately continue to claim to be professionals.

Nurses, on this continent, seem to be acutely sensitive to the problems of status in their profession. One evidence of this is the degree to which, over the past decade, they have launched studies aimed at exploring the sources of their discontent with their lot. These studies are aimed mainly at discovering the various kinds of subspecializations that have sprung up in the nursing field, and the relation of these to the larger world of work.

The claim of the nurse to professional status is a peculiar one. To begin with, the nurse does not make her livelihood by serving her own set of clients as an independent practitioner. Of the 1399 women in the nursing profession in Toronto listed by the 1951 census, every last one indicated that she worked for salary or wages. Moreover, with rare exceptions, nurses are trained, not in the university setting, but in the places in which they work. Their daily work involves them in taking orders directly from the supervisors in the hospital, or in slightly less direct way from the doctors on the staffs of the hospitals. Hence, in terms of both income and work organization, nurses lack the relative independence from an employer usually associated with professional status.

On the other hand, the nurse is closely associated with the drama of dangerous illness. As in the case of the undertaker and the pharmacist, some of the aura of prestige surrounding the doctor is cast over her. In the situations which she works in a hospital setting she has a peculiar relationship to the doctor. Although she is an employee of the hospital, she is also the right-hand man of the doctor, and therefore on occasion is entrusted with responsibilities far greater than those with which she is formally entrusted. This informal arrangement permits her to share in modest fashion in the prestige allotted to the doctor.

Nursing seems to have acquired a number of distinctive anomalies. The nurse is poorly paid, but her professional orientation prevents her from engaging in collective bargaining. She has employee status, but because of her distinctive relationship to the doctor she acts at times on the basis of her own responsible judgment. She is recruited often from the lowly ranks of society, and occupies a lowly position in the hospital hierarchy, but she associates with the figures of topmost power and prestige in the hospital setting. Each of these adds a peculiar dimension to her claim to professional status, and each is the source of status anxieties on her part.

The largest category of professionals, as listed in the census, is that of teachers, who comprise over 20 per cent of the total. As noted earlier, in this field of work the men are the invaders and seem to be displacing women to some degree. This tends to divide the field in a significant way, as is seen in the fact that the teachers' organizations tend to split into a men's and a women's model. On top of this the teaching body splinters along religious lines to some degree. These divisions along sex and religion tend to blur the unity of the whole group. Indeed, within the field of teaching many members express doubts as to whether there can ever be an organized profession. They note such things as the rapid turnover in positions of many teachers, the use of teaching as a door to the marriage market on the part of many women, the subordination of teachers to government officials at the municipal and higher levels, the highly varied levels of training undergone by the members. These things are seen as obstacles to the emergence of an organized and relatively autonomous profession.

In their efforts to achieve professional status, school teachers face difficulties which are much more fundamental than the above discussion suggests. To begin with, teachers are caught in a dual bureaucracy. The model of the autonomous teacher in charge of a one-room school is becoming an anachronism. Nor is this independent model any longer a major ideal. The major goal of teachers is to find a place in the large and increasingly bureaucratized schools in the urban areas. Work in such situations approximates to that of other large bureaucracies where the objectives of efficiency, economy, and uniformity set the tone of the daily activities of the teacher. Rules, regulations, and ritualized procedures take precedence over the interests and wishes of teacher and student.

In this context the machinery of bureaucracy grows with little encouragement. Administration becomes a large element in the daily work. Some teachers find that they are almost totally immersed in administrative tasks to the exclusion of teaching *per se*. The emergence of such a bureaucratic structure is apparently one inducement to men to enter what has been largely a feminine field; they see themselves as progressively emancipated from the teaching tasks, wearing the administrator's garments rather than those of the teacher.

The bureaucracy of the school system *per se* is paralleled by the larger bureaucracy of government within which the school itself operates. Whether or not the school itself is highly bureaucratized it is almost always part of a long and firmly established bureaucracy of the province which has organized the system of schools. Although this bureaucracy seems to be remote from the local scene on which the teacher carries on his work, still it decides in large measure what shall be the content of the teacher's work; it may also carry on an inspection concerned with the quality of the work performed. The very remoteness of this second bureaucracy may add to the sense of the teacher that the control of his work is vested in centres far beyond his own competence and initiative.

The existence of this larger bureaucracy has always been something of a threat to the emergence of a teaching profession of a self-controlling sort. The matter of what services the teacher provides, and, indeed, the matter of access to the field of work, have been vested in an outside body. Thus there have been serious limitations on the emergence of a definitely organized profession for teachers. As indicated above, the newer bureaucracy of the local system poses other threats, whose character can as yet not be clearly formulated. Indeed, from both directions, teachers seem to be becoming progressively enmeshed in bureaucratic machinery rather than moving towards the model of an independent profession.

Yet another feature of the position of the teacher remains to be noted. The relation of the teacher to the client is a peculiar one. Clients do not come to the teacher as autonomous persons in need of help. In most cases they are sent to school by parents, and the exchange which goes on involves both the student and one or both parents. This triadic relationship complicates the professional relationship of teacher and student in manifold ways. The parent may attempt to usurp the position of teacher; he may ally himself with the teacher against the student; he may ally himself firmly with the student against the teacher; or the two parents may split into separate camps and further complicate the professional role of the teacher. In general, one can say that the existence of any third party in the relationship poses very real difficulties for any practitioner of a profession. For the teacher this danger is endemic.

Furthermore, the third party may intervene at strategic points in the system other than that of the teacher-student relationship. The parent may intervene in the local system; he may go directly to the principal and thereby add another complication to the relation of teacher to the bureaucratic system of which he is a part. At another level, the parent as voter has power to intervene in the larger political system which governs the school; this also lies in the background as another complication in the roles played by the teacher. It is scarcely possible for the teacher to remain unaware of the varied ways in which parents act as a third party in the interchange that goes on between teacher and student (or client); the threats to the professional role are equally apparent.

In tracing a few of the troubles faced by the occupants of these various roles some common threads appear. In each case an effort is being made to maintain or achieve a professional model for its organization. A professional model is a blueprint of the hopes of an occupational group. One major element in the model is the client relationship, a delicate blend of the numbers of clients and their power relative to the practitioner. Presumably an ideal clientele for a true profession can be specified. It would comprise enough clients to provide a good living, but not enough to rob the professional man of control over his own time. Some should come from a social class permitting him to act as benefactor, some from a social level sufficiently high to add lustre to the practitioner serving them. Some should possess social power which can be used to further the interests of the profession; none should be strong enough to make the professional man subordinate to them. This list could be extended; it is sufficient to indicate some of the built-in hazards of professional life.

For some activities the number of clients is clearly inadequate to support their hopes to be recognized as full professions. In others clients are as powerful as the head of a giant bureaucracy, capable of transforming the would-be professional into a salaried employee. With others again, the potential client acts as only a customer in a market place should act. For still others the client and the practitioner are related through a third party who is able to modify the tone and character of the client-practitioner relationship. In all of these the achievement of the blueprint model collides with some of the stubborn facts of the social order in which it is set. However, even where the encircling social system hinders the anticipated emergence of the model, that system may be modified in crucial ways by the efforts of the occupation striving for professional status.

SELECTED BIBLIOGRAPHY

Ambridge, D., "Discard the Strike," *The Financial Post*, May 25, 1963.

Barber, C. L., "Canada's Unemployment Problem," *The Canadian Journal of Economics and Political Science*, Vol. XXVIII, No. 1, February, 1962.

Gzowski, P., "Hal Banks: The Fight to Break Canada's Waterfront Warlord," *Maclean's Magazine*, May 18, 1963.

Kovacs, A. E., (Editor), *Readings in Canadian Labour Economics*, Toronto, McGraw-Hill Company of Canada Ltd., 1961.

The Labour Gazette, "Facing Facts in Labour Relations," February 28, 1963.

Newman, P. C., "The Dilemma of Greater Leisure," *Queen's Quarterly*, Vol. 66, Spring, 1959.

Porter, J., "Concentration of Economic Power and the Economic Elite in Canada," *The Canadian Journal of Economics and Political Science*, Vol. XXII, May, 1956.

Smiley, D. V., (Editor), *The Rowell-Sirois Report*, Toronto, McClelland and Stewart, Ltd., 1963. (Chapter VI)

Watkins, M. H., and Forster, D. F., (Editors), *Economics: Canada*, Toronto, McGraw-Hill Company of Canada Ltd., 1963.

chapter seven

POPULATION AND IMMIGRATION

The phrase "population problem" has a premonitory meaning for many parts of the world — areas where the present excess of people, coupled with a constant increase in their numbers, suggests that all too soon the man-food ratio will become tragically small. By contrast, Canada *appears* to have vast resources and a relatively small population. Consequently immigration into this country, especially prior to the 1930's, has been encouraged, and we tend to think of population problems as alien to our society. But such is not actually the case. While some still argue that we should "open the floodgates and fill our empty lands", others insist that we already have more people than is desirable. Perhaps more important is the fact that as a nation which has grown to a large extent through immigration rather than "natural increase" (although Canada's rate of natural increase is relatively high), Canada faces a number of special problems, ones which grow out of the difficulties of welding a heterogeneous population into a single society. Not the least of these have been explored in chapters three, four and five, and others are considered here.

The first selection is a piece written especially for this volume by Warren E. Kalbach, a sociologist who specializes in the area of demography and population studies. "Population Growth and Ethnic Balance" is a detailed discussion of the current Canadian population picture, showing just how the present ethnic distribution has come about and suggesting some of the problems the society faces as a result of this development. A less recent article, "Our Older Population" by H. G. Page, gives the background to what is increasingly becoming a more serious social problem in Canada as well as

in most of the other industrial nations of the world. While this article concentrates on the demographic factors which explain the increasing proportion
of "senior citizens" in our communities, another selection in the following
chapter deals more with the social consequences of this situation.

Turning to the subject of immigration *per se,* we read next a report of a
study conducted by sociologist Frank E. Jones and psychologist Wallace
E. Lambert on "Attitudes Toward Immigrants in a Canadian Community". In
this study the authors have attempted to explain how "attitudes favourable"
and "attitudes unfavourable" to immigrants in a community come about
in terms of "the structure of interaction systems to which given attitudes are
relevant".

From the academic we next turn to the journalistic, and the last three
selections in the chapter all express opinions and concerns with Canada's
immigrant situation. Robert Jamieson, writing in 1958, not as a Canadian
but as an observer from Britain, suggests that if Canada really wants immigrants she is going about it in a rather poor way. She has never, he
claims, answered the questions of whether she needs them, or wants them,
or from where they should come. He concludes that Canada, for its own best
interests, would do well to freely accept "good people from southern
Europe", re-examine the rationale of the emphasis on "skilled" people, and
tone down what appears to be a rather haughty national attitude toward
people from Britain and northern Europe.

Major-General W. H. S. Macklin believes that "Canada *Doesn't* Need
More People" and, writing several years ago, argues that we should look
to solving our various economic, political and other problems, and concentrate on "improving the quality, standards, and the national cohesion of the
Canadian people rather than increasing the quantity by further dilution of
old stocks". Finally, Peter C. Newman asks "Are New Canadians Hurting
Canada?", especially in terms of the employment picture, and looks for his
answers to the comments of a number of apparently informed observers.

35. POPULATION GROWTH AND ETHNIC BALANCE*

Warren E. Kalbach†

In the hundred years following 1861, Canada's population increased more than fivefold, from 3,230,000 to 18,238,000. By January 1,1964, Canada passed the nineteen million mark, with prospects of reaching twenty-two million by the end of the present decade.[1] While the population doubled during the first thirty years of the twentieth century and increased another 75 per cent during the next thirty year period, Canada is not regarded as a country experiencing a "population explosion". It would be difficult to convince nineteen million Canadians living in an area of three and one-half million square miles of territory that there will soon be "standing room only". Considering the population-land ratio, resources, and level of economic development, it isn't too difficult to accept the point of view that "fears of overpopulation and underpopulation alike seem unreasonable in the next several generations".[2]

While Canada may be spared the spectre of hordes of humanity pressing against limited space and resources, it is nevertheless confronted with a multitude of serious problems created by differential rates of change within the population structure as a whole. While not as spectacular as an "explosion", the disruption of normal social, political, and economic activity resulting from these differential rates of change can be quite serious.

GROWTH AND DISTRIBUTION OF POPULATION

A general perspective of Canada's growth experience since 1901 is presented in Table 1. The largest percentage increase, which occurred during the first decade of the 1901-1961 period, was primarily a reflection of the population increase in western Canada. Subsequent to this

---

*Published here for the first time. Statistical data presented in this paper not specifically footnoted to other sources have been obtained from official 1961 Census publications, Annual Reports of Vital Statistics, and the *1963-64 Canada Year Book* published by the Dominion Bureau of Statistics.

†Dr. Kalbach, a specialist in population research, is Associate Professor of Sociology at the University of Alberta, Edmonton.

[1] Hood, Wm. and Scott, A., *Output, Labour, and Capital in the Canadian Economy,* Royal Commission on Canada's Economic Prospects, Ottawa, 1956, Table 4.1, p. 156, and Table 4A.3, p. 341.

[2] Ryder, Norman B., "Components of Canadian Population Growth," in Blishen, B., et al, *Canadian Society,* Toronto, Macmillan Company of Canada Ltd., 1961, p. 68.

period, the rate of increase declined until the great economic depression when the rate of growth reached a low of 10.9 per cent, and the prairie provinces, as a group, showed the lowest rates of any area in Canada. Since 1941, the rate of growth has been increasing, with Ontario, Alberta, British Columbia and the Northern Territories showing higher growth rates than Canada as a whole.

Table 1

CANADA'S POPULATION, 1901-1961

Year	Population	Percentage Increase
1901	5,371,315	11.1%
1911	7,206,643	34.2
1921	8,787,949	21.9
1931	10,376,786	18.1
1941	11,506,655	10.9
1951	14,009,429	21.8[a]
1961	18,238,247	30.2

[a]Newfoundland included in 1951 but not in 1941.

Associated with this pattern of national growth has been the massive redistribution of population from rural to urban areas, resulting from the revolution in agricultural technology and increasing industrial activity. Changes in definition of the terms "rural" and "urban" make the precise measurement of this shift rather difficult, but in 1901 only 37.5 per cent of the population lived in incorporated cities, towns, or villages, compared to 57.4 per cent in 1951. A revision of the "urban" definition in 1956 to include more of the population living under actual urban conditions (e.g., suburban areas adjacent to incorporated places) increased the urban population in 1951 to 62.9 per cent and indicated that by 1961, the proportion "urban" had increased to 71.1 per cent.

During this same period of time, the number of incorporated cities, towns, and villages increased greatly. However, a more significant aspect of growth than this has been the relatively recent and rapid population increase in a few metropolitan areas. By June 1, 1961, 45 per cent of Canada's total population resided within the boundaries of seventeen metropolitan areas. Of these 8.2 million people, 69 per cent resided within the five largest metropolitan areas of Montreal, Toronto, Vancouver, Winnipeg, and Ottawa.

The metropolitan area population increased by 44.8 per cent during the 1951-1961 period compared to an increase of 30.2 per cent for Canada as a whole. However, not all metropolitan areas experienced problems associated with rapid growth as considerable variation in percentage increases was reported. For example, Calgary and Edmonton metropolitan areas increased by 96 and 91 per cent respectively, while Saint John and Windsor increased by only 22 and 18 per cent. Similarly, for the various urban population size groups reported in 1961, rates of increase varied from 59 per cent for the largest size group of 100,000 and over, to 18.8 per cent for urban populations between 5,000 and 10,000. The type and severity of problems facing urban communities, whether it be a need for adequate police protection, efficient mass transportation, freeway networks, utilities, etc., is a consequence not only of specific rates of growth, but of the existing population and economic base as well as the socio-economic characteristics of the resident population.

BASIC COMPONENTS OF POPULATION CHANGE

Changes in population described in the preceding section are complex functions of fertility, mortality, and migration. Before proceeding with a consideration of the significance of these factors with respect to changes in the population's internal structure, a brief summary of their relative contributions to total growth is presented in Table 2.

Table 2

COMPONENTS OF POPULATION GROWTH: 1901-1961

(thousands)

Period	Births	Deaths	Natural Increase	Immi-gration	Net Mi-gration	Net Increase
1901-1911	1,931	811	1,120	1,759	716	1,836
1911-1921	2,338	988	1,350	1,612	231	1,581
1921-1931	2,415	1,055	1,360	1,203	229	1,589
1931-1941	2,294	1,072	1,222	150	-92	1,130
1941-1951[a]	3,186	1,214	1,972	548	169	2,141
1951-1961[b]	4,478	1,327	3,151	1,543	1,078	4,229

Dominion Bureau of Statistics, *Canadian Vital Statistics Trends, 1921-1954,* Reference Paper No. 70, Ottawa, Queen's Printer, 1956, pp. 7-9; and Department of Citizenship and Immigration, *1962 Immigration Statistics,* Ottawa, Queen's Printer, 1963, p. 7.
[a]Not including Newfoundland.
[b]Including Newfoundland.

It is interesting to note that for every decade since 1901, the main factor in population growth has been natural increase. For the last ten year period, 1951-1961, natural increase accounted for 75 per cent of the total growth. A long term decline in mortality, coupled with an increasing birth rate since 1937 has given Canada one of the highest rates of natural increase of any of the "developed" countries in the world. Canada's rate of natural increase of 18.4 per 1,000 population in 1961 exceeded that of the United States, U.S.S.R., Japan, and that part of India covered by registration areas. Only in the so-called "underdeveloped" countries such as Chile, Peru, and Ceylon could higher rates be observed.

Both Canada and the United States have been rather unique in maintaining birth rates at relatively high levels during the post-World War II period while rates in other developed countries have declined steadily from early postwar peaks. After achieving a postwar high of 28.9 in 1947, Canada's birth rate has remained relatively stable, varying between 27.1 and 28.5. However, the rate of 26.1 in 1961 was the lowest since 1945 and there is some indication that further declines occurred through 1963. Considering that an estimated 70 per cent of the rise in the birth rate during the 1941-1956 period was due to a sharp increase in the percentage married, it is interesting to note that the marriage rate for 1963 of 6.9 per 1,000 was the lowest on record in recent years and a continuation of a downward trend since the record high of 10.9 set in 1946.

Population growth during the 1951-1961 period may then be seen as the result of an unusual combination of high fertility, very low mortality, and a net immigration larger than that experienced during any other decade of the twentieth century. By way of illustration, 282,164 immigrants arrived in 1957, the largest number since the all-time record of 400,870 immigrants set in 1913.

CHANGES IN AGE-SEX STRUCTURE

If the present mortality and fertility rates were to continue, and if no further immigration occurred, Canada would in time develop a stable population, *i.e.* a population with a fixed age-sex structure and a rate of growth dependent upon existing mortality and fertility rates. Obviously, this has not been the case as the internal structure continues to be in a state of flux, a consequence of declining mortality, fluctuating fertility, and shifting patterns of immigration. Figure 1 shows the age-sex structure of Canada's population in 1961 resulting from its unique combination of mortality, fertility, and migration experience. The effects of low fertility during the 1930's are visible as are the effects of post-World War II increases. Not so easily discernible, but also a contributing factor to variations in size from one age-sex cohort to another, is net migration. Figure 1 also presents an approximation of a stable population based on recent Canadian mortality and natural increase experience which has been suggested as an ideal structure relative to the orderly development of the Canadian economy.[3]

Figure 1

CANADA 1961 CENSUS AGE-SEX DISTRIBUTION
WITH IDEAL MODEL SUPERIMPOSED

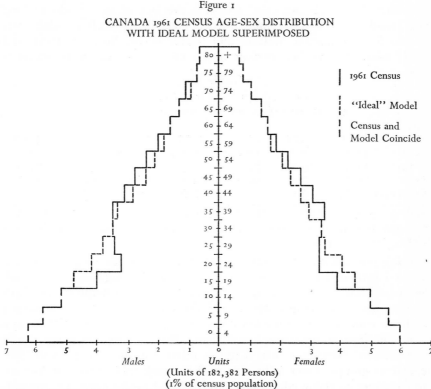

1961 Census

"Ideal" Model

Census and
Model Coincide

Males   *Units*   *Females*
(Units of 182,382 Persons)
(1% of census population)

Economic and Social Research Division, *The Basic 1961 Census Data on Immigration and Citizenship*, Report SR-2, Department of Citizenship and Immigration, Ottawa, Queen's Printer, September 1963, Figure 8. 111, p. 90.

One of the most significant age-sex group variations with respect to economic and social development is the changing proportions of dependent and economically active populations. In part, the burden of providing for either aged or young is a function of their numbers relative to the size of the economically active population and the rate of change in the ratio of dependent age groups to labour force. This is more clearly seen in

---

[3] Developed by the Economic and Social Research Division of the Department of Citizenship and Immigration and presented in the *The Basic 1961 Census Data on Immigration and Citizenship*, Report SR-2, Ottawa, Queen's Printer, 1963, pp. 89-91.

Table 3 which presents relative proportions of Canadian population within four major age groups for each census year since 1901.

A notable feature of Canada's age distribution over time, with the exception of the "65 and over" group, is the lack of any consistent long term trends. It is this variability which makes it difficult to adequately provide for educational, welfare and health needs. Between 1951 and 1961, nearly two million persons under 15 years of age were added to

Table 3
PERCENTAGE AGE DISTRIBUTION
OF THE POPULATION OF CANADA, 1901-1961

Age Group	1901	1911	1921	1931	1941	1951	1961
0- 4	12.1%	12.4%	12.1%	10.4%	9.1%	12.3%	12.4%
5-14	22.5	20.7	22.3	21.2	18.7	18.1	21.6
15-64	60.4	62.3	60.8	62.8	65.5	61.9	58.3
65 and over	5.0	4.6	4.8	5.6	6.7	7.8	7.7
Total %	100.0	100.0	100.0	100.0	100.0	100.0	100.0

Dominion Bureau of Statistics, *1961 Census*, Bulletin 1.2-2, Ottawa, Queen's Printer, 1962, Table 20, p. 20-1.

Canada's population, an increase of 46 per cent; while its proportion of the total increased from 30.4 to 34.0 per cent. During the same period, the population of working age (*i.e,* 15-64 years) increased by 22.9 per cent but declined in proportion to the total. In 1951, it constituted 61.9 per cent of the population compared to 58.3 in 1961. Without a favourable flow of immigrants to Canada, the working age group would have declined even more than it did in relation to the younger and older dependent groups. Essentially, this is the demographic basis for increasing resistance to rising educational, welfare and health costs, *i.e.,* proportionately fewer people are being called upon to carry an increasing tax burden. What is often not recognized is the need to spend more money just to maintain present-day standards for an increasing population. In addition, if it is recognized that present-day standards are in many respects grossly inadequate, any effort to correct the situation imposes an additional burden on the proportionately smaller labour force population.

A recent analysis draws attention to this shortage of persons in the younger labour force ages and estimates that approximately three-quarters of a million people between the ages of 15-19 (as of June 1, 1961) would be needed to provide a smoother transition from younger to older age-sex cohorts in Canada's population structure.[4] Reducing this deficiency

---

[4] *Ibid.,* pp. 91-93.

by encouraging immigration of economically active migrants in these age groups would tend to reduce the welfare cost ratio in terms of per capita income of the labour force, and at the same time contribute to a more orderly development of the economy.[5]

Another consequence of recent growth and changes in population structure is the impending impact of the postwar baby crop on both labour force and the job market. In the ten year period following 1951, Canada's labour force increased by 24.8 per cent, adding an average of 129,500 persons per year.[6] However, as a consequence of postwar fertility and on the basis of an assumed net immigration of 75,000, the Gordon Commission estimated that the labour force would increase by 27.4 per cent from 1960 to 1970.[7] If this increase in the labour force, amounting to 170,000 per year, is to be employed, it means that the economy must undergo a considerable expansion. The increase in "employed" labour force immediately following the war from 1946 to 1956 occurred at a rate of 91,900 employed persons per year, or an increase of 19.7 per cent for this ten year period.[8]

A possibility that the Gordon Commission understated the problem is suggested by a recent report that Canada would have to produce 450,000 new jobs during 1964 to keep pace with a growing labour force, and to offset an expected four per cent increase in productivity which would lead to the disappearance of 250,000 existing jobs.[9] Even allowing for possible labour bias, the problem of economic expansion appears rather formidable. Of course, there are those who hold the position that greater population increase will itself create greater economic development.[10] The experience of many rapidly growing underdeveloped areas would suggest that the validity of this position is dependent, in part, on the existing level of economic development as well as the demographic characteristics of the population increments.

---

[5] *Ibid.*

[6] Dominion Bureau of Statistics, *The Labour Force*, Vol. 20, No. 2, Ottawa, Queen's Printer, March 1964, Table 2, p. 5.

[7] Hood, Wm., and Scott, A. *op. cit.*, p. 188.

[8] Dominion Bureau of Statistics, *op. cit.*

[9] Report of an economic study presented to the United Automobile Workers convention in Atlantic City by Walter Reuther, U.A.W. president, in *The Globe and Mail*, Toronto, March 20, 1964.

[10] This point of view is reflected in a recent speech by Immigration Minister Tremblay in which he stated: "We are right in thinking that a still greater increase of the Canadian population could mean only a greater development of our economy." *Ottawa Journal*, March 18, 1964, p. 40.

CHANGES IN ETHNIC COMPOSITION

Interest in ethnic composition tends to be related to questions concerning the nature of Canadian society and problems of immigrant assimilation. The bicultural nature of Canadian society focuses attention and concern on changes in relative positions of British and French origin groups over time. Clearly, both groups are quite sensitive to any demographic trends tending to weaken their respective positions; and support or opposition to immigration policy and possibly to birth control programs often can be traced to the relative balance existing between these two major ethnic groups at any particular time.

The French in Canada, with the exception of the 1921 Census, have exceeded in number any of the separate component ethnic origins making up the larger "British Isles" category, and in this sense constitute the largest single homogeneous cultural group in Canada. Numbering 1,649,371 in 1901, the population of French origin increased 336 per cent by 1961, compared to an increase of 261 per cent for all British origins. These relative increases are all the more interesting when the primary sources of growth for these groups during this period are considered. The population of French origin was almost wholly dependent upon natural increase for its growth, while British origins were primarily dependent upon immigration.

Examination of Table 4 shows that during the past sixty years the French origin population managed to maintain its relative position of approximately 30 per cent of the total, while the British origins declined

Table 4
ETHNIC COMPOSITION, CANADA: 1901-1961

Year	British Isles		French		Other		Total
	Number (000)	Per cent	Number (000)	Per cent	Number (000)	Per cent	(000)
1901	3,063	57.0	1,649	30.7	659	12.3	5,371
1911	3,999	55.5	2,062	28.6	1,146	15.9	7,207
1921	4,869	55.4	2,453	27.9	1,466	16.7	8,788
1931	5,381	51.9	2,928	28.2	2,068	19.9	10,377
1941	5,716	49.7	3,483	30.3	2,308	20.0	11,507
1951	6,710	47.9	4,319	30.8	2,981	21.3	14,009
1961	7,997	43.8	5,540	30.4	4,486	25.8	18,238

Dominion Bureau of Statistics, *1961 Census*, Bulletin 1.2-5, Table 34, p. 34-1.

from 57.0 per cent in 1901 to 43.8 per cent in 1961. Clearly, this shift is due to changes in fertility as well as migration patterns which have resulted in rather rapid growth for ethnic groups other than British or French. In this period, the residual or combined "other" ethnic origin experienced a doubling in their proportionate share and now constitute one-fourth of Canada's total population. This rather rapid increase in the residual ethnic category poses some rather interesting questions regarding the nature of both present and future Canadian society.

With respect to future trends, it is interesting to note that the French origin component of the population has maintained its relative position through high fertility levels, a factor which has been relatively less important for British origins than immigration. On the other hand, it appears that both fertility and immigration have been significant for the rapid increase of other ethnic origins in Canada. Since fertility is less amenable to control than immigration, a closer examination of fertility differentials may provide insights into possible trends beyond 1961.

Keyfitz, in his analysis of Canadian fertility differentials, has shown a convergence of fertility rates among various social and economic groups.[11] Of special interest was his analysis indicating a convergence of fertility among British and French origin populations. Similar but more recent data for Quebec and several of the provinces with predominantly British origin populations continue to support the convergence hypothesis in general, but raise certain questions concerning its applicability to relevant age groups.

Quebec, for example, during the post-World War II period, experienced a crude birth rate of 30.7 in 1946 which subsequently declined to 26.1 in 1961. In contrast, Ontario, with a relatively high proportion of British origins, increased from 23.8 to 25.3 during the same interval of time. British Columbia also experienced a similar but somewhat smaller increase.

Inferences concerning ethnic fertility trends are somewhat tenuous when based on crude rates which are influenced by variations in the age-sex structures as well as distorted by the presence of other ethnic groups. However, to the extent that these particular provinces have heavy concentrations of the ethnic groups in question, such comparisons may have sufficient validity to provide tentative answers to the questions being raised at this point. With these limitations in mind, an examination of

---

[11] Keyfitz, N., "The Changing Canadian Population," in Clark, S. D., *Urbanism and the Changing Canadian Society*, Toronto, University of Toronto Press, 1961, pp. 13-15. Also, see his "Facts and Theory of Recent Trends in Canadian Fertility," in a report of the session on Canada, "Demographic Changes and Population Policy in Canada," held during a meeting of the Population Association of America, May 3-4, 1958, Chicago.

age-specific fertility rates for these same provinces minimizes the influence of age-sex variations while permitting a more detailed analysis
of fertility differentials as they may relate to ethnic differences. In this
case, the comparisons are limited to Quebec and Ontario because of the
similarity of Ontario and British Columbia relative to their proportions
of British origin population (59.4 per cent *vs.* 59.5 per cent) and
age-specific fertility rates.

Analysis of age-specific rates for Quebec and Ontario between 1931
and 1961 shows convergence only for those age groups over 25 years of
age. For the two youngest five-year age groups, fertility rates have increased in both provinces, but rates have increased faster and achieved

Figure 2

AGE-SEX DISTRIBUTION OF BRITISH ISLES AND
FRENCH ORIGIN POPULATIONS IN CANADA, 1961

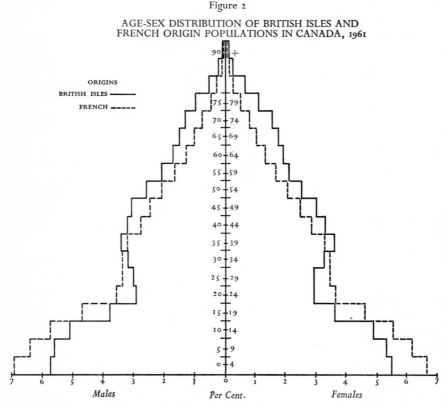

higher levels in Ontario, diverging rather than converging. For the intermediate ages between 25 and 39 years, convergence was apparent with

Quebec's rates higher but decreasing over time in contrast to Ontario's lower rates which remained either relatively constant or increased. For the older ages, Quebec's rates were higher, but both Quebec and Ontario showed consistent declines between 1931 and 1961, which tended to reduce differentials existing in 1931.

The combined effect, reflected in total fertility rates for women of child-bearing ages, shows definite convergence, with Quebec's total fertility declining from 4,001 to 3,700 during the thirty year period, compared to Ontario's which increased from 2,648 to 3,742.[12]

A measure of generation replacement, the gross reproduction rate, also shows convergence with Ontario's GRR of 1.824 now exceeding Quebec's rate of 1.787. In addition, the same trend is apparent when rates are computed for married women in child-bearing ages with Quebec decreasing to 167.3 per 1,000 from 225.3 in 1931, compared to an increase for Ontario from 129.9 in 1931 to 141.6 in 1961.

Net consequences of fertility, mortality, and migration differentials for the two major ethnic groups in Canada may be seen in the age-sex structures presented in Figure 2. Historically higher fertility of French Canadians is reflected in a larger proportion of its population in the age groups under thirty-five years, while the lower fertility and higher immigration of British origin population is apparent in the larger proportion of its population in the older ages. Now, if trends in Quebec and Ontario fertility allow valid inferences regarding ethnic differentials, then it would appear that the proportion of British origins in Canada would not be likely to continue its decline. However, considering the fact that both Ontario and British Columbia have experienced heavy immigration of non-British populations since 1946, it is entirely possible that their fertility experience has been significantly influenced by "other ethnics." In either event, the position of the French origin group in terms of its relative proportion, does not seem likely to improve in the immediate future unless some drastic change in immigration policy occurs. The problem of maintaining some degree of balance between the two "founding" ethnic groups will be increasingly complicated by the emergence of a sizable but heterogeneous third party with a growing interest in its share of Canadian identity.

In addition to problems of biculturalism or cultural pluralism suggested by recent demographic trends, there are other implications in the observed

---

12 Total fertility is the sum of the age-specific rates, *i.e.*, total fertility indicates the number of births which 1,000 women would have throughout their lifetimes, assuming no mortality, if they experienced at each age the fertility in effect during the period concerned.

age-sex differences of the two major ethnic groups. Any area, such as Quebec, with its high concentration of French Canadians, would be relatively more concerned with problems associated with a young dependent population than some other area, such as British Columbia, with a high concentration of British origins, hence large proportions of older people. Perception of "problems" at the provincial or local level, and definitions of self interests at the federal level, as well as the assignment of priorities in dealing with these problems would appear to be, in part, a function of the demographic characteristics of the provinces.

SUMMARY

While Canada appears to enjoy a rather enviable position in the world today with respect to its population-land-resource ratios, there is little justification for a complacent attitude founded on a naive belief that since there is no "population explosion," there is, *ipso facto,* no population problem. Quite to the contrary, analyses of relevant data show that Canada is faced with some very difficult problems arising from fluctuations in its fertility, mortality, and immigration experience.

Currently, Canada is faced with the task of developing efficient and healthy urban environments for increasing numbers of people crowding into relatively fewer metropolitan areas with high population densities. All areas are faced with the problem of providing adequate facilities for rapidly increasing cohorts of school-age children, university students, and retired people in the face of a proportionately smaller economically active segment of the population. There is also the challenge of expanding the economy to provide jobs for increasing numbers of young people entering the labour force, as well as for those now being displaced by automation and increasing productivity. If all this isn't enough to keep "Canadians" occupied, there is still the problem of ethnic balance as it applies to British-French Canadian relations. The issues are being complicated by an increasingly large number of other ethnic and racial groups who are beginning to show an interest in a Canadian society which cannot be contained wholly within either the British Canadian or French Canadian ethos.

36. *OUR OLDER POPULATION**

H. G. Page†

It is only in relatively recent times that the aged in our population have come to be considered as an economic and social problem.

Our industrial era and the present-day stresses have changed the entire pattern and philosophy surrounding old age. The industrial revolution, movement to urban centres, and resultant changes in economic and social values have also changed the concepts of old age dependency with more and more emphasis on community responsibility.

Three factors determine the age composition of a population at any point in time — births, deaths and migration. A relatively stable age structure will develop if birth and death rates remain fixed over a long period of time and the migrants in and out of the country balance each other age for age.

In an active country of present-day civilization such a static state of affairs is rarely if ever met — there are usually rising and declining cycles in one or all of these, influenced by economic, social, welfare and other factors, all interacting to produce varying proportions of the population at each age.

Two characteristics of a relatively new country such as Canada are *high birth rates* (which are common where there is virtually unlimited space and opportunity for population spread) and *heavy immigration* of young adults.

Both of these factors have been at work in Canada from the 1870's until not more than 20 years ago and have interacted to maintain a relatively young and middle age population.

A stable and relatively high death rate would have reduced the survivors of this era to stable proportions but the remarkable advances during the past generation or two in medical service, sanitation, curative and preventive medicine and medical care have reduced the risk of dying prematurely with resultant accumulation of aged persons in our population.

BIRTHS

Many of our present aged persons are survivors of the very high birth rates of the late 19th and early 20th century. Although official figures are

---

*From *Canadian Welfare*, May 1, 1955.
†Mr. Page is Chief of the Vital Statistics Section of the Health and Welfare Division of the Dominion Bureau of Statistics in Ottawa.

not available, it is safe to assume that birth rates of this period were of the order of 25 to 30 or more per 1,000 population.

Continued high birth rates of this order would certainly have the effect of producing large numbers of our present survivors despite any relatively high death rate.

MIGRATION

The most important *external* factor determining the high proportion of aged persons in our population today was undoubtedly the heavy surge of immigration between 1881 and 1931.

During that period over 5,800,000 immigrants entered Canada, over 4½ million between 1901 and 1931, most of whom were between 20 and 40 years of age.

DEATHS

The most important *internal* factor determining survival to old age has been the drastic reduction in death rates over the past one or two generations. It has been said that 30 per cent of the persons who reached 65 owe their survival to advances in public health and medicine since they were born.

Although the reduction of infant mortality mainly through conquest of infectious diseases has been a fairly recent accomplishment, there have been remarkable declines in mortality among adults as well, accounting directly and in large measure for the survival of our present aged.

During the last three decades alone mortality rates among men have been reduced by about one-half for all ages up to 50 with still higher reduction for women.

It is worthy of note that among women over fifty, reductions have been of the order of 15 to 20 per cent, but among men very little improvement over 50 is noticeable. This has had the effect of changing the present and future balance between men and women over 65.

LIFE EXPECTANCY

The net result of these mortality changes has been an advance in average life expectancy. In 1881 a boy who was fortunate to survive to age seven could expect on the average to live an additional 58 years; at present rates he could expect to live an additional 63 years. Most of this improvement has been at the infant, adolescent and young adult ages.

Today's newborn male infant can expect, if present mortality rates were to prevail for his lifetime, to survive to over 66; a newborn female infant to almost 71.

However, there has been very little gain in expectation of life at the older ages over those in effect 20 or even 50 years ago. On the average a man of 65 could expect then as now to live an additional 13 years; a woman on the other hand an additional 15 years. During the last 20 years a 65-year old woman's life expectancy has increased 1⅓ years.

From the welfare aspect these changes may be expressed more realistically in terms of number of survivors. If the children born in 1931, 1941 and 1951 were subjected throughout their life-time to the mortality rates in effect in these years, the following would survive to age 65 out of an original cohort of 1,000 babies.

	Males	*Females*
1931	587	617
1941	619	682
1951	658	755

A greater proportion of our population is surviving to age 65 — improvements since 1931 have meant that out of every cohort of 1,000 men, 70 more now survive to 65 than 20 years ago; almost 138 more women.

A man who now reaches 65 will survive beyond that age about the same number of years as his predecessors; a woman 1 to 1½ more years.

In the light of progress over the last 20 years in reducing mortality among older females, and present advances and interest in combatting disease associated with middle and old age such as cardio-vascular-renal conditions and cancer and the prevention of accidents, it is reasonable to expect that both the number surviving to age 65 and the years added beyond 65 for both men and women will be further increased.

It is essential in dealing with the statistics of old age to accurately define the "aged" population we are discussing. Since we are here concerned with survivors and since chronological age is involved in state and private social security benefits and concepts, the conventional age 65 has here been selected arbitrarily as the lower limit of old age for purposes of this article.

DEPENDENCE AND INDEPENDENCE

Since dependency of both the young and the old can only fall in the final analysis on the shoulders of the bread-winners in the population, in this article the population statistics have been divided for purposes of comparison into three broad groups: the dependent young, the bulk of whom are either at home or at school; the middle-age "bread-winning" group from 20 to 65; and the "aged" over 65.

Even a superficial inspection of the statistics reveals a very high rate of increase in the aged. The proportion of the population over 65 has steadily increased from 5 to 7.8 per cent in 50 years. This increase may not appear impressive at first sight but this must be considered in the light of the tremendous increase in the number of children since 1940.

During the last 50 years the number of aged has increased four times as compared with a total population increase of two-and-a-half times, about equally divided between men and women.

Most of the increase in the aged has, however, taken place within the last 20 years. While the total population has increased by a third since 1931 the proportion over 65 almost doubled, increasing from 576,000 to over one million.

However impressive these proportional figures may be, from the economic and social viewpoints we are primarily interested in the absolute numbers among our aged, and their dependence on and relationship to the bread-winner group.

In the early part of the century the ratio of aged persons to the middle age group in the population has been comparatively constant. However, in the last two or three decades the ratio of breadwinners to aged has been drastically reduced, as is here clearly demonstrated:

Ratio breadwinners to every aged person (over 65)

1901	9.9
1911	11.4
1921	10.8
1931	9.5
1941	8.4
1951	7.0

This, it is true, is an oversimplification of the number of persons on whom the responsibility for the economic or social care of the aged devolves in that it does not take into account, for example, the actual numbers gainfully occupied in the breadwinner group at every decade.

In this "middle" age group are included non-earning married women, the sick, disabled and unemployed, and unemployed widows. At the present time it is probable that a large number of married women are actually earners and that the burden of the aged is actually about equal to what it was in previous decades when the breadwinners were limited to employable men.

The simple ratio of aged to middle age population is still, however, a rough indicator that the balance is changing and will continue to increase for some time.

PROVINCIAL VARIATIONS

Although there has been an 85 per cent increase in the number of aged in the last 20 years for the country as a whole, this figure tends to mask the true picture of provincial patterns. The increase in the aged during the last two decades has not kept pace with the rest of the population in the Maritimes; in Quebec and Ontario the increase has been only slightly greater than the rate of total population growth.

On the other hand the increase in the proportions and number over 65 in the four western provinces has been phenomenal. In Manitoba and Saskatchewan the number over 65 has doubled; in Alberta it has increased two-and-a-half times, while in British Columbia the number has more than tripled!

There are several factors contributing to this situation, the most obvious of which is migration — the present aged are survivors of the heavy immigration into the Prairies during the last 50 years. The increase in British Columbia is a reflection of the recent heavy influx of older persons.

The net result of these developments is that, of all the provinces, Quebec now has the lowest proportion of its population over 65 (5.7) and British Columbia the highest (10.8).

MEN AND WOMEN

The sex ratio of the aged has also been changing in recent years; males still outnumber females and the trend is toward an eventual preponderance of females — a direct reflection of the reduction in mortality risk among females during the past generation.

The fact that more aged men are found in rural areas (about equally divided between farm and non-farm) than among the bread-winner group appears to be a natural reflection of the agricultural era. Migration to the city and town is characteristic of the young; the older farmer tends to stay on the farm unless widowed. More women are widowed than men and the tendency is for farm widows to move into the city, presumably to foster homes or to stay with their children.

One very important factor affecting the whole question of dependency of the aged is their marital status. For 10 out of every 100 women over 65 who are single, 12 men over 65 have never been married; 66 out of every 100 men over 65 are married and the remaining 22 widowed. As a result of the higher mortality risks among males, 48 out of every 100 women over 65 are widowed and only 42 married and living with their husbands.

At the present time about 575,000 of the 1,063,000 people over 65 are married, leaving ½ million single or widowed.

The implication of this picture for housing, income maintenance, and other social and economic factors affecting the aged are obvious.

It may be of interest to note that of the 540,000 males over 65 in 1951 over 208,000 or about 4 out of 10 were gainfully occupied; out of 523,000 women over 65, almost 27,000.

The ratio of aged employed to the total labour force has remained quite constant during the past 10 years at almost six per cent.

Among wage-earner families where the head of the family was over 65, over one-third earned less than $1,500 per year, and an additional 20 per cent earned less than $2,000. In almost 6 out of 10 such families the head earned less than $2,000 per year, and in 9 out of 10 less than $3,000 a year.

DISABILITY

Of the 1,063,000[1] aged in 1951, 263,000 were estimated to be physically ill or disabled, 162,000 severely, involving a chronic disability, deformity or amputation which might or might not confine the person to bed, wheelchair or sitting, but which in any case grossly interfered with the normal functions of life or in gaining a livelihood.

About 17 out of every 100 men over 65 were found ill at the initiation of the National Sickness Survey, over 50 per cent higher prevalence than among persons 46 to 64 and four times as high as among children.

Among aged women, over 21 out of every 100 were found ill on the opening day of the survey, almost 5 times the prevalence among girls.

One-half of all illnesses reporting among aged persons during the Sickness Survey were disabling illnesses, generally consisting of a heart condition, accident, arthritis or rheumatism, deafness, blindness or chronic disease of the nervous system.

On the average men over 65 are ill almost 92 days each year; women 112 days. Gainfully occupied men and women are away from their occupations 25 to 27 days.

FUTURE POPULATION

Estimation of the future total population of a country is fraught with dangers of misinterpretation since it is based on arbitrary assumptions of future birth and death rates and the extent of future migration.

It is somewhat less difficult to estimate the future population of the aged since this group does not as a rule emigrate and from past experience

---

[1] Less 36,000 who were in institutions.

it is possible to project what the probable maximum death rates of the older population will be.

Assuming therefore that there will be some reduction in death rates over the next generation, notably among women, and assuming that our present "upper middle age" population will not emigrate to any appreciable extent, some fairly broad estimates of the future population 65 and over in the next two decades may be useful for welfare administration purposes as a measure of the probable future "problem" of the aged:

ESTIMATED POPULATION (000's)

	Men	Women	Total
1951	551	535	1,086
1961	640-650	675-685	1,375
1971	740-750	860-870	1,610

These estimates predict an annual increment of 25,000 persons over 65 in the 10 years up to 1961 and closer to 30,000 in the next decade. Although these are only benchmarks based on our knowledge of past and present trends, the challenge to social workers is undoubtedly great.

37. *ATTITUDES TOWARD IMMIGRANTS IN A CANADIAN COMMUNITY**

Frank E. Jones and Wallace E. Lambert†

Approximately one in nine persons in Canada is a postwar immigrant. As a result, the public is very much interested in immigrants and immigration policy. The complexity of the reaction to the current situation prompted us to undertake research that would allow description and analysis of the attitudes of native Canadians toward immigrants.

We chose for the survey a town of 12,000 which had received a large number of immigrants after the war, chiefly from Holland and Germany.

*From *Public Opinion Quarterly*, Vol. XXIII, Winter, 1959.
†Dr. Jones is Chairman of the Department of Sociology at McMaster University, Hamilton. Dr. Lambert is Professor of Psychology at McGill University, Montreal.

As the native population of the town was primarily of British origin, we observed a situation in which there would be little variation in the ethnic background of our subjects and little variation in the ethnic background of the immigrants. Because the town was small, the natives would be more likely to be aware of the immigrants than in a larger city.

While this research is directly relevant to the adjustment of immigrants and to their integration into the community, it also provides a formulation of the relation of attitudes to certain basic characteristics of social systems which has broader applicability.

THEORETICAL ORIENTATION

Previous studies of immigrants have emphasized the importance of the behavior of the host population to immigrant adjustment or assimilation. Infeld regards the attitudes of native Americans as a main factor in the differential assimilation of his sample of German and Polish immigrants. Taft has proposed that "the effect of social interaction becomes of greatest importance in assimilation," a view supported by Richardson in his theoretical statement on assimilation, and in his report that the frequency of social participation between immigrants and natives is positively associated with assimilation. Warner and Srole include frequency and kind of participation as major criteria for their Scale of Subordination and Assimilation.

Our interest was consistent with the viewpoint expressed in the studies cited but we felt that it was worthwhile to direct attention to the relation between the attitudes toward immigrants held by the native population and the extent and kind of social participation these natives shared with immigrants. We took the view that a person's attitudes toward immigrants may be expected to vary in relation to the situation in which he interacts with immigrants.

Although several sets of questionnaire items previously employed in prejudice studies might have been used to measure attitudes toward immigrants, none of these satisfied the requirements made by our approach to the problem. The attitude schedule which we developed consisted of fifty-nine items constructed on the basis of Parsons' theory of social systems. Item analysis[1] reduced to twenty-nine the number of

---

[1] We used a procedure developed for this study by Professor George A. Ferguson, McGill University, whose generous assistance is gratefully acknowledged. A correlation coefficient, measuring the relation between responses to a specific item and the subjects' total scores, greater or equal to .50, and a variance, measuring variation in the distribution of responses in the five response categories of the item greater or equal to .90, were the arbitrary criteria for selection.

items with strong discriminatory power, and these provide the basis of our present analysis.[2] Preliminary study indicates support for our theoretically derived expectation that attitudes toward immigrants would vary in terms of the *functional dimensions* of social systems and in terms of the various *spheres of cooperative activity* in which immigrants and natives participated.[3] In this paper, however, we wish to present the results of an initial analysis in which variations in attitude were measured simply in terms of the subject's total scores on the twenty-nine items, and in which attention is directed to the relation between (1) variations in attitude and certain personal characteristics of the subject; and (2) variations in attitude and certain properties of the systems of social interaction in which natives and immigrants participated.

VALIDITY OF THE ATTITUDE ITEMS

Usually acceptable evidence for the validity of attitude items consists in demonstrating that respondents, known through other measures of their behavior to be favorable (or unfavorable) toward some object or event, are found to reveal favorable (or unfavorable) attitudes to the same object or event as measured by a set of items. A satisfactory procedure for validating our attitude items would be to have qualified judges observe and classify as favorable or unfavorable native Canadians who are in actual interaction with immigrants and then administer the questionnaire to the native Canadians. Plans to undertake this validation procedure in an industrial setting had, unfortunately, to be abandoned for reasons beyond our control. We can report, however, certain findings which suggest that our confidence in the attitude items is justified.

To our question, "In contrast to other Canadian communities, my community has received: too few immigrants, about the right number, or too many immigrants," 59 of the 78 respondents with favorable attitude scores on the Social System Items chose the first two categories as compared to 21 of the 79 with unfavorable attitude scores. This difference is statistically significant beyond the .001 level.

Respondents who gave favorable responses to SSI reported more voluntary and active contacts with immigrants (34 such contacts as compared

---

[2] We shall refer to these items as the Social System Items, abbreviated as SSI. An example of one of the questionnaire items is: In social clubs to which Canadians and immigrants belong, the immigrants should have the same chance as Canadians to hold responsible positions. 1. Strongly agree, 2. Agree, 3. Undecided, 4. Disagree, 5. Strongly disagree.

[3] In this study, social system dimensions were: goals, means, status, and solidarity; the spheres of activity were: work, neighborhood, social-recreational, commercial, family, religious, and educational.

to 14 reported by those giving unfavorable responses), and more voluntary but passive contacts (52 as compared to 42), while those with unfavorable attitude scores on SSI have disproportionately more involuntary contacts (62 as compared to 53) with immigrants. Over all, these differences are statistically significant at approximately the .03 level.

Respondents who gave favorable responses to SSI judge more of their contacts with immigrants to be beneficial, while those with unfavorable attitude scores evaluate contacts with immigrants more often as a hindrance. The difference in the distributions of judgment of reported contacts is statistically significant beyond the .001 level.

Of 144 contacts with immigrants reported by respondents with favorable scores on SSI, 99 were judged to be enjoyable and 40 as unpleasant or a matter of indifference (judgments on 8 contacts are lacking). The reporting 124 contacts, judged 41 to be enjoyable and 80 as unpleasant or a matter of indifference (judgments on 8 contacts are lacking). The difference is statistically significant beyond the .001 level.

In summary, those respondents who score favorably on the questionnaire in contrast to the unfavorable scorers, do not feel that there are too many immigrants in their community, have more voluntary contacts with immigrants, more often see their contacts with immigrants as beneficial, and enjoy their contacts with immigrants. In short, the subjects' responses to SSI were consistent with their judgments and actions relative to immigrants.

Analysis revealed a high association between favorable wording of items and favorable responses and between unfavorable wording and unfavorable responses. However, the favorable-unfavorable split of 33-26 for the 59 items used in the original questionnaire and the 15-14 split for the 29 items finally selected for analysis provided an adequate safeguard against wording bias. As it seemed possible that subjects might find the questionnaire long, we took precautions to test for subject fatigue, but statistical analysis revealed that the order of item presentation did not influence results.

SAMPLES AND FIELD PROCEDURE

The data were obtained from two probability samples[4] which will be

---

[4] City blocks drawn at random from a complete listing, and systematic sampling from a random start within blocks in proportion to block population density, were the main features of the selection procedure. Where there was more than one eligible subject in a selected household, one was chosen on a random basis. No substitutions were permitted if the relevant household yielded no eligible subject.

We gratefully acknowledge assistance from the Dominion Bureau of Statistics, Ottawa, especially from Mr. Douglas Dale, in the design of the sample.

referred to as Sample D, consisting of persons normally at home during the day, and Sample N, consisting of persons normally *not* at home during the day. In addition to the restriction concerning presence at home, each subject had to be Canadian-born or a naturalized Canadian citizen with fifteen years' residence in Canada. Sample D was composed primarily of housewives, although a few retired males and night-shift male workers were included. Sample N consisted primarily of married working males, although a few working females were included. The two samples yielded 157 subjects.

Collection of the data, undertaken by four interviewers who resided in the community during the field period, required two weeks. The interview procedure required the interviewer to read each attitude item to the subject and to check the response on the schedule (the subject was provided with a copy of the schedule so that he could follow the oral presentation of the items) and on completion of the attitude schedule, to obtain information, as directed by two additional schedules, concerning certain personal characteristics of the subject and the nature of his social contacts with immigrants. Approximately one hour was required to complete an interview. Most subjects readily agreed to be interviewed and showed a strong interest in the topic, usually volunteering opinions as well as responding to the prepared items.

ATTITUDE DIRECTION AND PERSONAL CHARACTERISTICS

Although we collected information on certain personal characteristics of our subjects, such as age and education, we had no adequate theoretical basis for predicting association between variations in attitudes toward immigrants and such variables, except those which serve as indices of social class level. We regarded such analysis, therefore, as a sheerly empirical venture which might yield some useful findings. In this paper, we wish simply to summarize these results.

A clear difference in attitude direction[5] occurred between Sample D, which showed 49.8 per cent of responses to all 29 items as favorable, and Sample N, which showed 61.1 per cent favorable, a difference significant beyond the .001 level.[6] Sample N subjects were found to be consistently more favorable than Sample D subjects when the items were ordered in

---

[5] "Attitude direction" is a term we shall use to refer to the assumed capacity of attitudes to vary from favorable to unfavorable. We recognize that in our analysis we may simply be reporting on variations in degrees of favorableness or unfavorableness, since we used no special technique to attempt to determine a zero point for each item.

[6] Unless otherwise stated, chi square was used to test for association between the frequencies of the various distributions.

terms of social system dimensions and in terms of spheres of activity, the differences in percentages favorable being significant at or beyond the .02 level in one instance and at or beyond the 0.1 level in seven of the thirteen possible instances.

We can only speculate about the reasons for the difference between the samples. It is reasonable to suggest that housewives, since they report fewer contacts with immigrants, are simply fearful of the unknown, but separate analysis of each sample reveals no significant association between contact or lack of contact and attitude direction. The role of the house-wife may restrict the range of activities of many women and be experienced as frustrating, possibly generating general hostility that in some circumstances can be directed against immigrants. Furthermore, since the wife is primarily dependent for her social-class position on her husband's occupational success, her relative incapacity to control her own destiny may be a source of stress which sharpens apprehensiveness toward her husband's possible occupational competitors. Unfortunately, we have no data to test such explanations.

Whatever the reason for the difference between the samples, separate analysis was clearly advisable, and the remaining findings will be reported separately for each sample.

The analysis showed little association between personal characteristics and attitude direction in either sample.[7] No association was found between attitudes toward immigrants and the subject's religious affiliation, ethnic origin, or length of residence in the community. No significant association was found between attitudes and the subject's age, sex, or marital status, although the data suggested a tendency for favorable attitudes to be associated with younger age groups, with married subjects, and with males.

A subject's level of education, occupation, and income were regarded as indices of social-class membership and, as we held that immigrants tend to enter a social system at its lower-class levels and are therefore a greater competitive threat to native members of such classes than to native members of higher social classes, we predicted a positive relation between attitude direction and social class. The data support our pre-

---

[7] To analyze the attitude data, the distribution of scores for each sample was divided at the quartile points, which yielded four equal-sized groups of subjects ranked from most to least favorable.

diction, as significant associations between education,[8] occupation,[9] and income[10] were obtained.

ATTITUDE DIRECTION AND SOCIAL INTERACTION

We assumed no necessary relation between attitude direction and the presence or absence of social contacts with immigrants in the sense that contacts necessarily generate positive or negative sentiments. It seemed more fruitful to think of social contacts between native Canadians and immigrants as occurring within systems of interaction and to analyze the attitude data in terms of selected properties of systems of interaction. We could not observe such systems directly, but with such analysis in mind we obtained from each subject information about the frequency of interaction, the number of spheres of activity in which interaction occurred, the subject's position in such interaction systems, and the rewards accruing from participation in such systems. Our prediction regarding the relation between attitude direction and the presence or absence of social contacts is supported by the data; they indicate that there is no association between absence of social contacts and attitude direction, although if contact has occurred there is a positive association, significant at the .02 level in Sample N, between attitude direction and the number of spheres of activity involved.

Frequency of interaction. Our theoretical viewpoint led us to predict associations between certain characteristics of interaction systems and attitude direction, but among such characteristics of interaction we did not assume a necessary relation between frequency of interaction and attitude direction. As it is reasonable to expect persons to develop either positive or negative feelings toward one another with increased frequency of interaction, we predicted no association between these two variables. The data support our reasoning, as there is no statistically significant association in either sample, although there is a tendency for subjects reporting less frequent interaction with immigrants to have more favorable attitudes than subjects reporting more frequent interaction.

Spheres of activity and interaction. We hold that the structure of interaction systems largely determine the actor's control of both the frequency and initiation of interaction and that such control will be closely associa-

---

[8] A marked trend in Sample D but not statistically significant; significant at the .03 level for Sample N.

[9] No association for housewives categorized in terms of husband's occupation; significant beyond the .01 level for Sample N.

[10] Significant beyond the .05 level for Sample D; beyond the .01 level for Sample N.

ted with each actor's attitudes to others in the system. In brief, we hypothesize a relation between the structure of interaction systems and attitude direction and specify the actor's control of the frequency and the initiation of interaction as two possible variables.[11]

Data relevant to the control of interaction include information about the spheres of activity where interaction occurs, the relative positions of the subject and the immigrants with whom he interacts, the subject's evaluation of the numbers of immigrants in such interaction systems, and the subject's pattern of initiating action. Analyses of these data, to be discussed separately below, provide a measure of support for our general hypothesis.

Among the interaction systems in the six spheres of activity for which information was obtained, the *work* sphere could be assumed to permit the individual the least control of interaction, while the neighborhood, club, church, and school spheres of activity, in varying degree, permit the actor a greater control over his pattern of interaction and the conditions under which he interacts with others. To predict an association between attitude direction and participation in these various systems required knowledge of the actor's personal control of interaction for each sphere of activity that we did not possess, but we felt safe in predicting an association between unfavorable attitudes and interaction occurring in the work sphere, where personal control was assumed to be lowest. Analysis reveals that Sample D subjects with unfavorable attitudes have disproportionately more interaction in the work sphere, while subjects with favorable attitudes have disproportionately more interaction in the club sphere. Sample N subjects reveal a similar association between the work sphere and unfavorable attitudes, while favorable attitudes are associated with neighborhood, business, and club spheres of activity. No statistically significant associations between sphere of activity and attitude direction, however, were found.

Voluntary and involuntary contact. In any interaction system we may expect to find involuntary and voluntary contacts between members but we may also expect interaction systems to vary in terms of the relative opportunities for either type of contact. We have presented evidence bearing on the relation between attitude direction and different spheres of contact which support our prediction of a negative relation between favorable attitudes and involuntary contact. We tested this hypothesis further with data which bear directly on these types of contact and found

---

[11] A number of studies support the view that the actor's position in the structure of a given interaction system influences his attitudes.

an association in the predicted direction, significant beyond the .01 level for Sample D but not significant for Sample N.

Authority. As superiors and inferiors may like or dislike each other, any association between the positions of incumbents, relative to the distribution of authority in interaction systems, and attitude direction must involve other variables. One such variable would likely be the actor's appraisals of the qualifications of incumbents of, or aspirants for, authoritative roles. In this respect, there is a general tendency for established members of a social system to be unwilling, under ordinary circumstances, to relinquish authority to new members. As actors who are in a superior authoritative position relative to others tend to control the initiation of interaction and the degree of intimacy which may occur, and as the established members of a group tend to prefer to control initiation and intimacy of interaction with new members, we predicted that favorable attitudes would be more frequently reported by natives whose positions relative to immigrants were superior rather than inferior or equal. The data reveal no trend in the direction predicted for Sample D but a clear association in Sample N; there subjects whose attitudes are favorable report disproportionately more situations in which they hold superior positions in interaction with immigrants, while subjects whose attitudes are unfavorable report disproportionately more peer relations. The association between interaction position and attitude direction is significant at approximately the .03 level.

Rewards. The distribution of rewards is a potential source of stress in any interaction system; this is especially true where it concerns new and established members of the system, as such contacts maximize the possibility of conflict between different conceptions of an appropriate distribution of rewards. In the present analysis, it is sufficient to observe that unless extraordinary circumstances prevail, the established members of a system define it as inappropriate for new members to have an equal or greater share of the available rewards until a considerable degree of socialization has occurred, and they tend to exclude new members from the exercise of authority. Interaction, therefore, in which one or more new members have the advantage with respect to rewards tends to be experienced as deprivational by the established members and to stimulate negative attitudes toward the new members. For our subjects, therefore, we predicted a positive association between position relative to rewards and attitude direction. We found, however, no consistent pattern of association between attitude direction and each subject's judgment of his job, his neighborhood living conditions, and the privileges available to him in his clubs as compared to those available to immigrants with whom he participated in common interaction systems. Sample D subjects whose reward position relative to immigrants is "higher" or "lower" reveal unfavorable attitudes, while those whose attitudes are favorable tend to report equality with immigrants with respect to rewards. Sample N respondents in the extreme directions of attitude show a slight but nonsignificant trend in the predicted direction. Field experience, however, revealed that the required information was difficult to obtain, and there is good reason to doubt the reliability of the data which bear on rewards.

EVALUATIONS OF PROPORTIONS OF IMMIGRANTS

Where social systems experience an influx of new members, the relative proportions of new and established members are likely to be a matter of concern to both categories of actor, since their proportionate numerical strengths have significance for the control of interaction and the distribution of rewards. On the basis of this assumption we were led to predict an association between attitude direction and our subject's evaluations of the proportions of immigrants in the interaction systems in which both participated.[12] The data clearly reveal that subjects whose attitudes are favorable more frequently express the opinion that there are "less than enough" immigrants while those with unfavorable attitudes express the view that there are "more than enough." This association between attitude direction and the evaluation of proportions of immigrants is significant beyond the .01 level in Sample D and beyond the .001 level in Sample N. As an analysis of attitude direction and subjects' *estimates* of the proportions of immigrants present in given interaction systems showed a trend toward an association, although not statistically significant, between favorable attitudes and reports of small proportions of immigrants and between unfavorable attitudes and reports of large proportions of immigrants, we may suggest that attitude direction is more closely associated with the evaluation than with the actual numbers of proportions of new and established members.

IMMIGRANTS AS FACILITIES OBJECTS AND REWARD OBJECTS

In interaction systems, actors may regard each other primarily as reward objects or primarily as facilities objects. This dichotomy can be applied to the orientations of native Canadians toward immigrants, where a ten-

---

[12] For reported contacts in a given sphere of activity, subjects were asked: "About how many immigrants are there as compared to the number of Canadians in this group?" Subjects were then asked if they would prefer to increase, decrease, or hold constant the stated proportion of immigrants to Canadians.

dency to regard immigrants as useful or valuable to the development of natural resources, to meet occupational shortages, to increase consumer demand (*i.e.* as facilities objects) can be observed as well as a tendency to regard immigrants as desirable simply as associates and friends (*i.e.* as reward objects). We hold that persons who regard immigrants primarily as facilities objects could hold favorable attitudes toward immigrants but, as the value of a facility object is a function of its utility in a given situation, there will be less stability or persistence in the attitude direction of such persons than among persons who regard immigrants primarily as reward objects. Our data do not permit us to compare our subjects in terms of these two actor orientations, but tests for association between each type of orientation and attitude direction show a clear positive association, significant beyond the .001 level in both samples, between these distributions, indicating a strong relation between the facilities and reward value of immigrants and attitudes toward them.

SUMMARY

We have advanced the view that there is a systematic relation between attitude direction and the structure of interaction systems to which given attitudes are relevant. This approach appears to yield a better understanding of variations in attitude than the typical survey analysis approach, where it is usual to look for relations between attitudes and age, sex, residence, and similar personal characteristics of the subjects. Our argument is supported by the present analysis, which yielded no significant associations between attitude direction and the familiar personal characteristics except educational and income level, and the association between attitude direction and either of those two variables seemed better understood by interpretation in terms of the structure of interaction systems. On the other hand, in each sample we found four significant associations out of a possible nine between attitude direction and characteristics of interaction systems.

In summary, the analysis suggests that attitude direction is associated with the control of interaction and with the type and distribution of rewards in the relevant interaction system. We conclude that further study of this relation by survey analysis procedures and in experimental situations would contribute to the understanding of the determinants of attitudes.

38. *DOES CANADA REALLY WANT MORE IMMIGRANTS?**

Robert Jamieson†

Canada just doesn't seem to know where it stands on immigration. I do not mean that many Canadians, official and unofficial, don't do a great deal for immigrants. But the whole approach seems to be inhibited, and Canada appears to have failed to reach clear conclusions on these basic issues:

Does the country need, and want, immigrants?

Does Canada want any particular kind of immigrants more than any other — e.g., northern Europeans, including people from the British Isles and France, rather than southern Europeans? If too few northern Europeans want to come, will Canada welcome more people from such countries as Greece and Italy?

What is the moral position of the country on immigration — is it merely conferring privilege of entry on the immigrant, who must then accept whatever is provided or not provided? Or does Canada really need the immigrant, as much as the immigrant may need Canada, and should Canadians be going out warmheartedly and unequivocally saying "Come and be part of us, and help us build up this great country of ours"?

I am not a Canadian, and it is not for me to answer these questions. But I suggest that it is in failing to answer them that Canada produces a frustrating situation for itself particularly in relation to immigration from Britain.

I know Canada could do well without journalists like myself, and I accept that in my case admission is a privilege extended: though one might point out that publishers have in recent years gone to the ranks of landed immigrants for their editors.

But whatever may be the situation in some fields, such as the newspaper one, there is just no hope at all of natural increase taking care of all of Canada's job needs over the next 20 years. She would also have to improve vastly her primary education and technical training facilities if she were to provide even the skilled labor section of her labor force. This

*From *Saturday Night*, March 23, 1959.
†Mr. Jamieson is Assistant News Editor for *The Financial Post,* Toronto.

is amply demonstrated in the Gordon report which, for the most part, assumes net average immigration of 75,000 a year. As there is an annual loss of around 50,000 by emigration, mostly to the United States, immigration of around 125,000 a year would appear to be Canada's minimum need.

And don't forget that nearly all long-range economic forecasting in the past has turned out to be underestimated. So Canada's immigration needs — if she is to take full advantage of the economic opportunity offered her — may be substantially greater.

Take a concrete example, the aircraft industry. For good or ill, Canada decided to build this to the point it has now reached, and committed a large part of it to building that nationalistic *jou jou*, the Arrow. Two-thirds of the workers on the Arrow came from Britain. Then Canada, now under a different government, dropped the Arrow, and 14,000 were thrown out of jobs with no hope of getting back into the aircraft industry. This appeared in British eyes as an affront to people who, most clearly of all, were invited to Canada, because Canada just couldn't have built up this size of aircraft industry without them. And, although nobody complained about it from the government side, it was an affront to the United Kingdom as a nation, for she freely allowed this large body of people to move to Canada, with very special skills developed mainly at public expense, after a good state education.

It was Canada's business whether she went on with the Arrow, but people in Britain are accustomed to see their governments looking at issues in the round, and working out broad solutions in the light of all probable consequences before announcing decisions. Does any Canadian seriously suggest this happened when the Arrow was dropped?

With the exceptions of 1956 and 1957, there has been no "mass" immigration from Britain to Canada in the postwar years. Many of those who have come have had friends or relatives, or contacts here, of one kind or another. To these people stories of distress can be confirmed or refuted in correspondence with people whom they trust. Yet it is probably just as well the articles were published,[1] for Canada had been considerably over-glamorized in the previous two or three years.

The articles might have had another value, if they had stirred some questioning in the hearts of men in authority here. You remember what the articles said: that there were large numbers of unemployed, bread-

---

[1] The articles referred to here were published in "The People", a British Sunday newspaper. (Ed.)

lines, many homeless, people raking garbage bins for something to eat, that British immigrants were among these unfortunates.

Canadians must admit the only thing which cannot be substantiated in this picture is the alleged suffering of British immigrants. For, so far as anyone can find out, no British immigrant suffered this degree of distress last winter, though some were in trouble after the big influx of 1957.

Even in early May — as I was coming to the office to write this article — I passed a breadline of destitute men in the heart of Montreal.

And only a few weeks ago, when the snows melted in Montreal, the body of a young European immigrant was found on a rubbish heap: the autopsy showed he had had no food for at least 24 hours before he died.

Such things should shock the conscience of a nation. But little action is taken.

These failures have relevance when Canada holds itself out as a good country to come to. Even where a prospective settler from Britain feels that he personally is unlikely to be in great need, he cannot help feeling unhappy in the presence of such great wealth as is displayed here, alongside a type of abject poverty that is now unknown in northern Europe. To almost anyone from this area, of whatever political complexion — I myself was a member of the Conservative Party in England until I came here — this appears to be a moral wrong, and as well an appalling waste of human resources.

No government would survive in Britain, Germany, Scandinavia, or the Low Countries that tolerated winter unemployment of the volume tolerated in Canada where one man in eight can be out of work.

Many Canadians will echo ironical cheers when I say that this is a country that doesn't think as people in Britain do. Your Establishment — the entrenched people with power who effectively influence political and social action — sneer at the Welfare State as you call it, and by implication at similar arrangements in most other northern European countries. These people do not know, I suppose, that the principles of the welfare state go back to the 16th century when, after the breakup of the feudal system, the central government appointed justices of the peace whose first duty was to maintain the King's peace, but whose next duty was to provide for the ablebodied unemployed. Parts of Canada haven't got that far yet, so do you wonder there is a conflict of ideas?

Don't count too much on another great swell of British immigration. Some will continue, but the broad flow will swing again towards Australia and New Zealand, where social ideas and political practices are closer to what British people understand.

Canada's problem, if it wishes to keep up total immigration, may be in becoming adjusted to accepting a very much heavier flow — numerically and proportionately — of immigrants from southern Europe. This is not too difficult. Australia was once very choosy about the sources of its immigrants, but it was logical, and when the flow from Britain didn't meet its needs, it opened the gates to people from central and southern Europe.

What prevents Canada drawing on the backlog of 100,000 or so of applicants in Italy? "There's a limit to the number of people one doctor can examine in a day," I have been told. Well, let's have some more doctors.

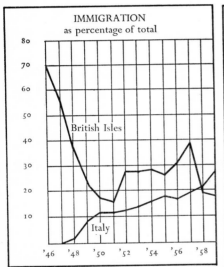

Immigration by two countries of last residence, British Isles and Italy, as percentages of total number of immigrants.

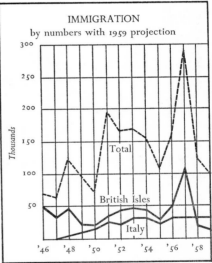

Number of immigrants coming to Canada from British Isles and Italy compared with total from all lands.

Just look at the Figures 1 and 2. With an enormous drop in total immigration last year and — according to shipping people — a further drop of almost a fifth in the first quarter of this year, the only country that is keeping up its numbers is Italy. And Italy is probably the only country with a colossal backlog of applicants. Yet from the evidence of the figures, if not from ministerial statements, there would appear to have been an informal quota on Italian immigration in the past two years of around 28,000. Can Canada afford to be so choosy?

It would seem to an outsider, for what his opinions are worth, that the actions that would best meet Canada's interests are:

(1) Lose your inhibitions about freely accepting good people from southern Europe — since this is your most likely source of substantial labor supply.

(2) Re-examine your demands for people with "skills" asking, first, are people who meet your requirements available and, secondly, is not your statement of requirements unduly exacting? Could not the degree of skill required be quite quickly acquired on the job, if you took a little trouble to instruct a man?

(3) If you really want more people from Britain and northern Europe, stop sneering at these countries, at their social arrangements and at their industrial and economic achievements. Be a little more humble about what you have to offer. Be warmer, and more frank, in your approach to the prospective newcomer.

I would send more of your people who have to deal with immigrants, and perhaps some of those who make policy, over to Europe, not to visit big shots and newspaper editors, but to see how working people live, and how unemployment and social security organizations work, how National Assistance (relief) is administered.

I would also, as some encouragement to those who might come here, sign reciprocal social security agreements with Britain and some other countries in Europe.

39. *CANADA* DOESN'T *NEED MORE PEOPLE**

W. H. S. Macklin†

Every time the Dominion Bureau of Statistics announces an increase in Canada's population it is a signal for widespread rejoicing. Shouts of "hosanna" and "hallelujah" are raised on all sides. Demographers rush to plot a new point on their graphs, and instantly proceed to project the

---

*From *Maclean's Magazine*, October 27, 1956.

†Major-General Macklin, C.B.E. (Retired) served in both World Wars and was formerly Adjutant-General of the Canadian Army.

curve of population into the future as far as their fancy takes them. The more steeply they think it will rise the better they like it.

We have the highest birth rate of any developed country in the world — more than twenty-eight per thousand per year. Our youths and maidens are marrying younger and having more children, and most Canadians think it's splendid. Since World War II we've imported some one million three hundred thousand immigrants, including our inimitable Mr. Pickersgill's inferior non-Canadian babies.

Yet many are not satisfied. Editors, prominent industrialists and politicians continue to agitate and to prod at the government for a speed-up in immigration. I think if some had their way they would build rafts and try to ferry over every human being in Europe this side of the Iron Curtain. I have heard it said in great seriousness that one half of the population of Great Britain should be transported to Canada. According to these enthusiasts, any Canadian problem — whether it be measles, inflation, or the national debt — can be solved by having more people.

I do not agree with them. I think this theory is an illusion, and that the old Boer, who complained loudly that his country was getting to be overpopulated because he could see the smoke of his neighbor's chimney, was much more realistic.

Looking at the matter from the broadest standpoint first, I reached the conclusion years ago that the most fundamental problem facing humanity today is neither racial, nor political, but biological; the seemingly insoluble puzzle of how to limit its own surplus fecundity. Of late years we have acquired a new basic problem: how to use and control atomic energy. I am afraid I do not think, as some do, that the solution to this second question will provide the right answer to the first, no matter whether the atomic energy is expended in hydrogen bombs or in industry.

The contention of the clergyman, Malthus, late in the eighteenth century, that the human race would outstrip its food supply, was discounted for two hundred years. But in the twentieth century science has greatly prolonged the average of human life, while there has been no corresponding inhibition in its reproduction.

So now, as Malthus foretold, the world's population is rising in an ever-steeper curve. There are no more virgin continents to develop, and multitudes are already hungry. When I hear of an increase in the birth rate, there rises a vision of the mountain of food each baby newcomer will eat if it lives to be seventy.

I have encountered this population problem at first hand in Asia. In the early 1930s it was my good fortune to spend two years in the Indian subcontinent. It occurred to me, from observations there, that whatever aspersions may be cast upon the system known sometimes as "colonialism," and sometimes, more accurately, as "imperialism," that system, in two centuries of British application, had wrought basic changes in India.

To simplify a complex matter, I will say that, under British rule, three things were introduced into India: transportation, sanitation, and irrigation. A great system of excellent railways was built, enabling the transfer of food from areas of surplus to areas of famine. Water supplies were purified, disposal of excrement systematized, drugs like quinine and the vaccines introduced. Gigantic dams were erected to water the desert and increase the food supply.

On top of this, peace succeeded a millennium of warfare, and thus the four horsemen of the Apocalypse — Conquest, War, Famine and Death — were restrained from their former devastating charges across the country.

Most people would call these things "benefits," but did all this increase the standard of living in India? It did not; it merely increased the number of Indians, which was rising in my time there by ten thousand each and every day and is now leaping up at around thirteen thousand per day. The Indians have continued to multiply right up to the level of the land's ability to maintain them at the lowest standard short of starvation.

When I asked a very prominent and very wise Indian what he thought would be the end of this trend, he answered that if the food supply is increased by every available means the standard of living may rise, the birth rate may fall, and the population may level off at six hundred million. It is a rugged prospect for a country where they already burn the cow dung for lack of other fuel, and so compound their impoverishment.

Twice in my life I have been privileged to see Japan, in 1935 and again in 1953. Between those visits Japan, in spite of war, added about twenty million people to her small, mountainous and infertile islands. I calculated that the population destroyed by the atomic bombs at Hiroshima and Nagasaki was replaced by natural increase in about three weeks.

Short of some completely new, scientific revolution in agriculture the Japanese cannot increase their production of food. They have to import it, and so they must export goods in a world of high tariffs and fierce competition. If that system fails them they must either control their birth rate, or expand at somebody else's expense, or starve.

As for Korea, the condition of humanity in the city of Pusan, when I saw it in April 1953, was so incredibly degraded, so appalling, and so hopeless, as to defy ordinary description; neither words nor pictures could portray it. It seemed to me to be the final result of centuries of over-population and depletion of a country's resources, followed by war.

"Well, what," you say, "has all this got to do with Canada?" The answer is that the disastrous effects of overemphasis on population, coupled with an almost total neglect of conservation, will in the end be the same here as they have been in those Asiatic lands. We cannot go on forever as we are doing, for instance, in the fertile semicircle between Toronto and Niagara — building factories, and houses to live in, on the land we have to live *on*.

In this matter of our population versus our resources we have forgotten that the commandments of the Almighty were never meant to be taken by halves, and we have elected to split the very first of all the great commandments, that which is written in the Book of Genesis, chapter one. "Be fruitful and multiply" is what it says to start with, and we have been multiplying like rabbits, or locusts, of late years, while totally ignoring the rest of the injunction: "Replenish the earth and subdue it." I see no notable signs of replenishment.

There are, of course, many aspects to this matter of population other than the depletion of resources. For one thing the sociological effects of the too-rank growth and urbanization of our people are numerous and serious. In achieving rapid growth we cannot avoid the urbanization; the record of history is that these two demographic phenomena invariably go together. Even Ghengis Khan, the all-conquering nomad of the thirteenth century, could not stop the trend. As fast as he overcame the cities of Asia and massacred their people, other cities sprang up in their places.

But urbanization brings plenty of troubles, for immense and growing congregations of humanity in cities strangle themselves, and they find that life becomes more and more expensive and less satisfying. Yet all the effort they can make never permits them to catch up to their basic wants in such facilities as housing, transportation, sanitation and recreation.

Thus Toronto spent about thirteen million dollars a mile on its five-mile subway, and the taxpayers of city and province are now putting up more millions for the express highways, designed to carry people past the place, instead of through it. As for Montrealers, they stagnate in their own traffic, and merely wish they had the subway and the by-passes.

Already our crisis in education, too, is pretty well national in scope because of the surging ranks of new school children and the hordes of young people who will soon be demanding entrance to our overburdened universities.

These things have placed a weighty and growing burden on our provincial and municipal governments. The faster their populations expand the worse they feel it. Ontario's premier has already pointed out publicly many times that the provinces face the paradox that "prosperity" is very expensive. This has now become a major political issue between provincial and federal governments. No matter which wins, the taxpayers won't.

All of these socio-economic problems, to be sure, would certainly be at least partially soluble given some applied political wisdom, and the will to make sacrifices. Unfortunately, in our free and democratic system of government applied political wisdom is rare. It is almost invariably strangled by an infinitude of vested interests and pressure groups. In many obvious ways it becomes next to impossible for government, at any level, to act consistently for the greatest good of the greatest number. The greater the number the greater the difficulty. A typical, if relatively minor, case in point is the uproar, frustration and procrastination that has attended efforts to establish a "green belt" around Ottawa.

There are other social effects of a nastier nature, and harder to cope with. I fear it is beyond dispute that there has been a disturbing increase in public disrespect for law and authority going along with the bigger census figures. As only one instance I cite the flagrantly lawless, reckless, boorish behavior of ten or fifteen percent of our motorists, and the resulting horrible accident toll, which is now accepted with resigned public apathy, punctuated by occasional futile outcries.

I scarcely need to harp on the very marked growth in the incidence of revolting crimes of violence, and as for juvenile delinquency, reams have been written on it and millions of words spouted without much effect. Prominent in the worst riots in Montreal in a generation, which occurred last year, were many youngsters in leather jackets. The press constantly records assaults, disorders, and wanton senseless property smashing by gangs of ruffianly scoundrels euphemistically called "teen-agers." A year or so ago in Toronto eight of these youthful and exuberant males chivalrously collaborated in a rape.

While the causes of these dangerous social aberrations are doubtless numerous and complex, I contend that they can be set down mainly to the too-sudden herding of too much humanity, of diverse cultures and backgrounds, into overswollen communities that are consequently almost totally lacking in communal cohesion and in even the rudiments of collective social responsibility. The quiet integrated life of farm and village has been replaced by the drab, neurosis-breeding existence of ugly, crowded suburbs, destined to be slums.

Lastly, before bowing to the clamor for faster immigration to augment our numbers, I recommend a long hard look at the existing standard of Canadian patriotism or zeal to defend the freedom, rights, privileges, and independence of this country.

"Patriotism," said Edith Cavell in her last message before the Germans shot her, "is not enough." She may have been right, but assuredly one of our weaknesses in Canada is that a great many of our people have acted for a long time — and still act — as if patriotism to the whole Canadian nation, or for that matter to any part of it, is a thing of no value at all, or even a positive evil.

There are certainly varied and cumulative reasons for this attitude, but I think the most important single one has been the importation of hundreds of thousands of people with not the smallest inkling of either of our two languages, or of our history, our literature, our cultures, or our political institutions.

I know of no other country in the world that ever attempted to absorb so huge a proportion of totally alien human stock in so short a time. For the benefit of the hecklers who would like to leap up at this point, shouting that I do not even know we took in a far bigger percentage fifty years ago, I will say that I am aware of it, and add that we are still digesting that lot.

Said Dr. Sidney Smith, president of the University of Toronto, proudly, "There is no Canadian race. There has never been a 'melting pot' policy toward newcomers. We have rejoiced in and been strengthened by their special contributions." And then he broke into a joyful recitation of the manifold and varied cultural and other benefits each of these incoming nationalities and races has bestowed upon us.

It is hard to quarrel with so eminent and humanitarian a Canadian. No doubt what he said is true, but it is not all the truth. I think Dr. Smith might feel differently, and less positively enthusiastic, had he had an experience such as I had in 1944, of commanding five thousand Canadian soldiers, of whom ninety percent were conscripts.

These were all very good men indeed, and had proved their endurance and bravery far from home, in the Aleutian Islands. While many of them were of European parentage they had all been born in Canada, and they had never lived anywhere else. Yet nearly all of them were totally lacking in any understanding whatever of the meaning or the price of freedom, nor had anyone ever taught them anything significant about this country. The parents of most of them knew naught of these things, and, clearly, neither did those who had given them such meagre schooling as they had had. So they had no patriotism — not any at all. How could they have any?

When a Greek Catholic priest came to camp to exhort and minister to the members of his faith, there were mutterings of discontent among them, because "the army has sent us a Polish priest." In short, such politics as these young Canadians had were not Canadian at all. They were still European.

I asked for some films calculated to arouse any love of country latent in these men, and was sent some reels made by our National Film Board, showing, among other things, the life of the Doukhobors, as typical, good, thrifty citizens of Canada. The films did not show any of the five or six hundred schools these people have burned down in the past sixty years, nor were any depicted in the nude.

I certainly do not discount the tremendous value of the science, the skills, or the artistic assets we have acquired from all the miscellaneous nationalities that have come here over the years. I merely note that there are also less attractive aspects to a rapid and wholesale immigration of mixed stocks, and there is no sense pretending there aren't.

In spite of the indisputable oriental industry so much admired by Dr. Smith, and the cultural and other merits of the Japanese in British Columbia, those people were not assimilated — not in three generations — and in 1942 the results to them were drastic.

The case of these Japanese, and several others like it, reminds me of a legendary tale:

A drop of oil asked sanction to mingle with the water in a jar, and the water said "No — for you can only rise to the top of the jar and spread, and even if the jar be washed, yea scoured, it will remain oily forever."

There were just over five million people in Canada 1901, and there are sixteen million much less homogeneous people now. In the interval we have acquired vast knowledge, but there has been no correspondingly remarkable increase in the sum total of our collective Canadian wisdom.

The expansion of the past ten years has been, I submit, too rapid. Anyway, it has presented us with a host of problems: economic, political, regional and national. My view is that we should now concentrate, for quite some time, on the solution of these vexing questions, and on improving the quality, standards, and the national cohesion of the Canadian people rather than increasing the quantity by further dilution of old stocks.

In ancient times neither cultured Greece nor mighty Rome proved able to survive the process of dilution indefinitely.

40. ARE NEW CANADIANS HURTING CANADA?*

P. C. Newman†

Almost two million people have crossed the Atlantic since 1945 to seek a better future in Canada. Most of them have found it. The newcomers have gradually been recasting their manner of life, have had nearly half a million babies, and have irrevocably diversified the character of this nation.

At the same time, an increasing number of Canadians, some in their official positions, many more unofficially, have been raising the cry that immigrants are snatching jobs away from native-born Canadians, lowering the standard of working conditions, and causing a shortage of housing. There are mounting charges that by allowing themselves to be exploited, the immigrants have made it easier for unscrupulous employers, landlords and others to exploit native-born Canadians as well.

Resented by some Canadians who treat them as second-class citizens, many of the new arrivals have chosen to withdraw into "ghettos" of their own ethnic groups, where at least their complaints are heard and understood. Many Italians, for example, are convinced that most Canadians regard them as inferior. "A sort of pizza curtain exists between us," says Arturo Scotti, editor of the Italian semi-weekly Corriere Canadese. "We're thought of as people who just like to sing and eat queer foods."

The ill feeling against immigrants by Canadians is increasing rather than diminishing. During the months of high unemployment last winter, second-, third-, and fourth-generation citizens without work tended to blame the newcomers. In queues outside Unemployment Insurance Commission offices there were ugly blusterings of "doing something about the damn immigrants." At union halls across the country indignant men drew up resolutions urging a permanent halt to immigration.

The antagonism toward New Canadians has not gone unnoticed across the Atlantic and has brought Canada sharp criticism. The People, a mass circulation British Sunday newspaper, recently published a series of articles accusing Canada of enticing England's skilled manpower "into a veritable man-trap." Such attacks, whether fair or not, will make it

---

*From *Maclean's Magazine*, July 18, 1959.
†Mr. Newman, author of *Renegade in Power: The Diefenbaker Years*, (Toronto, McClelland and Stewart Ltd., 1963), is currently National Affairs Editor of *Maclean's Magazine*.

harder to get immigrants when we need them — and most economists and many politicians insist immigration is essential for our long-range development.

Meanwhile, unless this country's business recovery speeds up, the complaints about New Canadians may grow even more vociferous in Canada next winter, and complaints abroad about Canada's treatment of immigrants may also become increasingly bitter.

How much truth is there in the accusation that Canadian business is ruthlessly exploiting immigrant labor? To what extent have New Canadians been grabbing jobs away from "Old Canadians?"

To obtain the answers to these questions, I have spent several weeks interviewing government officials, social workers, union leaders, immigrants, the officers of ethnic organizations and others concerned with the settlement of the newcomers. Their statements and the evidence I have found in investigating their statements have convinced me that:

Some shameful islands of European labor exploitation do persist in this country, mainly among the small sub-contracting firms in the big-city construction trades, and in the textile finishing shops of Vancouver, Winnipeg, Toronto and Montreal. With a few exceptions, the employers who take advantage of the newcomers' difficulties are fellow countrymen who preceded them to Canada and now operate businesses here. At a time when the average wage for a forty-hour week in Canada's manufacturing industries is seventy dollars, some newcomers are paid twenty-five dollars to work a weekly fifty hours. Immigrants have often had to pay exorbitant rents for inferior housing. They have frequently been victimized by real-estate sharks and used-car salesmen.

The unionized one third of this country's non-agricultural labor force has little realistic ground for claiming that immigrants deprive them of jobs. When industrial layoffs occur, they are usually on the basis of seniority; the newcomers are the first to be let out.

The unorganized, unskilled and semi-skilled element which swarms to temporary work of all kinds has been more seriously affected. Immigrants are in a preferred position because they will accept lower wages and are not prevented by family ties from working in remote areas.

Immigrants seldom take jobs away from Canadians well established in their trades, but their presence is beginning to weaken the bargaining power of organized labor.

Probably the most direct cause of conflicts between Canadian workers and the newcomers is that for some of the openings that do exist in times of increasing unemployment, immigrants are hired ahead of Canadians. "We find," says Mrs. Nel West, director of Toronto's International Institute, an immigrant employment agency and social centre, "that newcomers get preference over Canadians with many employers, because they realize that people who have left their homes to move here are serious in their approach to work and respect authority more."

The ambitious newcomer has little choice. With some exceptions, European degrees, trade diplomas and other qualification papers are not recognized by professional societies and unions in Canada. To advance, the immigrant must show evidence of Canadian experience. To get such training, he often feels that he has to compensate for his ignorance of language and work procedures by working harder for less money, and taking the jobs that Canadians don't want.

On-the-job tension grows when immigrants try to preserve inbred working habits. It's a custom in most central European plants to start the day by shaking hands with your co-workers. When Canadians coming on shift don't shake hands with them, then new arrivals think they're expressing hostility. "The perfectly understandable behavior of the newcomer in associating with fellow countrymen on and off the job also leads to great resentment," say Sid Blum, director of the Jewish Labor Committee and administrator of the human rights program for the Canadian Labor Congress.

The feeling of insecurity among immigrants employed in marginal jobs for marginal rates of pay is sometimes intensified by the fear of deportation. The Immigration Act provides for the deportation of immigrants who become public charges, and it is mandatory for municipal clerks to turn in reports on immigrants seeking aid. Although Ottawa seldom orders deportation unless the immigrant is obviously attempting to avoid work, Canadian Welfare Council officials report that the newcomers will sometimes endure near starvation, rather than risk investigation by approaching welfare agencies.

"The fear of deportation is also being used by foreign-born employers to prevent union recruiting among immigrants," charges Henry Weisbach, the education director for Ontario of the Canadian Labor Congress, who claims that foremen are sometimes ordered by management to tell newcomers that all Canadian unions are communist, and that they'll get into trouble with the police if they sign pledge cards.

Provincial government officials across the country say that the greatest number of complaints about immigrant exploitation involve small sub-contracting firms in the construction industry. Bruno Zanini, an Italian-speaking organizer for the Bricklayers, Masons and Plasterers Union, claims that in a survey he recently conducted among Italian sub-contractors in the Toronto area, he found that eighty-five percent of the bricklayers employed by the firms were not receiving holiday pay — compulsory under Ontario law. "Many of these men," he says, "have never heard of unemployment insurance — their employers haven't deducted the worker's share or paid their own." Eric Billington, chairman of Ontario's Industry and Labor Board, which investigates employer practices, insists that Zanini's claim is greatly exaggerated. "Certainly some of the Italian sub-contractors try to evade making holiday payments, but they're no worse than any other group," he says.

Small sub-contracting firms that sometimes disappear between jobs and keep few records are the worst offenders, according to government officials. The Manitoba department of labor recently discovered that a Yugoslav sub-contractor in Winnipeg was keeping the only data on his five-man crew of Yugoslav immigrant laborers on the inside cover of his cigarette-paper package. He had to pay a ten-dollar fine for failure to deduct income tax, unemployment insurance and workmen's compensation. "I don't know about the small firms," says George Playfair-Brown, general manager of Donolo (Ontario) Limited, a large Toronto construction firm that employs many immigrants, "but it would certainly be impossible for an employee receiving wages from us not to receive vacation pay or unemployment insurance."

Despite some flagrant examples of immigrant exploitation in the unskilled and semi-skilled categories of nearly every industry, the overwhelming majority of postwar newcomers to Canada have been absorbed relatively smoothly into the country's labor force. Most of them labor in jobs without heavy responsibility, but more and more of the immigrants have been gaining positions in the middle echelons of management. Except for some controlled by European capital, however, no major corporation in Canada is yet headed by a recent arrival from continental Europe.

As their jobs improve, many immigrants are assuming much more secure economic positions. The established newcomers put away an estimated hundred and fifty million dollars a year into their bank savings accounts, but recent arrivals have a tendency to purchase goods beyond their means. Immigrants from southern and eastern Europe, where there are fewer credit opportunities, sometimes translate their earnings from their first job into continental terms, decide they're doing very well, then load themselves up with installment debts. Parents of single men who come to Canada frequently receive in one of their first letters a photograph of their boy in front of his newly acquired used car. "Because they're so insecure, they become very materialistic and strive to collect symbols of their success as quickly as possible," says Dr. John Sawatsky, a University of Toronto psychologist who has studied immigrant integration. He claims one serious problem is that some of the smaller finance companies lure immigrants with easy loans, then hint at deportation if they fall behind on payments.

Just as some of the better-established immigrants most flagrantly exploit the newcomers as employees, they also are the worst offenders in selling newcomers things they neither need nor can afford. The immigration department recently ordered out of its immigrant coaches the vice-president of a German-Canadian club in Toronto, who rode the trains from Halifax, Saint John and Montreal as a welcoming ethnic representative. Federal officials discovered that he was simultaneously paid commissions by a Toronto store to sell the newcomers furniture. One German family complained that they had been signed up for fifteen hundred dollars' worth of furnishings an hour out of Halifax. The ethnic representative had told them that they'd have to own the essentials as soon as they left the train because all Canadian flats are unfurnished.

Some of the early misunderstandings between immigrants and Canadian merchants grow into charges of discrimination that turn out to be groundless. Immigration officials in Hamilton received one impassioned complaint from a recently arrived Italian family that Eaton's department store was discriminating against them. When government representatives investigated, they discovered that the Italian women were furious with Eaton's clerks because they refused to bargain over the price of merchandise — an accepted procedure in southern Italy.

The heads of immigrant families strive eagerly for the feeling of security afforded by home ownership, but they are often victimized by real-estate men who take advantage of their unfamiliarity with local conditions. "They're in such a rush to have a house, they'll believe almost anything they're told," says Julius Koteles, a Hungarian-born Winnipeg lawyer. In one case he recently investigated, he found that an unscrupulous real-estate agent had arranged for a Hungarian family to obtain a house for a down payment of only one hundred dollars, but the terms were such that the immigrants are now bound to pay off a mortgage for nearly twice the value of the house. The mortgage interest rate is eight percent.

A more spectacular plight was that of Ludwig Zsoldos, a Hungarian living in Edmonton, who bought a house for five hundred dollars last winter. The dwelling was obviously in bad shape, but Zsoldos thought he was getting a great bargain. He didn't notice that the sales documents only referred to the building. The lot on which it stood had already been sold to a brickyard. The house was in too poor condition for transfer to safer ground.

The exploitation of immigrants is not confined to cities. While the isolation of farm laborers makes them the least vocal of the immigrant groups, the leaders of ethnic societies claim that many newcomers who have taken agricultural jobs are being badly abused in terms of pay and working hours. One case recently investigated by social workers in Calgary involved a Spanish immigrant who had been kept for almost a year without pay on a nearby farm, working up to fifteen hours a day. The immigrant claimed the Canadian farmer had convinced him that he had entered the country illegally, that he was being sought for deportation, and that his picture was even hung with other wanted men in the local post office. The Spaniard eventually left to look for himself and told his story to a local welfare agency. It arranged another job, but no court action was instituted for back pay. The farmer claimed that he had rewarded his Spanish hireling with free board and clothing; the immigrant refused to take his case to trial.

Few wage disputes involving immigrants reach the courts. The amounts of money at stake are usually small and the newcomer is frightened of contacts with the law. There are still arguments about the extent of actual exploitation that took place in the most controversial postwar immigrant labor incident. This was the scheme of Ludger Dionne, who in 1947 flew in from European DP camps a hundred Polish women to work at his rayon spinning mill, in St. Georges de Beauce, Que. Those chosen had to sign two-year contracts for a forty-eight-hour week, at an initial rate of twenty-five cents an hour, then the province's legal minimum. They lived in the annex of a convent near the factory, had to call Dionne *Tatus* (father) and could only leave their residence twice a week until 11 p.m. Dionne personally approved their shopping lists and they had to submit any marriage proposal received for his sanction — a blessing seldom given. After paying rent and returning part of their trans-Atlantic air fare, their weekly wages averaged $3.60. The plan was so heavily criticized in the House of Commons, where Dionne was a Liberal backbencher, that nearly all of the women were allowed to leave within a year.

Another potentially explosive situation involving immigrant labor occurred in the summer of 1957, during the recognition strike by the United Steel Workers against Gaspe Copper Mines Limited, at Murdochville, Que. The new miners imported by the company to replace the strikers included a heavy representation of German immigrants. When Roger Provost, the president of the Quebec Federation of Labor, led a protest delegation to the mine site, the Germans lined up behind the barricaded fences, hoarsely repeating the illogical chant: "GO HOME DAMN CANUCKS!" Some violence followed, and most of the immigrants have now left the Gaspe.

These and similar embittering incidents are difficult to eliminate, but there is in this country an increasing realization that the immigrant is one of the indispensably valuable factors in maintaining Canada's economic and social development. "Our high standard of living," says Sid Blum of the Jewish Labor Committee, "could never have been developed without the human resources made available by large-scale immigration.

SELECTED BIBLIOGRAPHY

Aschmann, H. H., and Aitken, H. G. J., "Canada's Birth Rate," *The Canadian Journal of Economics and Political Science*, Vol. XXIV, February, 1958.

Barkway, M., "Can Immigration Solve Tomorrow's Problems?," *The Financial Post*, July 21, 1956.

Bladen, V. W., (Editor), *Canadian Population and Northern Colonization*, Toronto, University of Toronto Press, 1962.

Cahill, B., "Do Immigrants Bring a Mental Health Problem to Canada?," *Saturday Night*, June 22, 1957.

Corbett, D. C., *Canada's Immigration Policy*, Toronto, University of Toronto Press, 1957.

Hart, A. L., "Canada Doesn't Need More Immigrants," *Saturday Night*, March 3, 1956.

Jones, F. E., "A Sociological Perspective on Immigrant Adjustment," *Social Forces*, Vol. 35, No. 1, October, 1956.

Keyfitz, N., "The Changing Canadian Population," in Clark, S. D., *Urbanism and the Changing Canadian Society*, Toronto, University of Toronto Press, 1961.

McDougall, D. M., "Immigration into Canada 1851-1920," *The Canadian Journal of Economics and Political Science*, Vol. XXVII, May, 1961.

Peterson, W., *Planned Migration: The Social Determinants of the Dutch-Canadian Movement*, Berkeley, California, University of California Press, 1955.

Population Association of America, "Demographic Changes and Population Policy in Canada," (Meeting), May 3-4, 1958.

Roddick, P. M., "Immigration and the Canadian Employer," *The Business Quarterly*, Vol. 21, Spring, 1956.

chapter eight

FAMILY AND FAMILY-RELATED PROBLEMS

The family is probably the most consequential institution in the society in terms of the effect that it has upon our lives, and many of our social problems are directly or indirectly rooted in the family system. The relationship of family conditions and delinquency, for example, is well documented, and many of the attitudes we hold toward persons of different racial, religious or ethnic groups are the result of family experiences. While these particular problem areas, and some others which involve family to a greater or lesser degree, are treated in separate chapters in this book, there are yet other family or family-related problems which will be considered at this point. A number of these are set out by A. P. Jacoby, a sociologist at the University of Alberta, in a specially written article which reviews, comparatively, "Some Family Problems in Canada and the United States". His review reveals that there are some sharp differences as well as a number of similarities between the situations in the two countries.

A rather extreme form of family tragedy is revealed by Benjamin Schlesinger, a professor of social work, in "Families of Misfortune". This selection deals with those Canadian families, so maladjusted as to be referred to as "multi-problem families", who, although relatively small in number, account for rather large amounts of welfare expenditures. A picture of family disruption and the various social factors which relate to this disruption is presented from the point of view of the Family Court in an article by W. T. Little entitled "The Domestic Illness Profile Seen in a Family

Court Setting." Having collected a large amount of data drawn from families who have been involved in Family Court processes, Mr. Little is able to suggest a five-point program of recommendations for social policy to reduce the problem. Some of the more interesting current legal stipulations which bear upon family problems is presented in a rather light-hearted way by Frank Oxley in "Pity the Poor Husband on the Run." Mr. Oxley's point is to show that, in dealing with situations of family disruption, the law in Canada firmly protects the rights of women, but leaves the poor husband in a "pitiable" state as far as his legal rights are concerned.

The next article, by contrast, is not at all lighthearted, but rather a serious report of a scientific study of the characteristics of and relevant factors concerning ninety-six illegitimately pregnant women entering a Canadian hospital to have their babies. "Observations on Illegitimacy", by Dr. Solomon Hirsch, deals with one of the more important of the family-related problems, that of the "unwed mother", and presents some very worthy data on the medical and social-psychological characteristics of these women.

Not all illegitimately pregnant women choose to give birth to their babies, however, and they, along with a number of married women who likewise do not desire to bear the offspring they are carrying, seek abortions, both legal and illegal. Shirley Mair surveys the situation of the illegal or criminal abortion in Canada, and her article "National Report on the Abortion Mills and the Law" is probably best summed up by the quotation "Don't tell me your town doesn't have a criminal abortionist. You're just too naive to know who he is . . . ."

The final two selections in this chapter treat, respectively, two family problems which concern people at the opposite extremes of the life process: "What's Happening to Canada's Children?" and "The Problem of the Aged". In the first of these articles, Phyllis Burns reviews some of the needs of Canada's children, and the variety of services available to help meet some of these needs. But, she points out, "this picture also has a dark side", and she goes on to enumerate some of the weaknesses and difficulties in treating the many problems which children can present.

C. T. Andrews, writing about the problem of the aged, briefly describes the extent of this problem, and notes difficulties with regard to hospital treatment, nursing care, mental care, retirement and employment. He concludes that it is "along the line of increased productivity" that the solution to many of the problems of old age lies.

41. SOME FAMILY PROBLEMS IN CANADA AND THE UNITED STATES: A COMPARATIVE REVIEW*

Arthur P. Jacoby†

There exists a strong temptation to consider that for all practical purposes, the Canadian family and that to be found in the United States are very much alike. This is a convenient assumption, for data on family problems in the United States are readily available in the literature while statistics on the Canadian family and family problems are less easily come by. A comparison of these two countries with regard to family problems, where data are available, is the object of this paper.

Sociologists are fond of analyzing family systems from the standpoint of their structure and their function. Many books have discussed at length the changes in family function that have occurred in the United States during the last two centuries. Although statistical data directly indicating changes in family function are seldom found, it is the author's impression that similar changes have taken place in Canada. For example, changes in economic function probably derive, to a great extent, from the shift from a rural society to an urban one. In 1961 seventy per cent of the population of both countries was classified as urban.

From a structural standpoint, however, the Canadian family differs from its counterpart south of the border. The Canadian family is considerably larger: its average size in 1961 was 3.9 persons compared with the United States average of 3.3 persons.

Without doubt, one basis for the larger Canadian family is Canada's astounding (many would use the adjective "frightening") birth rate. Not only is the 1960 rate of 26.9 births per one thousand population greater than the U. S. birth rate of 23.9, but Canada outdoes all Western (and many non-Western) countries, with the exception of some in South America, in the rate of production of babies.

One response to the problem of potential over-population created by this high birth rate, and augmented by a high rate of immigration, has been the founding, within the last few years, of a Canadian Planned Parenthood Association with branches in many cities. A goal of first priority for this association is to bring about a change in that part of the

---

*Published here for the first time.

†Dr. Jacoby is Assistant Professor of Sociology at the University of Alberta, Edmonton.

Canadian Criminal Code which makes it a crime to distribute contraceptive materials, or information about contraception, unless it can be proven to be in the public interest. The founders of the Planned Parenthood Federation of America fought this battle successfully in most states of the United States several decades ago.

The legal status of contraception in Canada is at least as confusing as it is in the United States. There the perplexity stems from the fact that each of the fifty states writes its own laws regarding birth control. In some states it is government policy to distribute contraceptive devices to those who want them and cannot afford to purchase them privately. In other states it is illegal for even a physician to distribute these items under any circumstances. By way of contrast, the Canadian Criminal Code applies to all provinces. The difficulty in Canada seems to be that the code is administered differently in some provinces than in others and that no one seems to be very certain as to exactly what kind of behaviour is prohibited.

Distribution of contraceptive information is not illegal if it can be shown to be in the public interest. At present, some physicians are not willing to run this kind of risk. Recently a Planned Parenthood clinic in Toronto was closed by authorities acting under this section of the Criminal Code. This situation is equally ambiguous with regard to other methods of birth control: the legality of sterilization operations is questionable, and many physicians refuse to perform abortions (even with good medical reasons) for fear of legal punishment.

Although illegitimacy rates in Canada have shown a sporadic increase over the last fifty years, the 1960 rate of 4.3 illegitimate births for every 100 live births is not greatly different from that of the United States, which has been holding steady in recent years around four per cent. The rate of illegitimacy in both Canada and the United States tends to be on the low side when a comparison is made with other countries in which birth records are kept.

Many writers in the United States are expressing concern over the problem of "teen-age marriages." Since about the turn of the century there has been a decline in age at first marriage in both Canada and the United States, but the Canadian figure has invariably been several years higher than that for the United States. In 1959 Canadian females married at an average age of 23.1 years while their counterparts in the United States married at age 20.0. The corresponding figures for men were 25.9 and 22.6 respectively.

Why should such a difference in average age at first marriage exist between two countries that are, on the surface at least, so very much alike? Possibly the difference in the sex ratios (discussed below) of the two countries provides a clue. Perhaps the larger percentage of first generation immigrants in Canada's population helps to explain this difference in average age of marriage. The most likely answer, in the author's view, lies in Canada's stronger cultural ties with numerous European countries (backed, of course, by a continued high rate of immigration from those countries). Age at first marriage in most European countries seems to be much higher than in the United States and only a little higher than in Canada.

Textbooks on marriage and the family are fond of pointing out that the United States has one of the highest marriage rates, or conversely, one of the lowest rates of persons single, of any country. The indications are that Canada has a somewhat higher percentage of single persons in the population. An exact comparison is precluded by the fact that U.S. figures are reported in terms of persons fourteen years of age and older, while Canada's Dominion Bureau of Statistics reports on persons fifteen years of age and older.

About 26.5% of Canada's 1961 population 15 years of age and older was classed as single, whereas 25.9% of the population of the United States 14 years of age and older was considered single. A rough adjustment for the age differences noted above increases the Canadian percentage, however. Persons fourteen years of age in Canada in 1961 made up 1.86% of the population. Since almost all of these were undoubtedly single, we might tentatively consider about 28.3% of Canada's population fourteen years of age and older to be single.

The U.S. figure noted above excluded servicemen; presumably more men in military service are single than are married. Thus, the U.S. statistic, to be comparable to the Canadian, must be increased by some unknown amount.

Two explanations present themselves for the difference between the U.S. and Canadian data: (1) Since the older a person is, the less likely he is to be classified as single (never married), the older average age of the U.S. population would lead one to expect a lower percentage of the population to be single; (2) the earlier age of marriage in the United States, reported above, would also suggest that a lower percentage of this population would be classed as single.

One factor determining the number of people in a society that will remain single is the sex ratio (the number of males in the population per 100 females). Obviously, if the sex ratio departs markedly from

100, large numbers of persons must remain single due to the unavailability of mates. Both the U.S. and Canadian sex ratios have been declining in recent decades, but in 1961 the U.S. figure was considerably lower (97) than the Canadian (102). Since men have a higher mortality rate at all age levels the average younger age of the Canadian population is a factor in its higher sex ratio. Probably more important, however, is the fact that males tend to predominate among immigrants; Canada accepts far more immigrants today relative to its base population than does the United States.

The working wife and/or mother is frequently considered to represent a social problem area. A large percentage of married women in both the United States and Canada were employed outside the home in the early 1960's. About 25% of Canadian married women, ages 20-64, were included in the labour force, while about 33% of married women in the United States (all ages) were working. Although no exact comparison can be made because of the different age categories used, the above data suggest that employment of the married female is more extensive in the United States than it is in Canada.

The student of the family finds an outstanding difference between these two countries with regard to divorce rates and laws governing divorce. In 1959 the divorce rate (number of divorces per 1,000 population) in the United States (2.3) was about six times greater than that in Canada (0.4). In both countries the present rate of divorce represents a great increase over that of several decades past; in 1910 the U.S. rate was 1.0 divorce per 1,000 population while Canada's was under 0.05 divorces per 1,000 population. Thus, while the divorce rate in the United States doubled in this fifty year period, Canada's rate increased by eight times.

An important factor in accounting for this difference in divorce rates between two neighbouring and culturally similar countries is, undoubtedly, the differing legal provision for the granting of divorces. In the United States each state enacts its own laws governing divorce, while the federal government has jurisdiction in Canada. The grounds for divorce differ greatly. Canadian law specifies that divorces will be granted solely on the basis of adultery.[1] This is allowed throughout the United States. In addition, most states permit divorces by reason of cruelty, desertion, and drunkenness. States often add other grounds for divorce.

This brief review of family problem areas in the United States and

---

[1] In Nova Scotia, divorces are permitted by reason of cruelty (not the contemporary American "mental cruelty", but the wife-beating kind).

Canada has indicated a number of sharp cleavages and some similarities between the two countries. The dissimilarities reported above seem to be based primarily on differences in legislation between the two countries (e.g., regarding contraception and divorce) or upon such factors as the difference in sex ratios.

42. FAMILIES OF MISFORTUNE*

Benjamin Schlesinger†

The definition which is used most widely in Canada for the multi-problem family, is that formulated by the United Community Services of London, Ontario.

> A family is considered a multi-problem one if the following character-istics are present:
> a) Failure in functioning of the father such as alcoholism, criminal acts, desertion, mental illness and the like.
> b) Failure in functioning of the mother such as alcoholism, criminal acts, desertion, mental illness, child neglect, and the like.
> c) Failure in the functioning of the children such as criminal acts, mental illness, poor school adjustments, and the like.
> d) Failure in the marital adjustment such as out-of-wedlock children, promiscuity, severe marital discord.
> e) Economic deprivation and grossly inadequate housing.
> f) And as a result of three or more of the above listed, the family have been a chronic or intermittent undue burden to a community for over three years.

This definition thus includes only families which have come to the attention of community agencies due to their many problems.

In 1944, Wofinden in England wrote a description of the multi-problem family, which became a classic. He wrote:

> "Often it is a large family, some of the children being dull or feeble-minded. From their appearance they are strangers to soap and water,

---

*From *Canada's Health and Welfare*, Vol. 18, No. 5, May 1963, and No. 6, June 1963.

†Dr. Schlesinger, author of a recent book entitled *The Multi-Problem Family* (Toronto, University of Toronto Press, 1963), is Assistant Professor of Social Work at the University of Toronto.

toothbrush and comb; the clothing is dirty and torn and the footgear absent or totally inadequate. Often they are verminous and have scabies and impetigo. Their nutrition is surprisingly average — doubtless due to extra-familial feeding in schools. The mother is frequently substandard mentally.

"The home, if indeed it can be described as such, has usually the most striking characteristics. Nauseating odours assail one's nostrils on entry, and the source is usually located in some urine-sodden, faecal-stained mattress in an upstairs room. There are no floor coverings, no decorations in the walls except perhaps the scribblings of the children and bizarre patterns formed by absent plaster. Furniture is of the most primitive, cooking utensils absent, facilities for sleeping hopeless — iron bedsteads furnished with soiled mattresses and no coverings. Upstairs there is flock everywhere, which the mother assures me has come out of a mattress she has unpacked for cleansing. But the flock seems to stay there for weeks and the cleansed and repacked mattress never appears. The bathroom is obviously the least-frequented room of the building. The children, especially the older ones, often seem to be perfectly happy and contented, despite such a shocking environment. They will give a description of how a full sized midday meal has been cooked and eaten in the house on the day of the visit when the absence of cooking utensils gives the lie to their assertion. One can only conclude that such children have never known restful sleep, that the amount of housework done by the mother is negligible and that the general standard of hygiene is lower than that of the animal world."

Authorities in many countries, however, feel that this picturesque report is not fair and accurate. We in Canada are in the midst of examining the multi-problem family and its manifold implications for community welfare. Australia, Belgium, Britain, France, Holland, and the United States are all attempting to work out solutions to this problem which is costing communities a heavy toll in financial and human terms. We do know that these families constitute a small percentage of our metropolitan centers (4-8 percent), and yet they use about fifty percent of the health and welfare services and budgets.

The label which various countries attach to these families, seems to indicate that there is a universality in their living conditions, human welfare needs, and rejection on the part of the larger community. Holland calls them "asocial", Britain "problem", France "la famille inadaptée" (unadaptable) and "la famille sous-privilégiée" (underprivileged). On this continent we find such labels as "hard to reach", "resistive", "acting out", and "hard core" families. We seem to go along with Charles Booth, who in his classic study of Poverty in London in 1891 called them "the submerged tenth".

These families constitute the lengthy records in social agencies, the numerous visits to medical and psychiatric hospitals, the population of the worst slums of our cities, and they are the people for whom many members of our community have given up all hope, effort, and intensive service. They make up the families who are known to us from generation to generation as dependents on welfare, charity, and handouts. Unemployment, delinquency, illegitimacy, family breakdown, alcoholism, are all part and parcel of most of these families. We stood back for many years, closed our eyes and allowed the families to sink deeper into the slums of the body and mind. We felt that we could do nothing for them, that they were the lost cause.

Only within the last ten years, have we in Canada begun to examine this area of social welfare. We are at the stage of exploring and identifying the characteristics and needs of these families, before implementing any projects to work directly with these families on a concentrated basis, and to attempt to arrest this generational pattern of dependency.

We have considerable knowledge about the causal factors which seem to influence the growth of multi-problem families in our communities. We will briefly review the social and psychological factors which have been found to be almost universally accepted by professional persons interested in this area of human welfare.

SOCIAL FACTORS

There is increasing evidence that many of the parents of multi-problem families suffered considerable deprivation themselves during the early years of their lives. Many came from broken homes in which one parent, usually the father, had deserted or was imprisoned. Many of these parents, as children, had periods of institutional or foster-home placement or were brought up by a series of relatives. If they remained at home, their mothers were often employed and the children received inadequate substitute care. The mothers who had been deserted often entered into "common-law" relationships, sometimes bearing children by several men. In other words, the parents of the multi-problem family of today often have come from families that had similar characteristics. Case records show that asocial behaviour of families sometimes extends through several generations.

PSYCHOLOGICAL FACTORS

The social milieu of many multi-problem families suggests the nature of their psychological problems. Because these persons suffer such severe deprivation, they develop negative and hostile attitudes. Also, since they are often subjected to rejection by the community, they tend to isolate themselves from their neighbors.

The negative attitudes of the community toward these deprived families are likely to be heightened if the families belong to a race or culture different from the predominant one. Although persons of minority groups are often subjected to rejection in our society, the rejection is more overt if their standards of living or conduct deviate markedly from prevailing ones.

Lack of trust

One of the chief characteristics of both adults and children of multi-problem families is their lack of trust in others. They have few friends and little contact with social groups. They are mistrustful of neighbors, employers, physicians, nurses, school teachers, social workers, public officials, and so forth. In their dealings with health and welfare agencies, they may express interest in the service offered, but they tend to avoid personal involvement, often failing to carry through on plans that have been worked out with them.

Fear of authority

Because of their extreme mistrust of people, members of these families have an exaggerated fear of authority. All persons, of course, have some fear of authoritative agencies, particularly courts or other official bodies. Members of disorganized families, however, have greater and more pervasive fear; they feel threatened even by persons who have limited legal authority and whose approach is non-authoritative. Schools, churches, and health and welfare agencies are not only the symbols of community mores and social standards, but these institutions also have certain powers that can be invoked.

Feelings of hostility

Members of socially deprived families often have strong feelings of anger, aggression, and hostility intermingled with their mistrust and fear. Some persons are openly hostile and aggressive, while others attempt to hide their negative feelings behind a facade of friendliness and extreme politeness. Often these resentments go back to early childhood, when they were exposed to neglect, abuse, or abandonment by their parents.

Feelings of hopelessness

These persons have a sense of hopelessness which underlies all other feelings. These persons find temporary escape by going on a drinking or spending spree, by sexual promiscuity, by fighting, or by engaging in delinquent behavior.

Clinical factors

Any group of asocial clients will be comprised of persons with various degrees of mental health. Some may have relatively little pathology; their deviant behavior is largely a reaction to undue social strain and stress. Others may be psychotic or suffer from neurosis. A large proportion of asocial persons, however, fall into the category of "character disorders", the chief clinical feature of which is the arrest of the individual's emotional development. Because of inadequate parental care and guidance in early years, these persons retain many infantile attitudes and ways of behaving. In consequence, their responses are more appropriate to the pre-school age of development than to the adult level. They have difficulty in deferring gratifications, have little judgment about money and other practical matters, are selfish and self-centered, and tend to get into trouble.

What have we done so far in Canada in this area? The first prize must go to Vancouver, which was pioneered in this country in some pilot studies to identify and analyse multi-problem families in a metropolitan setting. In the month of June 1960, 1407 multi-problem families were identified in Vancouver, active with 14 social agencies. These families represented 21% of agency caseloads, and have been known on an average of 4 years by the agencies. The families seem to live mostly in a downtown section, characterized by deteriorated housing, high land value and low rentals. An interesting finding shows that these families are largely of Anglo-Saxon origin, and were residents of the city for a period of generations. Vancouver estimates that about twelve to sixteen thousand people are involved in the course of a year in these families.

In our own capital, Ottawa, a small study of multi-problem families sheds more light in this area. In 1961, the Welfare Council of Ottawa surveyed a group of 47 multi-problem families. These families are large, averaging 7.2 members per family (Canadian average 3.5), and all live in housing which is too costly, too crowded, or in poor physical condition. They are also in serious financial difficulty, in debt, and the education of the adults is limited to Grade 9 or less.

The families used 35 health and welfare agencies, and have been known to an agency for ten years or more. There is little co-ordination done among the agencies to help these families, and one finds a piecemeal approach, with each agency serving the family, and really not knowing what other agencies are doing with the particular family. The recommendations made in this report include co-ordination of services to these families.

Toronto and Windsor have done similar small studies of identifying multi-problem families. Toronto can be considered the pioneer in building an experimental two house unit for "troublesome families" in 1957. The final cost of the indestructible unit was $31,730.94. The house is described as "withstanding the rigours of hard wear", "free of infestation", and "fire retardent". The detailed description of the unit gives us a picture of an almost "atom proof" home, which even troublesome families can not destroy. It is felt that this experiment has helped multi-problem families in their adjustment to the community at large. It is part of the Human Rehabilitation of the families, who after a short time move out of the special unit to regular dwellings.

At the University of Toronto, School of Social Work, graduate students for their research requirements have been examining in detail the generational pattern found among problem families, and have examined the values held by these families.

The study of two generation families was undertaken in two social agencies in Metropolitan Toronto and consisted of a sample of 25 two generation families or 50 cases.

This study revealed a much larger size of family in this group of two generation families than the average Canadian family (3.5). The average size of the family in the first generation was 7.2 and 5.3 in the second generation. Most of the second generation families were still active with social agencies in Toronto.

The two generation families were confronted by a frightening array of problems. These included alcoholism, illegitimacy, marital discord, ill-health, unemployment, delinquency and crime, housing, financial problems and sexual deviation. There were also very pronounced problems in the area of care and training of children. Child neglect in the forms of physical abuse, lack of health supervision, lack of parental control and guidance, illegitimacy and desertion were present in most cases.

The problems that stood out sharply in the first generation were those of delinquency and crime, neglect and lack of parental control of the children. In the second generation the most frequent problem revealed was that of unmarried motherhood and illegitimacy.

The study also revealed that two generation families are mainly located in the downtown section of the city of Toronto, where there is a heavy population concentration. Residential mobility was very high in these families with an average move of more than once a year per family, but they moved largely within the same social milieu.

The data revealed that a high percentage of children of these families were cared for by social agencies. In the total number of families of both generations 57.7 percent of their children were placed with Children's

Aid Societies. In addition in both generations 38.7 percent of the children were placed by other means than Children's Aid Societies.

The average number of years a family was served by social agencies in the first generation was 7.2 years and in the second generation 3.8 years. Many of the problems confronting these families have come to the attention of a number of different health and welfare agencies in Metropolitan Toronto and outside Toronto.

What emerged from this study, was that if we do not make any concerted effort in preventing further dependency and do not help these families in an organized manner, the pattern of these families continues from generation to generation.

The financial cost to the community is staggering. Another recent graduate calculated costs for two Toronto multi-problem families. Family "A" had been receiving help from 16 agencies over a period of 17 years at a cost of $53,225 and family "B" known for 25 years had used up $61,700 of public and private funds. These costs did not include the price paid in human terms by these families, and the long array of professional and volunteer workers who had been in contact with these families.

From our experience in working with multi-problem families in Canada, we know that these families know that there are other ways to live, and basically they want to change. It is up to us to help these families out of the depth of despair, away from generational dependency and hopelessness and to rehabilitate them into the ordinary stream of life.

43. *THE DOMESTIC ILLNESS PROFILE SEEN IN A FAMILY COURT SETTING**

W. T. Little†

The Juvenile and Family Court of Metropolitan Toronto has been adjudicating domestic cases since 1929. From the beginning of the Family Court, the need for special domestic counselling was apparent.

*From *The Canadian Journal of Corrections,* Vol. 5, No. 4, October 1963.
†Mr. Little, a professional social worker, is Director of Social Services of the Juvenile and Family Court of Metropolitan Toronto.

When the advice of well-meaning friends, pastors, priests and lawyers failed to effect reconciliation among marriage partners, recourse to the Court became a means of settling bitter disputes regarding maintenance of wives and children by either reluctant or deserting husbands as well as many other problems.

This service has grown from one or two dedicated personnel with little formal training to a department of fifteen social workers with an intake section handling many thousands of cases a year.

Domestic counselling has become an important service to the Family Court, comparing in importance to that of the probation services, both juvenile and adult. Estranged partners, overwhelmed by circumstances they cannot cope with, are finding the courage and the insight to work out difficult family problems through the skilled and friendly help of professionally educated and qualified social workers.

In the Family Court of Metropolitan Toronto, domestic counsellors supervised by skilled supervisors with long experience and training, work with as many as 400 new families a month through the year.

These families come to the Court for help in resolving difficult marital problems either directly from the street, by telephone appointment or referral from social agencies throughout the city.

Although many reports have been undertaken by family agencies, planning council and others, very little reporting has come from the Courts regarding the nature of the cases before them or the profile characteristics of marriage partners undergoing domestic illness, a condition which is most prevalent in our society today.

With these facts in mind, the present investigation was undertaken. This is a study of 1,000 families in which one or more members of the family (more often the wife) has come voluntarily to the Family Court for some court action, or help to relieve the insufferable conditions of their married lives.

The objective of this study has been to identify the profile of a substantial sample of these families whose difficulties present us with the causation of many other social consequences such as juvenile delinquency, criminality, mental illness, alcoholism, transientism, to name only a few.

The material for the profile has been obtained from a questionnaire answered by the family members applying at the intake desks of the Domestic Counselling Department. Material from the case histories of families compiled by domestic counsellors and my own limited caseload has also been a source of information. Additional information was gleaned from intake information sheets used in the processing of clients to domestic counsellors from intake.

Any client applying to the Court has the fundamental right of swearing an information and instituting a court action without delay. However, in the majority of cases the complaining marital partner wishes to discuss his or her problem with some court officer prior to the laying of charges. It is at this point that the domestic counsellor comes into the court process, and will in many instances be the determining factor as to whether a court action will ultimately be undertaken or not by the client. The effectiveness of domestic counselling can possibly be estimated when we find that almost 90 per cent of all clients coming to the Court have been able to resolve their differences with the assistance of a counsellor without going before a judge. The remaining 10 per cent are referred to the Family Court judges for disposition of their cases.

It is realized by all counsellors that not every family difference or problem can be resolved out of the court room, or indeed should be.

THE AGE GROUP

Contrary to the general belief that marital partners in trouble are young, inexperienced teenagers, the truth is that the profile of the 1,000 cases observed between June 1962 and March 1963 indicate that the average age of husband and wife at the time of their marriage was 26.9 years and 23.6 years respectively. The ages of the spouses at the time their marital difficulties attained significance to the extent of being considered a court matter is on the average 7.7 years after marriage. In other words, the husband at the time of family breakdown is 34.6 years of age and his wife 31.3 years. This group can hardly be considered to be made up of young, immature couples.

Although no correlation has been established, it is interesting to note that marital difficulties and the "seven year itch" have something in common.

CHILDREN INVOLVED

As serious as marital bitterness between man and wife is, there is no real way of measuring the tragedy in the lives of children caught up in the maelstrom of domestic strife.

An average of 2.01 children per family that comes to the domestic court, gives us some idea of the social magnitude of this problem and the serious impact on little people under seven years of age (possibly the most formative years of their lives).

Although no study has been made as yet by the Court on a follow-up of such children, it is well known to us that many of them become known to our juvenile division and mental health clinics in later years.

NATIONALITY

Marital conflict is not restricted to any particular race or creed; however, as might be expected, Canadians are in the greatest number before our family courts and provide the largest single nationality representation in domestic counselling sessions — 81.7 per cent. The remaining 18.3 per cent of cases include members from all the immigrant groups admitted to this country with no defined pattern ascribable to any particular nationality. Italian, German, English, Yugo-Slav, Ukrainian and many others make up the foreign total. There are slightly fewer foreign wives than husbands — 17.9.

It is worth observing that among the cases under observation there are only 5.6 per cent of cases where the partners are of different nationality, i.e. Canadian-German, Dutch-French, etc.

MENTAL HEALTH

Many husbands and wives coming to the Court are in real need of psychiatric help and in many cases are referred to out-patient clinics and institutions on a voluntary basis. The real extent of this need, as determined by psychiatric assessment, is not known at this time. Although, we now have two psychiatrists attached to the Diagnostic Clinic of the Court, they have not been able to provide sufficient coverage of adults over a long period to provide reliable statistics.

We do know, however, that 5.3 per cent of all the husbands and 7.4 per cent of the wives in this sample, have been seen by psychiatrists on their own volition before coming to Court, in an endeavour to improve their mental health. We are aware that a much greater percentage of the total group are in need of such treatment at the time they are seen by the counselling service.

INCOME

Husbands and wives, who find their marriages in jeopardy, are among the low income earners as a group.

Classified under the following headings, we note that 98 per cent of the entire group earn under $5,000 per year and that almost 15 per cent earn less than $2,500 per year in a city that has one of the highest cost of living indexes in the country.

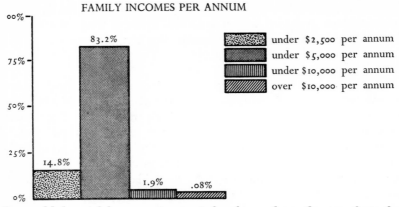

FAMILY INCOMES PER ANNUM

It would be a false premise to infer from these figures that almost all of domestic difficulties occur among those families within the low income brackets or in the same proportions. Such a deduction would quite wrongly lead us to believe that there is little or no domestic disharmony among the affluent or high income groups. Such is just not the case. There is a great deal of domestic illness in this group, but they resolve it differently than those who bring their trouble to the family court. Divorce is more easily available to those with high incomes, and any study of this group who resolve their domestic problems in this way will reveal that a much higher percentage of these people earn more than the average person appearing at the family court, which has sometimes been called the "poor man's divorce court". This is, of course, an ironic misnomer, as our family courts do not handle divorce cases. The wealthier class of citizens solve their marital disputes in other ways than using the family court. Private out of court settlements, legal agreements, higher court settlements with the aid of more experienced legal counsel excludes the low income earners as a group from such alternatives to their problems.

WORKING WIVES

The modern trend of wives working, as well as their husbands in an endeavour to establish a higher standard of living for themselves and their families, has not in itself given us any clear indication that this is a cause of family breakdown. It is significant, however, that 24.7 per cent of the wives of those families having marriage difficulties are working, and that even with this added income the total family income per annum falls within the pattern outlined above.

It is important to consider what is happening to the children of these families who are almost all under seven years of age, the majority being "pre-schoolers". In many cases the children are being left with relatives of the working couple, or with strangers on a day basis for which the parents pay a fee.

WELFARE

Not unrelated to the foregoing accounts respecting income and wives who work, is the fact that 31.1 per cent of the families observed have been, or are presently, receiving welfare money from municipalities within Metropolitan Toronto.

Many wives appear at the Court on the instructions of welfare officials advising that in order to receive welfare payments, they must lay charges against their husbands for non-support. This is a serious handicap to any domestic counsellor trying to work out a reconciliation with a problem family. Things that are said and done in court do not, as a rule, make for amicability between husbands and wives. At the same time, the problem is not easy of solution at the welfare level. Countless families have been known to attempt to obtain welfare payments while their husbands are earning enough money to keep the family. However, there are many needy families that have been eligible to receive welfare that should not have been obliged to prefer charges against a breadwinning husband simply to be eligible for welfare payments.

DOMESTIC PROBLEMS

The reasons given for marital discord are many and varied, but have been listed for purposes of this study under the following headings:

a) Desertion
b) Non-Support
c) Assault
d) Infidelity
e) Alcohol
f) General incompatibility

In most cases the presenting problem that is revealed at the point of intake at the Court is not always the same as that revealed after the completed intake interviews. Quite frequently there is more than one basic problem complicating family life. For example, I recall a case in which a wife who was severely beaten by her husband appeared at the intake desk requesting a charge be laid against her husband for assault. Before the summons could be issued, the wife withdrew the charge and asked for domestic counselling. In the course of one interview it was obvious that this assaultive behaviour of the husband was closely linked with (1) alcoholism, (2) non-support and neglect, (3) the alleged infidelity of the wife.

The following statistics have been compiled with these factors being equated; thus, there will be an overlapping of causes in the several areas under study.

Desertion by either spouse	6.3%
Assault	20.1%
Non-support	25.7%
Infidelity by either spouse	3.6%
Alcohol	44.0%
General incompatibility	14.8%

When we consider the part that alcohol plays in matrimonial disharmony it is important to understand whether domestic disharmony has brought on the alcoholic problem or perhaps the alcohol problem might be generic to the domestic situation. This could not be determined in this investigation, but would be worthy of a separate study in view of the high incidence of alcohol to marital discord.

Most wives who believed alcohol was a significant reason for marital strife felt that their husbands had always indulged to some extent, but at the time reported, drinking was severe enough to be considered jeopardizing family life.

Whatever the reason for drinking, there is ample evidence to show that alcohol is precipitating an inordinate amount of disharmony and unhappiness in those families coming to the Court for a solution to their domestic ills.

Infidelity of husband or wife does not constitute a large segment of the families in trouble. Husbands are slightly more unfaithful than wives, i.e. 2.0 per cent husbands and 1.6 per cent wives having sought other sexual partners and acts that have been uncondoned by their spouses.

Under the heading of general incompatibility have been included those of marital unions who have expressed the desire for separation, discontent on sexual grounds, marital problems based on personality differences, those who are already separated by mutual agreement, others wanting domestic counselling service, non-access to children (having been denied by one or other of the married partners).

SEX

Sexual incompatibility is seldom given as a basic cause in domestic relation cases. Domestic counsellors, who have observed thousands of families through the years, agree that from 30 per cent to as high as 50 per cent of their caseloads consist of married couples who have a serious unresolved sex problem.

This is not to say that the sex difficulty is in itself the primary cause or the presenting problem, but rather it is a natural reaction to a marital rift in other areas of domestic relations. For example, one wife stated, "I feel no obligation to get into bed with a man who comes home intoxicated and behaving more like an animal than a man". This is not a singular situation, although the reasons are not always the same.

If respect is lost by a wife for her husband, whatever the reason might be, a sexual coolness often follows and compounds the problem.

Sex problems seldom occur in marriages where no other problems exist. Conversely they frequently form part of a domestic situation that has for its base economic insecurity, alcohol, infidelity, etc.

RELIGION

Out of 1,000 cases studied, not one person mentioned that religion was a cause of marital disharmony or contributed to their problems in the intake interview.

This does not mean that domestic problems were not aggravated by religious differences. It does not mean that religious differences were not recognized as causes by many clients.

The following statistics would indicate religion is not entirely unrelated to some domestic problems. For example, one case I recall came to the Court on the complaint of a wife who charged her husband with assault. When we really had a chance to examine the facts behind the assaultive behaviour, it was found that this couple got married in an Anglican church as a neutral religious position between the Protestant wife's United Church background and the husband's Roman Catholic upbringing. The problem revolved around the baptism of their first child — the husband felt the child should be brought up in the Catholic faith, the mother felt this was a breach of pre-marital agreement, although there was nothing in writing to support this claim. The result was severe strain on this marriage, which eventually came to Court on an assault charge that did not reveal in itself the underlying factor of religious difference.

The following chart shows the religious denominations with comparative percentages, but does not compare the per capita relationship of denominations in the Metropolitan area.

Denomination	% of 1,000 cases
Protestant	57%
Roman Catholic	32%
Jewish	4%
Other	7%
	100%

Under the Protestant faith have been included United Church, Presbyterian, Anglican, Baptist, Lutheran, Salvation Army. Under Roman Catholic has also been included the Greek Catholic. Other religion includes Greek Orthodox, Mormon, Jehovah Witnesses, Apostolic, and one subscriber of "no faith whatever".

The general conviction that marriages between those couples of mixed religions does not contribute to stable family life has some foundation in the fact that 22 per cent of the total number of families in this study are of mixed religions.

The most common combination of mixed faith in marriage is between Protestant and Roman Catholic (17.5 per cent). In 5 per cent of these cases the wife is Roman Catholic and the husband Protestant. In 10 per cent of the same marriages, the husband is Roman Catholic and the wife is Protestant. Jewish mixed marriages are quite rare and make up .15 per cent of all cases observed.

SOCIAL AGENCIES

Even before a wife or husband appears at Court, more than one-sixth of our sample (15.5 per cent) have been to the Children's Aid or a family agency for some kind of help in their family matters.

This inability to cope with purely family problems would lead us to believe that there are personality inadequacies on the part of one or both marital partners, knowledge of which would be of great value to the domestic social worker. Thus, research into the areas of personality inadequacy would seem most profitable.

SUMMARY

In reviewing the findings of this paper, I believe we can discern a social profile of 1,000 clients who have come to the Family Court of Metropolitan Toronto for help in solving domestic problems.

This profile indicates that the average husband and wife are about 34 and 31 years of age respectively, and have been married for seven years before their domestic differences emerged into proportions involving their seeking assistance. They have two children, and earn considerably less than $5,000 a year. More than one out of every three families are having difficulty with the use of alcohol by one or both partners (more frequently the husband). Almost one in every three families has been, or is on some form of public welfare assistance, and one in every six has been to a social agency such as: a children's aid society or a family service association seeking help in one form or another.

The family is most likely to be Canadian born (81.7 per cent) and of Protestant or Roman Catholic religion (57 per cent; 32 per cent). A spouse of one out of every four families will be of different faith than the other in a marriage union. One out of every four wives is working. There is a need for psychiatric and domestic counselling support to a large, but presently unknown, number of unhappy people joined together in a marriage that is truly ill.

This profile leaves us with little comfort when we realize that the lives of almost 10,000 wives and husbands are falling into this pattern yearly in the City of Metropolitan Toronto in terms of Family Court domestic figures alone. We recognize that those from families of low income use the Court facilities when marriage fails. Those with more financial means utilize other facilities to resolve marital disputes — the divorce court — legal separation — agreements and private settlements, but the results are often remarkably the same — unhappy children, mental illness and anti-social behaviour.

There are many reasons to believe that a large number of marital problems stem from socially inadequate people joined in marriage. The solution to the dilemma will not be solved until adequate research defines these inadequacies and points the way to their correction.

IMPLICATION FOR SOCIAL POLICY

From the foregoing statements it would seem that if positive progress is to be made by reducing the number of seriously maladjusted marital unions with their consequent heavy toll on succeeding generations, the following recommendations could be considered:

1. Extensive research into the causative factors that are breaking down the stability of family life, some of which have been indicated in this paper.

2. The expanding of family services in a manner that will reach families when they need and can use help in solving marital problems, which is before court action becomes a necessary step.

3. Municipal awareness is necessary regarding the damaging effect on family life that accrues from poor welfare practices involving the sending of wives to family court to lay charges against husbands before welfare payments will be granted.

4. The establishing of the degree and kinds of social inadequacies of the people that make up the complement of our heavily burdened case-loads in domestic counselling services.

5. Recognition of the fact by governments that to date there has not been enough research consistent with the need in this area. One such

study should investigate the financial implications of domestic court action with and without professional counselling. In this way a clearer picture of the cost to welfare departments and taxpayers may be revealed and appropriate goals and procedures set for those charged with the responsibility of working with families having serious marital troubles, i.e., judges, court caseworkers and family agencies.

44. PITY THE POOR HUSBAND ON THE RUN*

Frank Oxley†

Canadian husbands who might be contemplating a fast and permanent getaway from home are hereby warned: Canada is not the best place in the world for an escape from women.

It's like the old story told in Britain about the foreigner in a rustic hamlet who asked a resident how to reach Stoke Poges.

"Well, sir," the local replied, "if I wanted to get to Stoke Poges, I wouldn't start from here."

All in all, Canada is designed for women — at least, so far as domestic desertion is concerned. The chips are stacked high on her side of the table.

For example, there is no such thing as the Deserted *Husbands* & Children's Act. And Vancouver is no longer a happy haven for fleeing heads of Ontario families who want to get away from them all. The long arm of Canadian law reaches out after male escapees from Newfoundland to B.C., and even a bit further than that. Reciprocal legislation with other countries makes marital meandering a tough task.

In the U.S., recent reports bring the long-suffering mother-in-law back into prominence. They really *are* the reason many husbands leave home. According to Tracers Co. of America, specialists in the art of finding men who prefer not to be found, the only "other woman" in the majority of recent missing spouse cases is the mother-in-law. It seems she makes a career out of telling her daughter that she married beneath

---

*From *The Financial Post*, April 27, 1963.
†Mr. Oxley, a journalist, is on the staff of *The Financial Post* in Toronto.

her. Usually, the son-in-law becomes fed up with financing the luxuries Mom insists her little girl deserves, and he beats it.

Ed Goldfader, Tracers' manager, says the typical man-on-the-run nowadays is 40-50 years old, holds an executive-type job, has traveled, is socially poised and friendly, has a good marital fidelity record and earns $12,000-$18,000 annually. The average intending escapee is spreading his horizons wider, looking for more and more distant places to hole up. In fact, Goldfader says, the man who leaves the country is the easiest of all to track down — he has to have a passport.

"The most successful disappearing act," Tracers' manager concludes, "is the one in which the husband stays in the same city but moves into a new neighbourhood, or remains in the same state but in a different medium-sized town."

In Canada, the picture is different.

✓ "One of the main reasons for men skipping home is money," B. K. Frankson, president, Frankson Investigation Bureau, Toronto, told *The Financial Post*. "Increasing debts, nasty letters from finance companies, inability to maintain a desirable standard of living — all make Canadian men pack a bag and run."

Frankson claims he set up Toronto's first organized tracing agency.

"I've spent many years tracing people," he says, "and I've come to the conclusion that Canada is a woman's country. If a woman leaves her husband there's not much he can do about it — unless there's another man involved."

But "cherchez la femme" still holds good, according to Frankson. When a husband disappears, he says, either another woman is involved or will be soon.

"A man who has been married won't be happy for long as a lone wolf," he told *FP*. "He'll yearn for the company, and the affection of a woman. It's in his nature. And when he yields to his instincts, he becomes easier to trace."

David Walfish, a Toronto barrister, widely experienced in domestic legal problems, says, "A man is legally responsible for his children until they are 16. If he leaves home, he retains that responsibility, and unless he can prove that he left with just cause, his wife may ask the courts to award maintenance for herself as well as for the children.

"If another woman is involved, the wife may seek evidence for a divorce, of course. If a wife leaves the home, there's very little a husband can do about it — assuming she hasn't gone off with another man. If the children are still at home, he has custody of them in fact, and it might not be a bad idea for him to seek legal confirmation of such custody after a while though it's not really necessary.

"Even if he suffers financial hardship, he cannot sue his absent wife for some contribution toward the family."

An official of the Metro Toronto Juvenile and Family Court confirmed this, but added that, in certain circumstances, a decision of the Supreme Court would make the wife pay up.

"Supposing she left her family in Toronto, went up to North Bay, started a business there and after a while, was making a substantial income from it," he said. "The husband might think he was justified in asking the Supreme Court to order her to make some contribution toward the cost of feeding, clothing and educating the children."

For years, Vancouver was paradise for an Easterner on the run from a woman.

"It was all a matter of expense," the court official told *FP*. "If the man was found there, he had to be brought back to his hometown before his wife could take him to court seeking maintenance. This cost the round trip for an official, his incidental expenses, and very likely the husband's one-way fare as well.

"It was not unusual to find the husband had few or no assets, so taxpayer's money was spent to no avail. Reciprocal legislation — initiated by Ontario — was completed between all ten provinces in 1953, and this resolved many practical difficulties."

It works this way:

Supposing a man leaves his family in Toronto, and after a few weeks, is found in Vancouver (or Moncton, or Montreal, Regina or Saint John). Evidence is given by his wife in Toronto, and the Attorney-General's department forwards the evidence to the province where the husband now lives. A temporary order for maintenance is sent along with the evidence. The husband is brought before a court in his own province and his evidence is heard. The judge may then confirm the Ontario order, vary it or dismiss it.

"The same thing applies within the province," the official said. "For instance, a husband who turns up in Red Lake, Ontario, may be brought to court there on evidence and a temporary order from Toronto."

A summons is issued in the first instance, giving the husband the opportunity of attending court in Toronto if he wishes. If he refuses, the procedure outlined above is adopted.

Reciprocal legislation exists between Canada and other Commonwealth countries, South Africa, Michigan State, and even the Channel

Islands (yes, even Sark, where a husband may still legally beat his wife, so long as he doesn't break any bones or draw blood).

Is there any way in which a skipping male may remain beyond the pale?

Well . . . uh . . . his wife must have an address for service of summons — the authorities cannot act without one. It's no help for a wife to say her husband is in Flin Flon. She must name a street and number or rural route.

The court is curt: no address, no summons.

(Memo to men: an insulated tent deep in the bush, maybe . . . ?)

Though mothers-in-law may be the king-size reason for marital discord in the U.S., there's a depressingly different reason quoted in Canada. Some private investigators had this advice to offer Canadian wives who want to keep their men happy and at home: Stop nagging!

(Psst! There's just one place in Canada where a man may sue his wife for money if she leaves him, and we're keeping this until the last. The North West Territories have an ordinance which reads, in part: " . . . a husband is primarily liable for the maintenance of his wife, and a wife is primarily liable for the maintenance of her husband.")

For men who are left, the queue for the N.W.T. forms on the right.

45. OBSERVATIONS ON ILLEGITIMACY*

Solomon Hirsch†

The writer was struck while working in a pre-natal clinic,[1] with certain similarities in the personalities of the illegitimately pregnant women, particularly in the way the women described and tried to explain their behaviour. There is a considerable amount of literature on this subject, both by psychiatrists and social workers and some discussion of differences in the course of the pregnancies of illegitimately pregnant and married women.

*From the *Canadian Psychiatric Association Journal*, Vol. 5, No. 1, January 1960.
†Dr. Hirsch is Associate Professor of Psychiatry at Dalhousie University, Halifax.
 1 Dalhousie Public Health Clinic, Halifax, Nova Scotia.

It was felt that another survey would be worth while for the following reasons:

(1) In the literature, it is commonly assumed that a basic factor in motivation is an unconscious desire for pregnancy, or that illegitimate motherhood represents the solution, or attempts at solution, of unconscious conflicts. It was felt that it might be of interest to check this hypothesis.

(2) More data are required on the comparison of married and illegitimate pregnancies, to establish whether or not differences in the course of pregnancy and in labour exist.

(3) Cultural factors are important in determining the attitude of the illegitimately pregnant woman and of society and therefore, a study in a different area might be revealing.

METHOD

It was decided to interview consecutive illegitimately pregnant women who were admitted to the clinic. Ninety-six women were interviewed one or more times. The interviews were centered around their motivation for having sexual relations, the neglect of contraception, their symptoms, particularly nausea and vomiting, their life history and their desire for therapy. An attempt was made to discover the drives responsible for their behaviour and to investigate the psychological effects of illegitimacy upon symptomatology and complications of pregnancy. The women's charts were studied after delivery to ascertain the number and kind of complications and to obtain data on their behaviour during their stay in hospital.

MATERIAL

The age range of the women was 14 to 38 years with a mean age of 21.3 years. Twenty-four of the women were 18 years or under. Almost no data could be obtained from six women because of very low intelligence or refusal to co-operate. Intelligence testing by the Weschler Bellevue test was done on fourteen women, part of a group who wanted their babies adopted. Of this group four were above average, three average, four border-line and three defective. A rough estimate of the intelligence of the remainder based on their school results and their verbalization are as follows: average or above 27, dull normal 23, borderline 23, defective 9.

MOTIVATIONAL RESPONSES

Almost all of the women showed some surprise at the question, "How did it happen?" The women were almost completely unaware of themselves psychologically. It had not occurred to them that they were in any way responsible for their own behaviour. Some protested that they were not unique in having had a baby before marriage, with statements like these: "You can't blame either of us, I'm not the first and I won't be the last." Some women vaguely blamed fate. For example, one said "all of a sudden it happened." Many of the women rationalized their behaviour giving excuses for having intercourse like the following: "I was tired of being a virgin," "I just did it to be mischievous," "I heard you had to try it out."

Forty-one of the women stated that they had had sexual relations because the man had desired or demanded it. Eleven of these women stated that they were in love with the man and would do anything for him. Most of the others of this group specifically mentioned that they wanted to please the man so that he would not reject them. This group of women made statements like this: "He might like me more if I did," or "I wanted to become more popular." The women who were "in love" stressed their devotion. For example, "I love him, I wanted to make him happy," "I pitied him when he got excited." Many of the women "in love" felt that it was permissible to have sexual relations if one loved the man.

This group was considered to be unusually dependent with a strong need for a dependent relationship with a male whose wishes had to be carried out at any cost. These women, contrary to what has been described in the literature, had a strong interest in the man and were badly disillusioned when the man left them following his learning of the pregnancy.

Sixteen women simply stated that marriage had been planned and it was impossible to get further insight into their motivation. These women seemed to feel that if marriage were planned, there was no question of not having intercourse.

Of the women who had been planning to be married, ten stated that they themselves had refused marriage after becoming pregnant. Several reasons were given for this latter behaviour of which the following are examples: "I'd never marry if I were forced to," "I now have another man. I don't have relations with him, he has too much respect for a girl."

The explanation of the behaviour of these ten women is not altogether clear. In some cases it seemed that the pregnancy made the women feel very guilty and contaminated, and caused such hostility to the father of the baby that their marriage to him was impossible. In other cases, the threat of motherhood and of being an adult woman seemed to cause such terror, that the baby was placed for adoption and the relationship stopped.

Sixteen of the women were obviously promiscuous. The reasons for their promiscuity were often obscure. A few of these were psychopathic in all spheres and others appeared able to relate to men on a sexual basis only and had intercourse with any man who took them out.

Six women stated that they wanted to get pregnant. One was a schizo-phrenic girl who stated that she wanted a baby but she did not want to leave her mother and did not want to be married. Two others said that they were sure they would get married if they became pregnant. One said flippantly, "I've always wanted a baby" but would not elaborate further. Another said "I love him. Now I can have his baby anyway."

Only five women implicated their own sexual desire as important in leading to sexual relations. Twenty women enjoyed relations and had frequent orgasms, thirty-three enjoyed relations but only rarely had orgasms, and thirty-seven were completely frigid, many stating that inter-course was painful or repulsive and that they hated it.

Seven women expressed overt hostility to their parents and it was obvious that this was a strong motivating force in their behaviour. Less overt hostility to the parents was a very common finding.

In a few women, curiosity or the need to test their ability to be mature women was important. (One, for example, told how after a childhood accident with injury to her external genitals, she considered she would never have children and had a strong desire to prove to herself that she could.)

It was difficult to get a satisfactory understanding of what was the main motivating force in the behaviour of the remaining women. It was the writer's impression that for the most part these women fitted into the group first described but they were so vague and unaware of their feelings that this could not be ascertained for certain.

The family backgrounds demonstrated, in general, marked rigidity in parental attitudes about sex. Almost all the women stated either that they had been taught nothing about sex or that sex had been stressed as something dangerous and wicked. They had been warned about men as follows: "You know what men are like, they are only after one thing, so be careful." Such teaching appeared to convince the women that by consenting to intercourse, they could satisfy a man's greatest desire and thus get affection from him.

It was considered that data about birth control would be important in revealing how the women dealt with their strong conscious wishes not to become pregnant. Again, their handling of this situation was illustrative of their extreme dependence on the man; all but twelve of the women assumed no responsibility whatever for preventive conception, yet blindly denied this eventuality to themselves. In fact, they denied responsibility for the occurrence of intercourse. If intercourse happened to them, as passive participants, it was acceptable; however, discussing or using contraception implied to them an active willingness for intercourse which was unacceptable because of the guilt aroused. Of course, cultural factors played some role in this. It is almost unknown for a single woman in Nova Scotia to ask her doctor for birth control measures. To several Catholic women, birth control seemed a greater sin than pre-marital sexual relations.

COURSE IN PREGNANCY AND PARTURITION

It has been mentioned by some writers that nausea and vomiting is rare in the pregnancies of unmarried women. In this series only thirteen women had no gastro-intestinal complaints whatever. Fifty-five women had nausea with or without vomiting. This varied in severity from mild nausea for a day or two to persistent nausea and vomiting for months. No case was severe enough to require hospitalization. The above figures are approximately what one would expect in a group of married women. There were no consistent psychological differences between the women who had nausea and vomiting and those who did not. Rejection of the baby or the pregnancy did not appear to be a significant factor in producing nausea and vomiting.

Few of the women had any desire for therapy. The few who did want help, had situational difficulties or chronic anxiety. None of the women felt that the fact of their pregnancy indicated a personality abnormality requiring therapy.

The case records of seventy-six of the women randomly selected were examined after delivery. There were thirty-nine female babies and thirty-seven male babies. The weights were in the usual range. It was the obstetrician's impression that there was no significant differences in labour but that the unmarried women seemed to expect less attention and complained less. There was no significant difference in sedation required.

Seven of the group were delivered by Caesarian Section — an unusually high number but hardly statistically significant. All the Caesarian Sections were done because of pelvic abnormalities. Two of the women had mild toxemia of pregnancy. There did not appear to be any significant difference in the condition of the babies on discharge from those of the babies of married women. (Discharge from hospital usually occurred in from seven to fourteen days.)

Many different cultural groups are represented in this area and even within similar groups there were various ideas of what was right or wrong.

Some of the women acted as if the doctor were somewhat naive in asking any kind of question about the subject. They felt that if a man and women were dating regularly, they would, of course, be having sexual relations. One women stated that a man certainly would not marry a woman who would not give in to his sexual demands. However, these ideas were the exception. It was the writer's impression that illegitimacy was more or less accepted by the coloured women and their families but strongly rejected by other groups. In many cases the girl was no longer accepted into the home.

DISCUSSION

In this type of survey one has to keep in mind exactly what group of women one is studying. Is one studying the small percentage of women who have intercourse who happen accidentally to get pregnant? Is one studying women who are unable to arrange for an abortion? Other pertinent questions of this kind could be asked. The present study concerns itself with women of a socio-economic group who cannot afford private care, who have, as a group, lower than average intelligence, who have had intercourse without the successful use of birth control methods, who conceived and who are unable or unwilling to arrange for an illegal abortion.

The acquisition of data in one or several interviews, may be open to argument, some feeling that this would be inadequate to draw conclusions about motivation for behaviour. Although there is some validity in this, often sufficient information can be gathered to question previous explanations and suggest a new possibility.

In the past, writers have stressed that since a woman behaved in such a way as to become pregnant, she must have unconsciously desired the baby, or that the pregnancy itself resolved some conflict. This type of hypothesis, very often used to explain behaviour in any area, must not be accepted blindly but investigated fully.

The concept that the ego is at fault due to deficiencies in some areas, might better explain the facts. This has some relevance to both prevention and therapy. The writer concludes that the commonest basic explanation for the pregnancy in this study is the extreme dependency of the women and a deficient ego, leading to poorly integrated behaviour.

The data concerning the nausea and vomiting are interesting and certainly suggest that strong conscious rejection of the pregnancy has little to do with its etiology. The writer has no explanation as to why the results of other investigators are so different in this respect.

SUMMARY

Many different personality types were represented in this study as has been described by various observers.

The major factor motivating the sexual behaviour of these women was the overwhelming importance to them of maintaining the dependent relationship upon a male with a total and blind acquiescence to his wishes. Of lesser importance were acting out against parents, a strong sexual drive, the need to prove oneself a woman and a desire, conscious or unconscious, to have a baby. Much guilt was aroused by the use of or insistence on birth control measures; these implied responsibility for sexual activity, the use of such measures was precluded. Contrary to other reports, nausea, vomiting and obstetrical complications occurred with the same frequency as in married women. The course of the pregnancy did not appear to be affected in any way.

It was concluded that a weak ego structure was more basic to their behaviour than the unconscious drive to have a baby, or the acting out of unconscious fantasies which often have been assumed in the previous literature. The results suggest that the mild nausea and vomiting of pregnancy is of physiological rather than psychological origin, and that the course of pregnancy is not as readily affected by unhealthy motivation for having the baby as has often been assumed.

46. NATIONAL REPORT ON THE ABORTION MILLS AND THE LAW*

Shirley Mair†

From early spring to late summer and into the fall, Canadians watched with increasing horror and sympathy while the toll of thalidomide-deformed babies mounted and then mercifully stopped short of seventy births. The dilemma of the babies' parents has made it impossible for the same Canadians any longer to avoid thinking and talking about abortion,

---

*From *Maclean's Magazine,* November 3, 1963.
†Miss Mair, formerly a Staff Writer for *Maclean's Magazine,* is currently an Associate Editor of *Chatelaine.*

a social and medical subject most people have shunned until now. Before abortion again becomes an unmentionable underworld practice, there are some facts that doctors, jurists, legislators and the rest of us should face about the 75,000 Canadian women who each year turn themselves over to hundreds of criminal abortionists.

• Hardly a social agency in the country will counsel or help a pregnant woman who needs, or thinks she needs, an abortion.

• Most doctors will refuse a woman an abortion when medical indications are that one is necessary.

• Police in Vancouver, Winnipeg, Toronto and Montreal try to track down and arrest criminal abortionists. Most of the country's other local forces don't bother to go after abortionists unless somebody makes a complaint and provides evidence.

• There is therefore a criminal abortionist available to almost any Canadian woman who wants the services of one, and in almost every case the abortionist's procedures are dangerous when they're not barbaric.

• Consequently, thousands of women who submit to criminal abortions hemorrhage, and some bleed to death; other develop uterus infection severe enough to sterilize or kill them; a few die instantly when the hack inadvertently allows air into their wombs where the bloodstream picks it up and carries it to the heart, causing it to stop.

Repeatedly in the past few weeks doctors who've seen bungled abortions have told me that most women are profoundly ignorant of the risks they take in making an appointment with a criminal abortionist. The same doctors privately admit that they sometimes turn over their own patients to these hacks even when the patient clearly needs an abortion for medical reasons. Under the vague law governing abortion in Canada almost no doctor can be confident that he will not be accused and convicted of carrying out an illegal operation if he performs an abortion, even in cases where the medical justification is clear.

THE PENALTY: LIFE IMPRISONMENT

Section 209 of the Canadian Criminal Code defines a legal, therapeutic abortion. It says that such an operation can be done only "to preserve the life of the mother . . ." Doctors frankly admit they can't decide how to interpret the word "preserve," and since Section 209 stipulates that any one found guilty of performing an illegal abortion is liable to life imprisonment, they're wary of doing the operation at all. Their hospitals are equally cautious of authorizing any of their physicians to perform an abortion in their operating theatres. The medical profession's fear is natural enough. Medico-legal experts disagree sharply on what the Code means, and some of them, like J. J. Lederman, a B. C. doctor-lawyer, say abortion — any kind of abortion — is illegal under the present law. In a recent issue of the Canadian Medical Journal, Lederman warned his colleagues, in an article called The Doctor, Abortion and the Law, that any doctor who performs the operation is leaving himself open to prosecution. A second authority, Dr. Kenneth Gray, a Toronto psychiatrist and lecturer in medical jurisprudence at the University of Toronto, disagrees. He has authorized abortion on psychiatric grounds and he says: "Abortion is legal. I teach my students it's legal."

A few other doctors say the Criminal Code adequately covers them to perform an abortion, not only to protect life and health but also to insure a mother's well-being. These doctors would abort thalidomide mothers and rape victims. Many other doctors might agree to do an abortion for these reasons once in a lifetime of practice. More likely they'd refuse for fear of being prosecuted.

In practice, therefore, a woman may be allowed a medical abortion — or she may be denied one, depending on her choice of doctor and his attitude towards the law. The majority of the women who took thalidomide found out about its tragic effects after the twelfth week of their pregnancies when it was too late to safely abort them. If some of the mothers found out early enough and did get abortions, both they and their doctors are telling no one.

Outside the spotlight of thalidomide, hundreds of other mothers have what is for them dire reasons for wanting to rid themselves of unborn children. Mothers who contract rubella (German measles) during the first two months of pregnancy are almost certain to bear a deformed child and a mother who gets the disease during the third month has very little chance of producing a healthy normal child. In recent years some non-Catholic doctors and hospitals have aborted rubella mothers, while others continue to refuse.

For whatever reason, only a very few therapeutic abortions are performed in any Canadian hospital. Women can enter hospitals for critical cancer, heart and kidney diseases and have an operation performed on the say-so of one doctor, but to get an abortion a women needs two, three and four signatures before a hospital will allow her the operation. Dr. John L. Harkins, an obstetrician-gynecologist at the Toronto General Hospital, estimated recently that there are between four and eight hundred therapeutic abortions performed in Canadian hospitals every year.

The 75,000 women who annually look outside a hospital for their abortions don't get the conscientious care of an antiseptic hospital or concerned doctors. These women get their abortions on kitchen tables, bathroom floors and beds laid out with plastic sheets. They usually don't know who their abortionists are, or even if they are skilled enough to avoid killing a client.

Actual statistics of women who get illegal abortions are impossible to tally, but 75,000 is a minimum annual estimate for Canada. In 1955 a group of American doctors, meeting for the Arden House conference on abortion, made an authoritative guess that there could be one abortion for every four live births and as much as twenty percent of the total abortion figure would be absorbed by women who had spontaneous abortions or miscarriages. Relating their estimates to the Canadian birth rate which is slightly less than half a million a year, 75,000 becomes a low figure for illegal abortions. Even allowing for more conservative Canadian mores, the figure is probably close to ninety thousand.

Criminal abortionists aren't difficult for these unknown thousands of women to find. Dr. Alan Guttmacher, chief of obstetrics and gynecology in a large New York hospital and easily the most outspoken authority on abortion in North America, told a group of American and Canadian protestant ministers recently, "Don't tell me your town doesn't have a criminal abortionist. You're just too naïve to know who he is . . . "

In large cities, half a dozen telephone calls will almost always track down a criminal abortionist who for $75, $100, $200 or $300 will "do something" to get rid of an unwanted pregnancy. Criminal abortionists seldom vary their treatment, but their prices slide up and down to accommodate their clients' budgets: women from prominent families are known to have paid thousands. An abortionist's greed can extend to deliberately risking his patient's life. An expectant mother, four-and-a-half months pregnant with twins, was recently killed by a criminal abortionist. Some incredibly irresponsible criminals have attempted to abort women six months pregnant.

A woman's best security lies with an abortionist-doctor who has a reputable practice as a sideline and the medical discipline to know what he does is dangerous. But amateur abortionists are much easier to find. According to the late Dr. Alfred Kinsey, director of Indiana University's Institute for Sex Research, men and women with no medical training comprise about eighty-five percent of criminal abortionists. Because desperate women clutch the first name or phone number that comes their way, their chances of being mangled, as one doctor says, "are excellent."

Who are the women who'll risk injury and death for an abortion, and take the chance of losing their reputations in a public scandal if they're caught? A police detective says they're "rich, poor, married, single, student, careerist, but the great majority of them are married women who've already had at least one child."

An unmarried Toronto career woman whose lover ditched her before she learned she was expecting a baby, got an abortion last July. Sitting in a Toronto restaurant two months later, she was composed and chic. Her job precluded any possibility that the woman wasn't efficient and responsible.

"It was rotten," she said. "I tried to think my way out of it, but there was no other way. First I went to a G.P., but he wouldn't help me. I tried a few obstetricians — went to them cold. They didn't know me and they wouldn't suggest anything.

"I had to protect my job but I had to chance telling someone. I picked friends outside the office that I intuitively felt might know of an abortionist. Three or four days later a woman called me and said she'd heard I was in trouble, that she'd help me. I asked who had said such a thing and who was she.

"She just said, 'I'll hang up if you're not going to be reasonable. How pregnant are you?' I gave in and told her eight weeks. That was fine. She told me not to eat dinner and to have $200 in cash ready the next night. I pleaded with her for the name of the person who'd told her, but it was no use. She hung up and the next evening I was ready. She called again, about ten-thirty and said to be ready after the eleven o'clock news. A cab driver took me in a roundabout way to an apartment house." (The abortionist often sends a middleman to make initial contact and if he suspects the woman is a police decoy, he ditches her. By cutting out the middleman, abortionists can make more money, but they then protect themselves by doing business only through trusted referrals.)

The woman continued, "The driver gave me an apartment number and the woman I'd talked to on the phone was inside. She asked for the money and then told me to lie down on a metal drop-leaf table in her kitchen. While I was getting arranged, she stirred a milky solution in a dishpan. She brought it over with a syringe and tube and said it might hurt and not to scream. I didn't look after that. I kept thinking, 'Lord, she didn't wash her hands after she took the money,' and then she was hurting me so much I just hung onto the leaves and prayed they wouldn't fall down."

Sitting at the restaurant table, oblivious of a handsome man at a neighboring table who was eyeing her appreciatively, the woman shivered and was silent. She stretched her tense legs and said, "When she was through the woman told me it would be over in about ten hours and I probably wouldn't feel like going to work the next day. How right she was. I didn't work for three days and I'll never forget it." She looked up from her coffee and saw the man watching her. In one motion she was on her feet — walking attractively toward the door.

There have been several housewives among convicted abortionists and an assortment of clerical workers, an unemployed actor, a salesman, a watchmaker, an ex-prison guard and a sex deviate. Anyone who passes along the name or phone number of an abortionist is risking some woman's life. In Montreal last year one woman led three of her friends to abortionists she'd tapped through a pharmacist. Two of them paid $300 and came through the procedure with no after-effects. The third paid the same price, but was later admitted to hospital hemorrhaging and when she was released three weeks later doctors told her she was sterile. In Winnipeg women are whispering about "magic-wand" abortionists. Translated, this means slippery-elm bark and when a Vancouver mother pushed a slab of this wood, wet with Lysol, into her womb a year ago, she died of gas gangrene only a few days after she was admitted to hospital.

Doctors and hospitals are tending thousands of less-than-fatal cases in silence. Last year Nova Scotia hospitals alone discharged 1,922 women after D and C's, an operation which is used for legal abortions and, more frequently to clean out an infected and bleeding uterus after a botched criminal abortion done outside the hospital. Saskatchewan hospitals discharged 2,730 D and C cases, B. C. 5,027 and Ontario coped with more than twenty thousand. A few of these operations were performed on women who started to miscarry, or for conditions that didn't involve pregnancy, but most of them were done to correct the mistakes of criminal abortionists. A young intern at a large Ontario teaching hospital says, "We've got women coming into emergency all the time with messed-up abortions. I don't know how many — maybe two a week." Actually his hospital's latest statistics show that in 1960, 873 women were discharged after "abortions: threatened and spontaneous."

Stewart McMorran, Vancouver's city prosecutor, accuses doctors of refusing to help police trap abortionists, by not reporting suspected cases to them. Most police forces, however, ignore abortionists and have certainly never asked for help or laid many charges. Vancouver, Winnipeg, Toronto and Montreal police make most of the country's abortion arrests; in 1959 not a single local force in Saskatchewan, Alberta, Newfoundland,

Nova Scotia or Prince Edward Island laid an abortion charge. New Brunswick handled just one case; Ontario, eighteen; and Quebec, Manitoba and B.C., split another eighteen between them.

Police laxity, nebulous laws and a public that's never wanted to mention the word "abortion" have all combined to make the problem a serious threat to thousands of Canadian women. In the last two years several groups and individuals — doctors, lawyers and interested laymen — have said they want the law clarified. Many of them want it liberalized. Dr. McCoy, in pointing out that the law restricted doctors from doing even necessary abortions, said he felt the operation should be allowed for broad physical and mental health reasons, and he included raped women who become pregnant. The Canadian Bar Association has since agreed that rape victims should be allowed to abort, and the lawyers also think mental defectives who become pregnant should be allowed the operation. Other doctors and lawyers have lengthened the list to cover abortion for a wide range of humanitarian and eugenic reasons and some suggest abortions should be allowed for women who have social or economic reasons for wanting the operation. A few have gone so far as to suggest that women in a "tired housewife" category be included.

The unfolding discussion has already split such normally united groups as the Catholic Women's League. In July the League passed an abortion resolution that was anything but bland ("abortion is murder, no matter what the condition of the living fetus") but, significantly, it did note that, "Many favor terminating pregnancy by abortion in cases in which it is possible the child will come into the world deformed." A month later, another ladies' group, The Canadian Federation of Business and Professional Women, came out with the strongest proposal yet made by any group. The women asked the federal government to establish a royal commission on abortion to investigate the situation in Canada. On making the proposal public the federation's president, Elsie Gregory MacGill asked, "If women won't ask for this, who will?" Who indeed?

47. WHAT'S HAPPENING TO CANADA'S CHILDREN*

K. Phyllis Burns†

To gain some perspective on the subject of Canada's children we can look first to the statistics provided in the 1951 census of the Dominion Bureau of Statistics. According to this report in 1951 there were 5,675,000 children under 19 years of age or 38½ per cent of our total population.

The 5¾ million children to whom reference has been made belong to 3¼ million Canadian families. It would be helpful to know what proportion of this total live as part of their own family groups and how many are being cared for outside their own homes in institutions, foster homes or elsewhere.

Unfortunately Canada as yet has no means of providing this type of information because there is no consistent compilation of statistics concerning the number of children requiring help from, or being served by, social welfare programs.

The collection of such statistics is only one part of the tremendous amount of research into the child welfare services needed urgently in the field of child welfare across Canada.

Without benefit of detailed statistics it is well known that many children in Canada are unable to live with their own families. It is known too that regardless of where these children live or with whom they are living they have common needs just as children the world over have common needs.

COMMON CHILDREN'S NEEDS

Much has been written and spoken about the needs of children and they are becoming so familiar that perhaps they are too readily taken for granted. A reminder may not be inappropriate.

First, every child needs a home of his own with all this implies of being wanted, loved and provided with an opportunity to put down from birth onwards those deep roots which are the only guarantee of the later full flowering of a mature personality.

Second is the child's need to have his physical needs met. Physical needs are not mere food, clothing and shelter, but also the opportunity to

---

*From *Canadian Welfare,* June 15, 1955.
†Miss Burns, formerly with the Canadian Welfare Council, is currently Social Affairs Officer with the Bureau of Social Affairs at the United Nations in New York.

be physically healthy, to have adequate nutrition, immunization and so forth.

Dr. Benjamin Spock has defined this goal for children as "good health is not just having a nose that doesn't run; it means feeling good enough to want to sing or whistle".

Third, every child needs room to grow, to develop competence and independence, to learn to take responsibility, and to gain satisfaction from it, to experience love and trust beyond his family circle as well as within it, and thus to learn the essential goodness of people and of living.

Fourth, every child needs education and training in accordance with his capacity. He needs to be prepared to fill a niche in life into which he will fit, be it large or small, unimportant or significant.

WHY CHILD WELFARE SERVICES?

Fortunately for many children, their own families can meet these needs of childhood without assistance. The community's concern is to see that *every* child is guaranteed the opportunity to have these needs met. Child welfare services are designed to give this guarantee to children whose parents cannot provide it.

If one generalization could be made about what is being done in Canada to guarantee these needs of children it would probably be that Canada is growing steadily in its determination to give real meaning to our belief in the child's own home as his best milieu.

Child welfare went through a phase of being "child-centred"; it is clearly now in the phase of being "family-conscious" and almost at a point where it is coming to be fully "family-centred". A long step forward has been taken even though in some ways it has been an awkward step.

FAMILY COUNSELLING

Family and child welfare services are now moving forward to offer service to families where there are difficulties, even though the parents are by no means neglecting their children, as this term is understood in our child welfare legislation.

As an example, the Children's Aid Society of Brandon developed a home-maker service as part of its program to provide a way of maintaining his own home for a child who might otherwise have to be removed because of his mother's inability to give him the immediate care he needs.

Also, while they are not new, the public welfare programs in British Columbia and Saskatchewan are enabled to provide a family counselling service for family groups where there is no neglect of children nor any economic problem, but where the solidarity and happiness of the family is threatened by quarrelling between husband and wife, poor child training, or strained relationship between parents and their adolescent children.

SOME WEAKNESSES

But this picture also has a dark side. It is well known that much neglect of children arises from poverty and destitution. A poor standard of living, malnutrition and poor housing sap initiative and self-respect and produce children who find it difficult to develop their full potentialities in school, at play or in employment.

These children when they grow up are likely to establish families in which they will perpetuate the vicious circle of poor living standards, malnutrition, poor housing, poverty, destitution and neglect.

Because we know how truly this pattern can repeat itself again and again, it is especially alarming that across Canada so little is being done to break the circle. Rates of social assistance and mother's allowances continue to be pitifully low, and needs which are basically the same are met on entirely different scales.

For example, a mother who was widowed by the death of her soldier husband overseas receives an entirely different type of allowance for herself and her children than the mother whose husband died at home from natural causes and who thus qualifies for a Mother's Allowance.

There is still no program in Canada to meet the needs of the employable unemployed who are unprotected by unemployment insurance.

A real glimmer of hope in the situation is the fact that in some places, of which the city of Vancouver is an example, social assistance is paid to employable unemployed persons with the province sharing some of the costs with the city. In other places such as Alberta and Manitoba no distinction is made between the employable and the unemployable group of unemployed for assistance purposes.

Even these provisions are seriously limited because the rates for this type of help are much less than adequate to meet family needs.

Preventive services to strengthen family life are also scattered. Canada's 3¼ million families are served by fewer than 50 private family welfare agencies. These exist in large centres or are provided by public services in some provinces which offer family counselling in the communities within their boundaries.

It is disturbing to consider the prevalence of legislative provisions to meet the cost of caring for children outside their own family while there is still such a dearth of services to keep children at home. It may well be asked, are we not really more ready to invest in breaking up homes than in building them up?

HOUSING

Housing in Canada is a tragedy in itself. What every family surely needs is a home in which to build a stable family life. Yet in Canada our standards of housing continue to be less than desirable.

For instance, 320,000 families in Canada, according to the 1951 census, live in shared accommodation, with relatives or as lodgers. This means that almost one in every ten Canadian families does not have the opportunity to shut its doors and work out its own problems in privacy. According to the census one third of Canada's population is living in what are described as "crowded dwellings".

WORKING MOTHERS

Eleven per cent of married women in Canada are working, a marked increase in the last ten years. The reasons for the employment of married women are manifold. The employment situation, the housing problem and the high cost of living are undoubtedly significant factors.

There is no way of knowing how many of these married women are the mothers of young children but it can safely be assumed that in a substantial number of cases they are.

In spite of this fact there is no appreciable increase in day-care facilities in Canada. Indeed, the only provinces in which this type of facility is licensed or supervised are British Columbia and Ontario. Furthermore day nurseries and foster day care exist only in metropolitan or highly industrialized areas in Canada.

FOSTER CARE

In the field of foster care of children some developments are very encouraging. Marked steps forward are being taken to employ the knowledge we have about how best to care for children who for one reason or another cannot be maintained by their own families.

Increased payments for care to foster mothers and fathers is a significant development. They are a recognition of the value of the service and of the devoted care which foster parents give to children in their charge. Mothering and fathering cannot be paid for in money but it does deserve recognition and adequate payment for out-of-pocket expenses which foster parents incur.

There is ample evidence too that greater thought is being given to the making of placements. This includes careful preparation of all those affected by the placement.

There is still an urgent need, however, as yet only partially met, to have equally careful work done with parents whose children are placed. This careful work is now taken for granted with foster parents and with children during the placement.

ADOPTION

In adoption service the most striking development is perhaps the increasing acceptance of the idea that every child who can never again live with his own parents is adoptable, provided a suitable home can be found for him.

This represents a fundamental change from the days when the obligation of the child-placing agency seemed to be the finding of perfect children for presumably perfect adopting parents.

A great deal of effort is being put into finding permanent homes for children whose own parents cannot provide one for them. Many examples might be cited, but one of particular interest is the "Special Needs Conference" which is held periodically in the Province of Saskatchewan. In a province-wide meeting of child welfare workers, the pertinent facts about the children awaiting adoption become known to all the workers. Strenuous efforts are made in every region to find suitable homes for these children, regardless of where they are living in the province.

In Quebec there is a steady and encouraging growth in the number of children being placed by the diocesan child welfare agencies. The fact that there are now twelve such agencies in the province, each carrying on an aggressive program on behalf of children resident in institutions in the province but for whom permanent family homes are required, is heartening.

INSTITUTIONS

The main concern now is to be sure that the child for whom placement is being sought can really be helped by the program the institution has to offer. This is surely a far cry from the days when institutions clamoured for children to "fill the empty beds".

There has been an interesting development of the use of the institution for observation and study in preparation for a long range plan for a child.

One of the more recent examples of this type of program is the new observation and treatment centre of Montreal's Children's Service Centre, where the combined skills of social workers, psychiatrists and psychologists are pooled to acquire a greater understanding of the individual child as a basis upon which to plan for him.

It is encouraging to see the time and care being put into the development of treatment centres for disturbed children. These centres are essential but caution is required in setting them up. They cannot be the answer for every "problem child" about whom the community is concerned and any treatment centre program can hope for success only if it is set up against a background of good service available to families and children in their own home and skilled foster care programs under the auspices of child welfare agencies.

Another requisite for a treatment centre program is good psychiatric consultation available to agencies serving children in their own homes or in foster homes and to the treatment centre itself. Another requirement is the facilities essential to carry on intensive and consistent work with the child's own parents so that, when his treatment has been completed and he is ready for return to the community, a home will be waiting for him to which he can go with some expectation of carrying forward the progress which has been made.

There is also increased interest and activity on behalf of exceptional children in Canada. There are institutions for children with special needs and also other specialized facilities for them within agencies and communities.

One example of this is the subsidized group home for troubled adolescent boys established by the Children's Aid Society of Vancouver. Here skilled people, supplementing the work of good foster parents, prepare adolescent boys to be self-supporting who might otherwise have found themselves in training school for delinquents.

OTHER SPECIAL SERVICES

There is an upsurge of public interest in mentally retarded children in Canada. This increased interest and understanding is largely attributable to the outstanding leadership which has been given by the parents of these children and which has tended to develop more varied resources to meet their needs.

It is encouraging to see the stigma so often attached to this group disappearing through public education, and to see that a principle is being applied to this group, which we have long accepted with respect to other groups of children, namely that no one type of resource can meet the needs of all.

There has also been a major growth in organization to meet the needs of crippled children. Councils for crippled children have been established now in almost every province of Canada. These, coupled with new provincial programs for crippled children's services, mean that greater opportunity is being provided for every crippled child to have whatever treatment, rehabilitation and education will be helpful to him.

The rapid growth of community psychiatric services cannot fail to have a good effect upon our overall child welfare program. In 1948 Canada had 17 mental health clinics; now we have 77 such clinics, and 18 clinics are set up exclusively to provide child guidance services.

The beginning of day-care service for disturbed children, a recent project of the psychiatric department of the Children's Memorial Hospital in Montreal is another move in a good direction. Perhaps the most significant aspect of this particular service is the fact that not only are the children receiving day-care treatment but the parents too are being helped on a regular weekly basis.

TENDENCIES

All these developments indicate trends which can be isolated for special examination. Legislation and regulations thereunder affecting children seem more and more to share the objectives of good social welfare practice.

Two examples might illustrate. First, a careful reading of the new Child Welfare Act in Ontario demonstrates the point. The agreement which has been in effect between British Columbia and Saskatchewan for the past year or more whereby residence qualifications for unmarried mothers between these two provinces have been abolished, is a further illustration.

This is an important recognition of the right of people to secure service when and where they need it, regardless of where their legal residence may be.

During recent years we have developed much greater objectivity in the social welfare field about relations between public and private agencies and this is a healthy and encouraging trend. In working out these relationships it appears that the child welfare field has lived through an experience similar to that of the institution-versus-foster-home struggle. It was thought then that a choice had to be made between them, but a more balanced view was eventually achieved which recognized that each had an important place of its own.

Across Canada there now appears to be general acceptance of the fact that neither public nor private services to children can exist in isolation, nor can any province have a well-rounded program if it does not have both public and private services of good standard.

There is a continuing urgent need for more personnel for the child welfare services as for all other fields of social welfare. Supervisors, case consultants and other senior personnel are needed to see that the best possible use is made of the vast reservoir of knowledge we have about how children can be helped, and to assist in the training and direction of young workers in the field.

As a contribution to a solution of this problem, fellowship plans have been worked out by some agencies to help their staffs get further training. The Department of Social Welfare and Rehabilitation in Saskatchewan and Children's Aid Societies such as that of Brantford, Ontario, are examples. Since all children have the same needs, they should have access to the same services whether they live in rural or urban areas, in a populous part of Canada or in sparsely settled regions. It is a real source of pride to some provinces that there is no real difference in quality between the services available to children in their rural and urban areas.

The need for more consistent and courageous planning in services for children is evident in many quarters. Errors may be forgiven, but errors made in planning for children affect human life deeply, and sometimes irrevocably. Their needs cannot be ignored nor can we delay, because the disturbing but undeniable truth is that children will not wait.

48. *THE PROBLEM OF THE AGED**

C. T. Andrews†

Canada today has three or four times as many old people as she had 50 years ago. Numbers are steadily increasing and the ratio of the working to the older age group is steadily narrowing. The same trend is seen in European countries.

Does it really matter? Numbers can be made to prove anything. Is not the old person today a much more useful citizen than he was 50 years ago? In an industrial and highly civilized community, experience and skill count much more than they did in the days of the nation's first

---

*From *Canadian Welfare*, December 15, 1953.

†Dr. Andrew, an English physician who was touring Canada at the time this article was written, is a Founder Member of the British Geriatrics Society and is still active in that field.

beginnings. Are we not in fact better off today? This question was seriously put to us on our recent tour of Eastern Canada.

In simple terms it may be answered that if in terms of health, happiness and productiveness, old people compare favourably with the rest of the community, then there is no cause for anxiety. Or in another way we may say that if they are not a burden to themselves, their families, and the community we may be happy with the present position. Let us therefore examine these points.

THE PRESENT POSITION

The increasing longevity of man today is largely due to the great discoveries in medicine in the last twenty-five years, to the sanitary idea in public health and to better housing and social conditions. By and large, however, these advances have been beneficial in the field of acute bacterial ailments including infectious fevers rather than in that of chronic disabling conditions such as are common in the aged.

Smallpox, diphtheria and cholera, pneumonia and meningitis, have been largely controlled; but chronic rheumatism, degenerative diseases of heart and blood vessels, and senile mental disorders have remained untouched by modern discoveries, and with larger numbers of old people in the community their total incidence is higher than ever. Every doctor of 25 years experience will have noticed the increasing load of this disability on the home, the hospital and the community today.

It is the home which takes the brunt of this problem in the first instance. But in the modern world families are smaller than in Victorian days; the daughter who stayed at home to mind the aged parents now goes out to work. There are more social and recreational attractions for young people outside the home, and the family tie has been weakened by two world wars.

The result is an increasing number of old people being cared for by a smaller number of young people. There are more old people living alone and therefore less able to fend for themselves when illness overtakes them. Much unhappiness results from loneliness and the feeling of being no longer wanted.

Side by side with this, industrial practice has forced on the community a fixed retirement age which in most cases takes no notice of the possible contribution in skill or experience of the older citizen of the community. The result is that many older people who might continue to support themselves for years are forced to accept a lower standard of living, and their care and maintenance becomes the responsibility of their families and the state.

A NEW OBJECTIVE

It would appear therefore that we have in fact only attained a limited objective by adding years to man's life. The objective that remains is that of lightening the burden on the community, relieving the strain on the family and making the extra years, years of happiness and fulfilment rather than frustration and loneliness. The task is difficult and complex. Let us examine some aspects of it.

THE HOSPITAL PROBLEM

On the hospital side the need for an active policy has been lost sight of. The disabilities of old age have been regarded as inevitable, and shortage of nursing staff has made it more convenient in hospitals and institutions to put old people to bed and keep them there, safe and warm. The physical and mental deterioration which has resulted from this policy is now well known.

But the trend is not easily reversed. Medical teaching in the last 30 years has neglected the preventive aspects of this problem and a generation of doctors has grown up without special knowledge of, or interest in, the problems of old age.

Hospital building tends to follow the traditional pattern with large and increasingly expensive buildings serving largely the younger age groups. The special needs of old people, who in England now occupy about 40 per cent of all hospital beds, are not met by the provision of large multipurpose hospital buildings. They are happier and less expensively cared for in smaller units designed to meet their particular needs.

These needs from the hospital point of view may be summarized as follows:

1. Active treatment.
2. Long-stay nursing care.
3. Mental care and treatment.
4. Substitute home accommodation.

THE ACTIVE TREATMENT UNIT

The modern active treatment unit is the only section of accommodation required which should be actively associated with the work of an acute general hospital. To this unit the special problems of the aged sick would be referred for advice, investigation and treatment. It should act as a consultative centre for other departments of the hospital and other specialties in its area, and the staff of this unit should be available for consultation in the home and for the provision of a domiciliary service in co-operation with the various agencies concerned with the service.

It should act as an educational centre to public and professional bodies in the medical problems arising in the care of old people and should organize research into these. In urban areas it may be desirable to arrange out-patient clinics, and the follow-up of patients who have been discharged from the unit will be a prime duty in all cases.

The staff of such a unit will include a consultant or specialist. The specialist in this field should be a general physician who may also have some responsibility for younger age groups. He would, however, require to devote a considerable part of his time to the work in order to achieve success. He will require to make effective liaison with the various bodies in his neighbourhood who are serving the needs of the aged. He will require to have the services of a general surgeon, orthopaedic surgeon and ophthalmic surgeon available and these should preferably make regular visits. Dermatologist, gynaecologist and a psychiatrist will also be required as occasion arises.

It addition to these and some junior medical staff he will require the services of physiotherapy, occupational therapy and chiropody. Most important of all his team is the social worker who will be the main agent concerned with placing those patients who have become fit for discharge.

LONG-STAY NURSING CARE

About 20 per cent of patients who pass through the active treatment unit will remain in need of nursing care and are too heavy a problem to be cared for at home. For these simple home-like accommodation is needed. It may, in cities or large towns, be in geographical relation to the active unit and active hospital but in rural areas where relatives' visiting becomes a problem it is better arranged in smaller units located throughout the area.

Patients should not be admitted to long-stay accommodation without adequate screening, both social and medical; and constant review and re-assessment should take place in order to ensure that remediable conditions are not overlooked. In the ordinary way admission to this unit would be by the authority of the physician in charge of the active unit and patients would first have a period of assessment and treatment in the active unit.

In England it is not usual to provide physiotherapy here but occupational therapy is very desirable. Quite apart from the psychological effect of occupation there are many cases in which the bedfast state can be avoided if activity is maintained.

MENTAL CARE

The care of elderly patients suffering from mental infirmity presents an urgent and increasing problem. In the past many of these have found their way, generally under certification, into mental hospitals. In England probably 25 per cent of old people in our mental hospitals have no need to be there if alternative accommodation can be found for them. The position is probably more serious in Canada.

Clinically they fall into three groups:

(a) those whose mental symptoms are secondary to organic disease. Many of these will die of their physical ailments, others will respond to treatment and recover;

(b) those who are impossible to control outside a mental hospital — a small group — and

(c) aged people who have progressively undergone mental deterioration at home to the extent that relatives are no longer able to look after them. Those in this group suffer from defects of memory, are sometimes untidy and dirty in habits, generally facile and emotional, sometimes garrulous and rather quarrelsome. They are often physically very well, able to be up all day, and require a minimum of nursing care.

It is desirable that the investigation and diagnosis of mental infirmity in old people shall be carried out as far as possible in the active treatment centre where special wards may be allocated for these patients. For the third group mentioned above some provision of long-stay accommodation is required. It should not be a part of the mental hospital but may be provided either in a separate annex or in association with other long-stay accommodation.

Small units of 30 to 40 beds with a homelike atmosphere are better than large institutions which tend to be impersonal and to take on the character of the mental hospital of the past. In this unit also occupational therapy is desirable.

Both types of long-stay unit mentioned above should be in close touch with the active treatment centre and the physician or his staff should make periodic visits to keep patients under review. The day to day care, however, in rural areas may be provided by a local practitioner.

UNIFIED SERVICE

It is necessary to emphasize the need for a unified service in each city or geographical area. For each hospital to try to act on its own, providing all types of service and accommodation, may be possible where the units are large, and the population served numerous and compact as in a city of one million or more.

Where smaller units attempt to compete in providing a service for all types, inefficiency and waste of resources are inevitable. In any area indeed a better plan will emerge if the various agencies can get together and pool their knowledge, experience and resources.

With an active policy in operation the need for beds should be considerably diminished. Our experience suggests that 9 beds per 1,000 of the population over 60 should serve for the above purposes, and that of these 75 per cent should be for long-stay patients. More accommodation will be required for women than for men but the exact proportion will vary somewhat from one area to another. In Cornwall it is 2.2:1 for the active treatment centre and 3.3:1 for long-stay care.

THE PROBLEM OF RETIREMENT

Figures published in England and America suggest that the proportion of elderly workers remaining in employment after the normal retiring age is steadily diminishing. In Canada we were told it is becoming very difficult to place men of 45 and upward in work of any sort. Some firms indeed will not accept men for employment in the first instance who are over 35. This trend is serious.

Apart from the general desirability that older citizens who remain mentally and physically alert should be able to find an outlet for their vitality, there is a danger that unless these men and women are permitted to continue in productive work, thus contributing to their own support, the maintenance of the aged will become such a crushing burden on the community as to force down the general standard of living.

Judged by the evidence available the bias in industry against the older worker would appear to be unjustified. Many, of course, are not qualified to do jobs in which physical strength is the prime essential. But where the job depends largely on skill and experience the evidence suggests that the abilities of the older worker are comparable to those of the younger. Absenteeism is not appreciably greater and reports from the Hudson Community Centre in New York suggest that health is markedly improved.

EMPLOYMENT OF THE AGED

But if the aged in considerable numbers are to be retained in industry it is necessary to ensure that pension and superannuation arrangements do not provide an obstacle either to acceptance of the older worker for suitable employment or to his continuance after pensionable age is reached.

Further it is necessary that industry should co-operate in the provision of special facilities and adjustments to suit advancing years. Such adjustments would include the finding of lighter jobs for a certain number doing heavy physical work; permission to start work a little later in the morning; special feeding arrangements; facilities for sitting at work where the job permits it; and rest periods. Wages can be adjusted to accord with the work done.

There is little doubt that along the line of increased productivity lies the solution of many of the problems of old age.

SELECTED BIBLIOGRAPHY

Anderson, O. W., "Health Needs of the Aged," *Canadian Welfare*, Vol. 26, October 15, 1950.

Beck, J. M., "The Canadian Parliament and Divorce," *The Canadian Journal of Economics and Political Science*, Vol. XXIII, No. 3, August, 1957.

Canadian Association for Adult Education, *The Family: Pressures and Problems*, January, 1963.

Canadian Welfare Council, *Family Desertion, Its Causes and Effects*, Ottawa, 1961.

Canadian Welfare (Special Issue: The Welfare of the Family), Vol. 40, No. 3, May-June, 1964.

Elkin, F., *The Family in Canada*, Ottawa, Canadian Conference on the Family, 1964.

Finlay, D., "Children Without Families," *Canadian Welfare*, Vol. 31, September 15, 1955.

Hatcher, G. H., "Some Social Problems of Canada's Aging Population," *Health*, November-December, 1950.

Lederman, J. J., "The Doctor, Abortion, and the Law: A Medicolegal Dilemma," *Canadian Medical Association Journal*, Vol. 87, August 4, 1962.

Schlesinger, B., *Multi-Problem Families*, Toronto, University of Toronto Press, 1963.

chapter nine

A CRISIS IN THE ORGANIZATION
OF HEALTH CARE

Men have always faced the problem of illness, and for most, illness has been the enemy to which they have finally succumbed. Today we are fortunate to live at a time when victory over many illnesses has been won, and the conquest of many others is imminent. What irony, then, to find that now that so much in the way of medical science has been made available to us, we often lack the *social ability* to take advantage of it. In many areas of Canada, for example, there are shortages of doctors, nurses, dentists and other health personnel. Often we have failed to provide sufficient hospital beds and equipment — equipment which was non-existent only decades ago, but now *could* be made available. For many the services and facilities are available, but the personal funds to afford them are lacking. Finally we find that disorganization, dispute and disagreement in the social systems which are vested with the responsibility of providing health care (and this includes professional organizations, governments, voluntary groups of a variety of types, and so forth) have become the social problem which has replaced what was previously mainly a medical problem — the prevention and treatment of illness.

Recently Canada was faced with a crisis situation which was the manifestation of such disorganization, and the effects of that crisis will be felt in this and other countries for years to come — the Saskatchewan Medicare dispute of 1962. The Saskatchewan Legislature had ruled that, as of July 1 of that year, compulsory government medical care insurance would cover each and every Saskatchewan resident, and physicians would be paid, not by the patient directly, but by the government from a fund to which each resident would contribute through a special compulsory insurance premium and from other tax monies. The Saskatchewan College of Physicians and Surgeons would not accept this plan, and the government would not withdraw it. An impasse was reached and a rare thing happened — Saskatchewan's doctors went "on strike". Many citizens joined together into voluntary groups to support their doctors; others formed associations which backed the government's plan. Saskatchewan was not a pleasant place in which to be in July of 1962, and the eyes of the world followed the dispute with keen interest and concern. Finally, on July 23, the legislators and the doctors, granting some concessions on each side, signed a compromise agreement. Medicare became a fact, but doctors would not be obliged to participate in it. Much of the tension subsided, but the issue is still far from being forgotten.

The four articles which together make up this chapter cannot be said to be representative of the many sides of the medicare dispute. They do, however, illustrate *some* of the more important occurrences, opinions and analyses which were part of, and have arisen from, this dramatic social controversy.

The first article, written just prior to the strike deadline, serves to introduce the problem. William Cameron, a radio and television news director in Saskatoon, saw medicare as a "Storm Over Saskatchewan" and reported in this article on the arguments backing each side of the dispute and on some of its immediate history.

Sociologist Henry Cooperstock, at that time a resident of Saskatoon, contributes an article called "Doctors On Strike". He offers a number of facts and some of his own opinions regarding the outcome of the dispute, and concludes with a discussion of the medical clinics which were set up, mainly by citizen's groups (opposed to the wishes of many of the doctors), to facilitate the workings of the government's health plan.

Almost every community in Saskatchewan was severely affected by the introduction of the medicare plan, and the opposition to it, but the small town of Biggar probably had a bit more than its share. A detailed and insightful article by Jeannine Locke tells why, after the settlement of the strike, one resident could meaningfully prophesy that "Our Town Will Never Be The Same."

Finally, James N. McCrorie, a sociologist currently employed as research director by the Saskatchewan Farmers Union, discusses some of the very important, though apparently little known, facts which help to explain how the medicare crisis in Saskatchewan could have happened and could have turned out the way it has. In "The Farmer and the Saskatchewan Medical Care Insurance Controversy" (an original article written expressly for this book), the author takes an historical-sociological approach and, after presenting some essential background information, is able to draw some worthy, if tentative, generalizations.

49. *MEDICARE: STORM OVER SASKATCHEWAN**

William Cameron†

All over Saskatchewan, a few days from now, doctors will close their office doors. The normal practice of medicine will cease. Saskatchewan is careening towards chaos in the care of the sick. The crisis over medical care is real: there is fear of what July may bring. July 1 is the day the provincial government's medical care plan is supposed to start. July 1 also is the day most doctors will withdraw from normal practice, and resort to as-yet-undefined "emergency services".

To the people of the Saskatchewan plains, for whom a sincere and lively concern for the sick is a tradition that was established with the first sod shacks of the homesteaders, the situation that has developed is incredible. The story of how Saskatchewan has come to this potentially tragic pass is long and complex. To the everlasting discredit of the press of Canada, it has been badly reported, grossly over-simplified, and totally misunderstood.

It may come as a rude shock to the press and public outside Saskatchewan to learn that there is no dispute over whether there should be prepaid medical care for all, with government involvement. Medical in-

*From *The Canadian Forum*, July 1962.
†Mr. Cameron, a journalist, is Senior News Editor for CFQC Radio and CFQC-TV, Saskatoon.

surance for everyone is not the issue. It is not even an issue. The end is not the cause of controversy. The quarrel — and a bitter and scarring one it is — revolves around the means, and the fundamental ideology behind the means. It would be difficult to find a doctor in Saskatchewan who opposes prepaid medical care for everyone, with a state-supported program. The College of Physicians and Surgeons of Saskatchewan is anything but the "rabble of anarchists" which it has been characterized by so distinguished a journal as the *Ottawa Citizen*. As long ago as 1948, it urged a "state supported program of medical insurance" in this province.

Why then the bitter struggle? In the Saskatchewan Medical Care Insurance Act, the doctors see, not a scheme of true insurance for all, but a device for all-out state control of their profession. In the unyielding opposition of the doctors, the government sees "an attempt by a privileged minority of 900 to dictate to a duly-elected government, against the expressed wishes of 900,000 others." The government, in other words, claims a mandate for its plan, a mandate acquired in the provincial election of 1960. In 1960, it made "medical care" the central issue of a campaign it fought and won handily, albeit with a minority of the popular vote. The opposition ballots, widely split among three fumbling and "me-too" shouting parties, comprised nearly 60% of the total cast. But Thomas Clement Douglas, the quicksilver little man who had been Premier since 1944, went back into power with a comfortably large line-up behind him in the Legislature. One year later, Mr. Douglas was gone, to head the New Democratic Party. But a few months after his departure, the Medical Care Insurance Act was law. Financed by a 6% increase in personal and corporation income taxes and a 1½% boost in the provincial sales tax, "The Plan" was to go into effect in 1962. The taxes did, on January 1. The plan was to start on April 1. It didn't. And no one has yet bothered to explain precisely why it was set back until July 1.

On May 3 and 4 of this year, 600 of Saskatchewan's 900 doctors closed their offices to attend an emergency meeting in Regina. Woodrow S. Lloyd, on whose more ample but at least equally able frame the Douglas mantle had fallen, addressed the doctors for more than an hour. He appealed to them to "give the plan a fair trial". He disclaimed all desire to interfere in "matters of professional judgment". Then he saw 595 of the 600 doctors leap to their feet with a roar when those who refused to work under the plan were asked by the chair to stand.

On that same May morning, with timing that almost everyone concedes must have been more than coincidence, J. Walter Erb resigned from the Lloyd Cabinet. If the timing was motivated by a desire for the maximum publicity, the choice by the Minister of Public Works was a master-stroke that even his former mentor, Mr. Douglas, could not have duplicated. The province sat and took notice, for this was the same man who only last fall — just before his demotion from the Health portfolio — had piloted the Medical Care Act through the Legislature. Mr. Erb, a handsome, burly gentleman with a good singing voice, sang in loud tones with charges of Douglas duplicity. His main reason for resigning, however, was the government's failure to honour a pledge never to introduce a plan that was not satisfactory to the medical profession.

This latter point is no flight of fancy. Repeatedly, in 1960 and later, Mr. Douglas and others enunciated five principles for a medical care plan. They are even set forth in Order in Council 729/60 as things the "government of Saskatchewan believes to be consistent with the fundamentals of responsible democratic government." Stated simply, the five principles are: (1) administration by a public body responsible to the Legislature; (2) prepayment through a personal tax; (3) universal coverage; (4) maintenance and improvement of the present high quality of service; and (5) acceptability to "those providing the service and those receiving it".

Principle number five, obviously, went out the window long ago. And there is no sign of its being revived.

The unacceptability of the plan to the doctors stems first from its general approach, and second from its details. The approach of the government has been to wipe out all that exists in the way of voluntary medical insurance — and there is much — in Saskatchewan, and substitute for it a monolithic system of state control. The control is vested by the state in the Cabinet-appointed Medical Care Insurance Commission. The powers of the Commission are set out in Section 49 of the Medical Care Insurance Act. That the powers are sweeping and all-embracing can scarcely be denied. All that is denied, by Commission or government, is that either body has any intention of wielding undue power over the profession. But the potential is still there.

The Commission, for example, may "make regulations prescribing the terms and conditions" under which insured services may be given by doctors. Plainly, this could mean whatever the Commission wishes it to mean, since all medical services are "insured services," and all citizens of the province are compelled to join the plan. It could mean supervision over medical procedures down to the size of the needle employed by a doctor. It may never do so, but it can.

The Commission is empowered to decide who may practice medicine in Saskatchewan. Under Section 40 (1) (b) it "may make regulations providing for the establishing, maintaining, and altering lists of persons entitled to receive payment under this Act." Sub-section (2) requires it to "consult with the appropriate professional body" before establishing or changing the lists. But "consult" is a virtually meaningless word in the practical realm. When it comes to deciding who shall practice medicine, a politically appointed body is all-powerful.

Without going into detail, let it also be pointed out that the Commission may decide not only who may be paid, but how much. It also is for the Commission to decide "the kind of information to be procured under any of the provisions of this Act," although penalties are provided for violation of medical secrecy by any government employee.

Early this year, the College of Physicians and Surgeons, having rejected the Act outright, announced that doctors would ignore the plan and continue to treat their patients outside the Act. The government, with as nimble a display of political footwork as was ever seen in the Douglas days, introduced amendments, which were rammed through the Legislature in the dying hours of the spring session. The amendments, among other things, make the Commission the legal agent of everyone who received a doctor's care. The Commission is your agent unless you sign a form saying you don't want it to be. The form-signing must be done separately for each service you receive. And you must make your own arrangements to pay the doctor, all the while continuing to pay taxes (with premiums still to come). Private practice outside the Act remains a theoretical possibility. But for all practical purposes, as the doctors point out, they will be accepting the control of the Act and the Commission the instant they look at a patient on and after July 1.

Hospital-based "emergency services", probably given without charge to steer clear of the Commission and its all-embracing agency powers, provide the only weapon left to the doctors. It is a powerful weapon. All over the province, people are demanding a further delay in the plan until agreement is reached with the doctors. The government is standing firm. So is the profession. And July 1 is almost here.

The popularity of the CCF-NDP government of Saskatchewan is at an all-time low. Most observers believe that given a chance through a provincial election, the opposition Liberals — despite apparent disunity at times, and a leader who has never caught on with the public — could topple the socialist regime. There is resentment over the arrogant way in which the Commission went about registering the populace for the medical plan. The act, in Section 24, clearly states that each person "shall register himself and his dependents." Perhaps fearing something less than a stampede to the registration desks, the Commission took it upon itself to save the citizens the trouble, and automatically registered everyone. The last chance to protest effectively (petitions having been ignored by the government) was snatched away.

During the last few weeks, the writer has talked with dozens of doctors about the seemingly desperate tactic of closing their doors. Harold D. Dalgleish, M.D., the Saskatoon surgeon whose burden this year and last has been the presidency of the College of Physicians and Surgeons, was one of them. Asked if the profession really believes it is better — in the interests of the patients — to give only emergency services than to practice under the Act, Dr. Dalgleish answered simply "yes". Dr. A. E. Buckwold, a kindly, widely-respected pediatrician who is anything but a politician, put it this way: "The doctors are fighting for the rights and freedoms that are the rights and freedoms of all." Contending that the government's entire approach to the problem is wrong, the College of Physicians and Surgeons has demanded outright repeal of the legislation, and a fresh start. To do so, the government claims, would constitute surrender to improper pressure.

The medical profession fears interference in professional affairs, and deteriorating standards when — inevitably — the day dawns that medicine is firmly in the hands of budgeteers and regulation makers, whose area of competence is dollars and cents and red tape, not the healing art. The government and the Commission insist that they "only want to pay the bill". In furthering that desire, the government has chosen the most extreme of many paths it could have followed. It has offered state control, not state support; it has acted as though a grave emergency existed in the care of the sick. There were gaps, but no emergency. The gaps could have been filled by a hand that helps, instead of a fist that dominates. The two-thirds of the Saskatchewan population already covered by schemes of their own choosing — in many cases of their own making — could have been left alone. The government could have turned its attention solely to those whose resources could not meet the need. It could have left the right of free choice. It chose, instead, to be Big Brother. Having so chosen, it has — in the space of some six weeks — spent an admitted $100,000 of public money on advertising, trying to convince the public of the merit of its plan — a plan for which the same government claims it received a mandate from the same public in 1960.

The plains of Saskatchewan bring forth men and women who learn early what it is to know struggle and discomfort. By her very nature,

Saskatchewan must produce a combative people. Controversy is as natural to them as their fierce love of the forbidding wilderness which they have tamed. But never has there been a greater controversy than this. All over Saskatchewan, her sons are taking sides as never before. And, like the cloud of an oncoming Saskatchewan dust storm, and with equal power to strike fear into Saskatchewan hearts, there looms ever larger the date that all Saskatchewan dreads — July 1.

50. DOCTORS ON STRIKE*

Henry Cooperstock†

On the Dominion Day week-end, the people of Saskatchewan braced themselves against the threatened withdrawal of normal services by the doctors. As families from the cities drove to the lakes, anxious mothers wondered whether the physicians of the province would make good their announced intention to boycott their regular practices.

The critical test did not come until July 3, for, although the strike was to have begun on the first of the month, doctors' offices are normally closed over the holiday anyway. Over the week-end, many still refused to believe that the doctors would really abandon their patients. They hoped to the last hours that the College of Physicians and Surgeons would ask the doctors to remain in practice while negotiations with the government were resumed.

Their hopes were dashed. On Tuesday, July 3rd, most doctors' offices were still closed.

The College had stated that it would organize emergency hospital services by staffing 31 designated hospitals out of a total of 147 in the province with some 240 doctors, but between 400 and 500 other physicians were unavailable to their patients. In some cases, listed phones were disconnected. In others, callers listened to the unsympathetic voice of a recorded announcement. Many of the doctors arranged to take holi-

*From *The Canadian Forum,* August 1962.
†Mr. Cooperstock is Associate Professor of Sociology at Brandon College, Brandon, Manitoba.

days at this time, although some had quite legitimately planned them months before. A physician who had intended to start his regular holiday on the week-end, was conspicuously present in his office on July 3rd so he would not be confused with the strikers, then set off for the country the next day. A few brave souls, prepared to defy the strike, either announced publicly that they would continue to see their patients or quietly went about their business of caring for the sick and pregnant.

It will take some good time to assess all of the implications and consequences of the doctors' strike, but certain observations may be made even now. There is little doubt that the prestige of the medical profession is in serious jeopardy as a result of the strike. While the College was astute in recognizing that the withdrawal of normal services was a potent political instrument, it lacked sufficient insight to sense that the strike was also a self-defeating weapon which could inflict grave damage to the profession. Either that, or the College chose to risk its honour by gambling with the psychological capital of doctors throughout North America and beyond.

The ideal image of the doctor includes the belief that he will never desert his patients, come hell, high water, or disagreeable legislation. The devotion of the doctor to his patients is widely regarded as sacred, and no discomfort to the physician, certainly no inconvenience or hardship created by legislation, can be allowed to suspend his availability to the sick. Indeed, this picture is reinforced by the humanistic tradition of the healing arts.

When the doctors of Saskatchewan withdrew normal services, a number of moral leaders in the medical community sternly repeated the obligations of the physician. Dr. Ernest Shortcliffe, executive director of the Presbyterian-University Hospital in Pittsburgh, said "It is unthinkable for Saskatchewan doctors, or any other health workers, to go out on strike for any reason whatsoever." Dr. Albert Sabin, famous for the oral polio vaccine, said the strike "is contrary to everything the practice of medicine stands for . . . . It seems to me that the doctors are false to their profession when they refuse to take care of the sick." Many others of like stature made similar comments.

The College insisted that the doctors were not on strike. They were only protesting a bad Act, and were now providing emergency service free of charge from hospital out-patient clinics. This was an obvious rationalization hastily contrived for public relations purposes. For one thing, the impersonal emergency service was no substitute for the much-vaunted doctor-patient relationship, which the College itself had only recently described as an intimate trust between a physician and his own client. Moreover, the hospital-based service was offered for emergencies only, and it was left to the layman to determine whether his complaint constituted an emergency. If an individual experienced a mere headache, which might turn out on clinical examination to be a symptom of a critical disease process, he could not justify asking for emergency care until the process had advanced to a dangerous stage.

Dr. J. Noel Doig, a Saskatoon general practitioner who had gone to the United Kingdom to plead the case of the Saskatchewan doctors before the British Medical Association, told a press conference in London that the doctors were not on strike. Speaking of the College's emergency services, he is reported to have said, "We have curtailed services from our surgeries [offices] and closed them and are now giving services from the hospitals. These services are in fact practically as comprehensive as those the patients were getting previously."

Dr. Doig's statement breaks down on closer inspection. How could services that are "practically as comprehensive" be provided by four to five hundred fewer doctors? Either the services were not nearly so comprehensive as Dr. Doig made them out to be, or the province has been supporting too many doctors all along, in fact hundreds too many. If so, this could turn out to be an unanticipated demonstration of Parkinson's Law, and some believe that under fee-for-service medicine, a law of this sort operates with little restraint.

Actually, by the time Dr. Doig made his statement, the province was reasonably well covered by physicians, mainly because the government had undertaken extensive emergency measures of its own to supplement those of the College. By July 20th, the College was serving some 40 hospitals, but all the other hospitals in the province were open save one, most of them staffed by doctors. The Medical Care Insurance Commission had brought in 70 physicians from the United Kingdom and about 10 others from other Canadian provinces and the United States who were deployed to points where medical care was lacking. Further, about 35 doctors were practising under the new legislation and some 70 others were in private practice outside the Act, all apart from the College's emergency service.

Had these additional services not been provided, the consequences might have been dire indeed. One physician brought in from outside the province to serve a rural community told this writer that he had just looked after a man who had been in a serious car accident, who would not have survived a trip to one of the emergency centers staffed by the

College; he would surely have bled to death on the way. This one incident was a telling commentary on the adequacy of the College's own emergency measures. Rarely have men charged with the care of the sick been so inhuman.

Perhaps even more significant than the moral crisis of the doctors in withdrawing normal services is the issue the strike posed for constitutional government. It is one of the grim lessons of the strike that the doctors have failed to learn, or to learn sufficiently well, that government in Canada is characterized by the rule of law and that without this principle there can be only anarchy. When a group of citizens believe a law to be pernicious, they test it in the courts or seek to defeat the government that enacted the legislation. They can also take their leave of the territory in which the law is in force. They do not withdraw their services from society as a means of demonstrating their displeasure or of forcing repeal of the legislation; to do so is to engage in a political strike against the government, a course which can be justified only when democratic rights have been destroyed and no legal means is available through which grievances may be redressed. This was hardly the case in Saskatchewan.

To be sure, the doctors were not breaking the law by refusing to work. From a legal standpoint, no man can be compelled to work. There is a sense in which some doctors might have been faced with legal sanctions if it could be shown that patients undergoing treatment suffered or died as a result of abandonment by delinquent physicians, and Dr. Richard Ford, Professor of Legal Medicine at Harvard University, offered his services to Premier Lloyd to investigate cases of this kind. Apart from such situations, however, doctors cannot be forced to work. Just the same, the doctors sinned against Canada's traditional constitutional processes quite as much as if taxpayers in the 40 per cent tax bracket and higher had refused to discharge their various duties to society simply because they were opposed to the Income Tax Act.

That Premier Lloyd was alert to the threat to constitutional government is clear from the fact that when the College said it would not call upon physicians to return to work until the Medical Care Act was either suspended or repealed, he refused to surrender. Every provincial government and the federal government as well must recognize that had he not taken a firm stand, the rule of law would now be a mockery.

It is a curious thing that the two major daily newspapers in Saskatchewan, the *Regina Leader Post* and the *Saskatoon Star-Phoenix*, both of them Sifton papers, failed to criticize the College either on the moral question of withdrawal of services or on the constitutional one, while editorial opinion in the rest of Canada, with few exceptions, saw these matters most clearly, regardless of their political complexions or their views about the Medical Care Act as such.

Quite sensitive to the editorial opinion of higher status newspapers, the *Saskatoon Star-Phoenix* berated the editors of newspapers outside Saskatchewan by saying, in a lead editorial on July 5th, "we would like to see our confreres in other provinces do some harder thinking than they have been doing on the crisis. For example, we would like them to tell us what law the doctors are breaking."

The same editorial implied that the outside press was simply not close enough to the scene to be adequately informed about the situation in the province. Why a newspaper editor anywhere should have to be right on the spot to recognize a moral question or a constitutional one when it jumps up at him is hard to fathom. Certainly, the *Star-Phoenix* did not disqualify itself from commending the Ontario government for passing legislation to prohibit a strike by hydro workers last April, but the shoe seems to pinch much too hard when it is on the other foot.

As a matter of fact, there has never been a Saskatchewan story that has been as well covered by correspondents on the spot as the doctors' strike. The three Toronto dailies, the *Vancouver Sun*, the *New York Times*, the *Herald Tribune*, the *Chicago Sun-Times*, the *Cleveland Plain Dealer*, the *London Daily Mail*, the *London Telegraph*, and the *Observer* are some of the newspapers which have had their top flight correspondents at the scene of the strike. One may be sure that their editors were better informed than the two Sifton papers would have us believe.

Many of these newspapermen were agreed that the Sifton press in Saskatchewan have allowed their long-standing hostility to the CCF-NDP government to cloud their objectivity. In this sense, perhaps they were *too close* to the scene. Never has this writer heard so much criticism of both the biased reporting and the editorial myopia of these newspapers.

The leader of the Liberal opposition in Saskatchewan was equally nearsighted. While Mr. Thatcher failed to utter a word of criticism on the constitutional question and in fact openly supported the doctors, his counterpart in British Columbia, Ray Perrault, took a responsible position by stating in Vancouver that the defiance of the Saskatchewan legislation could not be condoned. "When a law is duly passed by a legislature," he said, "it's a very serious thing for doctors to withdraw their services. Ultimately we could have a state of anarchy."

One of the exciting stories of the strike is the way in which citizens across the province have been attempting to fill some of the gaps created by the doctors' strike by establishing group practice medical clinics as permanent institutions. Clinics of this kind are widely regarded as an advanced form of medical care, but for all practical purposes there have been none in Saskatchewan in the past. Now there are some nineteen in various stages of organization. The first one appears to have started in Prince Albert and is now operating, with doctors hired on a salaried basis. Another is going strong in Saskatoon. In the rural town of Biggar, a citizen's group raised $40,000 in two days to establish a clinic. Others have been formed in Regina, North Battleford, Moose Jaw, and Swift Current. The clinics have banded together in an Association of Community Health Services and are exchanging ideas and materials. In every case, the clinic will be run by its members on a co-operative basis, and the doctors will be responsible to the membership through the clinical director. Whether these clinics will survive the return of regular physicians to their communities is an open question, but they have already shown that when Saskatchewan people are faced with a need, they know how to take co-operative action to meet it.

There has been an encouraging number of doctors who have expressed interest in working in these clinics. Doctors such as these make one realize that not all of the medical profession have escaped the civilizing influence of the human condition. Unfortunately there are too many who have been trained rather than educated, and who lack the qualities that make a practitioner of the healing arts a truly human being. We had better re-examine the education of our doctors before too long.

51. OUR TOWN WILL NEVER BE THE SAME*

Jeannine Locke†

At the junction of highways 4 and 14, 65 miles west of Saskatoon, a sign of triumphant civic waggishness proclaims to travellers: "New York

*From *The Star Weekly*, Toronto, August 4, 1962.
†Miss Locke, a journalist, is on the staff of *The Star Weekly*, Toronto.

is Big but This is Biggar, The Friendly Town." Beyond, as advertised, is a Saskatchewan "greater town," a proudly self-contained community of 2,800, important not only as a CNR divisional point but also as a commercial centre of satellite villages and hamlets strewn over a 35-mile radius of rich, grain-growing prairie. The town *does* have a famous reputation for fraternization. A year ago the Centre for Community Studies at the University of Saskatchewan uncovered in Biggar "the astonishing number of 139 voluntary associations . . . organized, joined and maintained by members pursuing a common interest." Community spirit, the stunned sociologists implied in their report, was not just urgently alive in Biggar; it was rampant.

Today Biggar is no longer a community in any except the geographic sense of the word. Its citizenry has been split into two utterly incompatible elements by passionate but only dimly understood differences over the Saskatchewan Medical Care Insurance act, which went into effect July 1. Even when differences are settled and Biggar is patched together again, the wound from this summer's civil war will still trouble the town. "Our town," in the words of an old-timer, "will never be quite the same again." In towns all over Saskatchewan, the hurt is as deep and will be as slow to heal as in Biggar.

The story of how this Canadian town, in crisis, was stirred to confusion by slogans and smears; how politics, the rule of law and standards of professional behavior were all frivolously debased and how, in panic, people abandoned both kindness and common sense, is uncomfortably at odds with the easy assumption that our way of life is, *per se*, the best of all possible ways. This summer there were both "Reds" and "Fascists" abroad in Biggar, by the townspeople's own account.

Medicare, at the start, was not a stirring issue in Biggar, although it was the main one in the 1960 provincial election. During that campaign, Allan Hooge, a general practitioner in Biggar for 22 years and acknowledged local leader — chairman of the school board and the United Church board of stewards, past president of the Liberal Association and the Kinsmen, former master of the Masonic lodge — made plain his own rejection of the CCF government plan for compulsory, comprehensive medical insurance. The Biggar Board of Trade brought a group of doctors from Saskatoon to explain the profession's opposition. Biggar, nevertheless, elected Woodrow Lloyd, the CCF member who had continuously represented the constituency since 1944 and who, when T. C. Douglas became leader of the New Democratic party in 1961, inherited the premiership of the province. The vote for Lloyd — and Medicare — was greater than the total vote for the other three candidates.

The following year, on November 17, the Saskatchewan Medical Care Insurance Act became law. It was to go into effect April 1, 1962.

By then Dr. Hooge and his associate of eight years, Dr. Lawrence Dunbar, a 33-year-old local man, son of a railroader, had been joined by two new doctors, Ian Burgess, 30, and Lyle Johnson, 27, both recent graduates of the University of Manitoba, who were to be salaried employees of Dr. Hooge. They developed quickly into a well-disciplined team. Their organization of staff meetings at St. Margaret's, the local 40-bed hospital administered by the Grey Nuns of Montreal, their devotion to raising the institution's standard of care and their awareness of their limitations as general practitioners, were much admired by Sister Bernadette Bezaire, director of nurses at St. Margaret's. It was a rare day in Sister Bernadette's experience that the local doctors did not consult by telephone with specialist colleagues in Saskatoon.

Early in March the government postponed the start of Medicare until July 1. The College of Physicians and Surgeons, representing the province's 904 doctors, had formulated a rival plan, an expansion of existing medical insurance schemes, administered by the doctors themselves, with the added cost to be met by the government and membership left voluntary. Premier Lloyd said no. Instead, his government amended its act to make it impossible for doctors to practise privately outside the plan. The college responded by threatening to strike July 1. Dr. Hooge told his patients: "We will close the clinic. It's impossible to work under a plan that doesn't comply with our ideals of medical practice." Asked what he particularly objected to in the act, he answered: "I'm not conversant with this act. The doctors had absolutely no part in drawing it up last fall. We simply can't work under a state-controlled medical scheme. We'll leave the province."

Late in May when signs went up in the Biggar Clinic announcing that it would close after July 1, there was still no organized alarm. It was unthinkable that the doctors would abandon their patients, who were also their friends. Dr. Hooge had delivered almost every student in the high school. His wife, Lorraine, was as busily involved in local causes as he. Their two daughters and son had all been born in Biggar and brought up in the big, solid, white-stucco Hooge house on the corner, one of the finest homes in town. The Johnsons and their two small children were without deep roots — they rented their house from Dr. Hooge, a man of property in the district. But, as Mrs. Johnson often remarked charmingly, they'd become "attached" to Biggar. The Burgesses were expecting their first baby in August. But it was Dr. Dunbar, a bachelor, who seemed the least likely to forsake the town. The town's trust in him was explained not only by his being a local boy but also by his plainly driven dedication to medicine. His old school friends could remember how, as a young boy, Laurie Dunbar had dreamed only of becoming a doctor. He'd devotedly tended most of his friends, at all hours, since. As one of them, Shirley Rowland, remarked to her railroader husband, Kelly: "Can you imagine Laurie Dunbar not coming if we needed him after July 1?"

Besides, Biggar was to be one of the emergency centres that the College of Physicians and Surgeons had promised to staff with two volunteer doctors, who would give their services free, if the town were without medical care after July 1. Having managed until 1954 with only two doctors, local people didn't panic at the prospect of being reduced again to that number.

Then, about 10 days before the June 18 federal electioon — when Biggar re-elected its Progressive Conservative M.P. — the temperature of the town began to rise. The Independent, Biggar's weekly newspaper, suggested that citizens return their Medical Care registration cards, with comments in support of their doctors, to Ross Thatcher, leader of the Liberal opposition in the Saskatchewan legislature, for presentation, in a bundle, to Premier Lloyd. The Independent's columnist, Pete Wentz, editorialized: "When a bunch of lying, two-bit politicians start to use their powers to threaten our honorable and dedicated doctors . . . it is time we get rid of them." The alternative, he predicted, would be Biggar's exposure to "some strange gook doctor from a foreign country."

No one wrote a letter to the Independent protesting those sentiments. Instead, the Biggar Board of Trade went into action. On June 10 Lloyd Hock, a member of the Board of Trade provincial executive and a well-liked Biggar merchant and restaurateur, was summoned by a group of businessmen in Saskatoon to a meeting of the provincial Keep Our Doctors Committee. He took with him fellow board members, Ivan Leslie, one of the town's two druggists and the president of its Board of Trade, Bill Morphy, editor of the Independent, and Glen Clements, proprietor of a real estate agency. The Biggar businessmen arrived at the meeting with a secure reputation for obedience to their parent Chamber of Commerce — their Board of Trade had stoutly supported Operation Freedom, the chamber's controversial campaign to alert Canadians to the danger of the free enterprise system being overwhelmed by socialism. They returned home convinced of the urgency of the KOD campaign.

That very night they organized their own committee. Forty turned out for the founding meeting. Their first act was to wire Premier Lloyd demanding he immediately meet a delegation from the Biggar KOD in Regina. The premier replied the next day that the committee had no right to order its MPP but that he would be available June 13, when he was scheduled to address an NDP constituency convention in Biggar.

Biggar proved, as usual, to be eminently organizable. A petition for presentation to Premier Lloyd, calling for delay in Medicare "until such a time as a plan can be prepared which is fully accepted by the medical profession or, failing this . . . a plebiscite," was circulated in a single afternoon through the town. At most doors the petitioners asked artfully only if the householders were "in favor of keeping our doctors." Eight hundred signed, many without pausing to read the text at the top of the petition. It was a badge of respectability to be on the doctor's side.

When the committee presented the petition to Premier Lloyd two days later, its content had become significantly swollen. The committee demanded not only a delay in Medicare or a plebiscite; it also notified Biggar's MPP that, having lost public confidence, he should resign and call an election. Lloyd's active supporters in the constituency, at whose meeting the KOD had been allowed to appear, were outraged. On that evening the battle lines were drawn in Biggar. It was henceforth to be a political fight between "that Liberal-infested KOD committee" and "that pack of NDP-ers." That neighbours and brothers were on both sides no longer mattered.

The KOD kept the offensive. In newspaper advertisements, reinforced by Regina and Saskatoon private radio and television announcements — as many as 13 a day on radio — the KOD pounded home its powerful message: "It can happen here! We will lose our doctors!"

In mid-June, without explanation, the College of Physicians and Surgeons withdrew its offer of two doctors for an emergency service in Biggar. The Independent announced: "There will be no doctors on duty in Biggar or in any of the other hospitals in the region under the emergency situation. At Rosetown only two doctors will be on duty, splitting a 24-hour shift daily." The Independent drove on despairingly: "The Health Region Board estimates there are between 50,000 and 55,000 people in the area. It has been stated by certain authorities of the region that it is doubtful if two doctors can adequately cope with the normal amount of confinements, let alone attend to other persons requiring medical attention." The Independent concluded ominously: "Hospitals in the region . . . will operate on an 'outpost' principle without the aid of doctors." The "legal position" of senior nurses' right to diagnose "had not been clarified and the regulations of the Canada Food and Drug Act will prevent administering of drugs."

During the following week Biggar druggist Ivan Leslie did his "biggest business ever," as his customers rushed to refill prescriptions. The Biggar Clinic was crowded every day during office hours between 1.30 and six. The three doctors still on duty — Dr. Burgess had taken holidays — were staggering under three times their normal number of appointments. Every bed in St. Margaret's was occupied.

On Monday, June 25, 18 hours of talks between the government and the council of the College of Physicians and Surgeons ended, without agreement, in Regina. That night a KOD delegation met the six-member Biggar Town Council and Mayor Lionel Jones, a hardware merchant, to "emphasize council's responsibility, to a certain degree, for the health of residents" after July 1. Council agreed it couldn't accept such a responsibility. The KOD then proposed that council advise Premier Lloyd by wire of *his* "direct responsibility" for "any unnecessary suffering and deaths resulting from the lack of proper and prompt medical attention" in his constituency. Mayor Jones obediently did. Premier Lloyd replied promptly that lack of medical care would be "due to the decision of doctors to withdraw their services."

Mayor Jones did not, however, act on the committee's suggestion at the same meeting that the council "contact the civil defence organization of the province asking about the possibility of evacuating children, expectant mothers and other persons requiring 'certain' medical treatment." No such request was ever sent, although it was reported in both the Independent and the Saskatoon daily newspaper, the Star-Phoenix, that Biggar had officially "accepted" the idea of an evacuation plan.

Only one citizen, a farmer in the Biggar district, Roy Atkinson, protested to Mayor Jones about the evacuation plan. It was "ridiculous," he said, and "could only cause panic."

On Tuesday afternoon, June 26, the medical director of the government Medical Care Insurance Commission, Dr. Graham Clarkson, telephoned Sister Bezaire to offer St. Margaret's the services of a British general practitioner, Dr. Ida Fisher, for the emergency period following July 1. Dr. Fisher was then on her way to Canada, Dr. Clarkson said. Sister Bezaire called a meeting of the eight-man hospital advisory board, under the chairmanship of Max Hock, father of Lloyd, and the board decided to accept the doctor "during the pending emergency."

That night, on radio and television, Premier Lloyd announced new orders-in-council that would allow Saskatchewan doctors to practise "without contact with the Medical Care Commission." They would be free to operate "entirely outside the act." Their patients would pay the doctors, then be reimbursed, according to the commission's schedule of fees, by the government. "This removes all reason for withdrawal of doctors' services and resultant punishment of the people of Saskatchewan," Lloyd concluded.

"It is financially impractical to practise outside the act in rural Saskatchewan," Dr. Hooge told his patients. Leaving only Dr. Dunbar to cope with the over-crowded clinic, Dr. Hooge and Dr. Johnson left Wednesday night for Dauphin, Manitoba, to investigate a practice there. "The for-sale signs will be on the clinic and on Dr. Hooge's and Dr. Dunbar's house this weekend," Clements announced in his real-estate office.

On Thursday, June 28, the Independent published a farewell message to the town from its doctors. It read: "This disaster which threatens to descend on July 1, 1962, is not our making. We cannot accept the rigid controls and loss of civil rights which the Medical Care act imposes."

The Independent noted that Dr. Burgess was on holidays. It neglected to mention that he would be returning to Saskatchewan, but not to Biggar, on July 1 to serve as one of the profession's emergency volunteers.

On Friday, June 29 — "Only One Day to MC-Day," the Saskatoon Star-Phoenix proclaimed in black letters — Dr. Hooge and Dr. Johnson were back in their offices. They had not been impressed by Dauphin, they reported to their friends, Hock and Morphy. The clinic and the two doctors' houses would not be for sale just yet, Clements said in a second announcement.

By Saturday, June 30, 22 patients had been discharged from St. Margaret's. One of them, Mrs. Frank Henrick, 59, was angry. She had been in hospital for eight days being prepared, because of a frail heart, for removal of gall-stones by a specialist in Saskatoon. "They chased me out of the hospital — everyone on his feet was chased out," she told her husband. "Then they tell me the Saskatoon doctor who was to do my operation has left. Now I have to suffer and the government is to blame."

In mid-afternoon Sister Bezaire was notified that the British doctor was standing by. "It would be better if she waited until tomorrow to arrive," Sister Bezaire suggested.

By 6.30 Saturday night the Biggar Clinic was closed to patients. "Have a good holiday," the receptionist called cheerfully to each of the doctors as he left. Dr. Dunbar reacted miserably. "It's a sorry mess," was all he could say. He and Dr. Hooge left by car for Winnipeg. Dr. Dunbar would go on to Ontario to visit relatives. Dr. and Mrs. Johnson would leave early the next morning for Winnipeg. Mrs. Hooge and her children were to stay in Biggar.

Between 7 and 8.30 Dr. Johnson made his rounds of the hospital, completed case histories of the remaining 18 patients in the wards, and phoned a colleague at the Rosetown emergency centre to report on one case, that of a woman whose heart condition was critical.

At a minute after midnight, Saskatoon radio and television stations announced: "The Medical Care act is in effect."

At noon on July 1, Dr. Ida Fisher, a 45-year-old London general practitioner and mother of five, arrived at St. Margaret's. Her contract with the government was for a month's service at a salary of $2,000.

During the remainder of the long holiday weekend, Dr. Fisher attended 20-odd patients who arrived at the hospital for treatment, admitted four and made half a dozen house calls, one in Landis, 20 miles away. Early Tuesday morning the heart patient suffered another attack. Dr. Fisher tended her and two other patients during the night. "Everyone," she found, "was most grateful. Some were indignant at the local doctors, not over matters of principle but because of their own personal involvement." Several weren't sick at all; simply afraid.

Tuesday morning radio station CFQC, in a news broadcast, described Dr. Fisher as "medical director" of St. Margaret's and remarked that town "officials" expected "violence among citizens with different views on the medical care issue in Biggar."

Sister Bezaire was "very concerned" about the report which, she was persuaded by the hospital advisory board, was directly and entirely attributable to Dr. Fisher. No one questioned Dr. Fisher herself or investigated the "officials" involved. Mayor Jones, as vice-chairman of the board, rushed out a news report that "Dr. Ida Fisher had not been appointed medical director of St. Margaret's hospital. The board's first concern," he said, "is for the return of competent and full medical services for our area."

At 11 a.m. Dr. Burgess, on his way to Kindersley, 100 miles west, where he was to serve as an emergency doctor, called at the Biggar Hospital. On the advice of Hock and Morphy, he had telephoned Sister Bezaire and volunteered to visit the heart patient. He told Morphy, for publication in the Independent, that he was "prepared to give free voluntary aid in Biggar community." Former patients should contact him by telephone at the Kindersley Hospital. He would "advise them to the best of his ability and, in the case of an emergency and where absolutely necessary, endeavor to come to Biggar." He also told his two friends: "Dr. Fisher hasn't had much experience in a hospital."

By noon, Hock was announcing to customers in his restaurant: "This woman doctor has never done an operation. She can't even do X-rays." Morphy, the editor, knew, for a fact, that "she couldn't thread a needle to stitch up a wound." He assumed that Dr. Fisher couldn't compose a coherent prescription — "they use different symbols in England."

The government commission offered a second doctor to St. Margaret's, a U.S. surgeon who had volunteered to serve in Saskatchewan. The rumor was that he practised in New York.

On Wednesday, the Independent reported, the hospital board had been informed that the second doctor "will only be sent if the hospital is willing to cancel all privileges held by the four doctors who were on staff at the hospital prior to July 1." That string had not been attached by the commission, according to Sister Bezaire. "Some members of the board heard about it," she announced with serene candor.

Wednesday night the Biggar KOD executive met in Saskatoon with other committees in the central Saskatchewan area. Twenty-five members of the Saskatoon Board of Trade attended the meeting and pledged financial as well as moral support for the KOD campaign, Hock reported when he returned home. Dr. Sam Landa, director of the College of Physicians and Surgeons' emergency service, addressed the group, Hock said, "inspiringly."

That same night, on the initiative of Roy Atkinson, the farmer who had protested the earlier evacuation plan, a meeting of 65 Biggar and district citizens was held in Oxborough Hall, some seven miles west of the town. Atkinson spoke to the group "as an individual — not as a vice-president of the Saskatchewan Farmers Union — who has come to the conclusion that the people who support the principle of universal medical care insurance will have to do something objective." There must be "no commotion about it," he insisted.

The only practical solution, the group decided, was to raise enough money to provide local facilities for doctors who would practise under the Medicare plan in Biggar. They set $40,000 as an objective.

Thursday at noon, members of the newly formed Biggar and District Citizen's Medical Health Association, without publicity, launched their campaign.

As they made their rounds, Lloyd Hock was in Regina at a meeting to organize a KOD cavalcade to Regina July 11. Seventy-five members of the Regina Board of Trade attended. They all decided, according to Hock, that "now we've lost our doctors the real fight in Saskatchewan is for our freedom." When Father Athol Murray of Wilcox told how "hatred is sweeping the province because of the medical care crisis," every man in that room, Hock reported, "had one hand on his hankie and the other reaching for his pocketbook."

Friday morning Dr. Landa telephoned Sister Bezaire to suggest that St. Margaret's would be "better off" without Dr. Fisher. The college's emergency service would provide a physician.

Almost immediately Dr. Burgess arrived at the hospital and the hospital advisory board assembled in Sister Bezaire's office for an emergency meeting. Hock confided over the counter in his restaurant that Dr. Fisher was "a card-carrying Communist; a fellow in Calgary is willing to sign an affidavit to that effect."

At 2 p.m. Dr. Fisher heard by telephone from Dr. Clarkson that she was being removed from St. Margaret's. She left by car for Saskatoon at 4. Immediately Morphy, on behalf of the hospital board, announced that "according to advice from prominent medical men assessing the situation the British doctor had not approached normal standards of practice and caution in treating injuries."

In Saskatoon Dr. Fisher learned for the first time the circumstances of her dismissal and the text of the hospital board statement. She replied in a statement of her own: "I am duly licensed to practise medicine by the Saskatchewan College of Physicians and Surgeons. I invite that body immediately to hold a proper investigation into the scurrilous allegations which have been made against me." Privately she said, "I'm weary of this war. But I shall stay."

Back in Biggar, news of the activities of the District Citizens' Medical Health Association had reached the KOD committee. The new group was dismissed as "a Red camp."

But by Saturday at noon the two-day-old DCMHA had collected more than $35,000 in cash and cheques and dispatched telegrams to all four local doctors at their Biggar addresses, asking them: "Will the Biggar clinic be open July 9? Would you be prepared to act under the Sas-katchewan Medical Care Act?"

Not at all to the association's surprise, Dr. Hooge answered in person. He met the executive of the association Sunday, July 9, and said no to both its questions. Dr. Dunbar, who was indeed in Ontario, was sent a second wire to his new address. He answered immediately, No. Dr. Johnson and Dr. Burgess were rumored on their way to Winnipeg, after a consultation with Dr. Hooge in Biggar. They could not be reached.

Monday night 250 members of the Citizens' Medical Health Associ-ation met in the town hall and announced its determination to "take all steps necessary to restore normal services to this district in both clinic and hospital." Their determination had grown out of "talk at street corners, in railway yards and on the farms in this district," according to their chairman, Lewis Craig.

"The progressive element of this community has come alive," Roy Atkinson and Alf Gleave, a farmer and president of the SFU, agreed. "Perhaps," said Atkinson, "there'll be a resurgence of the old progressive spirit in the whole province."

The two farmers meditated: "We've been brainwashing ourselves for the last 10 years — not only in Saskatchewan but on this whole con-tinent. We'd come to believe that ours is the best of all possible societies. Now the social forces that are really at war on the North American continent have come to grips in Saskatchewan. It's terrible. But who knows what may come of it?"

The Biggar Board of Trade was meditating, too. The next morning Mayor Jones, Clement, Leslie and a group of other businessmen asked to meet the board of the Citizens' Medical Health Association for "nego-tiations" in a room behind the barber shop on Main St. At the outset of the meeting the health association announced that negotiations could only begin when the businessmen had publicly dissociated themselves from the KOD committee. They all said they'd never belonged. But they declined to publish a statement, whereupon the meeting broke up.

Early Wednesday morning only a couple of cars followed Hock's into the Biggar cavalcade, bound for the "mass freedom rally" in Regina. Biggar's civil war was almost over. But everyone knew the peace would be as bitter as the fighting and not nearly as exhilarating.

52. *THE FARMER AND THE SASKATCHEWAN MEDICAL CARE INSURANCE CONTROVERSY**

James N. McCrorie†

The Saskatchewan Medical Care Insurance controversy of 1962 is an event in the history of the provincial community which will attract the attention of sociologists for years to come. The complexity of the issue can be simply demonstrated by posing a series of unanswered questions. For example: What was the nature of the ideological controversy between the provincial government and the medical profession? What was the relation of business, educational, labour and farm organizations to the medical care issue? How did the medical profession exert social control over its membership? What was the role of the press, both inside and outside Saskatchewan, in the controversy? What has been the impact of the medical care insurance controversy in other areas in Canada and the United States? What has been the pattern of immigration and emigration of doctors to and from Saskatchewan? What was the public's image of the doctors before and after the medical care strike?

Only time and attentive study will provide meaningful answers to these and other questions. The scope and depth of the issue forbids an ambitious and comprehensive statement on the medical care controversy at this time. In this paper we propose to introduce the reader to two, but not all, of the important facets of the issue, trusting that this introduction will serve as a stimulus and a guide to further interest, study and research.

The conflict leading up to and during the doctors' strike in July 1962 was intense. It has been reported elsewhere that families were divided over the issue, political affiliations were undermined, merchants were boycotted, many citizens were without normal medical services, doctors were torn between professional and business ethics.[1]

What is often overlooked in discussing the medical care controversy is that the people of Saskatchewan are not strangers to this kind of conflict. Since the turn of the century the history of Saskatchewan has been coloured with a number of conflicts which have divided the community

---

*Published here for the first time.

†Dr. McCrorie, a sociologist, is Research Director for the Saskatchewan Farmers Union, Saskatoon.

1 See preceding articles by Cooperstock and Locke.

on the one hand, and set some, if not all of the community at odds with other sectors of the economy.

The formation of the Grain Growers' Grain Company (now known as the United Grain Growers Ltd.) in 1906, the Saskatchewan Co-operative Elevator Company in 1911, the Saskatchewan Wheat Pool in 1924, and Federated Co-operatives in 1929 were all events in the history of the province that divided some in the agricultural community, and united others against those engaged in industries producing different but related goods and services.[2]

The sweep of the Progressive Party in 1921, and the separation of the Saskatchewan Provincial from the Federal Liberal Party in that same year were events which grew out of heated debate and dissension within the province on the one hand, and antagonism between the agrarian community and what came to be known as the "old line" parties, on the other.[3] The election campaign of 1944, which brought the C.C.F. to power for the first time in the province, was not without its drama and turmoil.[4]

The bitter controversies in 1946 over the farm delivery strike, and in the early fifties over livestock and egg marketing boards divided farm organizations and prompted an antagonism between agricultural producers and those engaged in the food processing industry.[5] The current hog marketing board controversy is but another and more recent instance of the kind of conflict which has been an integral part of Saskatchewan's history.

It would be misleading to suggest that an acquaintance and familiarity with intense kinds of conflict endeared the people of Saskatchewan to the medical care controversy of 1962. Such was not the case, but it may be said that events in the past prepared the people of this province, especially the agrarian community, for the kind of conflict which grew out of the dispute between the Saskatchewan College of Physicians and Surgeons and the Government of the province.

By withholding normal medical services, the doctors of the province hoped to exercise considerable pressure on the people and the govern-

---

[2] See J. N. McCrorie, *The Saskatchewan Farmers Movement: An Interim Report,* (Saskatoon, Center for Community Studies, 1964); H. Patton, *Grain Growers Co-operation in Western Canada,* (Cambridge, Harvard University Press, 1928.).

[3] W. Morton, *The Progressive Party in Canada,* Toronto, University of Toronto Press, 1950.

[4] S. Lipset, *Agrarian Socialism,* Berkeley, University of California Press, 1959.

[5] McCrorie, *op. cit.,* Chapter II.

ment. The deprivation, however, was not without precedence. One farm leader put it this way:

> "Ever since we settled these prairies sixty years ago, we have been skinned by grain traders, fleeced by packing companies, cheated by farm machine companies, tricked by politicians, and plagued with drought and grass-hoppers. These doctors are nothing new. We will win, the way we won the fight with the Grain Exchange."

It has been duly noted that Saskatchewan is the first political community in North America to adopt a *government* pre-paid, universal, comprehensive and compulsory medical care insurance program. It is also recognized that Saskatchewan remains primarily an agricultural community. Why should farmers, who are often associated with conservative views and tastes, lend their support to a government medical care insurance program? Again, a reference to the history and traditions of the agrarian community throws some light on the question.

As early as 1900, Saskatchewan farmers found themselves caught up in competition and conflict with industries producing different but related goods and services. For example, those engaged in the grain trade were interested in purchasing wheat at the lowest possible price, whereas the agricultural producer was interested in selling at the highest possible price. In order to protect their interests, the line elevator and grain trading companies pooled receipts, fixed prices, and attempted to keep farmers' marketing co-operatives off the Winnipeg Grain Exchange.[6]

In response to this kind of competition and conflict, farmers attempted to integrate the function of marketing with that of production. In 1906 they formed the first marketing co-operative, and between 1908 and 1910, they attempted to persuade the provincial government to nationalize the line elevator system, which, they claimed, was " . . . acting against the public interest by taking unfair dockage and giving inaccurate weights to grain delivered."[7]

In 1919 the federal government enacted the Canadian Wheat Board Act which marketed the entire western grain crop for that year. Initially, farmers through their organizations protested the action. However, within a year they came to realize that a Wheat Board gave them a fair

---

[6] See the *Report and Evidence of the Royal Commission on the Shipment and Transportation of Grain*, (Sessional Papers 81a, March 19th, 1900); *Report of the Royal Commission on the Grain Trade of Canada*, (Sessional Papers 59, 1907-1908); *Report of the Elevator Commission of the Province of Saskatchewan*, (Regina, Government Printer, 1910.)

[7] The provincial government refused to nationalize the elevator system, but agreed to pass legislation establishing a co-operative elevator company, and promised to underwrite the operations of the co-operative with public funds.

and stable price for their product. When the Board was disbanded in the following year there was general concensus in Saskatchewan that the federal government should continue in the field of marketing grain, and pressure was exerted to this end.

The federal government declined to re-establish a wheat board and farmers turned once again to co-operative action. In 1924, they established the Saskatchewan Wheat Pool, which removed the middle man and permitted the producer to market his product directly to consumers in national and international trade.

The Wheat Pool failed in the crash of 1929 and once again farmers turned to government for action. A voluntary board was established in 1935, and deliveries of wheat to the board were made compulsory in 1943. To the Saskatchewan farmer, a compulsory government marketing board was an acceptable alternative to a marketing system which placed the producer in competition and conflict with those traditionally involved in the grain trade.

Ever since the settlement of the west, Saskatchewan farmers have been in continual conflict with railway companies. The Canadian trans-continentals did not provide a cheaper transportation alternative to the American network. As Fowke has pointed out, they were built for defensive and economic reasons pertaining to the development of a national industrial economy.[8] The farmer, however, continually argued that rail transportation should operate in the interests of the shipper, and to this end, he was prepared to encourage the federal government to nationalize rail transportation in Canada.

In his efforts to cope with and temper competition with industries producing different, but related goods and services, the farmer initially looked to co-operatives for an answer. However, he found in time that co-operatives were limited in their functions. Government action — either in the form of regulations or ownership — offered him an acceptable alternative. During the short sixty years of Saskatchewan's history then, government participation in certain sectors of the larger economy became compatible with the economic interests of the individual agrarian entrepreneur.[9]

---

[8] V. Fowke, *The National Policy and the Wheat Economy*, Toronto, University of Toronto Press, 1957.

[9] It should be noted that other industries have also welcomed "limited" government participation in the economy. See for example, E. H. Carr, *The New Society*, (Boston, Beacon Press, 1959); G. Cole, *Principles of Economic Planning*, (London, Macmillan & Co., 1935); L. Hartz, *Economic Policy and Democratic Thought*, (Cambridge, Harvard University Press, 1948).

But there is a second and more important aspect to the Saskatchewan farmer's acceptance of government activities. Unlike those engaged in other productive industries, the Saskatchewan farmer employs his family in the operation of his enterprise. Leaving aside the rhetoric which has become associated with the family farm, it must be recognized that agricultural production in Saskatchewan is carried on in most cases by a family unit, and the costs of operating a farm are seldom distinguished from the costs of providing for the family welfare. So, for example, the farm family must meet the costs of purchasing seed, fertilizer, and farm machinery, as well as the costs of food, clothing, and medical care for the family.

The tendency on the part of the farmer to think of his farm operation and family as one enhanced his interest in and commitment to the medical care insurance program. The government insurance plan, which included complete and comprehensive coverage at the cheapest possible cost, promised to reduce the farmer's investment in medical care for his family, leaving aside monies to be invested in other phases of family life or the farming operation. "Compulsion" and "government control" were not the central issues in the controversy for most farmers. Complete medical care at the lowest possible cost was the issue.

Any generalizations we can entertain at this time are tentative. However, given the medical profession's fear of and resistance to government-sponsored health programs, our analysis suggests that the Saskatchewan community contained two conditions which were essential to the successful implementation of a government medical care insurance program:

1. The kind of conflict we can expect to be associated with the implementation of government programmes of this kind was not novel to Saskatchewan. If it was not welcomed by her citizens, this kind of conflict was not without historical precedence. The Saskatchewan experience has included a great number of conflicts in the past which were gradually and successfully overcome.

2. The relationship of the individual farmer and his family to the productive processes of the agrarian economy enhanced his interest in and commitment to a medical care insurance program sponsored by a provincial government. The farmers' ideological commitment to government medical care insurance was rooted in economic considerations.

SELECTED BIBLIOGRAPHY

Canadian Medical Association Journal, (Editorial), "Unjust Laws Exist", Vol. 87, July 28, 1962.

Edmonds, J. K., "Saskatchewan Doctors Regroup While the Fires Smoulder On," *The Financial Post,* February 9, 1963.

Gregory, E. G., "Impact of Medicare; Address," *Industrial Canada,* Vol. 64, July, 1963.

Hall, O., "Some Problems in the Provision of Medical Services," *The Canadian Journal of Economics and Political Science,* Vol. XX, No. 4, November, 1954.

Hall, O., "The Informal Organization of the Medical Profession," *The Canadian Journal of Economics and Political Science,* Vol. XII, 1946.

McLeod, J., "Medicare: Round Two," *The Canadian Forum,* September, 1962.

Report of the Thompson Advisory Planning Committee on Medical Care, Regina, Queen's Printer, 1962.

Taylor, M. G., "The Role of the Medical Profession in the Formulation and Execution of Public Policy," *The Canadian Journal of Economics and Political Science,* Vol. XXVI, No. 1, February, 1960.

Tollefson, E. A., *Bitter Medicine,* Saskatoon, Modern Press, 1964.

part three

PROBLEMS
OF
INDIVIDUAL DEVIANCE
AND
PERSONAL DISORGANIZATION

chapter ten

THE PROBLEM OF ADDICTION

It is usual to think only of the narcotic drugs (e.g. the opiates) when one speaks of addiction, but for the purposes of this chapter we shall consider alcoholism to be a state of addiction as well. Of the three articles included in the chapter, two deal with alcoholism, one with the problem of narcotic drug addiction. Both problems are by no means unique to Canada, although there are certain aspects to each (e.g. their relationship to the law, treatment facilities) which are, to some extent, peculiar to this country.

In the first article, written especially for this book, Robert J. Gibbins of the Alcoholism and Drug Addiction Research Foundation of Ontario describes the nature of "The Alcoholism Problem in Canada." He compares alcoholism rates by province, then compares the Canadian rate to that reported for eleven other countries, and finally discusses some of the social effects of this disease. Robert E. Popham, associated with the same Foundation, contributes the next selection, a comprehensive discussion of "Some Social and Cultural Aspects of Alcoholism." He offers a "definition" of alcoholism, some other factors about it, and, in comparing rural to urban alcoholism rates, some statistics for the various provinces. He concludes with the presentation of a theoretical hypothesis regarding the nature of alcohol addiction which attempts to take into account both the sociological and the psychological aspects of its etiology.

A. M. Kirkpatrick, of Ontario's John Howard Society, examines the problem of narcotic addiction in an article entitled "New Views on the Narcotic Problem." Here he treats the subject in terms of definition, and from the statistical, criminal, legal, economic, medical, and therapeutic points

of view. His final comments, regarding treatment of the problem, are at the
same time critical, controversial, and constructive.

53. ALCOHOLISM IN CANADA*

Robert J. Gibbins†

The word "alcoholic" as applied to a person means many things to many
people. Unfortunately it is a term that is used very loosely not only in
everyday conversation but also in lay and scientific literature. Undoubtedly
this fact has contributed much to the confusion that exists in the minds
of many Canadians about the problem of alcoholism. Since the purpose
of this article is to provide information about the prevalence of alcoholism
in Canada, it is necessary to define at the outset what is meant by the
term "alcoholic". An alcoholic is defined as an excessive drinker whose
dependence upon alcohol has reached such a degree that it results in a
noticeable mental disturbance or an interference with his bodily and
mental health, his interpersonal relations, and his smooth social and
economic functioning, or who shows the early signs of such developments.[1]

Until 1954, estimates of the prevalence of alcoholism among Canadians were based largely upon incompletely verified U.S. figures. This
practice, which was due to the absence of adequate Canadian studies,
was based upon the popular but erroneous assumption that the two
countries were similar with respect to percentage of persons who drink
abnormally. It is now clear that the application of U.S. proportions to
Canadian populations resulted in a grossly distorted picture of the problem
in Canada.

This note of warning is sounded here since there are those in Canada
who, in their zeal to initiate what they believe to be ameliorative programs,

---

*Published here for the first time.
†Dr. Gibbins is Director of the Psychological Laboratory at the Alcoholism and
  Drug Addiction Research Foundation, Toronto.
  [1] Based on the definition of alcoholism adopted by the Alcoholism Subcommittee
of the Expert Committee on Mental Health of the World Health Organization.

feel free to disregard factual information and foist off on an unsuspecting and often uncritical public greatly exaggerated estimates, some of which are based upon nothing but a fallacious analogy, and some of which have no apparent basis at all. On the other hand, of course, are those who, because of wishful thinking, self interest, lethargy or lack of information, tend to underestimate the size of the problem.

In order to provide a reasonably sound basis for an estimate of the prevalence of alcoholism in the Province of Ontario, a field survey was conducted during 1952-53 in an Ontario county which was selected because its population was closely comparable to that of the province as a whole with respect to rural-urban distribution, sex ratio, ethnic and religious composition, and percentage of persons 20 years of age and over.[2] Because of this similarity it was possible to estimate a rate of alcoholism for Ontario on the basis of the county rate.

In 1951 there were 43,606 persons 20 years of age and over in the county investigated. The survey detected 698 alcoholics. This means that in the county in that year there were approximately 16 alcoholics for every 1,000 persons 20 years of age and over. Applying this rate to the adult population of Ontario (3,042,543 persons 20 years of age and over) gave 48,681 alcoholics in the province in 1951. These figures compare very closely with estimates for the same areas based on the Jellinek Estimation Formula, namely 696 for the county and 48,898 for the province.[3] Lest the reader feel that his credulity is being strained by such close similarity between the two sets of estimates, it must be pointed out that undoubtedly the survey did not detect all of the alcoholics residing in the county and consequently the survey figures for the county and the province probably represent underestimations. The significant fact is not that the two sets of estimates are so close numerically, but that they are of the same magnitude.

In 1961, a second survey of the same county was begun, and has recently been completed.[4] This survey detected 1,249 alcoholics. Since there were 53,138 persons 20 years of age and over in the county in 1961 the rate is 24 alcoholics for every 1,000 adults. Because the procedures used

---

[2] Gibbins, R. J., "Alcoholism in Ontario: A survey of an Ontario county", *Quarterly Journal of Studies on Alcohol,* No. 15, 1954, pp. 47-62.

[3] For a detailed consideration of the Jellinek Estimation Formula see Popham, R. E., "The Jellinek Alcoholism Estimation Formula and Its Application to Canadian Data", *Quarterly Journal of Studies on Alcohol,* No. 17, 1956, pp. 559-593.

[4] Newman, A, *A Re-Survey of Alcoholism in an Ontario County,* Alcoholism Research Foundation Substudy 2-N-64.

in the second survey were in all important respects similar to those used in the first, the increase in rate is not accountable in terms of differences in method. Application of the county rate to the adult population of Ontario (3,791,400 persons 20 years and over) yields an estimate of 89,120 alcoholics in the province in 1961. Again there is an impressively close correspondence between estimates based on the survey and estimates based on the Jellinek formula. According to th Jellinek formula, the 1961 rate for Ontario was 25 alcoholics per 1,000 adults, which gives a total of 93,450 alcoholics in the province in that year.

Because there have been six other instances in which estimates based on the Jellinek formula have compared favourably with independent estimates[5], there is some justification for using this procedure to calculate rates of alcoholism for Canada and the provinces. The results of such calculations may be seen in Table I.

Table 1

ESTIMATED PREVALENCE OF ALCOHOLISM IN CANADA
AND THE PROVINCES 1961.

Area	Alcoholism Prevalence	
	Alcoholics per 100,000 Aged 20 and Over	*Total Alcoholics*
Canada	2,140	230,025
Ontario	2,440	93,450
British Columbia	2,380	24,200
Quebec	2,340	69,940
Manitoba	1,970	10,930
Prince Edward Island	1,640	960
Alberta	1,550	12,100
Nova Scotia	1,460	6,130
New Brunswick	1,230	3,945
Saskatchewan	1,170	6,290
Newfoundland	915	2,080

Ontario, British Columbia and Quebec rank highest and New Brunswick, Saskatchewan, and Newfoundland lowest with Manitoba, Prince Edward Island, Alberta and Nova Scotia occupying intermediate positions.

---

[5] Popham, *op. cit.*

Although at present an adequate explanation for this inter-provincial variation in rates cannot be offered, it is worth mentioning that the more urban provinces tend to have higher rates.[6]

Table 2[7] depicts Canada's rate of alcoholism compared with that of the United States and certain other countries.

Table 2

ESTIMATED NUMBER OF ALCOHOLICS PER 100,000 OF
THE POPULATION OF 20 YEARS OF AGE AND OVER
IN CANADA AND IN VARIOUS OTHER COUNTRIES*

Country	Rate of Alcoholism	Year
France	5,200	1954
United States	4,760	1956
Chile	2,960	1950
Sweden	2,580	1946
Canada	2,140	1961
Switzerland	2,100	1953
Denmark	1,950	1948
Norway	1,560	1947
Australia	1,340	1947
England and Wales	1,100	1948
Finland	1,100	1957
Italy	700	1954

* Latest available year in each case.

The marked difference in rate between Canada and the United States clearly exposes the fallacy of applying American figures to Canadian populations. Table 3[8] shows that Canada and the United States differ not only in rate of alcoholism but also with respect to percentage of persons who drink. From the table it is apparent that a larger percentage of Canadians than Americans use alcoholic beverages. Of considerable interest is the finding that, in comparison with American women, a larger percentage of Canadian women drink.

---

[6] Schmidt, W., *The Ecology of Alcoholism,* Alcoholism Research Foundation, Substudy 5-4-63.

[7] Most of the data in this table were extracted from Popham, R. E. and Schmidt, W., *Statistics of Alcohol Use and Alcoholism in Canada 1871-1956: First Report,* Toronto, Alcoholism Research Foundation and University of Toronto Press, 1958.

[8] The data in this table were taken from Bennett, R. S., *Statistics of Alcohol Use and Alcoholism in Canada 1951-1961: Second Report,* Alcoholism Research Foundation Substudy 1-B-62.

Table 3

PERCENTAGE OF USERS OF ALCOHOLIC BEVERAGES AND OF TOTAL
ABSTAINERS IN CANADA (1958) AND THE UNITED STATES (1957)
AND ESTIMATED NUMBER OF ALCOHOLICS PER 100,000
ADULTS IN THE TWO COUNTRIES (1956)

	Canada			United States		
	Users	Abstainers	Alcoholism Rate	Users	Abstainers	Alcoholism Rate
Total population	65%	35%	1,890	58%	42%	4,760
Men	70	30	—	67	33	—
Women	60	40	—	50	50	—

The facts that a larger percentage of Canadians than Americans drink and that Canada has a much lower rate of alcoholism than the United States add support to already existing evidence which suggests that the relationship between the size of a drinking population and its rate of alcoholism is not direct and simple as it might superficially appear to be.

Let us recapitulate some of the things that have been said about the population involved in the problem of alcoholism. In Canada there are approximately 10,593,200 persons 20 years of age and over. Of these 6,885,580 use alcoholic beverages; and of these an estimated 230,025 become alcoholics.

If the problem is expressed in relation to the users of alcoholic beverages only, instead of the entire adult population, we find that of 1,000 alcohol users approximately 33 are alcoholics. Thus it would seem that alcoholism is not the inevitable end of every Canadian who drinks, but that it occurs in only a fraction of the population of users. However, since the majority of our adult population drinks this fraction of it is numerically large.

Alcoholics are persons who, because of their illness, contribute a disproportionate amount to absenteeism, accidents and wastage in industry, neglect their families, cause hazards to traffic, and populate our jails. They become seriously ill with the diseases of chronic alcoholism, and continually suffer mental and frequently physical pain.

In relation to the size of the drinking population the number of alcoholics is small, but it is a number of sufficient size to play a significant role in the mental and physical health and in the social and economic welfare of the nation.

54. *SOME SOCIAL AND CULTURAL ASPECTS OF ALCOHOLISM**

Robert E. Popham†

ORIENTATION

Among some of those who are primarily concerned with the treatment of alcoholics, there is a tendency to take what appears to be a rather one-sided and short-term view of the nature of alcoholism. To such workers, who necessarily are "individual" or "case history" oriented, the data generally subsumed under the "cultural and social aspects of alcoholism" usually seem of little relevance.

The attitude to which I refer is reflected very clearly in a remark which a fellow student at the Yale School of Alcohol Studies once made to me during an anthropological lecture on Jewish drinking habits. As is now quite well known, the Orthodox Jewish population has a very low rate of alcoholism. He said: "Why do they waste our time with this? I don't expect to see any Jewish patients in my hospital."

This view, and the milder versions of it found among many therapists, is quite understandable, though not particularly desirable. Thus psychiatrists, for example, are faced with particular individuals — across the desk here and now — and these persons want and expect to receive help with their particular problems. Under these circumstances the findings and theories of the social scientist, who focuses on *group* differences and mass trends in drinking behaviour, and not primarily on individual differences, must appear of little or no practical value. But when attention is shifted from particular alcoholics to the nature of alcoholism in general, and from the immediate problem of giving service to the long term goal of prevention, the relevance of social and cultural factors soon becomes evident.

DEFINITION OF ALCOHOLISM

Let me illustrate this first with reference to the problem of defining alcoholism.

If one reads through a sample of the case records of alcoholics admitted to a clinic such as Brookside in Toronto, one is struck by the fact that

---

*From the *Canadian Psychiatric Association Journal,* Vol. 4, No. 4, October 1959.
†Mr. Popham is Associate Director of Research (Behavioural Sciences) at the Alcoholism and Drug Addiction Research Foundation of Ontario.

neither their social nor their psychiatric histories are particularly distinctive. That is to say, there does not appear to emerge anything in the order of a cluster of personality traits, or childhood or adult experiences, which you could say were characteristic of alcoholics, being only or largely found among alcoholics, and not about as frequently in psychiatric patients not labelled as alcoholics.

Putting the matter on a more objective basis, this impression is supported by the essentially negative results of a number of attempts to distinguish alcoholics from psychiatric populations at large, by means of psychological tests and the like. Thus up to the present time data have not been obtained which would permit the formulation of a definition of alcoholism in terms of psychological or psychiatric criteria of etiological significance.

It is presumably this state of affairs which leads most workers to fall back on definitions based on the drinking behaviour of alcoholics: the one thing they do have in common and which sets them apart from the rest of the psychiatric population.

However, as soon as this approach to definition is adopted, the sociocultural context of the drinking has to be taken into account. For example, if we speak of *excessive* drinking as a characteristic of alcoholics we have to know what is meant by excessive. The implication is that the consumption of alcoholic beverages is greater than that constituting the norm of the society in which the alcoholism occurs. This is essentially the core of the definition adopted by the World Health Organization (Expert Committee on Mental Health, 1952). But then it is necessary to know what the norm is and presumably this is a sociological problem.

PHASES OF THE DRINKING HISTORY OF ALCOHOLICS

Another closely related approach is to describe alcoholics in terms of the various characteristic phases through which their drinking history passes.

According to Jellinek, the alcoholic has passed through a sequence of stages in his history such as 'blackouts', 'sneaking drinks', 'increased tolerance', 'loss of control', 'the development of an alibi system', 'going on periodic benders', 'regular matutinal drinking', and so on.

Although this has proved a useful way of describing alcoholic drinking in this country, it is important to keep in mind that these phases represent consequences, or perhaps one might say *symptoms* af alcoholism, and not etiological factors. It may well be just such confusion of symptoms with etiology which accounts for the persistence with which many still search for a distinctive alcoholic personality.

It is also important to recognize the fact that this description of the alcoholic in terms of his drinking history depends at least in part on the socio-cultural context. Thus, for example, the French alcoholic typically has a quite different drinking history. In France the dominant pattern seems to be inveterate drinking and what French writers call "l'alcoolisme sans ivresse".

The French alcoholic tends to drink steadily through the day but not sufficient quantities to grossly incapacitate him. He does not commonly exhibit the pattern of "bender drinking" so familiar in the North American alcoholic. In this country the alcoholic is thought of as one who has "lost control of his drinking". That is, when he has had one or two drinks he is compulsively led to go on to a bender: to drink himself into a stupor. In France and other wine-drinking countries, it is necessary to speak of "inability to stop drinking" rather than "loss of control". Thus the French alcoholic apparently requires a certain quantity of alcohol each day but one or two drinks does not lead to a bender. His object is to maintain a certain relatively low blood alcohol level continuously, rather than to achieve a state of acute intoxication periodically.

In North America, regular morning drinking is almost by itself considered to be evidence of alcoholism. In France such behaviour is not thought of as unusual and drinking throughout the day is socially acceptable.

The alcoholic in France tends to be labelled as such when he has drunk enough, for long enough, to have developed an organic complication such as cirrhosis of the liver or one of the alcoholic psychoses. As a result, alcoholism is there generally considered a problem in physical medicine and not a psychiatric problem at all.

Parenthetically, it is interesting that only in the French literature does one find a treatment for alcoholism recommended which is designed to permit the patient to continue daily drinking. It is suggested that the antabuse dosage be so regulated that a reaction will not take place unless consumption goes beyond what is considered a 'healthy' amount.

Let me give a final example of the possible role of socio-cultural factors in defining the symptoms of alcoholism. The Doxa survey of drinking habits in Italy showed that only one percent of the population consumed alcoholic beverages "outside of meals". This is, of course, just the reverse of the practice in this country. It is interesting that the estimated prevalence of alcoholism in Italy is also about one percent. Whether the same people are involved in both cases is not known, but it is quite possible that regular drinking unaccompanied by the taking of food is regarded in the same unfavourable light as regular matutinal drinking in North American communities.

Thus, at the present stage of knowledge it would seem that what will be labelled "alcoholism", what will be regarded as symptomatic of this condition, what kind of problem it will be considered, and perhaps even approach to treatment, are at least in part determined by the socio-cultural situation in which the drinking takes place.

SOCIO-CULTURAL FACTORS IN ETIOLOGY

It begins to appear that socio-cultural factors have, in addition, a major role in the determination of the *prevalence* of alcoholism in a given population or cultural grouping. Three examples may serve to illustrate why this is thought to be the case.

(1) *Rural-urban differences in alcoholism prevalence*

Some time ago, Jellinek noted that the combined rate of alcoholism for American urban areas (over 100,000 population) was slightly more than double the combined rate for rural areas (under 2,500 population).

More recently this finding offered a possible means of explaining inter-provincial differences in Canada. The percentage of urban residents (based on the Census definition of "urban") and the rate of alcoholism in each province is shown in Table 1.

Table 1

Province	Estimated Alcoholics per 100,000 Adults	% Urban Residents in Adult Population
British Columbia	2,285	70.7
Ontario	1,780	73.1
Quebec	1,760	71.4
Nova Scotia	1,450	55.0
Alberta	1,420	51.3
Manitoba	1,420	60.7
New Brunswick	1,180	45.8
Saskatchewan	1,140	32.8
Newfoundland	640	43.7
Prince Edward Island	520	26.9

It can be seen that, although by no means a perfect relationship, there is a clear positive association: the more urban the province, the higher the prevalence.

It might be supposed that this rural-urban difference could be accounted for on the basis of higher rates of psychosis and neurosis in cities than in rural areas. Indeed, this may be partly the case, but it also seems likely that attitudes play a part.

Towards the end of national prohibition in the United States (1919-1933) a plebiscite was held in each state to determine whether prohibition was to be repealed or retained. The proportion voting against the repeal of the Eighteenth Amendment provides a rough index of dry sentiment.

In a recent investigation, a highly significant *negative* correlation was found between degree of dry sentiment as measured in this manner and degree of urbanism. Thus American areas which had a high degree of dry sentiment appeared to be relatively more rural and to have lower rates of alcoholism. This suggests that prevailing attitudes or, one might say, the average degree of acceptance of drinking has something to do with the prevalence of alcoholism in a population or a particular segment of a population.

(2) *Sex differences in the prevalence of alcoholism*

A problem which has interested clinicians as well as social scientists for some time is the reason for a difference between males and females in the prevalence of alcoholism. In Canada and the United States the ratio is about six male to one female alcoholic. But it is interesting that there are apparently international differences in this ratio. In some of the Scandinavian countries it is said to be as high as twenty-three to one; and in England only two to one.

It seems hardly reasonable to postulate that women are somehow less subject than men to neurotic conflict, anxiety states and other personality disturbances, especially in view of the international variation in the ratio. Again the possible role of community attitudes comes to mind as an explanation.

In our own society we have, as has often been pointed out, a *double standard of morals,* which in its simplest terms is the attitude that it is less acceptable for a woman to sin than for a man. In the sexual area, for example, pre-marital affairs among males are at least condoned, if not considered desirable: "he is just sowing his wild oats". But females are supposed to be virgins when they marry; those who do engage in pre-marital sexual activity are labelled: "promiscuous", "vulgar", "lower class", "immoral", etc.

The double standard is equally evident in the case of drinking behaviour. Men are expected to get tight if not "roaring drunk" on occasion. The ability to consume large quantities of liquor seems to be a source of kudos and a demonstration of masculinity. But drunkenness among women is regarded with great disapproval as a sign of moral degradation.

(3) *Cultural group differences in the prevalence of alcoholism*

The most frequently noted example of a marked difference in the prevalence of alcoholism among different cultural or ethnic groups is that which obtains between the Jews and the Irish. The former rank among the lowest of all groups and the latter among the highest. According to available empirical data Jewish groups appear to have at least as high frequencies of psychosis and neurosis as are found in groups which have much higher frequencies of alcoholism. Moreover, clinical impression has it that anxiety states and drug addiction may occur with greater than average frequency among Jews. Thus it would not seem that the relatively low prevalence of pathological drinking among them can be attributed to a lower prevalence of mental disorders. On the other hand, it would seem increasingly clear that Jewish attitudes towards the use of alcoholic beverages are of considerable importance in this connection.

It has been pointed out that the Jew has a ritual attitude towards drinking. Thus one or another type of alcoholic beverage figures in all aspects of the religious life. In the circumcision ceremony a benediction is said over a cup of wine; a few drops are place on the infant's lips and the godfather drinks the remainder. After the Bar Mitzvah, the Jewish equivalent of the Christian confirmation rite, wine is drunk at the feast of celebration. In the marriage ceremony, the bride and groom drink wine from a common cup; and in the old days one of the rites performed at funerals consisted in washing the head of the corpse with wine. Apart from its use in ceremonies marking major events in the life cycle, Snyder estimates that alcoholic beverages figure in routine religious ceremonies about 250 times a year. Hence wine has a symbolic and sacred character for the Jew, and accordingly, drunkenness is condemned as a profanity and an abomination.

Further evidence of the importance of the ritual attitude is found in the differences in drinking patterns which occur *within* the Jewish population. Snyder compared Orthodox, Conservative, Reform and secular groups (that is, those Jews who have left the synagogue altogether) and found that the prevalence of drunkenness tended to increase the further the group was removed from orthodoxy. It may be supposed that the trend from the Orthodox to the secular groups reflects increasing assimilation of the culture of the majority gentile community, including drinking habits. But this trend also may be seen as partly a function of changes in attitudes towards the larger gentile population and in the degree to which they fear loss of identification as Jews, or, conversely, desire to avoid such identification. For example, the attitude of the Orthodox Jew towards drunkenness, in addition to being conditioned by the role of alcoholic beverages in religious life, may be affected by anti-gentilism. Thus, for him, to be drunk is to behave like a "goyisha kopf" — an opprobrious term for a gentile.

The attitudes of the Irish toward drinking, in contrast to those of the Jews, may be characterized as predominantly *utilitarian*. Bales illustrates this with reference to drinking in Irish rural communities as follows:

" . . . At the fairs where the livestock is sold, there is usually a long, heated argument about the price. When an agreement is finally reached, the bargain is sealed with one or more drinks. Sometimes the seller takes his customer to the public house before the agreement is reached and treats him a few times to 'soften him up'. In making the bargain for a marriage it is necessary to reach extensive economic agreements in the evaluation of the farm and livestock, since this determines the amount of the dowry which the young lady's father will give. In one of these matchmakings the bargainers treat back and forth until all are well fuddled. One writer says, 'To one who has lived for some time in England, the mixture of tippling and business seems like some incredible dream. Little bits of business get in, as if by stealth, between the drinks during the day!' The farmer typically comes home from a day at the fair in a very intoxicated condition indeed. His wife does not usually complain. In fact, if she is a good wife, she may treat her husband the next morning with 'a hair of the dog that bit him'. Drunken men are usually treated with care and affection in Ireland. To the mother the drunken man is 'the poor boy'. Laborers seeing an intoxicated man coming home from the fair are prone to regard him with envy, rather than pity, since he is in a much better state than they."

As Bales further points out drinking "to get over a hangover . . . is a pure example of individualistic utilitarian drinking" — and, one may add, a practice by no means unknown in North American communities. Expressions familiar to us which include the word "need" with reference to alcohol reflect the utilitarian view. We say we *need* a drink: "to buck us up", "to get feeling good", "to relax after a tough day", "to drown our sins and sorrows" and so on. All of these indicate the utilitarian attitude in placing the emphasis on the drug properties of alcohol, that is, on its physiological effects as a means to an end.

THE VULNERABILITY-ACCEPTANCE HYPOTHESIS

In attempting to illustrate the role of socio-cultural factors in the etiology of alcoholism, I have mentioned only attitudes. I do not wish to give the impression that this is the only such factor involved. But it is probably one of the most important of those so far investigated to any extent. Moreover it leads nicely to one final theory which I would like to outline briefly.

However, let me first clear up another impression which I may have given, namely, that I believe the problem of alcoholism to be really one for the social scientist to solve and not the psychiatrist. On the contrary, I believe that sociology and anthropology, on the one hand, and psychology and psychiatry, on the other, are strictly complementary approaches to the problem. Take, for example, the group differences which have been discussed: rural-urban, male-female, and Jewish-Irish, and assume that it is established beyond doubt that these differences are due to social and cultural factors. There would still remain a problem, and a very large and complex one at that, namely, to explain why certain individuals and not others enter into the statistics of alcoholism in any one of these groups: why Bill Smith and not Tom Jones. This, as I see it, is the psychiatric and psychological side of the problem of alcoholism; group differences are for the social scientist to explain.

A theory which brings these two approaches together and which may be called the "Vulnerability-Acceptance Hypothesis", was formulated by E. M. Jellinek in an effort to account for some of the international differences in prevalence and type of alcoholism which he had observed. The idea involved may be schematically represented as shown in Figure 1.

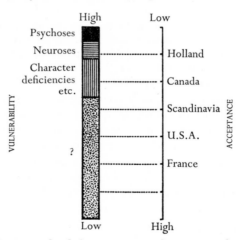

The vertical line on the left represents the range of vulnerability in a population. The psychotics are most highly vulnerable; then come those suffering from the classical psychoneuroses followed by individuals customarily placed in one or other of a large number of more vaguely defined psychiatric categories such as "psychopathic personality", "personality trait disturbance", etc. Presumably, at the present stage of psychiatric knowledge it is not known whether there is a more or less continuous gradient of maladjustment with, for example, the psychotics and neurotics at one extreme differing from those at the other end of the scale only in degree, and separately labelled merely for convenience, or whether there are fundamental qualitative differences. However, for present purposes it is convenient to think of the members of any given population as ranged along such a scale.

The vertical line at the right represents the degree of acceptance of drinking to be found in a population. In practice, this is not easy to measure. It would have to be determined on the basis of an overall assessment of the prevalent attitudes towards drinking in a population: the maximum quantity of an alcoholic beverage which it is generally considered acceptable for an individual to consume at any one time, the degree and frequency of intoxication which is tolerated, and the like. However, largely on an impressionistic basis some European and other countries may be placed at various points along this theoretical scale of acceptance.

Holland appears towards the lower end of the acceptance scale. In this country it appears that little drunkenness is tolerated and, as a result, alcoholics tend to be defined as such relatively earlier in their drinking history. Moreover, because of the attitudes strongly opposed to heavy drinking, only the more highly vulnerable would be expected to succumb to alcoholism as a rule. Thus, assuming that the vulnerability factor is more or less constant from country to country, one would expect to find: a relatively higher frequency of psychosis and neurosis and lower frequency of physical complication among Dutch alcoholics and, accordingly, that alcoholism was generally defined as predominantly a psychiatric problem.

In France, at the opposite end of the acceptance scale, relatively heavy regular consumption is generally approved, as noted previously. And as would be expected in terms of the hypothesis, the prevalence of alcoholism is very high, the proportion of alcoholics suffering from alcoholic psychoses, cirrhosis of the liver and other organic complications is also high and, in contrast to Holland, the proportion of highly vulnerable individuals in the alcoholic population is relatively low. For the latter reason, alcoholism tends generally to be defined as a medical rather than a psychiatric problem.

Countries such as Canada and the Scandinavian countries which have experimented with prohibition, have fairly restrictive liquor legislation, and relatively active temperance groups, tend to fall between these two extremes. Perhaps the moral is that we should think very seriously before accepting the frequently heard view that there would be no problem of alcoholism in this country, or that it would be much less serious if alcoholic beverages were as readily available as soda pop, and that the source of the problem lies in the propaganda of the "Drys" and in repressive and old fashioned liquor legislation which together make drinking a sinful and guilt ridden activity.

Let me conclude by pointing out that Jellinek's hypothesis need not be confined to international differences. It may well be applicable to such problems as rural-urban, sex and ethnic group differences, mentioned earlier in this paper. For example, if the difference in prevalence of alcoholism between males and females is in fact due to the operation of the double standard, then a relatively higher frequency of the more serious personality disturbances might be expected among female alcoholics. This may explain the widespread impression of clinicians in this country and elsewhere that the female alcoholic tends to present a more difficult or complex treatment problem.

SUMMARY

The emphasis of the social scientist on group differences and mass trends in drinking behaviour in contrast to the "individual" or "case-history" orientation of the psychologist and psychiatrist was noted. The relevance of the former approach is chiefly evident when concern is with the nature of alcoholism in general rather than with particular alcoholics, and when the focus of attention is on the long term goal of prevention rather than on the immediate goal of giving service. It was suggested that what tends to be labelled "alcoholism", what are regarded as symptoms of that condition, what type of problem it is considered to be (e.g., medical versus psychiatric), and even approach to treatment are at least in part determined by the socio-cultural situation in which the drinking take place. It was further suggested that socio-cultural factors might have a major role in the determination of the prevalence of alcoholism in a given population or cultural grouping. This was illustrated with reference to the role of attitudes in rural-urban, sex and Jewish-Irish differences in prevalence. Finally, the "Vulnerability-Acceptance Hypothesis" of Jellinek was discussed as a potential means of bringing together the two complementary approaches to the problem of alcoholism represented by the social scientist, on the one hand, and the psychiatrist and psychologist, on the other.

55. NEW VIEWS ON THE NARCOTIC PROBLEM*

A. M. Kirkpatrick†

WHAT IS ADDICTION?

Drug addiction exists when a person's behaviour and way of life are determined by his dependence on and the availability of narcotic drugs which are harmful to him and hence to society.

Administratively there are three general classifications of addicts. First are those called medical addicts who have become addicted as a result of a medical condition in which drugs have been legitimately administered for the relief of pain. Secondly are a number of persons called professional addicts, medical practitioners, nurses, dentists and veterinarians, who, having access to the drugs, have become addicted to them. The third group with which we are concerned consists of those who obtain their supply from the illicit market and are called criminal addicts.

It is essential to differentiate between the first trial or use of drugs and the actual causes of addiction which are apparently psychological, physiological and pharmacological. It is unlikely today that the initial contact with drugs for the criminal addict is through legitimate medical treatment. Initiation usually occurs in a social situation through association with users. Pedlars are most wary of supplying anyone not known to them, because of the danger of apprehension and conviction. Hence the first "shot" is usually obtained in an encounter with addicts at a party, through prostitutes, or through introduction to a "pusher" by someone who will vouch for his curiosity and his fraternity with the criminal fringe.

HOW MANY ADDICTS HAVE WE?

The statistics presented in 1955 to the Senate Committee on the "Traffic in Narcotic Drugs in Canada" indicated a known addict group of 3212 persons comprising 515 medical addicts, 333 professional addicts and 2364 criminal addicts. Because of the legal sanctions, addicts do not willingly reveal their identity, and since three years have elapsed it must be assumed that these figures would not exaggerate the present situation.

In the same enquiry it was revealed that of the 2364 criminal addicts, Montreal was known to have some 200, Toronto about 400 and Vancouver about 1100. The balance are presumably either in prison or in other

---

*From *The Canadian Bar Journal*, November 1959.
†Mr. Kirkpatrick is Executive Director of the John Howard Society of Ontario.

areas probably adjacent to these cities. It is common to rationalize the large number in British Columbia as being due to easier living conditions or a less expensive and more readily available product. But Dr. G. H. Stevenson, actively engaged in drug addiction research, believed that this was due rather to the social and cultural development of the province as a frontier area and to its having had in early years the influence of Chinese immigration which had brought in opium smoking. He indicated that 82% of those addicts he had studied in British Columbia had started their addiction in that province.

Court and prison statistics are the main sources of information on addiction, so that the unconvicted always constitute an undisclosed fraction of the total. This makes it most difficult to determine the true statistical situation and the rate of increase. We are, in fact, discussing the control of a phenomenon whose proportions are not known with accuracy.

HAVE ADDICTS CRIMINAL RECORDS?

Commissioner Nicholson of the R.C.M.P. reported to the Senate Committee that of 2009 cases studied 1668 involved persons who were very probably criminals before they became addicts. In fact, only 341 had been first convicted under the Opium and Narcotic Drug Act.

Dr. Stevenson reported that three-quarters of those he had studied had been delinquent or had a criminal conviction before they went on drugs. He said the addicts had in the main been poorly adjusted before taking drugs and that the general causes of delinquency must be thought of as predisposing to addiction those personalities requiring this form of "crutch" to assist them through life.

This picture of the addict as both criminal and addicted tends to confuse the issue. Both criminality and addiction are symptomatic and should be dealt with as behavioural entities. There is increasing experience that criminality can be corrected even though it may have sociopathic or psychopathic involvement. Hence the addict's criminality and relationship to the illicit traffic should not deter his treatment for addiction even though this may be complicated medically by powerful social and legal factors.

WHAT DOES ADDICTION COST?

A capsule of heroin, which is the most common narcotic drug illegally used, costs upwards of $6.00 on the "street", and a "hooked" or "wired" addict may need upwards of ten "caps" a day to maintain the drug balance he desires.

To obtain this amount and enough for food and shelter, he must clear over $60.00 per day. Female addicts obtain this mostly by prostitution and males either by living off the avails of prostitution or by theft. To clear this amount by theft he must actually steal a great deal more since he will not usually obtain more than 15% from a "fence" or perhaps 30% by direct sale on the "corner".

At any given time, of the known criminal addict group numbering about 2400, some 400 will be in the penitentiaries and a similar number in provincial penal institutions. Hence the number of illegal purchasers of drugs currently out of prison in Canada may be about 1600. Assuming that 600 are females and males living off the avails of prostitution, there remains an active predatory group of about 1000 either peddling drugs or stealing upwards of $600.00 per day, if they can, to maintain themselves. The loss to business and the householder, though seldom realized, due to the criminal depredations of this group is of staggering economic significance.

IS THE ADDICT SICK?

Regardless of the criminal associations which may have led to the initial taking of the drug, of the prior delinquency which might have led to these associations, or of the subsequent criminality to maintain the habit, the addict is, in a very real sense, a sick person and in need of the help of the medical profession in co-operation with various adjunctive professions, such as social work and psychology. The addict is in the grip of a disease which has a pathological effect on him beyond his power to control.

This is evidenced first by the compulsive need he has for drugs. All normal considerations of truthfulness, honour and integrity are as nothing before this need, which is not less powerful than hunger. The addict, when on drugs, becomes a scheming, conniving person driven by an overwhelming need to secure satisfaction for this craving which, though it may be psychological in its origin, appears to involve changes in the body chemistry. The second characteristic is the inevitable increase in tolerance and hence in intake of the drug. This may build up very quickly and result in the diminution of the effectiveness of the drug owing to repeated use which develops the need for increasingly large dosage. A person may become addicted with a very few shots in the course of a few days.

It must be remembered that having become addicted and regardless of his past criminal record, if any, criminal acts of the addict result from the craving for drugs and his obsession with obtaining and maintaining a source of supply, rather than from any organic mental deterioration.

WHY NOT GIVE HIM THE DRUGS HE WANTS?

Unlimited, free, unrestricted use of drugs of a prolonged nature would lead to a compelling addiction and would provide no realistic solution but an intensification of the effects on the addict. Apart from the constant danger of overdose, there is the risk of infection from unsterile methods of intake and most addicts are heavily scarred. The more indirect effects are due to neglect of self-care and hygiene.

In his personality he would become intensely preoccupied with self and indifferent to normal living, to proper standards of behaviour, to the discipline of work or to the need for realizable goals and achievements. He would avoid situations involving mature sexuality, social responsibility and competitiveness. At the best of times, his world is made up of himself and his problems; he has largely lost the capacity to give, even to his loved ones. His illness has destroyed for him the possibility of achieving the customary rights of freedom, happiness, friendship, work, security and health. He is engaged in a course of self-destruction and is to be pitied rather than feared. The unlimited and prolonged use of drugs would intensify this profile of psychic and social misery.

ADDICTION TAKEN FROM MEDICAL CONTROL

In Canada, the Opium and Narcotic Drug Act provides a mandatory minimum sentence of six months in prison for possession and a maximum sentence of 14 years for trafficking. It is not a crime to be an addict, but to have possession of drugs. Even if the drugs are obviously not being made available for sale, as long as they are in a quantity susceptible to analysis, the magistrate has no authority to award probation or to suspend sentence even if treatment were available and requested by the addict.

The present punitive approach has been no effective deterrent to the addict motivated by the need for drugs, or to the non-addict dealer in pursuit of substantial profits. The illicit traffic has not been suppressed, nor has the spread of addiction been prevented. This is not to suggest that the law enforcement efforts to control should not be continued to contain this social peril within the smallest scope. The higher-up supplier is rarely, if ever, caught, and the street pusher is usually the one on whom the force of the law descends. In a majority of cases pushers are themselves addicts forced to sell to assure their own source of supply or by other underworld pressures persuasively effective.

JURISDICTIONAL RESPONSIBILITY

The enforcement of the Opium and Narcotic Drug Act is the responsibility of the Federal Government. The R.C.M.P. seek to control the illegal importation and sale of narcotics. The Department of National Health and Welfare, through the Division of Narcotic Control, is responsible for the legal importation and distribution of drugs.

In Canada, the treatment of illness is a provincial responsibility and, since drug addiction is considered to be a form of illness, its treatment would be under provincial jurisdiction. A number of provinces have provided for treatment, usually in mental hospitals, but such legislation has been in the main ineffective because it has failed to meet the basic difficulties inherent in treatment and in the attitude of the addict himself. Treatment facilities have been provided within the penal systems at Mimico Reformatory in Ontario and at Oakalla Prison in British Columbia. The Narcotic Addiction Foundation in Vancouver has been established and is obtaining important data for study and planning.

TREATMENT

Legal sanctions and the full weight of the law are massed against the addict, who is forced to live a fugitive, hounded, transient life, truly without a place to lay his head, and in constant fear of arrest. He is in a sense an outcast and his inept attempts to solve his problems keep him in the world of his fellow addicts who alone, he thinks, can appreciate his problems. He insulates himself and does not seek or avail himself of available help owing to his need for anonymity and his association with the illicit drug traffic.

Unless he is in a state of severe distress due to lack of drugs, his appearance is not likely to be unusual. He has no defined mannerisms, tics, postures or speech impairment. His behaviour will probably be serious and co-operative; but his emotions may appear blunted and not appropriate to the intensity of the difficulty he describes.

The professional worker must remember that the addict is no amateur and consumes much time and effort in disguising the truth behind the façade he is building to obtain his ends, which are usually either drugs or assisted withdrawal. He may, in fact, really want withdrawal and cure, he may feign illness to secure drugs, he may use severe withdrawal symptoms as an appeal for medication, he may merely be "casing the joint" (particularly the physician's office) with a view to later theft of narcotics, prescription blanks or other valuables.

It is within such a frame of reference that treatment considerations must be undertaken. Such proposals should start with the humane withdrawal from drugs, a period of medical convalescence and pre-discharge preparation, and a period of post discharge control including a long period of supervision in the community. The addict should have the right to return to the institution following the almost inevitable relapse.

Withdrawal symptoms are noted within about 12 hours after the last administration of drugs. These are acute for a few days and cease in a week or ten days in most cases, but a period of about two months is necessary to ensure recovery from the physical effects of drugs. Medically assisted withdrawal is individualized to the need of the patient, but usually involves substitute drug therapy or gradual reduction of dosage. It is essential to prevent the patient's access to drugs other than those prescribed, and this involves some custodial measures.

At present, withdrawal is usually done "cold turkey" in the city or county jails with little supporting medical treatment. This is a most agonizing process for the addict, characterized by severe twitching, shaking, sweating, vomiting, abdominal cramps and, in some cases, severe hallucinations.

The period of pre-discharge preparation may be from a few months to a year, depending on the patient's reaction to treatment and his capacity to plan for discharge. He should at least be kept in hospital until he can sleep without medication and has received necessary dental and medical care to regain weight and appetite. During this period the clinical team may engage in psychotherapy, supportive treatment by developing educational and vocational skills, and practical planning for the re-establishment of the patient in the community.

The period of post-discharge control should continue the supportive treatment and help the patient test his plan, which should be readjusted as necessary to the experiences of competitive living, the securing of accommodation, of employment, of friends and group associations. On casual observation the addict may at this time seem self-possessed and even boastful; but his self-esteem is often low, as revealed in his running away from occasional failures or what he interprets as rejection. This low self-esteem may prevent him from functioning long enough to obtain some successful experiences which might help disprove his inner feelings. During this period constant supervision and support are desirable to bolster this sagging self-esteem and develop broader tolerance for tension, pressure and frustration.

Such treatment and re-establishment should preferably take place in his local community rather than in some central and isolated "addicts' island". He needs easy access to withdrawal in the event of relapse and the support of the climate of the institution and its personnel, which should be small enough to personalize its treatment. Hence the major municipalities (Montreal, Toronto, Vancouver) might well develop treatment centres and discuss the co-operative financing of these with more senior levels of government. The incidence of addiction may largely be in these municipalities, but the problem is much broader in scope and responsibility.

SPECIAL FACILITIES FOR TREATMENT

It is important to provide facilities for the treatment of the addict outside the penal institutions. These should be under medical control where the type of treatment described above (in very general terms) might be provided. Rather than leave the matter to private physicians or to general or mental hospitals, it would seem desirable at the present stage of the illicit drug traffic to set up resident rehabilitation centres which would focus the most informed and specialized medical and professional interest and knowledge on this problem. The necessary supportive restraints could be ensured in such a setting, as they are in mental hospitals.

The objectives of such rehabilitation centres might well be to reduce the addicts' suffering, to engage in treatment linked to research which would bring more complete understanding of addiction and enable us to speak of "cure" rather than "arrest", to prevent the spread of addiction, to offset the illicit drug traffic, to reduce the amount of criminal activity engaged in by the addict, and to restore addicts and their families to a state of social and economic health and well-being.

It is not suggested that such rehabilitation centres should be dispensaries to which people might apply for a regular dosage of drugs, but rather that they be centres in which the purpose would be to bring about "cure" and not merely to maintain a habit of addiction. It is probably unwise to use the word "cure", since it is more likely that, at the present stage of understanding, the course of addiction can only be "arrested". Even to accomplish this requires a milieu therapy involving the whole person and his relationships in the community to which he will return. Preparation for discharge should involve visits into the community with social workers to enable the patient under guidance and with protection to pick up the threads of his affairs and to develop effective plans and relationships.

Dr. Harris Isbell of the United States Public Health Hospital for Addicts at Lexington, Kentucky, made follow-up studies of addicts treated at the hospital and believes that the recovery rate will be between 15% and 25% over a five-year period following treatment. He believes that this is an important result and that the problem of relapse should not be allowed to discourage the development of treatment programs and facilities.

An experiment at Hollywood Hospital in Vancouver with the use of LSD (lysergic acid diethylamide), which creates artificial psychoses, has resulted in a group of addicts remaining "off drugs" for over 12 months. This is a valuable clinical development which might be incorporated into rehabilitation centres as part of a complete treatment program.

The objection to rehabilitation centres may be made that addicts would seek to enter them only to obtain assisted withdrawal in order to reduce their tolerance and enable them to start the habit again on a minimal and less costly level. The extent of such improper motivation is a matter for conjecture, and under medical supervision, with the safeguards proposed, should be kept minimal.

With some exceptions experience has indicated that the addict would like to "kick the habit" and stay off, but, though there is some evidence that ageing and maturity may help, few are convinced that they could really do it and that it would be worth trying. Though the addict may have been properly motivated to enter a rehabilitation centre, the phenomenon of relapse must be anticipated. This is one of the realities that make treatment of the addict so difficult.

The real aim of the program should be to help the patient master his desire for drugs. While this means depriving him of drugs at the start by coercion to get him through the agonies of his need, he must be able to summon the strength eventually to deprive himself. When his gratifications have increased to the extent that they constitute a positive force, the addict may be reluctant to exchange the pleasures of his new reality for the certain destruction of his old way of life.

If the relapse is genuine, the patient should have the right to re-enter the centre and again receive assisted withdrawal, which should take only a few weeks before return to productive employment. If advantage were being taken of these facilities, the patient concerned should be treated as a law-breaker.

THE LAW-BREAKING PATIENT

Where the patient misuses or abuses the treatment opportunities, refuses treatment, or is convicted of a criminal offence concurrent with active addiction, there is no other course but to treat him as a law-breaker and, if necessary, to sentence him to probation with a condition that he accept treatment. If he refuses this opportunity or is otherwise criminally charged, he should be sentenced to a medical correction centre, with a drug addiction unit, and thus perforce must be treated as a prisoner within the penal system.

In our custodial institutions there are at present few facilities for the treatment of addicts. Federal medical correction centres, including drug addiction units, should be established as part of the new development which proposes that the federal institutions will receive all men sentenced to over six months. Addicts from these institutions, when considered ready, should be returned to the community under parole supervision by way of the rehabilitation centres. They would thus profit by the post-discharge control for addiction under experienced workers co-operating with the prison after-care workers in regard to their criminality and total re-establishment.

Addicts are being paroled from penal institutions at the present time under the supervision of after-care agencies like the Elizabeth Fry Societies and the John Howard Societies. A reasonable proportion have refrained from further criminal activity and have abstained from drugs. A chemical test has been developed, which indicates the presence of drugs in the body, and a condition of parole may be that the parolee consent to the performance of such tests. If these are positive the parolee has obviously violated the conditions of his parole and must again accept medical treatment, if possible through the rehabilitation centre rather than being returned to prison, though his violation of parole conditions may lead to this action by the parole authority.

VOLUNTARY OR COMPULSORY TREATMENT

Treatment in medical correction centres as part of the penal system obviously involves compulsion in absolute terms. Treatment in rehabilitation centres of addicts on probation would similarly involve external motivation. But even for the addict who enters voluntarily with inward motivation, a degree of supportive restraint and some custodial features to prevent illicit access to drugs would be necessary. The power of individual motivation can rarely cope with the fixation of drugs. Like many other sick people, including the mentally ill, addicts may not have the will-power to go through a course of treatment without a degree of supportive coercion.

It should be possible for an addict to commit himself by civil proceedings as under the Mental Health Act. But there should be a restriction on his right to sign himself out immediately after withdrawal, before the period of convalescent and rehabilitative treatment has taken place. He should be required also to accept the post-discharge control.

It should be possible for a magistrate in a criminal court to suspend sentence for possession if the addict agrees to treatment in a rehabilitation centre rather than being sent to prison with all the stigma of a jail sentence and the added problems of re-establishment.

THE CANADIAN DILEMMA

To treat addicts as patients and to place them under medical attention rather than in prison is the desirable goal. But we must accomplish this in the presence of a very active illicit market, including that in the United States, to which the patient may revert for supplementation of dosage or for complete dosage in the event of a relapse. Hence for a time the element of restraint to support voluntary motivation may prove essential in the medical management of the case. So might a system of photographic registration to prevent mobility between centres and an influx from other countries despite the penalty of immediate deportation.

It is relatively easy to effect withdrawal and by proper safeguards to ensure drug-free convalescence, but the difficult task faces all concerned when the addict returns to the community where there is an available supply. For this reason he must be willing to accept protective supervision with reasonable control of his activities and, if necessary, submission to tests for the presence of narcotics.

The process of law enforcement should be continued vigorously to bring about the identification of addicts and addict-traffickers. These should be referred for treatment either through civil or, if necessary, criminal proceedings. The non-addict trafficker and the suppliers at various levels should be rigorously pursued and sentenced under the Criminal Code, which appears to provide adequate sanctions with a maximum sentence of 14 years at the discretion of the magistrate.

GET THE ADDICT OUT OF HIDING

Addicts are not a homogeneous group. All they have in common is their addiction. Each individual is his own therapy problem. Not all will voluntarily agree to undergo treatment. Not all who do so will be able to continue unless aided by some compulsion to support the regimen imposed.

Physical dependence on drugs can be removed by withdrawal treatment but the mental and emotional dependence can be overcome only through the individual's own efforts and desires. He must want to "kick the habit" and must realize that it may be a slow process in which there may be relapse. There should be no premature termination of support to the patient lest he return to drugs under stress situations.

But suppose he does! One ex-inmate of a penitentiary, with the help of an after-care society, remained off drugs and held a responsible job for over two years. He was a happy man, producing in the economy and maintaining himself and his family. He relapsed and was resentenced to prison to be maintained at a cost of $2000 per year. A few weeks of treatment in a rehabilitation centre most probably would have enabled him under supervision to resume his life as if he had had an absence due to ordinary illness. Now once again he has had the devastating experience of failure, and he emerges again with the stigma of an "ex-con."

Much about the treatment and medical control of addiction is uncertain largely because of the presence of the illicit traffic which mocks the control efforts of law enforcement and the efforts of the professional worker in treatment and re-establishment. In the past we have conveniently let it be the patient that has been at fault and not our methods of control and treatment. It is now most important to agree on some basic plan which will involve a treatment approach.

In no other way will we get the addict out of hiding so that we can not only count him but obtain accurate information on relapses, "cure", and re-establishment. There will be kinks and "bugs" to be ironed out in any such plan, but given the opportunity and freedom to develop under medical control a positive answer to addiction in Canada can be found.

Can we escape the individual and social responsibility of helping others to reach their highest potential?

SELECTED BIBLIOGRAPHY

Cook, S. A., "Criminal Behavior and the Use of Beverage Alcohol," *The Canadian Journal of Corrections,* Vol. 4, No. 2, April, 1962.

Gibbins, R. J., "Alcoholism in Ontario: A Survey of an Ontario County," *Quarterly Journal of Studies on Alcohol,* Vol. 15, 1954.

Kirkpatrick, A. M., "New Approach to Drug Problem Suggested," *Criminal Law Quarterly,* February, 1960.

Long, V. H., "Alcoholism in Canada," *Canada's Health and Welfare,* June, 1961.

MacDonald, R. St. J., "Narcotic Drug Addiction in Canada," *Current Law and Social Problems,* Vol. I, Toronto, University of Toronto Press, 1960.

Macdonald, R. St. J., "Controlling Narcotic Drug Addiction in Canada: Recent Developments," *Current Law and Social Problems,* Vol. II, Toronto, University of Toronto Press, 1961.

MacLeod, A. J., "Custody for Treatment Under the Narcotic Control Act," *The Canadian Journal of Corrections,* Vol. 6, No. 1, January, 1964. (See also other articles in this issue.)

Martin, M., and Dancey, T. E., "A Review of Contemporary Management of Narcotic Addiction," *Canadian Medical Association Journal,* Vol. 86, February 17, 1962.

Popham, R. E., "A Statistical Report Relating to Alcoholism and the Use of Alcoholic Beverages in Canada," *International Journal of Alcohol and Alcoholism,* Vol. I, 1955.

Popham, R. E., "The Jellinek Alcoholism Estimation Formula and Its Application to Canadian Data," *Quarterly Journal of Studies on Alcohol,* Vol. 17, 1956.

Popham, R. E., and Schmidt, W., *Statistics of Alcohol Use and Alcoholism in Canada, 1871-1956,* Toronto, University of Toronto Press, 1958.

Potts, F., "Drug Addiction in Ontario," *The Canadian Journal of Corrections,* Vol. 1, No. 2, January, 1959.

chapter eleven

OUR MENTALLY ILL AND DISORDERED

Mental illness is now one of our most serious social problems and promises to become, in our rapidly changing society, even more and more severe. Add to the ranks of the psychotic and the severely neurotic (these being what are usually inferred by the term "mentally ill") the retarded and the ever increasing number of senile (ever increasing due to the growing number and proportion of the elderly in our population), and we find that hardly one of us can avoid some contact with the problem. The three articles which follow were selected to represent some of the more important dimensions of the problem.

In 1963 the Canadian Mental Health Association published a study of psychiatric services in Canada entitled *More for the Mind*. From the prologue of this book we have selected a section entitled "Extent of the Problem of Mental Illness" as our lead article. Here statistics are presented regarding patients in Canadian mental hospitals, and current public attitudes toward mental illness are reviewed. Next, Angus M. Hood (Director of the Toronto Mental Health Clinic) discusses mental ill health and emotional instability as "Canada's Largest Health Problem". His message is directed particularly toward the business and industrial world, but it is equally meaningful to every member of the society.

389

The final article, "Canada's Alarming Suicide Pattern" by Julien Bryan, is included here not because it details a very important aspect of the general problem of mental health (in Canada, in fact, suicide is legally considered to be part of the *crime problem*), but because it does represent a condition which probably *should* be considered in a health-illness rather than a legal-illegal context. In this article Bryan explores such questions as cause of suicide, Canadian statistics and legal status, "popular" techniques of self destruction and societal attitudes toward the problem.

56. *EXTENT OF THE PROBLEM OF MENTAL ILLNESS**

Canadian Mental Health Association

National statistics on the prevalence of mental illness are limited to studies of annual admissions, re-admissions, discharges and the year-end patient population in residence or "on the books" of mental hospitals, psychiatric units and special institutions for the care and treatment of disabilities such as mental deficiency and epilepsy. Some of these statistics have been summarized for the years 1955 to 1961 inclusive in the following table, although figures quoted are incomplete. It is estimated, for instance, that at the end of 1960 there were actually nearly 68,000 patients in hospital, with another 8,000 patients on probation or trial convalescence, but still carried officially on the hospital books, making a total of 76,000 patients.

Admissions to mental institutions have shown a significant increase in recent years. In the period recorded here, this increase amounted to more than 34 per cent. However, when allowance is made for the population growth of Canada, it is seen that the admission rate remained about the same during the five-year period. The annual increase in the number of patients in residence during the period was slower, and when related to the population growth, actually showed a steady decline. These trends are also observed in British and United States mental hospitals.

*From *More for the Mind*, a report of the Committee on Psychiatric Services (Dr. James S. Tyhurst, Chairman), Toronto, Canadian Mental Health Association, 1963.

PATIENTS IN MENTAL HOSPITALS§

	1955	1956	1957	1958	1959	1960	1961
All admissions	32,222	36,438	37,672	40,296	43,184	43,121	47,758
First admissions	21,774	25,097	24,582	26,536	28,066	26,935	29,719
Rate per 100,000 population	139	156	155	156	161	151	163
Re-admissions	10,448	11,361	12,090	13,760	15,118	16,182	18,039
Discharges	26,158	30,974	31,836	35,481	37,058	36,768	43,215
Deaths in hospital	3,642	3,724	4,312	4,041	4,448	4,512	4,462
Resident patients at year end	63,683	65,107	65,768	66,213	66,433	66,399	66,546
Ratio per 100,000 population	406.4	405.7	397.2	389.4	381.6	372	365
Personnel employed full time at year end	18,543	20,596	23,095	24,773	26,005	27,197	29,019
Ratio per 1,000 patients	295	316	351	369	389	415	451
Operating costs-total millions of dollars	69.8	78.9	86.6	97.8	109.3	117.8	132.2
Percentage change	+13%	+13%	+9.1%	+13%	+11.2%	+7.8%	+12.2%
Per patient per diem cost-dollars	3.05	3.37	3.70	4.14	4.66	4.99	5.37

§This table is taken from another C.M.H.A. source to replace the one in the book **More for the Mind**. It is almost identical to the original but slightly more up to date. (Ed.)

These trends are even clearer if institutions which care for mental defectives — Hospital Training Schools — are separated from the statistics. There are 11 of these, accounting for 10,751 patients. Movement of patients in and out of these institutions is much slower than in the other psychiatric hospitals.

Hospitals caring for the mentally ill are thus gradually becoming more active as treatment centres, with a larger annual turnover of patients admitted for treatment and discharged again. Slowly, the tide is turning from the traditional use of mental hospitals as custodial or residential institutions. Nevertheless, the haunting vision of seemingly endless lines of anonymous faces, representing the aged and the chronic mentally ill for whom nothing seems to remain but custodial care, is a challenge to the present system of treatment if not an indictment of it.

Apart from patients treated in psychiatric hospitals and institutions there are an unknown number, estimated to be very large indeed, treated privately by psychiatrists or family doctors. Recent British studies indicate that "in any group of sick people something like 30 per cent will be found to be suffering from conditions about which it would be helpful to have psychiatric advice". United States reports indicate that 30 to 50 per cent of patients consulting the family doctor or admitted to medical wards of general hospitals suffer, either essentially or as a complicating factor, from psychiatric problems.

Attempts have been made to measure the proportion of the population with psychiatric illness. A random sample of the population of Baltimore was examined by internists of Johns Hopkins Hospital during 1953-55. Their diagnoses of psychiatric illness were carefully reviewed by a panel of psychiatrists. It was established that 11 per cent of the population examined had such illness. Comparative findings were:

	Prevalence per 1,000 population
Psychiatric illness	112
All heart diseases, including hypertension	92
Arthritis	84
Diabetes	23

A Cornell Universtiy group studied psychiatric illness in urban and rural areas of New York, Nova Scotia, Alaska, Mexico and Nigeria. In one such typical study, only 19 per cent of the population was psychiatrically symptom free, while 31 per cent presented a history of psychiatric symptoms impairing working capacity or life adjustment. Major mental illness was found in only 0.8 per cent of the population; the overwhelming proportion of psychiatric illness comprised neurotic and psychosomatic disturbances.

Studies in Canada have shown that in the period 1955-56 in the Canadian Civil Service psychiatric illness accounted for 8.9 per cent of the days of female sick leave and for 5.2 per cent of male sick leave.

In one U.S. company recently studied 15 per cent of the workers were responsible for half of all absences in one year. This group was prone both to bodily illness and to disturbances of mood, thought and behaviour, i.e., psychiatric illnesses.

In Canada, 1,271 suicides were reported in 1958 and it is suggested there were many more not reported. Suicide accounts for 6 per cent of the male deaths in the 25-44 age group.

These are but a few reasonably reliable indices of the extent of mental and emotional illness. Prevalence can be shown to vary with socio-economic and educational levels, age and sex. Emotional disorders increase in a rapidly changing social or technological environment.

No mention has been made of the prevalence of emotional and mental disorders of children, estimated at from 5 to 10 per cent for school groups; nor to mental retardation, affecting at least 3 per cent of the population. The extent of mental and emotional disturbances leading to alcoholism, drug addiction, broken homes and social misery of all kinds can only be guessed. Certainly, the frequently quoted "one person in 10" seems a very conservative estimate.

CURRENT PUBLIC ATTITUDES

Important scientific advances undoubtedly have been made in the treatment of mental illness. Have public understanding and attitudes kept pace with these advances?

Attitudes change slowly. Many people still have deep feelings of apprehension about mental hospitals and patients. The hospital all too often is still regarded as a custodial institution designed to protect the community as much as the inmates. The patient is often considered little different from the criminal. Many commonly believe that only paupers go to government mental hospitals, which are in some way less desirable than private medical services or general hospitals.

Evidence exists that the following misconceptions are still commonly held in Canada. It is erroneously believed that:

— mental illness is a sign of moral weakness or poor character, and therefore carries a stigma;

— mentally ill persons are disturbers and offenders and should be so treated — as if they were totally responsible for their behaviour;

—mental illness is almost always hereditary — a sign of weakness in the family tree;

—once mentally ill, a person always has a "weakness" in spite of apparent recovery; he is a poor risk for employment and may become a problem or a trouble maker;

—Provincial mental hospitals are a last resort and used for only the "chronically insane" and "demented old people" who can afford no better care, that is, for indigents;

—psychiatrists are different from "real" doctors in some undiscoverable way — they are not fully qualified as physicians or not to be trusted.

Thus, the stigma extends beyond the patients to the treatment, to the mental health services and to the professionals concerned. It calls forth negative reactions occasionally even from other physicians.

It is interesting to observe the elaborate ways in which people will deny the existence of mental illness in their family, among their friends or in themselves. Often it is referred to obliquely as a "breakdown", or associated with laudable but usually incorrect causes: thus, "he cracked up from overwork". Even when there is surface acceptance of mental illness an underlying ambivalence and ingrained prejudice are often detectable.

Ask the man-in-the-street seriously about mental illness and he will often agree that it is an illness, that it should be treated like any other illness and that chances of recovery are good under modern conditions. Yet, he will just as quickly reverse this attitude and talk scathingly of some unprepossessing individual as a "nut" or a "queer" or a "psycho", readily indicating the undesirability of these qualities.

During the war mental and emotional breakdown was commonly experienced by army personnel and treated by psychiatric specialists, but in public it was only occasionally referred to as mental illness. Instead, terms like battle-fatigue, combat-neurosis and "neuro-psychiatric" casualty were the World War II substitutes for World War I "shell-shock". The more "tough-minded" services such as the RCAF were inclined to deny the existence of mental and emotional breakdown and spoke instead of "lack of moral fibre".

Reminiscent of the attitude of those "tough-minded" war-time officers is the approach of some senior business executives. Their knowledge of and understanding of mental illness and mental health is apt to be incomplete, negatively structured and rigidly held. They are more inclined to discriminate against mental illness and the mentally ill than is the man-in-the-street or than are certain other professional groups such as teachers and clergymen.

How then is the public attitude changing?

More publicity and information of one sort and another are undoubtedly being directed to the public today than ever before. Television, radio, newspapers, popular magazines, women's journals and the digest periodicals all carry material on mental illness. All of this information is by no means accurate according to present psychiatric understanding. Nevertheless, the public is reacting to it and the image of mental illness is changing.

Studies show that, generally speaking, the public today is not so much misinformed as uninformed. Important gaps exist in public knowledge; for instance, about psychiatric services in the community. Mental illness is often unrecognized and misjudged. While many people readily acknowledge that mental illness is an illness, they are still inclined to punish a person showing unmistakable signs of schizophrenia rather than to send him to a doctor. The stigma associated with being "mental" has stubbornly persisted. In no other illness is the personality of the patient so fundamentally altered that close friends and even relatives have difficulty in relating to him and feeling about him as they used to.

Along with the feeling that the patient is "different" there is the notion that he is irresponsible; hence, legal action is taken to restrict his freedom and reduce effects of his irresponsibility. At the same time the public finds it hard to accept the patient's apparent irresponsible behaviour as an effect of illness — a symptom. His offensive and sometimes damaging actions are regarded as something he could control if he only wanted to, something for which he should be held responsible. These attitudes often create real difficulties in the occupational rehabilitation of patients.

The medical profession, odd as it may seem, has not always been in the forefront of public opinion in promoting an objective scientific attitude towards mental illness. It has actually been reluctant to accept mental illness as a group of diseases meriting a comparable investment of professional time, training, research and public money to that given to physical illness — and this in spite of the fact that it has long been known that the morbidity and disability from mental and emotional illness is much greater than from most physical illnesses.

Various reasons account for the medical profession's hesitancy to accept mental illness as a health problem meriting its closest attention. Psychiatry until recently has seemed rather unspectacular, vague — even unscientific and unrewarding — compared with the rapid and striking advances made in control of contagious diseases, in management of many illnesses of internal organs and in modern surgery. Efforts to pinpoint exact organic pathology as the cause of mental illness have been unsuccessful, except in a few striking, and relatively rare, diseases. Nevertheless, the conviction remains that sometime, somehow, the true organic causes, either in cell pathology or in pathological chemistry will be discovered. Meantime, the interest and energy of medicine seem to have been largely directed elsewhere.

The status of physicians who have made a career of the specialty of psychiatry, either in mental hospitals or in research, also seems, until recently, to have suffered in comparison with other specialties. It has been suggested that this has led to the development of a certain defensiveness and aggressiveness on the part of psychiatrists in private practice or in university posts. At the same time it has been mooted that physicians working in government services, including most of those in the field of psychiatry, are inclined to be passive and lacking in initiative. Both of these stereotypes are probably wrong. Yet, until recently the field of mental health has apparently not been as attractive to young physicians and other professional personnel as other health fields.

A noticeable turn for the better, however, has occurred during the past 5 to 10 years. With the new developments in diagnosis and treatment, with new patterns of care stressing the development of community services, with new opportunities for careers in psychiatry and other mental health professions, and above all, with a vigorous program of public education and citizen involvement, Canada may indeed be on the threshold of a new deal for the mentally ill. The spectre and the old image of mental illness may be banished once and for all.

57. CANADA'S LARGEST HEALTH PROBLEM*

Angus M. Hood†

The year 1960 was World Mental Health Year. It was so designated by the World Health Organization and the World Federation for Mental

*From *The MacLaren Advertiser,* Vol. II, No. 4, Winter, 1960.
†Dr. Hood is Director of the Toronto Mental Health Clinic and an Associate in the Department of Psychiatry, University of Toronto.

Health. Some of the topics selected for study in many countries were The Needs of Children, National Surveys of Mental Health, Teaching of the Principles of Mental Health, The Problems of Human Relations Occurring in Industries and Other Occupations, and finally The Psychological Problems of Immigration.

These meetings are but one evidence of the growing concern of nations for the mental health of their peoples. No one can doubt that it is justified. To quote from a World Health Organization Seminar: "If the amount of bodily disease in the world reached the proportions of many of the existing social ills with mental and emotional causes (delinquency, alcoholism, drug addiction, suicide, etc.), not to mention classical mental disease, an epidemic state would be declared and strong measures taken to combat it."

It is clear that the costs of emotional ill health in dollars, man-hours, and personal and family happiness are staggering in our own country as elsewhere. This year 75,000 of our fellow citizens will spend an average of six months in mental institutions. To these who are so ill must be added the numbers whose symptoms have led them to seek treatment from psychiatric clinics and private psychiatrists. But the largest group of all are those who seek or receive no treatment. They continue to attempt to cure their ills with patient nostrums, or take out their conflicts on family, in the job or society at large. Mental ill health and emotional instability is Canada's largest health program.

Although the problems are large and far from solved, there is much progress to record. One of the most significant and promising changes is the spirit of enlightenment that is growing in the public attitude toward the disturbed person. The mentally ill are less and less viewed as evil or dangerous or possessed of devils, but as people who have fallen ill and can be helped to return to their families and communities. The rising clamour in this century by an aroused public for humane treatment of the mentally ill has led to salutary changes in treatment concepts in our mental hospitals. The last ten years has probably seen the greatest progress in this regard so that our hospitals are becoming centres of hope rather than the dungeons of despair. The greater understanding of emotional illness by the man in the street has similarly led to earlier treatment and a demand for community mental health services for less disturbed patients. We also find a yearly rise in the number of patients voluntarily requesting treatment in psychiatric hospitals in contrast to being committed by legal process. The formation of volunteer groups of hospital visitors through the White Cross Service of the Canadian Mental

Health Association is another indication of the lifting of the curtain of fear. Many of our mental hospitals hold an Open House Day so that the public may come and see for themselves the treatment facilities for the mentally ill. These are but a few examples of the effect of the changing climate. One must sadly note, however, that areas of prejudice and superstition still prevail and education must go on.

A major effect of public concern has been the tremendous increase in treatment resources now being provided and planned by all levels of government. The pressure of increasing population and rising rates of hospital admission strengthened the demand for action. It has inevitably led to new hospital construction to relieve, to a degree, the desperate overcrowding of our mental hospitals. But even today most still have more patients than the capacity for which they were designed. The new hospitals are not just new copies of the old. There is a growing feeling that smaller hospitals located close to communities are preferable to large, centrally located institutions. New concepts of patient environment and well equipped treatment units are replacing the former utilitarian, custodial type of mental hospitals. Of course, better buildings without adequate staff help the patient very little. Thus governments have had to concern themselves with training psychiatrists, social workers, nurses, psychologists, occupational therapists and other ward personnel. Through Federal Health Grant assistance and expanded University training facilities, larger numbers of professional workers are becoming available. Although psychiatry is attracting more young physicians for specialist training and is gaining in respectability, the demand far exceeds the supply. In all disciplines, the numbers are still woefully short. However, between 1947 and 1957 the staff to patient ratio in our hospitals increased from 227:1,000 to 351:1,000.

Two other developments which have gained tremendous impetus with government support are worthy of note. First is the establishment of psychiatric units in our general hospitals. Fifteen years ago no such wards existed. Today they are found side by side with other medical services in over forty general hospitals across Canada. This is a notable achievement and indicates again the growing acceptance of psychiatry by the medical profession and public alike. Here milder cases can be admitted, treated and discharged just as the patient with a peptic ulcer or a broken leg. In 1957 some 35% of all psychiatric in-patients were treated in such units.

The second development has been the setting up of community mental health clinics. In the last ten years the number has increased eightfold until now there are more than 150 in all of the provinces. Here the patient who is able to remain in the community can receive the treatment he requires if he cannot afford the expense of private fees. Here, too, children come with their parents for the treatment of emotional and behavior problems. These are the centers of early treatment and prevention. A breadwinner can be kept on his job, a mother in her home, a child helped to grow. Although great strides have been made in a short span, inquiry would reveal that each clinic has waiting lists of patients for whom there is no time and that all feel the shortage of trained staff.

We have been speaking of progress and there is more to report. In the direct medical-psychiatric treatment of the patient the advent of "tranquilizing" drugs has nigh revolutionized the approach to patients. One cannot attribute therapeutic optimism to any single factor, but this new group of drugs has done much to quickly relieve the suffering of the mental patient and made him more quickly accessible to measures for his rehabilitation. Combined with improved patient environment, enlightened staff attitudes, the prospect for early discharge from hospital has improved immeasurably.

The notion of rehabilitation is the most lively issue in patient care today. It is no longer sufficient to think of providing protection for and against the disturbed person. The job of the hospital is to get him out of hospital. Moreover, to get him out is not enough. We must help him, wherever possible, to find a useful place in his family and community. This obviously means that rehabilitative efforts must include his family and the community as active partners in his return. There is a conscious move on the part of the mental hospitals to work more closely with the communities they serve. There is room for much greater mutual understanding. Not only immediate family members, but public health personnel, employers, White Cross associations, churches and other groups can be involved in the re-establishment of the individual. It is a slow but eventually rewarding task that is now beginning as the mental hospital seeks to integrate itself more closely with the community. Much encouraging progress has been made in this direction in Great Britain and has been a stimulus to similar efforts in Canada.

So far we have been addressing ourselves to the care of people who in varying degree have become admittedly afflicted with emotional disturbances. Comments have been made to point out both problems and the progress in attempts to restore these people to health. But what of prevention? This opens up even larger and more overwhelming challenges. The dual approaches of research and education on a vast scale are what are needed. At this time this is clearly impossible and so we struggle to make small inroads here and there.

In the field of medical research into the causes of some of the major mental illnesses such as schizophrenia, new doors are slowly being opened to reveal intriguing vistas for further exploration. Biochemical investigations are showing promise that this dread disease may have specific and remedial causes. New discoveries in genetics and chemistry are shedding new light on mental deficiency. Yet, here again, the research in mental disorders suffers from a paucity of funds, while these same disorders continue to be the largest single cause of illness in our land. Perhaps the glimmer of hope will stimulate more research previously withheld because of ignorance and pessimism.

Great as are the needs in the area of physical research, the need for social research into the causes and remedies for prevalent social ills is as great, if not greater. We know illness rises in times of high unemployment; that alcoholism, divorce and broken homes contribute to, as well as are caused by emotional disorders. The sins of the father are visited on the children and it is often difficult in an individual case to clearly discern who is victim and who is victimized. The provision of reasonable security and wholesome living conditions for its citizens must surely be reasonable, if evasive, goals in a democratic society. We believe that such efforts contribute in the long run to the mental well-being of the individual. There is thus a need for us as citizens to keep alive a strong social conscience in our own communities.

Education for mental health is a formidable undertaking. It is hoped that each generation will be more successful than the last in making appropriate and mature adjustment to changing times. This begins with our children and is mediated through the family, the school and the church. In a changing society families are cut off from tradition and are often confused as to what they want to teach their children to equip them for adult life. They often feel the need of guidance and the mental health educators are striving to meet this need — to give young parents guideposts in child-rearing which we hope will help them to raise children who believe in their own worth as individuals and as contributing members of society. These principles are being offered to our teachers through courses in colleges, through school mental health consultants and by seminars. The concern with educating the whole child and with his individual assets and problems is slowly permeating the classroom. Much, much more could be said about the problems of the families of today and the aims of education. Suffice it to say that efforts are being made on many fronts to help parents and teachers more fully comprehend the psychological needs of children. Too often, however, the neurotic patterns are carried on, or the child gets lost in the mass and problems are perpetuated just as are our myths and half truths from one generation to the next.

In industry and business there is growing awareness of the importance of human relations in the maintenance of high productivity at all levels. Since the Hawthorne experiment of the Western Electric Company, it has been clear that the physical environment and the physical health of the worker may be of little avail if his mental attitude is poor. His relations to fellow-workers, superiors, his family, his aspirations and frustrations all have a bearing on his work. Although few industries employ psychiatrists, more of them through supervisory staff, personnel departments and medical services are cognizant of the emotional problems of employees and seek to help either directly or by referring to psychiatric resources. Thus industry, too, can contribute to prevention of human breakdown.

These have been brief observations of the problems and progress of mental health. There is a surging interest in this field which is long overdue and much still to be done. It will require the active support and the best efforts of us all to lessen the burdens of human suffering caused by mental ill health.

58. CANADA'S ALARMING SUICIDE PATTERN*

Julien Bryan[†]

Suicide, however incomprehensible it may seem to many of us, set a new record total of 1,271 deaths in 1958[1] — a more potent killer than tuberculosis or drowning, a toll twice that of fire. And even this figure is in reality only an estimate since, for every suicide reported as such on

*From *Saturday Night*, November 12, 1960.

†Mr. Bryan is an author interested in social and economic research, especially in the areas of demography, population, economic welfare, criminology and statistical presentation.

[1] The number increased to 1,287 in 1959 and to 1,350 in 1960. (Ed.)

the death certificate, there are two other "accidental deaths" reported that are in all probability suicides.

Who commits suicide? It is sobering to reflect that 60 per cent of suicide victims are between 35 and 64 years of age and thus bring their lives to an end in the fullness of adult life. In Canada, as indeed generally throughout the world, about four times as many men as women commit suicide. However, more than half of all suicides occur among persons 45 years of age and over, although this group constitutes less than one-quarter of the total population. Comparatively rarely do children or adolescents kill themselves. Apparently it is more generally the result of the weariness, disillusionment and hopelessness of the later years of life rather than the disappointments of youth.

No simple assessment of the character and temperament of the suicide victim is possible. There is practically no psychiatric condition in which suicide may not occur, though it is most common in patients suffering from severe depression. Suicide represents a man's total retreat from the vicissitudes of life, a failure in his mechanisms of adaptation and an escape from reality.

In many cases suicidal persons are victims of strong and powerful aggressive impulses which they fail to express outwardly and which they consequently turn inwards against themselves. While the problem of estimating suicidal intention remains a difficult challenge, it is worth noting that the suicidal attempt is the most common emergency for the psychiatrist in private practice.

What drives people to suicide? It is motivated by a host of sociological, cultural, ecologic, psychological and other factors. Family trouble, pain, remorse, drunkenness, abject poverty and numerous other situations have been adduced as the causes of suicide but at best such formulations can generally be based only on the opinions of others. With our modern industrial-scientific civilization, social and personal adjustment is a process of unequal difficulty that some find impossible, and some will prove to have a breaking point. A change in status, being unemployed, or even winning a promotion, may lead to suicide.

Divorce plays a significant role and general loneliness is often fundamental. Even changes in weather may play a part and one observer found that sudden peaks in curves for suicide coincided sharply with low-pressure barometric readings. Among men, financial troubles, "executive" frustrations, physical diseases, acute panic over unsuspected homosexual feelings, have caused suicides. Women are more disturbed by domestic troubles and unsatisfactory love affairs. But practically all of us have suicidal tendencies buried deeply within us.

Strangely enough, it is in the Spring months of March, April and May that most suicides occur, although suicide is a problem in all seasons. Regionally speaking, residents of British Columbia and Alberta are more likely to kill themselves than those of any other province and those of Newfoundland least likely. The city dweller is more apt to kill himself than his country cousin. Foreign-born people are more vulnerable than native-born. Divorced and single people have higher rates than those who are married.

How do they commit suicide? While we have all heard of unusual, dramatic methods of suicide, four simple means account for over 90 per cent of suicides. Most frequently they come about through firearms. (In 1958 about 444 such deaths accounted for 35 per cent of all suicides). Hanging and strangulation account for over a quarter of all suicides. The third most lethal agent is poison of all kinds and the fourth drowning.

The methods of committing suicide change over the years and are different for men and women. While men are more likely to hang or shoot themselves, women prefer more passive techniques such as sleeping pills or gas fumes. Shooting is more popular than it formerly was while poisoning has lost favor and new methods have come into vogue such as asphyxiation by plastic cleaning bags.

Statistics show that while firearms account for 40 per cent of male suicides, only 13 per cent of female suicide victims choose this means. After poisoning, women prefer hanging and drowning. Hanging is the second most popular method for males and accounts for over a quarter of such deaths.

Age, in many cases, determines the method of suicide. Young people kill themselves more impulsively than do adults and take the first means at their disposal — often resorting to hanging or using their father's gun. While firearms comprise the leading method generally for adults, after 60 years of age hanging and strangulation become the most widely-used method. Poisonings are widely scattered in all age groups while drownings are significant in all the adult years.

Canada's suicide rate in the 5-year period 1954-58 averaged about 7.4 per 100,000 persons. While countries such as Denmark have rates in excess of 20 and the United States and England have rates of around 10, other countries such as Ireland, Mexico and Egypt, have rates below 3. The incidence of suicide is low in the less developed countries, high in the more; and in some countries of very high living standards it has become a problem of major proportions.

The overall rate of 7.4 for Canada masks the fact that the male rate was 11.4 compared with a female rate of only 3.3. In addition, the factor of age is highly significant with male rates per 100,000 population varying from 0.2 for ages under 15 years to 32.4 for the age group 60-64. In the 60-64 age group the rate is also the highest for females even though it stands at only 8.5 — a rate exceeded by males from 25 years of age onwards.

Canada's lowest recorded suicide rate per 100,000 population was 5.7 in the year 1921, the first year for which national statistics are available. The rate rose almost to 10 in the depression and dropped to nearly 6 in World War II. This wartime decrease appears to be a very general phenomenon and has been observed in almost all belligerent countries. Two particular factors help account for this experience. Improved economic conditions result in a very high level of employment with a consequent easing of financial burdens and worries which are known to play an important part in many suicides.

A less obvious but perhaps even more significant factor is the psychological impact of war on emotionally disturbed individuals. It gives them a new sense of community with their fellow men facing a common danger and provides a new and concrete purpose and goal. After the War the suicide rate resumed its upward course and has shown an immediate response to even minor upheavals of economic activity.

Morally and legally there is no sympathy for suicide in Canada. It is condoned by no religious faith and Section 213 of the Canadian Criminal Code states: "Everyone who attempts to commit suicide is guilty of an offence punishable on summary conviction". This can lead to two years in jail and makes doctors even more reluctant to report suicide attempts.

It was not always like this. While Aristotle condemned the practice of suicide, it was enforced by the Greek state for political and military offenders. Seneca stated, "If life pleases you, live; if not, you have a right to return whence you came". St. Augustine was one of the first to postulate suicide as a sin and the early Christian Councils decreed suicide as the work of the devil. Plato was inclined to believe that suicide was a dishonorable act since a citizen had no right to deprive society of his civil life without the permission of a magistrate.

In the old days in England, the estate of a suicide (unless he was proved insane) reverted to the Crown, and the bodies of the victims were buried at crossroads with a stake driven through them in an attempt to pinion the "evil spirit". The word suicide was introduced to the law about 1700 A.D., coupled with the phrase, "while temporarily insane". The latter statement was added as a "pious perjury" on the part of the jury to save the family from poverty and disgrace.

Modern research has removed the stake and the evil spirit as psychologists and sociologists seek suicide's hidden meaning. It is their recent findings, coupled with statistics, that make possible a partial understanding of suicide which in turn offers opportunities for prevention. It has been found, for example, that suicide is caused by a variety of factors, psychological, cultural and situational. But the chief factors appear to be a personality defect occurring in early childhood, plus the stress of life situations on the defective personality. Sometimes the personality weakness is dominant while in other cases life situations seem so crushing that even the "normal" person thinks suicide is logical. At the present time statistical investigations are being combined with detailed individual clinical studies to study the problems of social integration and cohesion. The aim is to shed light on the relative importance of such aspects as bereavement, loneliness, poverty, awareness of declining faculties, decreasing vitality, impairment of physical health, and mental disease.

Society's feelings about suicide are confused. For example, suicide is often considered to be a coward's way out and at the same time it is believed to take courage to kill yourself. Much of the responsibility for preventing suicide must rest with the family and the family physician. (Ironically enough, among occupational groups MD's are most prone to suicide.) The success of voluntary societies in protecting potential victims has been indicated in a number of stories in the world press.

Sometimes clerical advisers have been phoned in critical hours and have talked many out of taking the final act. It is important to realize that emotional conditions that have been clearly linked with suicide are capable of study and understanding. The bulk of suicide victims are both clinically and psychiatrically ill and until better means are devised would benefit by closed-ward hospitalization, with particular attention paid to manic-depressives and alcoholics.

D. A. E. Bennett, associate professor of psychiatry at the University of California Medical School, has made practical suggestions for suicide prevention. The public generally must be educated to recognize suicide danger signals, such as depression, anxiety, loss of appetite and insomnia. Treatment should never in any case be attempted by amateurs. Police officers should be more thoroughly instructed in dealing with suicide attempts. We need stricter control of dangerous and addictive drugs, particularly barbiturates.

The registration of all suicide attempts together with followup supervision would help too. But the greatest need of all is public understanding so that our efforts to give effective psychiatric treatment to people of suicidal tendencies or who have actually attempted suicide will not be blocked by either legal proceedings or outdated prejudices.

SELECTED BIBLIOGRAPHY

Cahill, B., "Do Immigrants Bring a Mental Health Problem to Canada?" *Saturday Night*, June 22, 1957.

Coburn, F. E., "Psychiatry, the Family Doctor, and Public Health," *Canadian Journal of Public Health*, Vol. 54, No. 2, February, 1963.

The Financial Post, "Bold New Approach Sought to Mental Illness Program," June 9, 1962.

The Financial Post, "What Mental Illness Costs," June 9, 1962.

Gregory, I., "Factors Influencing First Admission Rates to Canadian Mental Hospitals," *Canadian Psychiatric Association Journal*, Vol. 4, April, 1959.

Jones, C., "Suicide — A Disease That Can Be Treated," *Maclean's Magazine*, April 8, 1961.

McConnell, R., "The Shame of our Hospitals for Retarded Children," *Chatelaine*, June,1960.

Canadian Mental Health Association, *Mentally Disordered Children*, (Submission to the Royal Commission on Health Services), Toronto, May, 1962.

Dominion Bureau of Statistics, *Mental Health Statistics*, Ottawa, Queen's Printer, 1960.

Roberts, C. A., "Mental Health Services," *Canadian Medical Association Journal*, Vol. 85, May 14, 1961.

Tyhurst, J. S., et. al., *More for the Mind*, Toronto, The Canadian Mental Health Association, 1963.

chapter twelve

SEXUAL DEVIANCE

Straddling the problem areas of Mental Illness on the one side and Crime and Delinquency on the other, we find ourselves concerned with the issue of sexual deviance. In this chapter we have, first, an article by Kenneth G. Gray who is both a psychiatrist and a lecturer in medical jurisprudence. In "Sexual Deviation: Problem and Treatment," he defines or describes the principal types of sexual deviation (homosexuality, exhibitionism, fetishism, voyeurism, sadism and pedophilia), suggests some of the popular misconceptions regarding these problems, and recommends a four-point set of principles to guide a plan for dealing with sex offenders.

Next an Edmonton psychiatrist, writing in *The Canadian Medical Association Journal* on "Deviant Sexual Behaviour and the Sex Criminal", discusses some of the causal theories involved (incorporating several reports of research done by others). While limitations of space have prohibited incorporation of all of Herbert Pascoe's worthy article (we have had to omit some statistics and some very interesting case histories), the sections presented here do shed a great deal of light on the problem from the psychiatric point of view.

One important Canadian effort to treat the problem of sexual deviance, the Forensic Clinic of the Toronto Psychiatric Hospital, introduced in Pascoe's article, is discussed in a popular vein in an article by Franklin Russell entitled "Clinic to Curb Sex Crimes Before They Happen". By tracing the efforts of the Clinic to treat the problems of one "patient", the article aptly describes one approach to the treatment and prevention of sexual deviance.

What is it like to be a "deviant"? The life and problems of a young male homosexual are graphically portrayed in an autobiographical article (anonymous) entitled "Living With Homosexuality". The author shows keen insight into his own problems, and an awareness of the medical, psychological and sociological aspects of this condition. He despairs at the limited possibilities of "treatment" and suggests that he is actually lost with regard to solving the problem of how to live in this society.

59. SEXUAL DEVIATION: PROBLEM AND TREATMENT*

Kenneth G. Gray†

Sexual deviation is the term used by psychiatrists to describe abnormal sexual conduct, that is to say, an act performed for sexual gratification other than sexual intercourse with an adult of the opposite sex. A sexual deviate is a person who engages in such conduct.

The term sexual deviation is used in preference to sexual perversion because of the legal, moral or social condemnation implied in the word perversion. The role of a psychiatrist is to understand and treat patients, not to judge them.

This amoral attitude may give rise to misunderstanding. For example, psychiatrists may be accused of advocating that courts and prisons be replaced by psychiatric clinics.

No Canadian psychiatrist is likely to recommend any weakening of the administration of justice in dealing with sex offenders. The community is bound to rely upon the police, prosecutor, judiciary and penal institutions to protect women and children from the harmful acts of certain sexual deviates. Psychiatrists can participate in the judicial process, but there is no suggestion that they can replace it.

Before discussing the nature of psychiatric participation, it is necessary to say something about the principal types of sexual deviation.

Homosexuality: This is a sexual attraction of one man for another or

---

*From *Saturday Night*, November 26, 1955.
†Dr. Gray, who is professionally trained in both medicine and law, is Professor of Forensic Psychiatry at the University of Toronto.

one woman for another. In some cases, a homosexual person has no sexual interest in members of the opposite sex and is impotent with them. In other cases, the person may be bisexual, that is to say he derives sexual pleasure from contacts with members of both sexes. The condition may be temporary or permanent. *→on the contrary women do it all the time but to a lesser degree.*

Exhibitionism: This is a condition found only in men. Some men get sexual pleasure out of exhibiting the sexual organs publicly to women. The exhibiting is pleasurable in itself and is not a prelude to other sexual overtures or attack. The exhibitionist may arouse disgust or fear but he is not dangerous. *← fashions such as mini skirts & low cut tops etc. just this.*

Fetishism: Like exhibitionism, this condition is found only in men. One form of fetishism is a sexual interest in women's clothing. A fetishist usually shows a preference for some particular article of clothing, for example, a woman's shoe.

Transvestitism: A transvestite prefers to dress in female rather than male clothing. He may be charged with an offence because he steals the clothing or in situations where he poses as a woman.

Voyeurism: A voyeur is sometimes referred to colloquially as a "peeping Tom". A voyeur derives pleasure from spying on women.

Sadism: A sadist is a man who derives sexual gratification from inflicting pain and suffering on some other person, usually a woman. The acts of cruelty may be mental or physical. The sadistic acts may serve to arouse or intensify sexual excitement as a prelude to sexual intercourse. On the other hand, some sadists get complete sexual satisfaction out of the sadistic acts themselves.

Sadism is sometimes confused with sex murders in which the murder is committed in panic or to escape detection.

Sadism is one of the two most socially dangerous deviations, the other being pedophilia.

Pedophilia: In this condition, a man is sexually attracted to young boys or girls. Most pedophiliacs are middle-aged or older. Frequently they are impotent, sometimes alcoholic.

Careful and wise handling by parents can minimize the shock of this premature sexual experience for a child so that no permanent damage will ensue. Fortunately, there is no reason to expect that a child is likely to become a sexual deviate in adult life because of such an experience.

These are some of the types of sexual deviation that psychiatrists see in practice. In addition, there are instances of anti-social conduct which, on the surface, are not sexually motivated but on investigation prove to be types of sexual deviation. When a fetish steals a woman's shoe, he may be charged with theft. He is not charged with a sexual offence but the underlying reason for the crime is erotic satisfaction.

When a psychiatrist is asked to examine a sexual deviate, he will classify the abnormal sexual conduct in accordance with the foregoing or similar classification. The next step is to ascertain why the person engages in the abnormal conduct. He will try to determine the cause of the sexual deviation. This means utilizing every available diagnostic tool, including psychiatric examination, psychological testing, physical and laboratory examination and where required, such procedures as X-ray films, electroencephalograms (electrical recordings of the brain) and many others.

A small proportion of the cases are found to be suffering from a disorder of the mind of a kind which necessitates treatment in a mental hospital. In other words, a small percentage of sexual deviates are found to be mentally ill, mentally defective or epileptic to such a degree that confinement in a mental hospital is needed.

The great majority of cases are not in this category. They do not show any signs of obvious mental disorder. They are of normal intelligence and are accountable for their conduct.

For this reason such terms as "sex maniac" appear ridiculous to any one with experience with sexual deviates. They are not madmen or raving. There is nothing about their appearance or conduct (except their sexual conduct) to distinguish them from other people in the community.

As a rule there is no physical or organic basis for the sexual deviation. In most cases, the cause of the sexual deviation is a deep-seated and obscure psychoneurosis, the origin of which may commence in early childhood or adolescence.

The question is often asked, what treatment is used for sexual deviates? From what has been said it is apparent that surgery, drugs, hormones or other forms of physical treatment are rarely the answer. The cases that belong in mental hospitals will benefit from the improved forms of treatment now available — but they are a small proportion of the total. In most cases, the treatment is psychological, involving a long, painstaking effort.

Whether treatment should be given in a jail, hospital or clinic depends upon the kind of person to be treated. It should be noted, too, that some cases are not good subjects for treatment: some sexual deviates are unlikely to benefit from any known method of treatment. In the case of a sexual deviate who is not mentally ill or defective and is a menace to others, treatment (if any) should be carried out in a jail and the deviate should be imprisoned as long as he is a menace. If he is mentally ill or mentally defective, he should be treated in a mental hospital. If he is not mentally ill or defective and not dangerous, he should be treated in a clinic in the community.

In order to ensure a wise sentence for a person convicted of a sexual offence, it appears obvious that psychiatric facilities should be available so that courts may obtain the requisite information. Facilities for treatment should be provided in jails, mental hospitals and community clinics.

A few popular misconceptions are worth mentioning.

One of these misconceptions is the idea that psychiatrists can pick out sexual deviates in the general population or predict that an individual is likely to commit a sex crime. Community plans for dealing with sex offenders should recognize that the first chance to do anything about a sex offender is when he is convicted of his first offence.

Another popular fallacy is the idea that a man who emerges in one form of sexual deviation is likely to progress to a more serious form. Thus, some people believe that an exhibitionist is likely to attack women or children. The fact is that sexual deviates usually adhere to the type of deviation they have found most satisfying.

It should be recognized that sex offenders make up a rather small proportion of criminal offenders. Statistics also show that sex criminals repeat their crimes less frequently than other criminals.

Plans for dealing with sex offenders should be founded on these principles:

1. Continuation of traditional facilities for the administration of justice, utilizing psychiatric facilities when necessary;
2. Indeterminate sentence to penal institutions for dangerous sex criminals who are not mentally ill or defective with treatment of those who can benefit by it;
3. Treatment in mental hospitals for mentally ill or mentally defective sex criminals;
4. Utilization of probation and suspended sentence in the case of sex criminals who do not require imprisonment or treatment in mental hospital and who would benefit from treatment in a community psychiatric clinic.

60. *DEVIANT SEXUAL BEHAVIOUR AND THE SEX CRIMINAL**

Herbert Pascoe†

While it is true that the average man in our Western civilization spends a great deal of his waking life fantasying and ruminating over sexual matters, it is difficult to estimate just what proportion of his time this occupies. It is likely true that the time spent thinking about such matters is markedly disproportionate to the time spent in real sexual activity. It is also true that one of the striking differences between the commission of a crime and the restraining of oneself from such commission is merely the difference between thinking a thought and acting out a thought. The inhibiting effect of social and moral conscience is usually the differentiating factor. If the thinking about criminal deeds was equally as much a crime as the commission of such deeds, then we would likely all be criminals at one or other time in our lives.

Where social and moral conscience is weak or absent, a psychopathic or sociopathic personality is usually in existence. Or to put it in a simpler manner, whereas a normal person respects and is aware of the difference between right and wrong, so too is a psychopath often aware of social wrong, except that he does not *care* about it. He is thus able to carry out antisocial behaviour without the pangs of conscience that most "normal" persons would experience. Where such activity involves sexual behaviour, he may become a sex criminal (but such criminals are not necessarily all psychopathic personalities). This will also depend upon whether or not he is discovered by the law, or apprehended by the law. This raises a perplexing question. Does a crime occur whenever behaviour described as criminal by a criminal code takes place, or only if law enforcement bodies know of it? For the answer to this, we must ask help from our legal colleagues.

The element of conscience need not be involved in a so-called sex crime, however. Even if this action follows mutual consent between two adult homosexuals and neither calls upon the law to intercede, the action can still be considered criminal if a legal officer learns of it. In some states in the U.S.A., various deviant sex practices between a man and

*From *The Canadian Medical Association Journal*, Vol. 84, January 28, 1961.
†Dr. Pascoe is in private practice in Psychiatry in Edmonton and is also Clinical Instructor in Psychiatry, Faculty of Medicine, University of Alberta, Edmonton.

women are punishable by law even with mutual consent between the the two, should the law be informed.

The increasing overt interest in our civilization regarding sexual matters in the past few years (as witnessed by the popularity of certain novels, plus the sexual themes of the majority of successful motion pictures) is commonly accepted, but not without concern, by many. It is difficult to believe that such public interest was not as marked in the Victorian era, although of course in a more subdued manner. So often, "wrong", "guilt", "sin", and similar terms are applied to sex, and being a "good" or "bad" person involves one's handling of one's sexual activities, thoughts and interests.

A combination of public concern over sexual matters in general, plus mounting interest in the causation of sex crimes, disposal and rehabilitation of the criminal population and the sex criminal in particular, has led to the writing of this paper.

What follows below combines the author's experience in the treatment of patients with sex deviations (with some personal reflections therefrom), plus gleanings from the reports of colleagues and other authors who have dealt with similar patients in recent years.

The public reaction to sex deviation of any sort — always stronger when children are involved — is one of alarm, resentment, and disgust, and with varied prejudice against the one who commits the deed. For years now, the public trend has been turning to the realization that such persons are ill — socially if not medically — and that prison alone is not the answer to their problem.

The inflammatory reaction of such deeds upon the public may produce temporary chaos and emotional turmoil, but may often bring about a worthwhile outcome, as happened in the city of Toronto six years ago. Three Toronto housewives, as a result of their concern over several sex crimes involving children in that city in 1954-55, banded together to found the "Parents' Action League", a lay organization dedicated to the pursuit and dissemination of knowledge about sex crimes, and research into treatment and possible prevention of such phenomena. An impressive list of psychiatrists, medical men, psychologists, legal personnel, politicians and lay persons were involved in the creation of the body, which received much public support, and support from the lay press. As a result of its efforts, and pressure directed by it upon the Ontario Provincial Government, the "Forensic Clinic" — an affiliate of the Toronto Psychiatric Hospital and the University of Toronto Department of Psychiatry — was born. The clinic was not entirely oriented to sex deviates even at first, although interest was predominantly in sexual deviation at that time. The Parents' Action League branched out, as a lay organization, to concern itself also with juvenile delinquency, salacious literature, education in the schools regarding accepting rides from strangers, and other pertinent areas of concern. Chapters formed throughout the province, and interest in the organization spread through the nation and to the U.S.A.

Why do (usually) men commit sex crimes, and what are the most common types? The breakdown of statistics for new cases seen in 1958 from the Forensic Clinic in Toronto indicates that the most common types of antisocial sexual behaviour are homosexuality, exhibitionism, and pedophilia. Of 179 new patients seen in 1958, only six were suffering from psychoneurotic disorders and 13 were schizophrenic; the majority of the remainder were persons with disorders of character, behaviour and intelligence, but not necessarily victims of mental or emotional illness as we know it.

Hammer and Glueck studied 200 male sex offenders at Sing Sing Prison, under a program sponsored by the New York State Department of Mental Hygiene, over a period of five years, and concluded that sex offenders have *castration fears* (but not necessarily consciously) in the following order of increasing intensity, according to the crime committed: (1) rape, (2) heterosexual contact with adolescents and children, (3) homosexual actions with adolescent partners, and (4) homosexual action with child partners. [*Castration fears* refers to the conscious or subconscious anxiety experienced by men with reference to loss of, or threats to their masculinity, virility, physical appearance, etc. Men with such a problem often have difficulty relating easily to women, feel inferior, and so forth.] The continuum, from rapist to homosexual pedophilia, appears to represent in parallel fashion the increasing intensity of castration feelings on the one hand, and the correspondingly greater distance from the mature female as a potential sexual object on the other. Incest subjects were found to be the most overtly psychotic, and also to harbour the most intense castration feelings. The view held by these authors is that the sex offender presents an attempt on the part of the offender to employ *substitute sex* outlets for the mature female, because of the threatening potential, both psychosexually and psychosocially, with which she is endowed. Almost every one of the subjects exhibited feelings of fear (as a reaction to massive Oedipal entanglements) of approaching *mature* females psychosexually.

As in the case of obesity, hopes for endocrinological causation of sex deviation are legion, but rarely realized in fact. So also is the case in physical treatment of sexual aberration, especially with the use of hormonal substances.

Castration of sexual offenders is permitted by law in many countries, notably Norway. If it is effective, likely its value is due to the psychic trauma and fear inflicted, and not to specific physiological or psychological treatment as such. This practice in some ways resembles that of some ancient civilizations, which amputated the hand of a criminal because of theft.

Lieberman and Siegel reported on a program for the treatment of sex offenders at a state hospital in California over a period of two years from 1952 to 1954. In 284 patients involved, 50% of the crimes were perpetrated upon children below the age of 14. For the most part, this did not involve sexual intercourse. About one-half were returned to the courts after a 90-day observation period as untreatable. Of the remainder, the results of an intensive treatment program proved gratifying — centring mainly on group psychotherapy. Three-quarters of the group were discharged as improved and preliminary studies showed a low percentage of recidivism.

In contrast, Glueck studied 30 pedophiles, 30 rapists, and 50 non-offenders as controls. Among other features, a serious impairment of social and moral conscience formation and resultant impairment of the restraining effect of conscience on overt behaviour was noted (this smacks strongly of the psychopathic personality). Because of the *lack* of improvement in the majority of men treated in individual group therapy in his series, organic therapies of various types were employed. The immediate post-treatment results in a group of sex offenders treated intensively with electroconvulsive therapy showed more promise than other measures. This is remarkable in view of the fact that few psychiatrists would ever consider this treatment for sexual deviation *per se*. The author noted that the serious character of the psychopathology in sexual offenders made psychotherapeutic approaches quite ineffective. In psychiatric research, particularly in the therapeutic area, personal bias and faith by the worker involved, often plays a part in the outcome, so far as opinion about "improvement" is concerned.

The Forensic Clinic in Toronto reported a high percentage of failed appointments in 1958 — 23% as against actual attendance. A similar finding is noted in the 1959 Annual Report from the clinic. This is not surprising in view of the high degree of character disorder present. Such persons often fail to develop close relationships with their doctors in a treatment program, and often fail to accept responsibilities of many kinds, including the keeping of appointments. The majority of new patients in 1958 were young; only 10% were over 40 years, 24% being between 20 and 24 years, and 20% between 16 and 19 years.

In group therapy with voluntarily referred homosexuals, sexual relationships between members have developed. One aggressive member had to leave when he began acting out against passive members. Difficulties developed because of strong resistances offered by many men with character disorders. It was felt that a few, but by no means all of the group, were being definitely benefited by treatment.

There seemed to be general improvement in a group of exhibitionists, and also in a group of pedophiles, but repeat offences took place, although the incidence was low. Eight of twelve voyeurists were treated, and three improved.

The Clinic, created originally under the leadership of Dr. Peter Thomson, and now directed by his successor, Dr. Edward Turner, is enthusiastic about the future, in terms of its potential for research, teaching and treatment.

DISCUSSION

The number of children and adults who die annually from sex crimes is minimal, compared with the number who die from other crimes, accidents and diseases. There is a common misconception on the part of the public that exposure to sex deviates in childhood, of itself, will lead to later neurosis or emotional and/or sexual maladjustment. Isolated episodes such as these do not likely have lasting effects, if the child involved is basically emotionally healthy. Prevalent concern over sexual sensationalism is a characteristic of our society, and may well belie our own inner anxiety about sexual matters. To think of sex deviates as being "ill" and requiring treatment as well as, or rather than, a prison sentence is humane.

Since most sex deviates are *not* inclined to violence or assault (excluding rapists and deviates with sadistic tendencies), there would seem to be no need for mass removal of such persons from the community for a prolonged period of time. A great deal needs to be done as yet regarding public education in this matter, and it goes without saying that a wealth of research is yet required in this field. Research helps often to determine *what* is going on, but unfortunately does not always tell us what to do about it.

The problem of sex deviation and the sex criminal is not unlike other social and medical problems. Constitutional and environmental factors are likely both present in varying degrees in each offender. Cultural, religious, philosophical, moral and economic factors may well play a part in varying degrees.

Johnson and Robinson feel that perverse sexual behaviour develops from unconscious or, less frequently, conscious pathological fostering of deviant sexual behaviour, early in life, within the family setting. A parent may either act openly seductive towards a child, or may, by equivocation, foster behaviour oriented towards sexual deviation. This writer agrees with their opinion that definitive psychiatric therapy is a prodigious task in both the adolescent and adult sexual deviant, and that *it is futile in patients who show no compelling motivation for treatment.* They feel that there should be education of well-intentioned parents who do not observe proper and healthy rules of modesty in the home. They admonish pediatricians and family physicians to face the unequivocal truth that all degrees of seduction and sexual stimulation occur all too commonly in the home, and in families which exhibit every *outward* aspect of respectability, decency, and conformity with convention.

Ellis, Brancale and Doorbar of the New Jersey Diagnostic Center for Sex Offenders suggest certain recommendations for the prevention of sex crimes: (1) To reduce drastically the number of sex offences on the statute book (e.g. why should sex perversion between two *mutually consenting adults* be considered a crime?). (2) To increase the amount and objectivity of sex instruction. (3) To encourage a much more liberal, socially sanctioned heterosexual participation on the part of young people.

(The author of this paper does not necessarily agree with the last recommendation of Ellis *et al.*, in terms of its potential to reduce the number of sex crimes.)

The core of sex crime, then, is that of inability to appreciate oneself as being "masculine" in one's own eyes, and to be inadequate sexually to a degree that one is unable to form satisfactory relationships with the opposite sex. There may be marked hostility directed to women in general, or the individual involved may derive sensual pleasure from inflicting violence upon others. Should this hostility erupt in an uncontrolled fashion, the beating of one's partners may take place, and rape, or the murdering of one's victim — a woman or child — may be the outcome. Such assaultive sex crimes comprise only a minority of all sex crimes, but these naturally receive the major share of publicity in the lay press.

Let it be stressed that all sex deviates are not sex criminals, e.g. a fetishist is not a sex "criminal" as such. Certain types of deviation are listed in the criminal code, and if a deviate commits one such type of act he becomes a sex criminal, whether or not he is apprehended. The majority of sex criminals are not dangerous in terms of being potential murderers, contrary to popular belief. In criminal sex acts, attention is usually "forced" upon the victim — as in the case of rape, exhibitionism and pedophilia.

When criminal sexual behaviour takes place, it is perpetrated upon a woman, a man or a child, but in all cases, sexual gratification is attained from a goal less than the ideal, mutually acceptable, heterosexual relationship. Hopefully, such a heterosexual relationship is complete with sincerity, mutual respect, compassion and love.

To hope that in the immediate future all sex deviates and sex criminals can be "cured" with "treatment" is at the present time to be naïve and idealistic. We are undoubtedly heading in the right direction, but society's hoped-for goal in this problem area remains as yet distant, and perhaps not completely attainable.

61. *CLINIC TO CURB SEX CRIMES BEFORE THEY HAPPEN**

Franklin Russell†

Late last February, a Toronto accountant named William Garçon was having a bad day working on income-tax figures and worrying about meeting a special mortgage payment. He was feeling unwell. His mother-in-law showed no sign of returning to her home in a nearby town after staying for three months.

When he got home that night, Garçon (a pseudonym) was upbraided by his wife for forgetting to buy bread. His mother-in-law said, "It's little things like that which break up marriages, William."

Garçon said nothing and went upstairs to change his clothes. As he took of his coat, the sleeve knocked a bottle of nail polish, spilling it on the bedspread. Garçon was stunned. Then he jumped to his feet, ran downstairs into the street, "in search" as he said later, "of a little girl."

*From *Maclean's Magazine,* September 23, 1961.
†Mr. Russell, currently resident in New York City, is a Canadian author on natural history, science and travel subjects.

This was the mechanism of a sex crime in the making. Last year between 2,000 and 3,000 Canadians were indicted for sex crimes and probably double that number were never caught or reported to the police. Their crimes ranged from peeping through bedroom windows to murders. They are Canada's least understood criminals and, in most parts of the country, they can expect a lifelong succession of prison terms without ever understanding why they commit their repugnant crimes or knowing how they might stop.

THE PATIENTS: SEVEN HUNDRED DEVIATES

Fortunately, Garçon lives in an enlightened province, and as he ran down his quiet suburban street on his bizarre search, he saw a phone box. He stumbled into it and called a psychiatrist at the Forensic Clinic of the Toronto Psychiatric Hospital. After a few minutes of conversation, he walked home relatively calm.

The Forensic Clinic has, in five years of its life, treated nearly 700 sexually deviated people. It is pioneering a new approach to the problem of sex criminals. It is unique in Canada and, in some respects, unique in the world. "These deviates need not be regarded with abhorrence and fear," says the clinic director, Dr. R. Edward Turner. "They can be treated."

Backing his statement are the results: about eighty-five percent of the clinic's patients have learned to control their perverted drives. The clinic, however, may be performing an even more important service. In a field that is markedly barren of reliable research, the clinic's workers, every year, move closer to accurately predicting the behavior of deviates. (And it has found a few facts about the victims — some young girls deliberately tempt pedophiles (child molesters) to make attacks.)

Dr. Turner feels a major duty facing the clinic is public education. "Sex deviation has been shrouded in superstition, in hatred and fear for centuries," he says.

The clinic is trying to help some of the thousands of Canadians who live in strange fantasy worlds of deviated sex impulses. Many of these people live perpetually on the verge of committing large or small sex crimes. "The real extent of the sex-deviate problem in society," says Dr. Stuart K. Jaffary of the University of Toronto school of social work, "is like the iceberg — nine tenths hidden below the surface." It is now recognized that nearly all men have sexually deviant thoughts. Fortunately, most men have control. For those who haven't the clinic is becoming a sort of safety valve, a place they can turn to for free treatment, secure in the knowledge that it is run by the Ontario Department of

Health and has nothing to do with the police or the reform system. The clinic is also a watchdog for faint signs of schizophrenia or psychopathic traits which are warnings that a deviate may become a sex murderer.

Garçon's sex problem started in his teens. He was attracted to little girls but never molested them. He did not analyse how he felt about them but he knew his thoughts were wrong. He found, when twenty-one, that his form of sexual abnormality was called pedophilia and that he was sexually linked to the exhibitionists, who expose themselves to shock women in public, and to the peeping toms, who may take fantastic risks to spy on people undressing. He knew he was not a dangerous sexual pervert, but he lived in constant dread.

For ten apprehensive years, he controlled himself. He married and had two children, but marriage did nothing to alleviate his deviate urges. One day in 1956, while watching a small girl paddling at a beach on Lake Simcoe, fifty miles north of Toronto, he suddenly grabbed her by the shoulders. The child cried out, the mother came running up, and Garçon only extricated himself from the situation by saying he was trying to protect the girl from a bee.

THE SUPREME EFFORT OF SELF-CONTROL

He was really frightened now. He recalled reading that a Forensic Clinic had recently been opened in Toronto, following a series of savage sex murders in the province. He decided to make a supreme effort to control himself and succeeded for five years — till his rush into the street.

After his telephone call, during which the psychiatrist calmed him and made a clinic appointment, Garçon's treatment was routine. He was first interviewed by Valdemar Hartman, chief social worker. What were his relations with his wife, children, mother, father, relatives, employer? Hartman was looking for environmental stresses, hatred, frictions, tensions. He discovered Garçon was terrified of his mother-in-law, and frequently resented his wife and his employer. He was insecure. He had wanted to be a doctor but his mother had insisted on accountancy. Hartman's skill in appraising Garçon's social problems would be vital in later treatment. "It has been said," he says, "that a good environmental history in sex cases is half the battle of diagnosis."

Garçon soon realized that his sex problem was buried deep in his past and was related somehow to his parents; and that this was true of all sex deviates. A week later, he kept an appointment with a senior clinical psychologist, Dan Paitich, when, under psychological testing, he proved to have an IQ of 125, and answered 227 questions about his relations with his parents and 115 questions about his sex life.

Unlike about twenty percent of the 200-odd sex offenders sent to the clinic yearly by probation officers or courts, Garçon was not resentful. He wanted to co-operate. He revealed that his father had been weak, dominated by his aggressive mother. According to one clinic worker he was proving to be a routine pedophile with a desire to behave toward little girls with some of the affection he once wished his mother had given him.

Like all sex deviates, Garçon was deeply ashamed of his perverted drives and thought his case was the worst imaginable. He confessed this to Dr. Harry Hutchison, the chief psychologist, who had Garçon's case history before him and who had to decide whether group or individual therapy was to be used. But despite his sharp feelings of guilt, Garçon's problem was almost superficial compared with the deep-rooted case of exhibitionism treated earlier by Dr. Hutchison and Dr. Ian C. Lond of the department of psychiatry of the University of Toronto.

A twenty-five-year-old man came to the clinic after the most extraordinary record of exhibitionism. He first exposed at thirteen, made lewd telephone calls to girls at fifteen, became a peeping tom for a year and by his early twenties was constantly tense, as he said, "with a fever to expose." He would strip off all his clothes, hide among trees, and spring out at girls as they passed. He hid in girls' school cloakrooms and exposed when girls came in. He was a public menace while driving because his wild fancies frequently caused him to swerve off the road to a spot where he could expose.

The presence of his wife did not inhibit him. She told the psychiatrists that when he wanted to expose he would look paralyzed and his eyes would become glazed. She would grab him and drag him away. The patient said he felt excited before exhibiting, and full of awful dread and a grim determination "to go ahead regardless." Everything became unreal as though he were watching himself in a dream, a familiar symptom to clinic workers.

The force driving sex deviates is often irresistible and all of them speak of it with awe or horror. One peeping tom, terrified of heights, climbed a one-hundred-foot elm half a dozen times to look into a girl's bedroom in an apartment building. "Once I get the urge to look for a child," Garçon told Dr. Hutchison, "it's absolutely compelling, impossible to resist."

The exact reasons for sex deviation aren't known but all sex offenders are thought to behave in a manner symbolic of disorders created in their childhoods. A highly successful thirty-five-year-old salesman came to the clinic voluntarily because his work was deteriorating due to his sex-sadism fantasies. "I imagine myself lashing women with a whip," he confessed, "ripping off their clothes and punching them." He was a mild man, seemingly normal, but his preliminary psychological report showed his father often used to thrash his mother into unconsciousness.

Sometimes a crime may be even more directly symbolic. The clinic, which also handles cases of compulsive theft or assault, recently treated a woman who used to steal belts; psychologists found her father used to beat her with a belt.

Despite some of the more obvious symbolism, the causes of sexual deviation are still shadowy. "It's amazing the dearth of information on the subject," says research associate Dr. J. W. Mohr. In practically any other field of psychiatry, Dr. Mohr would have ten to twenty years of research material from which to work. As it is, he has five years of clinic research material and a trickle of information from a few clinics elsewhere in the world.

He is trying to answer dozens of basic questions about sex deviation. He doesn't know yet, for example, why exhibitionism in men reaches a peak in their mid-twenties, falls away in the mid-thirties, and almost disappears after forty-five. Again, no one knows why pedophilia occurs predominantly in three age groups — late teens, mid to late thirties and mid to late fifties. Another surprising and still unexplained finding in Dr. Mohr's research was that pedophiles, more frequently than other deviates, reported long service in the armed forces or merchant marine.

Deviates occur in all religions, races and income brackets. "If it's possible to make one large generalization about them," says Dr. Paitich, "it's this: their relations with their fathers determine *whether* they will be deviates; the relations with their mothers determine what *sort* they'll be."

Soon after he was accepted for treatment, Garçon was startled to hear that he would be joining a group for therapy. "But I could never face the others," he protested. Dr. Turner, the clinic director, disagreed. "You'll be surprised how much it will help," he said.

Garçon *was* surprised. The clinic runs seven therapy groups, two for homosexuals, two for pedophiles, one for exhibitionists, one for patients' wives, and one for adolescents. At the first group meeting under the direction of psychologist Arnold Lupmanis, Garçon got insight into the problems of others and this diminished his own. One man confessed he had hated his father so much "I wanted to kill him." Patients freely discussed their "crimes" and the peculiar strength of the forces that drove them to commit these crimes. They warmed to one another, recognizing each insecurity as their own. The therapist guided the discussions, and encouraged patients to talk themselves out.

"It's hard to be dogmatic about treatment when so little is known about sex deviation," says Dr. Turner, "but the therapy here is based first on a thorough analysis of the patient to find his problem, then on encouraging him to recognize it, accept it and master it." Drugs are rarely used to help this process.

The case of the exhibitionist who exposed even before his wife demanded special methods. After some trial-and-error private treatment, he was put under light hypnosis at the clinic. The therapist described the type of woman that had led him to exhibit. After several experiments, the patient could relax at the thought of an exposure-prompting situation. His wife was then instructed to take him to a department store where he could see many women. He endured agonies, but was able to ignore all but one woman. His therapy had taught him sufficient self-control to turn his back on her.

A key to recovery is the patient's recognition of the "trigger" that sets him off. For Garçon, it was the knowledge that feelings of frustration and inadequacy could start him thinking of deviate behavior. For others it might simply be the sight of an undrawn shade, a girl with high heels or a certain type of dress. One thirty-year-old man committed incest with his ten-year-old daughter immediately after every argument with his wife.

Garçon's wife was called in to the group therapy sessions where it became clear that she too had psychological problems, some of them sexual.

Despite the widespread ignorance surrounding sexual crimes, the clinic has made a start in teaching understanding. Already, Ontario police are becoming much less antagonistic to deviates. In the past, they might beat deviates in disgust. Today, some patients report the exceptional sympathy of arresting police, a sympathy for which they are deeply grateful since most sex offenders are terrified of authority. Recently a police constable found a man in a Toronto alley in suspicious circumstances. Instead of arresting him, he said, "Why don't you give them a call down at the clinic. They might be able to help you.'"

Dr. Turner has lectured at the annual meeting of Ontario magistrates and advised them on ways of recognizing deviates. His colleague, Dr. A. B. Stokes, professor of psychiatry at the University of Toronto, recently addressed cadets at the Ontario Police College.

Dr. Turner doesn't claim to be stopping sex crimes though the clinic undoubtedly is doing so. He knows the clinic has only just begun its real work. "We are pushing deeper and deeper into the problem" he says, "and eventually we may reach those deviates who cannot yet be treated away from hospital or jail." He is speaking of those with schizophrenic or psychopathic traits which, combined with their misdirected sex drives, can turn them into incomprehensibly savage murderers.

The rapist too is an urgent subject for research. Technically he is not even classed as a deviate. Dr. Mohr, in a recent visit to Kingston penitentiary, found most rapists there were married men but little further research has been conducted.

Little, if anything, can be done to prevent sexual deviation till family life has been strengthened, says Dr. M. D. Tuchtie, director of the clinic's in-patient unit. "We must break the vicious circle of character-damaging influences," he says. "These are produced by parents whose own thoughts have been distorted by *their* parents."

William Garçon still attends the clinic once a week and is making excellent progress in group therapy. "The compulsion is easing," he says. "I still have some urge but it's easy to control." He's been greatly helped by the fact that his wife is sticking with him. His mother-in-law left the house. Disgusted, she tried to persuade her daughter to leave Garçon, but failed.

"Bill Garçon is a good example of rehabilitation," says Dr. Turner. "He shows how, with the right treatment and understanding, the average sex deviate can be steered back into a normal life."

62. LIVING WITH HOMOSEXUALITY*

Anonymous

As a healthy young male of 30 handicapped by homosexuality, I would like to state some of my views on the problems involved, both for the individual and for society.

According to Allen, five theories are worth considering regarding the etiology of homosexuality:

(a) That it is a form of vice indulged in by decadent rakes satiated

*From *The Canadian Medical Association Journal*, Vol. 86, May 12, 1962.

by other sexual pleasure. This view is not supported by clinical evidence about known homosexuals.

(b) That is it a genetic aberration due to inherited and constitutional factors. Kallmann in a study of twins found that if one twin was homosexual, the occurrence of homosexuality in the other twin was 50% for binovular twins and 100% for uniovular or identical twins. This finding appears to support the hereditary theory, but other workers have questioned the validity of these findings. It is beyond the scope of this paper to consider the arguments involved.

(c) That it is a glandular or endocrine disease. This explanation was a popular approach to the problem, and a number of investigators claimed to have found some basic hormonal imbalance but their findings have been largely discredited. The lack of success in the treatment of homosexuality with glandular extracts leads one to doubt that this is a significant causative factor.

(d) That fundamentally it is an acquired psychological disorder.

(e) That it results from a combination of two or more of the foregoing factors.

The theory that homosexuality is due to a psychological disorder seems to be a most reasonable one, but still leaves a great many questions unanswered. It is proposed that the main psychological factors involved in the genesis of this disorder are: (a) hostility to the mother, (b) excessive affection for the mother, (c) hostility to the father, and (d) affection for the father. This proposal seems so broad as to be meaningless because if this hypothesis was valid, almost everyone would be a homosexual. At present all that can be said is that the cause of homosexuality is probably psychological, but the factors involved are extremely complex and may be different for each individual.

Some writers claim that one of the causes of adult homosexuality is an early homosexual seduction, but this seems unlikely as a basic cause. Kinsey reports that 37% of American males have had some variety of homosexual experience to the point of climax. Despite this, only about 4% are true homosexuals in that they prefer and have sexual experiences with other males only. If anyone does become a homosexual after an early seduction, it is probably because the tendency was there in the first place.

In my own case I have been attracted to members of my own sex for as long as I can remember. Memories of attraction with distinct sexual connotations even as far back as 5 years of age confirm, if that is necessary, Freud's ideas on childhood sexuality. I can remember becoming excited by other boys to the point of feeling a sensation similar to the desire to urinate. By the age of about 14 or 15, I began to realize that there was something wrong with my desires and dreams. To all outward appearances I was quite normal, but my desire troubled me. Where other boys were forming heterosexual relationships and going out to school dances, I never felt comfortable when I was expected to have physical contact with a girl. This was in spite of the fact that I had three sisters, had attended a coeducational school and felt at ease in feminine company. By the time I was 16 and in my final year at school, I was very much in love with one of the boys in the class but could not understand why, and was too ashamed to let him know. At that time, I didn't know that there were such people as homosexuals but had worked out in my mind that something had gone wrong in my development. I was having dreams about boys which were followed by emission, but this experience disturbed me so much that I trained myself to wake up in time to control and prevent ejaculation. I came to believe that although physically I was a male, emotionally I was a female, and many times felt ashamed to the point of considering suicide.

I went on to university after high school, but the feelings of guilt over my condition were becoming greater. I felt that I must be mentally diseased, immoral and sinful to have such desires. Plans to castrate myself or to end my life altogether were frequently in my mind. To make matters worse, life at home was not easy because my parents were constantly fighting; the next year they were divorced.

During a lecture in psychology at the university, I first heard that there were others like me. Previously, I had heard smutty jokes about "queers" but hadn't quite understood them. After learning that there were such people as myself, I devoured every psychology book I could lay my hands on in order to find out more about this condition. None of them told me much that could help, although they did reassure me that others were in the same predicament.

I finally summoned up enough courage to visit the lecturer in psychology and ask her if I could see the pyschiatrist at the clinic attached to the university. It took all the courage I possessed to tell her why, but I finally managed to come out with the dread word "homosexual", and an appointment was made for me. The visit to the psychiatrist's office was a nightmare during which I blocked so much that I could hardly tell him anything. But at last it was over. The psychiatrist told me he could do nothing for me at the clinic, but made an appointment for me with a psychoanalyst in private practice. Another agonizing visit followed, at the end of which the analyst informed me that because of my lack of finances, he could not accept me as his patient.

I had never been able to confide in my parents. I had always been a "good, quiet boy who never got into any trouble" and the thought of telling them and asking for money for treatment was unbearable. It still is.

The guilt feelings remained and I still had no answer to my problems. Pressure from friends at university forced me to take girls out an dates, but when I was expected to pet them in the car, it was impossible; my social life became limited. Yet despite the fact that I didn't go out very often, I still couldn't get much studying done.

In my final year of teacher training, one of our assignments in psychology was to write a psychological treatise on our own childhood and adolescence, so I gave a full report on mine. The result was an interview with the lecturer. His advice was to try to adjust to what I was, accept myself and live with homosexuality. He even went so far as to arrange for me to have a talk with an acquaintance of his who was "gay". It was after this that I had my first sexual experience, at the age of 22. Psychiatrists I have spoken to since have criticized the psychologist for his advice, but to my mind he was taking a realistic view. My guilt feelings and the frustrations of life made suicidal thoughts a constant companion, and as there was no chance to obtain treatment, I feel that his advice was reasonable. Until then I had not even indulged in masturbation.

During this time and over the next two years, I fell in love with one of the men I had met at university and we became very close friends. On looking back, I think that he probably had strong latent homosexual tendencies, but as he often made derogatory remarks about such people I never attempted any intimacies. The friendship broke up gradually, probably because he felt threatened by his own feelings. During this time I had come in contact with a group of homosexuals but couldn't bring myself to feel close to them. To me they were shallow and affected, and what I wanted was a stable person that I could love and "marry".

I taught school for three years. During this time I was also flying part-time with the Air Force and working weekends in a store. I was trying to keep myself as fully occupied as possible to escape the inner turmoil. But once again a friendship with one of the men in the Air Force was developing within me into something more than friendship. I knew that I was powerless to control the emotions building up within me, and that they could never be expressed overtly. I then decided that geographical escape, although it would never solve my problems, was the only answer.

I gave up teaching, emigrated, and joined the Air Force full-time. I knew that to love the way I do takes a year or so to build up, and because the Air Force constantly moves its people from one place to another, I was unlikely to become involved with anyone. Also, as a homosexual, I did not consider it right to go on teaching, even though children do not attract me and I can keep my overt behaviour under rigid control. This control is very strong. Because of my guilt feelings during adolescence I had tried to kill all emotion within me and to censor consciously all verbal and nonverbal expression. This is what Cory refers to as wearing a mask. The result of this rigid control is a lack of spontaneity and difficulty in conversing or behaving in anything like a natural manner.

The geographical escape worked well for almost five years. Once again I fell in love; I couldn't restrain my emotions but their expression was under my control and nothing happened. The man to whom I was attracted was transferred and I was left nursing another broken love-affair that not even close friends knew about. For the first three years in this country I had no contact with any "gay" life, and after that it was only when I was on leave. The last year while on leave I met another "gay" person whom I felt I could love and who loved me. For the first time in my life I was happy, having found what I had been looking for; even though it lasted only a short time before I had to return to duty, I knew that this was what I had always wanted. But about a month after my return the authorities found out about my friend, his room was searched, my letters were found and led to a phone call to my Commanding Officer. The result was disgrace for me and a prompt discharge from the Air Force; this in spite of the fact that I had worked hard and had a respected and responsible position.

Where to from here? There seem to be three courses open: (a) try to get psychiatric help; (b) give up all ideas of ever having sexual relations; (c) defy the law and live as a homosexual.

The first course I have considered and discussed with a number of psychiatrists, psychoanalysts, psychologists and doctors. Some have told me to seek treatment; others have advised me to accept my homosexuality and live with it. Treatment is long and expensive, more expensive than I can afford, and here a simple socioeconomic factor creeps in. On this matter it is said that "the patient should preferably be young rather than middle-aged . . . the less he has put his homosexual urges into practice the better chance of a cure." The problem is that in the early years of full psychosexual development few are in a position to afford psychiatric treatment. Only later in life, when the individual has worked out an adaptation to life in the only way he knows how and has followed this for a number of years, is he in a position to finance treatment. By this time he has accepted homosexuality as a part of his personality, and Allen describes this type as "too ill, too grossly deviated and lacks the urge to be cured."

Another factor to be considered is the simple one of numbers. If Kinsey's figure of the number of homosexuals can be applied to this country, there are about 350,000 male and female homosexuals between the ages of 15 and 60 years in Canada. This is a staggering figure, and if they all sought treatment it would probably take up the working time of all the therapists in the country. Finally, in reviewing the literature on the subject, most psychiatrists report results that are not encouraging. Wolberg reports that "These conditions [sexual deviations] are among the most difficult of all syndromes to treat . . . . In treating perversions, the therapist must prepare himself for a long struggle. Resistances are usually intense . . . . While the ultimate outlook is not as favourable as in other problems, there is no reason why patients who become motivated . . . cannot achieve a good result." Thus, I could obtain treatment if I had the money, but there would not be much cause for optimism about the results.

Most psychiatrists will probably read in this a lack of motivation, and they are probably right. But what provides the motivation? Is the homosexual's predicament comparable to that of the alcoholic who has to lose everything in life and "hit bottom" before motivation is achieved? But the alcoholic who is drinking is destroying himself and hurting those around him. Whom would I be hurting if I lived as a homosexual? I can see nothing basically bad or sinful in homosexuality. I do not want to hurt anyone in my adjustment to life. A "marriage" such as the one I desire would be more difficult than a normal marriage, but it would make two people very happy and would hurt no one. Such marriages are known in "gay" life and they do work.

Again referring to Wolberg's text, it is stated that "they [perversions] serve as avenues of discharge of deep needs other than sexual." While this is in keeping with my personal experience, it still does not follow that homosexuality is wrong. In considering "straight" people who are married, Kinsey has shown that the amount of sexual deviation as defined by the legal code is high, and that these people are using sex as "a discharge of deep needs other than sexual". They are adjusting to the minor maladjustments that constitute part of their personalities. No one is perfectly normal in every aspect and it seems to me that we can and must accept a less-than-perfect adjustment provided that society does not suffer in the process.

A charge usually levelled against homosexuals by many is that homosexuality is usually associated with other abnormalities. Granted that the incidence of neuroses, psychoses and suicide in homosexuals is higher than normal, could it not be that these aberrations are caused by the difficulties the invert has to face? The majority of inverts battle through a very difficult life trying to adjust, and fact that in most cases they make a reasonable go of it argues for their mental health. In my case, attempts at self-analysis carried on over the years have understandably not been effective, and even with the help of a number of LSD-25 experiences I could find greater self-acceptance but could not even approach the core of the problem.

The second approach to my problem, to adjust to my abnormality but never to enter into any sexual relationships, I have also considered. I have told myself that if priests and nuns can cut themselves off from "sex", then I could too, but the sex drive is extremely powerful when frustrated for no apparently good reason. It is easy for a psychiatrist to tell me to give up sex completely, and then go home to his wife. If there are thousands of others like me, why is this necessary? The only answer I ever get is "because it's the law". Another suggestion has been to sublimate my sexual desires into socially acceptable forms, but sublimation is on an unconscious level and my desires are very much within the conscious.

The third approach, to live quietly and discreetly as a homosexual is the course I would like to follow, but the law forbids it. I have already gone through the disgrace and humiliation of being exposed and dismissed from employment. This was not for some specific act, but just for being what I am. Living under the constant threat of disgrace, imprisonment and loss of employment is not a pleasant way to live. The law in this country forbids, on pain of 10 years' imprisonment and whipping, one man having relations with another even if both parties are in consent and the act is in private. The law regards such an act as "unnatural"; but this I am unable to understand because to me it would be natural whereas a heterosexual relationship would be unnatural. Incidentally, there is no such law for women. The Wolfenden Report strongly recommended that homosexual behaviour between consenting adults in private should no longer be regarded as a criminal offence. The Church of England does not regard homosexuality as a sin and has recommended a change in the law in this respect. Almost every book written on the subject by professional authorities likewise advocates such a change. Why has there been no action on these recommendations? I think the answer to this question was summed up by Mr. R. A. Butler, the Home Secretary, when he said that the issues raised by the Wolfenden Report are in advance of public opinion in England.

Society is strong in its condemnation of homosexuality, but the majority of homosexuals are unobtrusive and ask just to be left alone. I am not asking for a miraculous change in society's attitudes, but I do ask support, from those who are in a position to give it, for a more enlightened legal code. The laws dealing with this matter make blackmail a lucrative business for unscrupulous people and also preclude a homosexual from holding a job of worth. Modern versions of witch-hunting are carried on in both government and private business. In this respect the statement of the United States Civil Service Commission with regard to the employment of homosexuals is typical: "There is no place in the United States Government for persons who violate the laws or the accepted standards of morality, or who otherwise bring discredit to the Federal service by infamous or scandalous personal conduct." This Committee stated that its primary objective was "to determine the extent of the employment of homosexuals . . . in Government; to consider reasons why their employment by the Government is undesirable; and to examine into the efficiency of methods used in dealing with the problem".

CONCLUSION

Where does this lead me? I don't know. With the law as it stands, it can only lead to a constant fear of being found out and imprisoned; or to a very lonely existence made lonelier by the knowledge that there are thousands like me forced to suppress, reject, and feel guilty about emotions that we had no part in creating and have no power to direct. We can control our overt behaviour but it makes us less human and there does not seem to be any good reason why this should be necessary except that "it's against the law". The only conclusion to which such reasoning leads me is that it is wrong because it is against the law, and it is against the law because it is wrong.

This problem, which so often confronts physicians and psychiatrists, is a cause of much unhappiness. Most workers admit that their knowledge of the problem is meagre, so is it not time to rescue it from the morass of Victorian taboo? It has not been the aim of this article to criticize the medical and other professional workers in the field of mental illness, for whom I have the highest regard, but to draw the attention of the profession to the problem through personal testimony. Progress can only come after all concerned discuss it freely, so that a more enlightened view can be achieved. Continued study directed toward revision of existing laws and education, to disperse the general prejudice against the publication of authoritative information, may stimulate much-needed research into the nature and causes of homosexuality. The amount of human suffering caused by this affliction certainly warrants the undertaking of extensive research. Given freedom, there are many who would gladly work to help others similarly afflicted.

SELECTED BIBLIOGRAPHY

Fulford, R., "What We Can Learn from the Tragic History of a Sex Criminal," *Maclean's Magazine*, September 21, 1963.

Lexnoff, M., and Westley, W. A., "The Homosexual Community," *Social Problems*, Vol. 3, April, 1956.

Report of the Royal Commission on the Criminal Law Relating to Criminal Sexual Psychopaths, Queen's Printer, 1958.

Sturup, G. K., "Correctional Treatment and the Criminal Sexual Offender," *The Canadian Journal of Corrections*, Vol. 3, July, 1961.

Turner, R. E., "The Group Treatment of Sexual Deviations," *The Canadian Journal of Corrections,* Vol. 3, October, 1961.

Turner, R. E., Hutchison, H. C., and O'Donnell, L., "The Forensic Clinic of Toronto Psychiatric Hospital," *The Canadian Journal of Corrections*, Vol. 1, October, 1958.

chapter thirteen

CRIME AND DELINQUENCY

Unquestionably the problems of crime and delinquency, and the subsequent difficulties involved in the areas of penology and corrections, are among the most important in our society. According to the most recent figures presented in *Canada Year Book* these were, in 1960, 35,443 adults convicted of *indictable offences* (which excludes all minor, traffic and civil convictions), and a year-end total of 6,344 adults in Canadian penitentiaries. Another 10,896 were in reformatories and jails. All of these figures are increases over previous years.

The number of legally defined juvenile delinquents (who would be under the age of 16, 17 or 18 depending upon provincial definition) totalled 13,965 in 1960, more than twice the number recorded a decade before. Training schools for boys and girls in 1960 held a total of 3,388.

These figures, while giving some indication of the seriousness of the crime problem, probably represent only a fraction of the actual occurrences of criminal and delinquent behaviour in the nation, since they are drawn from among the last stages of the judicial process. Another rough indicant of the scope of the problem is the huge volume of literature which continuously appears in books, magazines, professional journals and newspapers dealing with various phases of criminality, delinquency, penology and correctional services. These media, however, tend to emphasize subjects of popular interest and consequently yield a rather distorted picture of the nature of the crime problem.

The six articles which make up this chapter are not intended to "represent" this many-faceted social problem, but simply to sample some aspects of it. The important question of "The Persistent Offender" is explored in the first article, by Dr. Bruno M. Cormier and associates. This is a report on the following factors as they relate to the recidivist or criminal repeater: family and social background, education and intelligence, work history, sentences imposed, record of violence and the offender's attitude toward sentencing.

Stuart Jaffary, a professor at the University of Toronto School of Social Work, offers some challenging commentary on the current Canadian system of criminal law in the selection entitled "A 'System' Riven by Conflict". He charges that "our archaic 'system' of the criminal law is the major contributor to delinquency in Canada", and goes on to discuss the implications of his claim, especially with regard to the Juvenile Delinquency Act and the Juvenile Courts.

At this point the "History of Treatment in Canadian Penitentiaries" up until 1953 is reviewed in an article by Walter F. Johnstone and B. W. Henheffer. To facilitate this review they divide the development into four stages or periods: the pre-Confederation era, 1867-1938, 1938-1946, and 1946-1953. This history is brought up to date, in part at least, by J. W. Braithwaite in a selection entitled "The Revolution in Corrections", which describes British Columbia's Haney Correctional Institution as an illustration of modern correctional trends.

The next article turns our attention to the problem of child offenders. W. T. McGrath presents "A New Look At Juvenile Delinquency", which is rather optimistic in tone but points out some of the inadequacies and inconsistencies in facilities for and treatment of delinquents.

Finally we turn to capital punishment, a subject which many Canadians have become concerned with recently. Eric Nicol writes that while he does not believe that the death penalty serves the function for which it is most commonly defended (deterrence), it does exist in Canada as a fact. Therefore, for the sake of argument, he is willing to grant its alleged deterrent value, on the condition that, "If Hangings Continue — Make Them Public". His article, while being satirical and witty to a large extent, presents at the same time a starkly meaningful argument.

63. THE PERSISTENT OFFENDER*

Bruno M. Cormier, Jadwiga M. Sangowicz,
Raymond Boyer, André Thiffault,
Miriam Kennedy, and Anton Obert†

Terms such as the Habitual Criminal or the Hardened Offender are used very commonly by all those concerned with criminology, whether in law and the administration of justice, or in such fields as sociology, psychology and psychiatry. What must not be forgotten is that it is only recently that we have studied the man himself, the persistent offender, rather than concentrating on his offences. Furthermore, the science of human behaviour was not sufficiently advanced to study crime as a human phenomenon. There are many reasons for this new development, an immediately striking one being history itself. During the larger part of our western civilization, so many crimes were punished by the death penalty that it eliminated the possibility of recidivism for many offenders. The problem was thus summarily solved for the offender, and for society. Today, in our most civilized countries, capital punishment is either absent or imposed for very few defined offences, but in the not too remote past, hundreds of offences which we would describe as petty were punishable by death.

The study of the problem of recidivism became possible in our society with a convergence of three trends. One was the shift in thinking from the crime to the offender; the second was the increasing use of deprivation of liberty as the major form of punishment; the third was the setting up of well-documented police and prison records which allow us to study a criminal career. However, we have to some extent been handicapped by the fact that psychiatrists and other clinicians have in the past tended to overlook the field of criminality. Even the ones who are interested have found the study of recidivism a difficult one. The psychiatrist, in his practice, meets patients with recurrent illnesses, and can observe

*From the *Canadian Journal of Corrections,* Vol. 5, No. 3, October 1963.
†Dr. Cormier is Associate Professor at the Department of Psychiatry, McGill University, Montreal, Associate Psychiatrist at the Royal Victoria Hospital, Montreal, and Psychiatrist in charge at St. Vincent de Paul Penitentiary, Montreal. His associate authors (J. M. Sangowicz, M.D.; R. Boyer, Ph.D.; A. Thiffault, L.Ps.; M. Kennedy, P.S.W.; A. Obert, P.S.W.) are all at the McGill Clinic in Forensic Psychiatry.

them, not only during periods of sickness but in health. The criminal, when he is found guilty (and especially if he is a repeater) is withdrawn from the community, and therefore not easily available for observation and treatment. He is observed neither in prison nor during periods of liberty. Only recently have research workers entered our prisons to study men serving their sentences, and after.

This study of the persistent offender is much concerned with the emotional states that precede, accompany, and follow each criminal act. Instead of concentrating on one criminal act, we take a longitudinal approach which includes every offence and takes into account the total life and personality of the offender. We have made a study of 173 offenders whom we describe as persistent recidivists — men who are repeatedly in trouble with the law, who associate mainly with other criminals, and spend a large part of their life in prison. Those offenders fall into three groups:

1. Those who develop a pattern of persistent delinquency very early (as early as ages 8-10), and from then on become juvenile delinquents, and eventually adult criminals — Primary Delinquents;
2. Those who are first persistently delinquent in adolescence, and continue into criminality — Secondary Delinquents;
3. Those who manage to avoid serious delinquency till reaching maturity, but after this fail to conform to a normal social code and become persistent offenders — Late Delinquents.

This summary will describe some aspects of the offender's background and criminality, including such factors as social and family history, schooling, intelligence, work, types of criminality, sentencing, imprisonment.

FAMILY AND SOCIAL BACKGROUND

As sociologists and others have already reported, persistent offenders usually come from poor economic and social background, with much physical and emotional illness; they belong to the under-privileged. We cannot isolate one single factor, even extreme poverty or great emotional deprivation, as being decisive. A social disorder as severe as persistent criminality must be studied in all its dimensions. We have noted, however, that where many adverse factors co-exist, the tendency towards delinquency starts earlier, and the more likely such families are to produce many delinquent sons. However, it is not sufficient to point to negative features without also studying the strengths. We must emphasize that there are many families, in fact the majority in what are called delinquency neighbourhoods, who are equally handicapped, yet manage to bring up non-delinquent children with a sound value system.

EDUCATION AND INTELLIGENCE

The great majority of our persistent offenders have not reached beyond Grade 8; fewer than 10 per cent have gone beyond Grade 9; and, even more revealing, nearly 25 per cent have not reached Grade 5. This poor showing is not for most of them related to low intelligence. The distribution of the intelligence rating of our 173 persistent offenders, taken as adults, is within normal range. Their poor scholastic achievement is an important symptom of their total problem of maladjustment as children, revealed at school in learning difficulties, in an inability to get on with other children, and very often in their poor control of aggressive drives. We have noted that the earlier clear-cut delinquency began, the more serious was the maladaptation prior to the appearance of delinquency.

It is generally believed that the I.Q. changes relatively little. This may be true for those who develop normally, both intellectually and emotionally. It is not invariably valid for our research subjects. We have information of intelligence ratings of some of our persistent offenders over a period of many years, as reform school and clinic records were available to us. We made a study of a small group whose I.Q. testing was very low in childhood and adolescence, and whom we now see as adults. That inability to learn and low intelligence is for some only a symptom is borne out by the fact that in this particular small group the I.Q. level increased remarkably in time, from very low to average and higher. A good number who were diagnosed in their childhood as mental defectives proved to be normal. One pseudo-mental defective was later rated at the penitentiary as intellectually superior.

Another perhaps unexpected observation is that the possession of high intelligence does not guarantee that a persistent recidivist will spend fewer years in the penitentiary than the less gifted ones. Other emotional factors tend to counteract his superior ability.

WORK

The work history parallels the poor scholastic record. We note that those whose delinquency began the earliest generally have the poorest showing. The incapacity to work, however, is not permanent. Regardless of the severity of the criminality, the potential to change with time exists, and this includes work potential. As our subjects spend so much time in confinement, we have studied their work habits in prison and in the community.

There is a kind of feeling among these serious offenders that they owe it to themselves not to work, or that they will work only if they can get an exceedingly well paid job. Some of these men are capable and quite skilled. No matter what the intellectualization, the truth is that they cannot cope with the disciplines and demands of a job. There are others who are prepared to take on any job, even an inferior one, on release, but they fail to hold it, being ineffective and inadequate and they revert to criminality, where they are equally inept and are quickly returned to the penitentiary.

If we take our most extreme cases, we see what appears in each adult life a total lack of interest in work, whether in prison or out. Gradually, work in the penitentiary improves — not necessarily a liking for work in itself, or as a training for living on the outside, but because it makes the prison life easier. Even where there is a first extreme resistance to work, there is a surprising change by the time a man is nearing the end of his 20's, when he may develop a positive satisfaction in some kinds of employment. This again does not mean that he is motivated for work on the outside. Work in the prison and work outside are entirely different. In the penitentiary, work does not involve earning a living, providing for oneself and one's family, taking responsibility, and here is where a change must occur.

The attitude towards work on the part of penitentiary authorities requires overhauling. Work in the prison must be neither a punishment, a pastime, nor a hobby. It must assume the same meaning as it does on the outside, that is, earning, living by his work, and taking responsibility for himself and others.

SENTENCING

The 173 subjects in our research sample received a total of 500 penitentiary sentences. Most of these, 85 per cent, were for five years or less, and ten-year sentences were, as a rule, imposed for offences like robbery while armed, or robbery with violence. Sentences tended to grow longer with increasing appearances before the courts. For example, 75 per cent of those serving a fourth penitentiary sentence received a longer one than the first, and in most cases longer than the second or third.

An attempt was made to measure and compare the proportion of their life these persistent offenders have spent in prison. We have formulated what we call the Incarceration Coefficient. This is a correlation between the total time an offender has spent in jail or penitentiary after reaching age 16, and the time he has spent outside. Minimum figures were used, that is, the exact time spent in the prison, not the length of the sentence, which permits time off for good behaviour. (For example, a man with a two-year sentence may actually serve only nineteen or twenty months.) Nor did we take account of the time spent in the trial wards, often a period of many months. *We discovered that nearly two-thirds of our subjects have spent more than half their life since age 16 in incarceration. More than 30 per cent (about one-third) have been in prison for 70 per cent of their life after age 16, and very few indeed, 8 per cent, spent 30 per cent of their life or less in confinement after this age.* Moreover, the ones who have spent the greater part of their life in the penitentiary after 16 are those who spent more years in institutions, orphanages and reform school before the age of 16. *In other words, those in prison the longest in later life tended also to have been confined longer in their early life.* Most of our subjects have spent tragically few years of their entire life outside of confinement.

A rather puzzling datum in the case of persistent recidivists is that the length of years spent in penitentiary appears to bear little relation to the severity of offences. We are not here speaking of the kind of persistent offender who spends a large part of his life in short prison terms for vagrancy, loitering, and other petty offences, but of those who receive penitentiary sentences for infractions like simple theft, breaking and entry, theft of auto, up to robbery while armed or with violence. Men can spend as long years in penitentiary for a succession of relatively minor offences as those who commit very major ones.

Having established the proportion of life spent in prison, an attempt was made to establish the time a criminal spends in liberty between sentences. We can give only an approximate picture as our figures on length of time spent in liberty are conservative, based on official records, and leaving out periods, frequently long, spent awaiting trial and sentence. Our data indicates that the majority of offenders below the age of 30 lived only *18 months or less in liberty between prison or penitentiary terms.* However, the picture after age 35 changes, and the period of liberty lengthens. *Out of 49 men over 35, 19 have remained at liberty for at least three years, twice as long a period as the under-30 group. In the 20-30 age group, only 6 men out of 89 succeeded in attaining this 3-year figure.* We consider this finding of great importance, confirming our view that the propensity for crime decreases, as shown by the fact that a man is able to stay out of trouble for longer periods as he grows older.

VIOLENCE

The image of the persistent offender as a violent man is commonly held. We studied our 173 offenders in three groups:

1. Those who never resorted to violence;
2. Those who, although basically non-violent, committed the occasional violent act; and
3. Those whose crimes were exclusively or predominantly violent.

It should be added that an offender is considered violent if he carries an offensive weapon, whether or not violence is committed. In our sample, 83 (that is, 45 per cent) showed no violence whatever, and 23 could be classed as basically non-violent.

Of the 83 non-violent, 45 were below age 30 and 38 were above. The factor of age must be taken into consideration, and the possibility that offenders under age 30 may become violent later in their criminal career. We have noted, however, that for those who are first violent after age 30, the quality differs from offenders with a consistent history of violence. It is much closer to the kind found in the incidental offender, who in a state of depression, or out of despair, may commit a violent act. For the offenders under 30 who have been occasionally violent, it is difficult to predict at this stage what their future will be. A trend emerges, however, that the ones who have seldom used violence early will not tend to resort to it later. *This contradicts the generally-held belief that sooner or later a recidivist will resort to violence as his mode of criminality.*

ATTITUDE TO SENTENCING

The attitude of prisoners towards their sentences was studied. Their widespread feeling that they are sentenced on their record is confirmed in our data. It remains that for certain types of recidivists, the sentence is based not entirely on the offence as on the whole previous record. A persistent offender, therefore, could spend most of his life in a penitentiary, regardless of whether he commits very serious offences which are highly detrimental to society or much less dangerous ones. In our sample, of the 173 subjects, we found that for an offender, after his first penitentiary offence (usually before age 20), the chances for his receiving anything less than another penitentiary sentence are small, irrelevant of the seriousness of the offence. There is at present in sentencing a shift from the traditional practice of sentencing a crime to sentencing by the previous criminal record. The use of the criminal record can represent an advance only if the total life of the man is also examined as a point of departure for a meaningful punishment and treatment, along with the number of previous convictions. This is a contemporary trend but it is certainly not reflected in our sample.

COMMENTS ON OUR FINDINGS

We are accustomed to thinking of an offender in a single dimension as one who repetitively breaks the law. We tend to assume that his whole life centres about his criminality. This is far from the whole story. We believe that the criminality in persistent criminals is only one manifestation of an emotional disorder involving the whole personality.

A persistent recidivist differs from other deviant personalities in that, among the many other anomalies in his makeup, the one that makes him different and outcast is his recurrent anti-social behaviour. Society takes measures to deal with this particular aspect and concentrates on this area. The persistent offender is isolated and this is one of the reasons why he is difficult to reach for the psychiatrist and clinician. Recurrence is not in itself a state exclusive to criminal behaviour. Recurrent depressions and repetitive neurotic conditions are well known to psychiatrists. They have been able to study them and observe the patient before, during and after their breakdowns; in health as well as in sickness. As a result, preventive and therapeutic measures are available. Above all, in contemporary psychiatric thinking, the prejudice no longer exists that if patients have been ill once or twice, they must be labeled forever as psychiatric cases. A different attitude holds for the persistent offender. He is believed to be a chronic and permanent state, without alternation between anti-social behaviour and periods when he is law-abiding.

This assumption is not too reasonable in the light of statistics which show that recidivists spend most of their adult life, and often a great part of their youth, in institutions. They can, therefore, hardly be continuously anti-social, having been removed from society. The classic reply to this is that if they were not removed, they would be permanently and continuously criminal.

A refutation of such attitudes can be possible only in the close observation of the persistent recidivist, both in prison and between sentences in free society. Our research had this in mind, and our aim was to study such offenders not only in the penitentiary, but to follow them after. We could then determine whether there were shifts, that is, whether there were what might be called peaks of a drive to criminality and periods of subsidence.

As every individual is unique, we have seen a variety of states and many shadings. There are also fluctuations and a change with the passing of time, and the serving of many sentences. Nevertheless, there is a consistent pattern. Let us look at a man in his late 20's who has spent most of his life in institutions. He may be a good prisoner, a well-behaved citizen of the penal community he inhabits; he may even play a constructive part in it. Yet, from time to time, he will become tense, depressed, or over-active. Sometimes these symptoms are intolerable enough to bring him into difficulty with prison authorities, who resort to disciplinary measures. We can, therefore, say that even in prison a recidivist does not present an unchanging picture, and we have learnt to recognize, in following the course of a long sentence, periods when he would have been more predisposed to anti-social activity if he had the opportunity. We also see the contrary, states comparable with good social adjustment. We believe that similar changing emotional states correspond to similar episodes on the outside.

When we are in steady contact with persistent recidivists at liberty, we find the same kind of fluctuation. As they grow older, most of them experience a great wish to conform. They even make considerable effort, but they sometimes break down under recurrent stresses from within the personality, which are aggravated by outside factors. For some, the abnormal personality itself is more significant than outer circumstances, while for others it is the opposite; but for all, a relapse takes place when there is a combination of both factors. In a criminal's early life, the character deviation is the most decisive factor, while later on, the environment takes on greater importance.

Since the establishment of probation and parole, the fact has become known that many persistent offenders are by no means continuously criminal. It is clinical research, however, that has brought to light the many drives, both constructive and disruptive that operate in the psyche of these individuals. As well as destruction and damage to themselves and others, there is self-healing. While this becomes more apparent with the years, nevertheless, the potential has been there from the beginning. In taking the history, it becomes abundantly clear that it was not the potentials which were lacking, but the individual's incapacity to use, or even to recognize them, and the corresponding inability of others to do as much.

What do we mean by self-healing? From the view of society, it is the attainment of acceptable social behaviour. We are not in a position to say that our persistent offenders end by becoming what can be called "normal" and well-adjusted. We must study to what extent years of criminality, accompanied by emotional as well as physical banishment from the community at large, has affected the personality and how permanently. Among those who have ceased to be criminal, we are aware of two extreme types of adjustment. There are some people who have made a good and contented life for themselves, becoming responsible citizens, and there are others who, while no longer actively criminal, are socially derelict. We are sure that there are many other possible adaptations, and this will be a future area of our research.

The conviction that the persistent offender between sentences is merely an uncaught criminal is unfounded. This may be true in the case of exceptionally serious cases, but the fact that older offenders after age 35 manage to stay out of prison for periods twice as long as the young ones is in itself an indication of change and increased ability to stand stress. In this research, where behaviour has been followed in the prison and out, we have been able to trace, especially in the period between sentences, both the strength of the struggle to avoid criminality and the temptation to act out in an anti-social way.

Persistent criminality is thus not a specific state, but one symptom among many others of an englobing personality defect manifesting itself in every sphere of the individual's life. The hopeful aspect is that with time, healing forces within the personality come to the surface. A major research project is to study more closely and intensively, not only the criminal behaviour, but all the other manifestations and qualities which make up the total man we call the persistent offender. A real impediment has been the fact that the administration of justice has failed to integrate what knowledge is already available.

Finally, we would like to emphasize that one of our statistical findings ought to trouble the popular conscience — the fact that the persistent offender spends only a few months here and there in liberty up to the time he is middle-aged. For those who remain in prison because they are no longer equipped to live in free society, the least we can do, in the name of charity, is to think of them as no longer habitual offenders but as habitual prisoners.

64. A "SYSTEM" RIVEN BY CONFLICT*

Stuart Jaffary†

In Canada our criminal law and its machinery is in the grip of a serious internal conflict. Its thinking, and some of its practices, are a century

*From *Canadian Welfare*, July 15, 1962.
†Dr. Jaffary was formerly Professor of Social Work at the School of Social Work, University of Toronto.

behind the times. In the rapid pace of today's social change the criminal law stumbles along with a philosophy and policy of punishment enunciated by Jeremy Bentham in 1840, written into the law of England soon afterwards and continued in Canada virtually unchanged ever since.

ARCHAIC "SYSTEM"

Occasionally a member of the Bench expresses pained surprise that our prisons are failing to reform criminals. Of course they are — our archaic "system" of the criminal law is the major contributor to delinquency in Canada.

A disturbing aspect of this situation is that our senior law enforcement officials seem to be unaware of this damaging conflict at the very heart of the criminal law. A "minor" result is that we waste millions of dollars of the taxpayer's money annually. A major result is that we are gradually undermining the citizen's trust in our system of criminal justice. Both results are serious, the first in an economic way (leaving aside for the moment the inestimable human damage which is caused), the latter in a sinister undermining of our national morale.

This deep and serious conflict, running throughout the criminal law, is the conflict of punishment versus treatment.

Punishment is the cornerstone of our present criminal law, in theory and practice. In recent years treatment has at least gained recognition as one purpose of the law — but one to be overweighed by punishment when a choice has to be made, which is frequently.

At the same time we are expanding some facilities for treatment — juvenile courts, adult probation services, the forensic clinic and the parole board — with demonstrable success. But their very success serves to sharpen the conflict with the basic punitive action of the criminal law.

Evidence of the conflict is apparent throughout the whole range of the operation of the law; sharp questions occur at every stage. Police forces have to decide whom they shall arrest, for what reasons, and at what points they shall exercise their wide discretion. What shall be their attitude and policy toward the prostitute? Toward gambling? Toward the sex offender? Shall youths in difficulty be handled by counselling — or by prosecution?

The conflict continues at the court level. Shall juveniles charged with murder be tried in juvenile or adult courts? In magistrate's courts, who shall be placed on probation and why? Who shall be sent to prison and why? Is an "exemplary sentence" really exemplary in effect, or is it merely a defeatest admission of the magistrate's conflict, recognized or not, and his exasperation? What shall be done about the glaring futility of repeated short sentences for inebriates?

In the prisons the conflict continues further. Prisons are obviously intended to be places of punishment, if only by their main function as places of banishment from society. But by filling them with repeaters we destroy much of the deterrent effect of punishment. Many of our prison inmates look on prisons as home and are incapable of living in the free community. Quite a number deliberately commit offences in order to be returned to prison. Is this deterrence?

RETURN TO TREADMILL?

What shall be the deterrent regimen in a prison? Humanity and common sense dictate that the inmate must be given adequate shelter, food, and medical care. What about less basic needs? Dental care is an example. Nearly every inmate needs it, for health reasons if not for his later re-habilitation. But it is expensive. Should we "not waste money on these bums" or should we provide dental service that will keep them free of pain, healthy, and on the job? Another statement of the dilemma is: Does the institution exist for the man or the man for the institution? If the former, it will have a full complement of treatment services, and they will be used. If the latter, all you need is a 19th century rockpile and treadmill.

Within the institution the most glaring aspect of the conflict is the matter of time, the length of sentence. The law, and the bench, following the law, assesses time on a frankly punitive base — small offence, short time; serious offence, long time.

TIME ESSENTIAL

For the institution attempting to operate some form of rehabilitative program, time is the essential element in it. When sentences are short — 87 per cent were under 12 months in Ontario prisons in 1961 — the time is too short to engage in any effective instructional program. If, by accident, the needs and potentialities of the man happen to coincide with the time needed to complete a course of instruction, whether this is the completion of Grade 8 standing or an apprenticeship rating as an electrician, man and instructor are perhaps fortunate; enough time is available for the objective.

But the main result of the varying lengths of sentence is frustration for the institution attempting a training program. The men most suitable for the program cannot engage in it, and the schoolrooms and shops are filled with less suitable students who happen to have been given longer sentences. Even with this compromise their instruction may be cut short at any point by the stupid clemency of a royal visit or a national celebration, the unwise action of a parole board, or other factors.

Even the penitentiaries, which have built sound training programs on the expectation of a minimum two-year sentence can count on the two-year man for only a minimum of some 16 months. For a first offender, subtract from this period the initial several months of his stay — during which he is learning to accept his situation and work in it — and little enough time is left for training. Thus the training institution's fine intentions and hard work also become a partial victim of a punitive law.

"OUTSIDE"

The sharpest point of the conflict comes when the man leaves the institution and returns to the community whether by discharge or parole. The community still resents him — he is the scapegoat who has returned to remind it of its own guilt. He is labelled a jailbird, ex-con, or bum. Doors are closed in his face — doors of employment, association with his former groups — yes, even the doors of churches.

Facing this mountain of stigma and hate, "rehabilitation" almost becomes a mockery because its prime conditions are lacking, namely acceptance by the community and interest in the man. Suspicion and refusal are the ugly realities which confront him.

The causes of this widespread stigma lie deep in the community and in the hearts of its citizens.

But the criminal law must accept part of the responsibility. On his discharge from prison, the law says he is a free man, one who has paid his debt to society, and who starts with the slate clean.

The facts are cruelly opposite — he is a hounded man, with prison memories seared in his soul and all the cards stacked against him. What does the law do to reconcile this glaring conflict between its pious declaration and the ugly facts of life? Is it even aware of a conflict? Is it aware of the hard facts of life which face the dischargee or the parolee? Does it ever recognize that its punitiveness extends far beyond the sentence which the court imposes; that it can, and does, haunt and damn a man for his lifetime? Is this its intention?

So, if the law, constantly asserting its high purpose in safeguarding the community, remains firmly punitive, is it reasonable to expect that the citizen will be otherwise? There is urgent need here for honest and thorough soul-searching into the actual effects of the cardinal doctrine of punishment, the corner-stone of the Canadian criminal law.

Canadians, or at least the welfare segment of us, tend to pride themselves on our good child welfare services. In some areas — child protection is one — there is cause. We like to believe that our handling of the juvenile delinquent is generally humane and effective. Some of it is.

But the conflict in our criminal law is also readily apparent in the juvenile field. In all of Canada, how many juvenile courts have we that really carry out the intention of the Juvenile Delinquents Act? How many have full-time, trained judges? How many have a sufficient and well-trained probation staff? How many have access to clinics for careful personality assessment of the child before them? How many have facilities for carrying out the recommendations?

JUVENILE COURTS

On the contrary, how many juvenile courts are mere shadows of the magistrate's court, presided over by a judge or a magistrate in another hat, in hurried sessions, with time squeezed from a busy day on the bench?

Does the magistrate really acknowledge and believe that "as far as practicable, every juvenile delinquent shall be treated, not as a criminal, but as a misdirected and misguided child, and one needing aid, encouragement help and assistance?" (The Juvenile Delinquents Act, Section 38).

Or does he carry over to it the prevailing attitude and practices from his main job in the criminal court? In many of our juvenile courts, is conviction in fact not the primary purpose and achievement? Does the work-a-day magistrate really accept that the court stands in the place of the wise parent to a child in deep trouble and need?

If he does, what facilities does he have to act as such a parent, apart from his own experience and wisdom? Has he the benefit of a thorough report from a probation officer on every child before him? Does he read it, and weigh it? Has his court, or his community, facilities for carrying it out — for securing helpful supervision of the child in his own home, in a suitable foster home, in a children's institution equipped to deal constructively with the child's needs? Or is his hard choice a much cruder one — thin probation service or a commitment to a distant, crowded, provincial training school?

COMMUNITY ATTITUDE

Does our basic conflict really have to do with all this? Indeed it does, it is central to it. What about the attitudes in the community toward the child in trouble — are they concerned and helpful or are they punitive, either frankly so or in the thin disguise of apathy, rumour, or prejudice?

The child is likely to have been a nuisance — or more. He has caused trouble at school; he is the bane of the local police force; he affronts the community by damaging property, stealing cars, setting fires, and assaulting girls. The community's reaction is likely to be punitive: get rid of him, banish the young punk to the training school — we've had enough of him. In Ontario the training schools are bursting with children so committed, many without even a scanty report accompanying them.

Does such a situation come under the heading of "contributing to delinquency"? Then who will charge our communities with the offence?

NEED KNOWN

Should our juvenile courts do so, as they deal with the results of it every day? Hardly likely, as they themselves are creatures of their communities.

Or our attorneys-general, who are charged with the enforcement of the Juvenile Delinquents Act in the spirit as well as the letter of the law? They seem strangely oblivious to the situation — could it be that *we* have failed to draw it forcibly to their attention, clearly and firmly documented?

If this indictment is accepted, even in part, we will hear the immediate response: "We know we need better services for children. But they cost a lot of money and we can't afford it". The reply is so ready and so familiar! And we blush in shame (or should) as soon as we have said it. Children are expendable, dollars are not. So we go on building more training schools and more prisons.

Forty years ago, in passing the Juvenile Delinquents Act, we congratulated ourselves that we had at last removed the child from the criminal law. What naïve optimists we were — and are! It is again time that we frankly admitted our failure and looked hard at the reasons for it.

Let us recognize that a declaration of intention, even on the statute books of the land, is meaningless unless we relentlessly see that it is carried out. Dare we take an honest look at what punitiveness is doing to Canadians — of all ages?

65. HISTORY OF TREATMENT
IN CANADIAN PENITENTIARIES*

Walter F. Johnstone and B. W. Henheffer†

The success of any penal system must always be measured by the degree to which it achieves its primary purpose — the protection of society and the reformation of those entrusted to its care. The histories of penal systems show transitions through stages marked by brutality and excessive and inhuman punishment to the present stage where more concern is being shown towards individual treatment and respect for the rights of those unfortunate enough to be inmates of prisons.

Canada's penal history shows that many practices (both good and bad) of the American and British systems have been adopted. At the time when prison building was contemplated, the trend was towards the Auburn or Congregated System, and Canada, influenced by those in this System, adopted this method of prison administration. Prisoners were permitted to work together in shops during the day under a strict rule of silence and at night were locked up in individual cells. To maintain this System, it was felt that rigid discipline and severe forms of punishment were required to imbue in the inmate the fear of committing further offenses.

An analysis shows that Canada has developed through four main stages in penal thought:

1. Pre-Confederation
2. 1867 to 1938
3. 1938 to 1946
4. 1946 to 1953

PRE-CONFEDERATION ERA

During this period, the prisons were the responsibility of the individual provinces. It is difficult to visualize a more repressive regime, with concentration on the degradation of the human being and an attempt to deprive the individual of every facet of social living.

The Royal Commission of 1849 highlights many of the flagrant abuses to which inmates were subjected. Corporal punishment was widely used. Of 2,012 punishments in Kingston Penitentiary during the year 1845,

---

*From *Canadian Welfare*, September 15, 1953.

†Mr. Johnstone is with the Department of Justice in Ottawa. Mr. Henheffer is Correctional Program Director of the Province of New Brunswick.

1,877 were floggings with a rawhide or "cat" consisting of a number of strands of twine. With the population then numbering about 480, each prisoner, on the average, was flogged four times that year. This coupled with the complete lack of segregation paints a very black page in the annals of Canadian penal history. This report shows boys as young as eight years freely associating with older criminals and subject to these brutalities for the most trivial offenses such as talking, shouting, laughing, whistling, and quarrelling.

A case is cited of a boy, aged 11 when he entered prison, who has three long columns of offenses and punishments over a period of three years (38 floggings with the rawhide and 6 with the "cat"). Another case shows that a boy of ten was flogged 57 times in eight and a half months. One can only agree with the Commissioners when they say "it is very clear that if the individual was not naturally bad, such a frightful amount of punishment must assuredly have made him so . . . we can only regard this as a case of barbarity, disgraceful to humanity".

These, along with bread-and-water diets, were the formal forms of punishment. Yet there were many other methods of this era which were every bit as disgraceful and inhuman. The Commissioners describe such practices as shooting arrows at the convicts, throwing stones, snowballs, and potatoes at convicts, requiring convicts to open their mouths on the pretense of searching for tobacco and then throwing salt, snow, or mud into the mouth, and "ducking" in cold water in the winter — truly some of the most inhuman practices, carried out by supposedly humane prison officers against those unable to object!

It was shown also that political patronage and graft were common, with the Warden of the Penitentiary drawing up bills for presentation to Parliament by the member of the district (who happened to be the Warden's son), and improper use of prison goods and money.

The general principle appeared to be that incarceration meant punishment only, and that if an individual could be reformed it was only by repressive and barbaric techniques. Any officer who did not abide by this rule was usually discharged summarily or, through a process of false charges and discrimination, life was made so miserable for him that he soon left.

With the appointment of new prison officials, many of these evils were partially overcome, yet the supposedly humane treatment in 1856 (quoted by the new Warden) included 1,600 deprivations of bed with bread-and-water diet, 735 confinements in solitary dark cells, 111 convicts punished by water shower, and numerous lashings.

At completion of sentence, and garbed in the clothing of some newly arrived felon, the ex-prisoner was presumed capable of returning to the community from which he came, able to abide by the laws which emphasized honesty and decency, yet which permitted cruelty, abuse, and dishonesty to be a part of its punishment system.

1867 TO 1938

With Confederation, the administration of the penitentiaries came under the Federal Government. There appreared to be a shift towards more humane treatment although resort to corporal punishment was frequent, and so were many of the other punishments of an earlier day. Although many amenities came with the change in trend, emphasis was still focused upon close confinement with rules of silence, and the ever present conformance demanded by the threat, and use, of corporal punishment.

Speaking at the Canadian Penal Congress in May, 1942, Judge F.A.E. Hamilton of the Winnipeg Juvenile Court stated "the major developments in Canada have consisted of enlightened statements by administrators and commissioners rather than in the application of enlightened policy to curative treatment".

During the years 1927 to 1938, no fewer than eighteen disturbances occurred in the penitentiaries, with numerous small disturbances in the industrial farms and reformatories. These were brought about by injustices in the administration and by the prisoners seeking privileges which in most instances were given them only after rioting had occurred.

Tobacco was issued in the prisons, yet the necessary cigarette papers were withheld and inmates had to use toilet paper to make their cigarettes. After the riot in Kingston Penitentiary in 1932, cigarette papers became an issue and have remained since. Of these conditions, the Royal Commission of 1938 stated:

> It is unnecessary to state that this method of prison discipline is highly undesirable. Good prison management should have recognized injustices existing in the prisons before being driven to recognize them by riotous conduct resulting in the destruction of life and property. Amelioration of the rigours of prison life following these demonstrations indicates a weakness in the prison administration. If prisoners were entitled to the ameliorations of these conditions, the administration is gravely to be censured for allowing such conditions to prevail. On the other hand, if the prisoners were not entitled to the amelioration of these conditions, they ought not to have been granted concessions because of their mutinous behaviour. Nothing is more destructive of discipline than to grant privileges that are not in the interests of the administration of justice, merely for the purpose of preserving contentment among the prisoners. It is equally destructive

of discipline to drive prisoners to violence in order to draw attention to injustices that ought to have been promptly recognized.

The culmination of these injustices, the disturbances, and the eventual recognition of the inadequacies, was the appointment in 1936 of the Royal Commission to Investigate the Penal System of Canada, known as the Archambault Commission, whose report was the death knell of the failures and archaic treatments used in Canadian penal institutions. Its 388-page report indicated the gross error of assuming that reformation can be brought about by fear of harsh, punitive treatment, while the eighty-eight recommendations of the report could be the blue print for effective prisons and prison treatment.

1938 TO 1946

With the publication of the Archambault Report in 1938, changes in the administration of the penal system of Canada were contemplated, but these recommendations were shelved, by necessity, with the outbreak of World War II and the subsequent all-out war effort. It was a quiescent period, but one during which many of the old-time policies of prisoner treatment were evaluated and plans formulated for carrying out the required reforms.

1946 TO 1953

With the termination of World War II, the Archambault Report came off the shelf and shortly thereafter the appointment of Major-General Ralph B. Gibson as Commissioner of Penitentiaries, with Mr. Joseph McCulley (since succeeded by Mr. Ralph E. March) and Dr. L. P. Gendreau as Deputy-Commissioner, heralded the New Deal in Canadian prison administration. The accomplishments of these men in instituting the recommendations of the Archambault Commission are evidence of what can be done, even despite the necessity of using out-moded physical plants.

Emphasis has been shifted towards the treatment of the individual prisoner. Some of the changes include a system of classification, partial segregation, vocational training of those capable of learning trades, and the establishment of an officer training college. But the greatest change has been in the attempt to find solutions to the problems of each individual inmate. Through this system, the convict in our prisons is becoming equipped to handle many of his problems when he is released. No longer does the prisoner leave the prison with a twisted and warped personality brought upon through the brutality of prison officials.

In addition, there has been encouragement to outside agencies, such as the John Howard Societies and National Employment Service to become interested in the prisoner, both in prison and when he leaves, thus continuing the process of rehabilitation and reform until the ex-prisoner becomes assimilated into his rightful place in society.

A medium of expression is provided through the prison publications and radio programs, thus eliminating the riot as the only means of bringing the prisoners' problems to the notice of the public. Sports and hobbies are encouraged in order to give the prisoner something to do in his spare time, rather than having him in idleness or fomenting trouble for himself and the prison administrators.

The philosophy behind this program is that the prisoner is not considered merely an outcast from society, something to be shunned and maltreated, but rather a human being who may be reformed by individual and humane treatment. Many people will say such a system is costly or that the prisons are coddling the prisoner. Certainly such reforms cost money, but if the money and effort spent to place a man behind bars were to be spent on keeping that man a productive unit of society, then the gain would outweigh the cost.

These reforms cannot be carried out without the support of the general public, yet the public must be kept informed. We can hardly consider the historical development and these penal reforms without paying tribute to those agencies such as the Canadian Penal Association whose aim is the reduction of recidivism through a better treatment of the prisoner and the elimination of many of the contributing factors to delinquency and crime. Individuals, too, are making their contribution, such as that of J. Alex. Edmison, whose voice has been heard across Canada in the interest of penal reform and a better deal for the ex-prisoner.

These gains have been made with a great deal of effort and we must be certain that we do not regress. The greatest threat would be public apathy — the taxpayer pays the bill and he should know what is happening to his money. But there are still many improvements which can still be made. Some of these would include:

1. An expansion of the facilities and services which have proven useful tools in the rehabilitation and reform process including the introduction of a system in which more adequate segregation could be carried out, enlargement of treatment facilities, and expansion of the training facilities so more men can be placed in positions where they can be assured of a decent living.

2. Expansion of officer training. One poorly trained, sadistic officer can undo all that a dozen good officers will achieve. This training

could ensure a pool of well-trained officers to take the place of those who leave the service.

3. From the custodial point of view, good officers must be secured and retained. This will necessitate salaries which will attract high calibre men to a career in the service and build up a pool from which suitable officers can be selected.

Canada's penal history up to 1946 was nothing of which we could be proud, but the many improvements augur well for the future. The leader in this movement must be the federal authorities who can advise and assist our provincial governments in many of their problems. In this way, a uniform and humane system can be developed across Canada. Such a system will not tolerate brutality, because brutality is not a deterrent or reformative influence. We must have a system which attempts to return its convicts to society, better men for the experience.

66. *THE REVOLUTION IN CORRECTIONS**

J. W. Braithwaite†

In the past, our prisons resembled feudal fortresses; there existed within them a separate, strange, unnatural culture. Few visitors entered or wished to enter; their inhabitants were able to venture forth only upon discharge. Although supported entirely by the local community, these institutions made little or no contribution to the community life beyond their walls.

Prisons have not been overly successful, because they have been concerned with teaching men to live in the wrong environment, i.e., a prison culture. If we are to break with the past, then we must re-create the prison culture, making it at the same time more realistic and more therapeutic. As Sir Alexander Patterson said: "The man who comes in as a criminal is made into a prisoner. All initiative and self-reliance is lost. He becomes more useless and dangerous because he has cloaked his dis-

---

*From *Canadian Welfare*, November 15, 1961.
†Mr. Braithwaite, a professional social worker, is Warden of the Haney Correctional Institution of British Columbia.

honesty with the paint and plaster of a well-behaved inmate of an institution".

Fortunately, the situation is changing. Public dissatisfaction with traditional methods of handling the imprisoned offender has given rise to a greater public desire for a new approach. The increased use of social workers and other professional staff in the correctional field has brought further pressure for change. Another impetus towards more enlightened programs has been the great strides made by our fellow workers in the field of mental hygiene. A changing philosophy of corrections is emerging throughout Canada.

New minimum-security units have been opened at William Head and at Agassiz in British Columbia, and others will follow across Canada. On the provincial level, Ontario, Saskatchewan and British Columbia continue to make exciting contributions towards the development of a modern correctional program. Other provinces are exhibiting a growing interest. In New Brunswick a new institution is being built by the inmates themselves. Alberta is planning to open five small minimum-security camps this year.

These are only a few examples of the current revolution in corrections, but there is much yet to be done. Many of our present institutions are backward when compared with probation and parole services. The problem, however, is not to remove prisons but to reform them. We take an offender and remove him from his family, his friends and home, and place him in a setting where he has little or no opportunity to exercise initiative, and which gives him even more disreputable associates than he would have in the community. We permit time and monotony further to erode what still remains of his character, and then, on release we ask the parole service or the John Howard Society to make him into a responsible citizen.

We need in corrections the type of social revolution that has occurred in the field of mental health, where obvious, onerous custodial features have been drastically reduced, and the whole atmosphere approaches normal community living and is primarily concerned with therapy.

Men are sent to prison *as* punishment, not *for* punishment. The punishment comes from the loss of personal privacy and freedom — this is punishment enough. All other efforts should be focussed on solving the problems that caused the initial incarceration.

While we agree that an adequately staffed probation service should be our first line of defense, we must have in reserve appropriate institutions to meet the challange presented by those who fail on probation. If we are to return the offender to the community better equipped to cope with his problems, then we must place greater emphasis upon training him to live in a community and less emphasis upon how to exist in prison.

Knowing that the offender will return to the normal community, we must develop institutional programs that are community conscious. We must, first of all, create what has been referred to as a therapeutic community within the institution. This can only be done by making institutional living a much more normal experience than it is today. Secondly, we must be eager to involve the community in our overall program. Finally, we must give the offender the opportunity of practising responsibility and initiative within the community beyond the fence or wall.

COMMUNITY WITHIN WALLS

A more realistic institutional community is not too difficult to attain. Let us consider the institution with which I am most familiar — the Haney Correctional Institution. This is a relatively new institution designed to accommodate 380 men in the main building, 60 men in the Honour Camp, and 60 men in the Pre-Release Camp. The average age of these men is 20.

Unlike many prisons, the Haney Correctional Institution is not an all-male world. We have approximately 15 women on our staff. The majority of these are stenographers and secretaries, but we are fortunate in having three who are social caseworkers. We have found, in dealing with the male offender, that there is a definite advantage in assigning certain clients to a female caseworker.

Sometimes prison administrators create unnecessary problems by over-emphasizing traditional concerns. Thus many institutions are embroiled in internecine strife between so-called custody and treatment groups. All staff at Haney who deal directly with the offender belong to one of two large staff groups — either the Correctional Program Department or the Specialized Program Department. The former is concerned with the general work program, individual lay counselling, recreation, and most of the group counselling program. The latter includes all professionally trained personnel.

As Correctional Program staff become more experienced and knowledgeable, they move into areas of program pioneered by the Specialized Program Department, which is responsible for all specialized services, as its name implies, and for leadership in the development of program. In this way *all* staff members assume responsibility for security and the treatment of the offender.

There are many ways in which the institutional community can be made to approximate the normal community. We must look at every aspect of our total program and relate it to community standards. We cannot merely employ guards, place them in a vocational shop, and deceive ourselves that by doing this we have vocational training. If we have vocational or academic programs — as we do at Haney — then we must have fully qualified instructors who are subject to inspection by the Department of Education. All men completing vocational or academic courses receive certificates that are identical to those received by citizens in the community.

The inmate's individual initiative should be encouraged through freedom of choice. Self-determination should be practised in all areas, whether it be the choice of vocational training, the development of parole or release plans, or whether or not to go to church. Too often, institutional programs create dependency and produce superficially cooperative serfs.

Not only must self-determination be encouraged on the individual level, but it should also be fostered on the group level. At the Haney Correctional Institution the members of each living unit meet regularly in a community meeting with the officer in charge of the unit and the caseworker assigned to that unit. In such meetings personal problems and problems of policy are discussed with equal frankness and freedom. In this way, all members of the community are enabled to play a part, not only in institutional management, but also in assisting each other to develop more positive attitudes.

Each living unit now has a staff team headed by an experienced senior member of the Correctional Program Department. On the team are work supervisors, recreational leaders, vocational instructors, and a hospital officer who acts as a consultant on all matters of hygiene. In addition, there is a Parole Officer who, while not a member of the Institution staff, is assigned to the unit to serve as a consultant on pre-release planning. The final member of the team is the Counsellor — a trained, experienced social worker whose role is to serve as a staff development and resource person.

All the men living in a specific unit share common work or training placements and, in effect, the unit becomes a small institution or community within the total program. Each trainee must work with this staff team and all his requests — for transfer to the Honour Camp, for parole consideration, or for changes in his individual treatment plans — must be discussed with, and approved by, the team.

In addition to weekly meetings devoted to evaluation of the unit community and its individuals, each team spends one whole day a month free of its routine work commitments, and this day is devoted to a planned program of staff development, utilizing resource people from related agencies, the university, and/or the community at large.

LINKS WITH THE OUTSIDE COMMUNITY

Making the institution more normal fulfils only part of the required new approach. We must also make our institutions part *of* the community and not apart *from* the community. There are numerous ways in which this may be done, and one of the most important is to attract visitors for the institution.

The most desirable and important visitors are, of course, the family and friends of the inmate. Considerable thought goes into the development of the visiting programs at Haney. The visiting rooms are bright, colourful, and attractively furnished. There is a notable absence of wire screens, glass walls or other similar dividers. In the summer months, visiting is conducted on the lawn of the Institution and the men have purchased almost $400 worth of garden furniture for this purpose. At certain times of the year we have special church services for inmates and members of their families.

An attempt is made to enlist the active support of the family in the offender's program. When Parole Board meetings are held at the institution, family members are invited. Here they have an opportunity to meet with the prospective parolee's counsellor and the Parole Board and learn how they can actively assist the inmate not only to attain, but also to maintain, parole status.

Another important group of visitors includes ex-inmates who have attained a degree of success within the community. They return to discuss problems encountered "on the street". They also attempt to assist the discharged offender upon his release.

Other visitors include volunteers who come to assist in the institutional program. Students from the School of Social Work at the University of British Columbia complete their fieldwork requirements at the Institution. Outside athletic teams, speakers from the community, and all other visitors enrich the institutional program and make the public more aware of the problems encountered in the field of corrections. Without the support and interest of the local community, an institutional program is likely to become stereotyped and stagnant.

COMMUNITY OUTSIDE THE WALLS

Not only should the modern institution receive from the community, but it should also give to the community. We are fortunate in having at

Haney some of the best vocational shops in the province (14 in all). With the cooperation of the Attorney-General's department and the local school board, we have been able to conduct a night-school program for citizens of the local community. This program is now in its third year and offers courses ranging from home baking to welding. Many of the better hostesses in Haney, when complimented on their fancy pastries, smile and confess: "I learned that at the Institution."

The final step in this revolution in corrections is to take men out into the world beyond the institution. This is the world to which they will eventually return and from which they must never be totally divorced. Re-entry into the community at various times during a man's sentence serves to enhance the possibility of his success after discharge. Movement into the community from the Institution, the Honour Camp and, of course, the Pre-Release Camp, is frequent and well planned.

But practically all institutional programs have their community counterparts. For example, our athletic teams participate in community leagues and play Home and Away games. Members of the Institution's Alcoholics Anonymous group are encouraged to visit similar groups outside, in the hope that, once introduced to the community group, they will maintain their membership upon discharge.

The Institution Drama Group has been active and successful for several years now. One of its crowning achievements occurred when it won the British Columbia One-Act Play Festival with its comic presentation of a nineteenth-century melodrama, 'Lady Audley's Secret'. In Victoria, where the finals were held, the usually reserved press wrote of this success under the headline — PRISONERS STAGE SUCCESSFUL RIOT!

All our outdoor work programs at the Institution are devoted to the cooperative development of a 13,000 acre forest reserve. In carrying out this forestry development work, the trainees have every opportunity to abscond if they so wish, but it has been our experience that a man is able to take much more pressure in terms of treatment and program if he knows that he himself has the responsibility or opportunity to decide at what point he may remove himself from the situation. Many of our trainees have gotten over 'rough spots' in their institutional program on the basis of knowing that, if it gets to be more than they can stand, they can always 'take off'. Their decision to remain is, therefore, a necessary step towards maturity.

The Honour Camp has been developed as an intermediate objective for all trainees prior to the pre-release phase of their sentence. This gives to the individual who has met the challenges of institutional life the opportunity of living in a minimum-security setting, but at the same time, being able to participate in the rich training program that can only be found within the Institution building itself. (Thus, men in the Honour Camp come and go freely to the Institution for vocational, academic, and other programs, and they assume full responsibility for their own security at all times).

If it is felt that a man has obtained the optimum benefit from his program before the time he is eligible for parole, then it may be possible, in the setting of the Honour Camp, for him to obtain employment in the community during the day and return in the evening. Each man involved in this program is responsible for paying room and board at the Honour Camp and for helping to support his family.

When a man is permitted access to the community, he finds it possible to cope with certain of his problems before he is discharged. Some of the men go to the John Howard Society to meet with their wives and the J.H.S. caseworker. There they can discuss family problems while they are still serving their sentences.

At the same time, not all trips into the community are for the primary benefit of the trainees themselves. Service to others is a concept that must be emphasized. What better way to do this than for the men to go out to complete projects for the good of the local free society. Each major unit has a community service project on which the men work voluntarily during their leisure hours. The three current projects are: for the main Institution, the development of a municipal park; for the Honour Camp, the landscaping of the local hospital grounds; and, for the Pre-Release Camp, the development and maintenance of a Y.M.C.A. Camp. In this way the men learn to serve others while serving their sentences.

Most outings from the Pre-Release Camp focus on the day of release. In this minimum-security camp men serve the final portion of their sentence. They work to a large extent under the supervision of staff from the Department of Recreation and Conservation in the development of Garibaldi Park. In this way, they are conditioned to work under the direction of a person who is primarily interested in production rather than in the personal, positive development of the worker himself. This helps in the transition from the therapeutic community to the competitive community we all know.

All men in the Pre-Release Camp go to the National Employment Service offices prior to release and register for employment. Occasionally, a man will be permitted to go to the office of a prospective employer without an escort. Once the employer gets over his initial surprise, he realizes that this approach is the best recommendation that can be given to the trainee.

If a man finds employment before discharge, he may, with the cooperation of the B.C. Board of Parole, shorten his stay at the Pre-Release Camp by as much as one month. This serves as an incentive for the man and his family to cooperate actively with the Parole Officer in finding suitable employment for the day of his discharge. In these times, when unemployment is still fairly high, our goal is for each man to have a job by the time he leaves. Despite periods of economic depression, and despite the lingering prejudice against hiring ex-inmates, we have been able to find jobs for roughly two-thirds of the men discharged.

This movement to the community is the final test, not only of the inmate's sentence, but also of the 'new look' in Corrections.

If we are to develop this new approach, we must reflect community conditions in a more realistic way within our institutions. The public must see the Institution as part of *their* community. And the offender should be permitted the occasional return to the outer world in order to maintain the bridge between the prison and the public.

All institution personnel face limitations in their efforts to be progressive. Few people are more dedicated than those who work in corrections. They suffer set-backs but they continue to do the job. Their progress is limited by their budgets, the maturity of the inmates for whom they are responsible, and the degree of public support. However, there is a growing desire for change in our approach to the imprisoned offender, which, while exemplified in the Haney program, is not exclusive to it.

If you find correctional workers in institutions looking a little more hopeful these days, in spite of the fact that, owing to the increased use of probation services, they have a somewhat more difficult group of offenders with whom to work, you will, I am sure, be able to understand why.

67. A NEW LOOK AT JUVENILE DELINQUENCY*

W. T. McGrath†

Before the beginning of the present century, child offenders were dealt with in much the same way as adults. They were subject to the same laws, their cases were heard in the same courts, and they suffered the same punishments. (Some shocking examples of the results can be seen in the early records of Kingston Penitentiary.) In 1893 the province of Ontario passed the Children's Protection Act, which provided for the establishment of children's aid societies and for commitment to them of neglected and delinquent children by court order. The following year the federal parliament passed an act to provide for the private trial of offenders under 16 and for their detention prior to sentence separate from older prisoners. Canada's first comprehensive Juvenile Delinquents Act was passed in 1908, and was replaced in 1929 by the Act that is still in force.

The effect of these developments was that juvenile delinquency was separated from adult crime, with its own philosophy, its own legislation, its own courts, and its own treatment services. The time now seems ripe to review what thirty years of experience has taught us. (It should be emphasized that this study is not made timely by any deterioration of the delinquency situation in Canada. There has been no increase in the delinquency rate in this country since the end of the last war.)

The first and most fundamental problem to be solved is when a child should be considered delinquent, and when he should be considered neglected, disturbed or defective.

The fact that a child has committed an act which is technically against the law does not mean that the best approach to him is as a delinquent. He may be a mentally retarded child who does not understand the seriousness of what he has done. He may be an emotionally disturbed child who is best dealt with by a child guidance clinic. He may be a child whose parents are not giving him proper care, and his great need may be for substitute parents. To deal with one of these children as a delinquent may not only mean a failure to give him what he needs, but it may do unnecessary harm by giving him a reputation to live up to.

*From *The Canadian Forum*, Vol. 42, June 1962.
†Mr. McGrath is Executive Secretary of the Canadian Corrections Association, Ottawa, and author of a number of books and articles in the area of crime, delinquency and corrections.

Then, too, there are many normal, well-behaved children who commit technical delinquencies that can and often do land them in juvenile court. No child grows up without getting involved in some of the simple acts that are against the law, and to brand these children delinquents can be a dangerous mistake.

How, then, do we separate those various categories? A useful beginning would be to raise the lower age limit used in defining juvenile. At present the age is 7, and any child of that age or over may be declared delinquent. There are obvious reasons for arguing that a child as young as 7 can hardly be delinquent in any real sense, and he might be better dealt with as neglected. Probably the age should be raised to either 12 or 13, with the higher age preferred. Of the 11,686 children who were found delinquent in 1959 (the latest year for which figures are available), 12 per cent were under 12 and 23 per cent were under 13.

Another desirable amendment would be to redefine what actions should constitute a delinquency. According to the Act,

> *juvenile delinquent* means any child who violates any provision of the *Criminal Code* or of any Dominion or provincial statute, or of any by-law or ordinance of any municipality, or who is guilty of sexual immorality or any similar form of vice, or who is liable by reason of any other act to be committed to an industrial school or juvenile reformatory under the provisions of any Dominion or provincial statute.

This is very wide. Municipal by-laws, for instance, include such things as riding a bicycle without a license, or playing truant. It is not necessary to point out that a very large proportion of our children could be classified as delinquents under such provisions.

Even some charges laid under the Criminal Code seem misplaced in regard to children. During 1959, for instance, 222 children were found guilty of vagrancy. Surely if a child under 16 is a vagrant he is better classified as a neglected child rather than as the subject of criminal proceedings.

One of the difficulties is that no matter what action brings a child before the court, he is found guilty of having committed a delinquency, not of the specific action. If one child comes before the court for armed robbery, and another for having ridden his bicycle on the sidewalk, both are found guilty of the same offence, delinquency, and their legal status before the court is exactly the same.

These amendments would help keep out of court many children who should be dealt with otherwise, but they would not solve the whole difficulty. There would still be children appearing in court who have committed a relatively serious offence, but who would probably be better dealt with in some way other than criminal proceedings.

What is probably required is some discretionary power resting with the court. The province of Quebec has legislation called the Schools for the Protection of Youth Act. When a child is involved in some minor delinquency, the court has a choice of proceeding under this provincial legislation, which calls the child neglected, rather than under the Juvenile Delinquents Act. All these cases, whether of neglect or delinquency, are heard in the juvenile court; so sorting out the various cases presents no administrative problem.

The reason why the juvenile court was given such wide powers originally was that these minor offences *may* indicate the child is out of control, and the court can then take action to prevent serious delinquency developing. However, this is a perversion of criminal legislation. If a child needs this kind of help he should be reached through child protection legislation, amended if it cannot cover all proper cases now.

There is some disagreement as to the extent the juvenile court should function as a legal tribunal, with full regard to proper legal procedures, and to what extent it should function as a clinic or a social agency. It would appear that the Act means the court to be a court, because it says that proceedings "may be as informal as the circumstances permit, consistently with a due regard for a proper administration of justice." However, this is not always applied. It is, for instance, only rarely that a child appearing in juvenile court is represented by counsel, and when a child is defending himself in court it is difficult to maintain that we have proper administration of justice. The judge, of course, may watch out for the child's interests, but that is not the same thing.

Many people think it is better if children appearing in the juvenile court are not represented by counsel, on the ground that we may give the child a "big-shot" complex. However, protecting the rights of the individual may be more important than giving the child a proper sense of his own importance.

The matter of appeals is also pertinent here. There seems to be no good reason why a child convicted of a delinquency should not have the same right of appeal as an adult convicted in the adult court. It may be that if we were more careful to keep inconsequential cases out of juvenile court, the application of due procedure would be more practical.

Wide variations exist across the country in the way in which we deal with children who have committed an offence. The Juvenile Delinquents Act is not in force in all parts of the country, and where it is not in force children appear in the adult court in the same way as do adults. The Act is in force only where it is proclaimed. This means that considerable areas of some provinces do not have juvenile courts.

This is national legislation and should apply equally to all Canadians. It is unjust that a child in one part of the country should appear in juvenile court, while another child in similar circumstances in another part of the country should appear in adult court.

The reason why provision was made to permit this piecemeal proclamation of the Act was the shortage of facilities in this country fifty years ago to care for children. It appeared more practical to allow those cities that had such services to introduce the new program immediately, without waiting for all areas to catch up. That situation no longer exists. The more populous areas are already covered under the Act, and sufficient facilities are now available in all parts of Canada to make national proclamation feasible.

Another variation is in the upper age used in the definition of juvenile. The Act says that a province may set the age anywhere between 16 and 18. Again, it is unjust that national legislation should apply to Canadians unequally. If a boy of 17 is a juvenile in one province, he should not be an adult in another. British Columbia, Manitoba and Quebec have set the age at 18; Alberta at 18 for girls but 16 for boys; Prince Edward Island and Newfoundland at 17; Saskatchewan, Ontario, New Brunswick and Nova Scotia at 16.

A more difficult problem is the discrepancy in the functioning of individual courts, the extent to which due procedure is followed, the attitude toward treatment and punishment, etc. With several hundred juvenile courts in Canada uniformity in these matters is very difficult to achieve.

Combining a number of smaller courts into one circuit court, conferences and training courses for juvenile court judges, and literature that can be made readily available to them, are all ideas that should be considered in the cause of greater uniformity. Once the question of the extent to which the juvenile court is a legal tribunal is settled, the problem of uniformity would be greatly simplified.

No matter what age is selected in defining juvenile it will fit uncomfortably in the individual case. Children mature at different rates, and some children reach adulthood some years earlier than others. Some flexibility is therefore needed. One suggestion is that instead of a two-court system — juvenile and adult — we might have a three-court system — juvenile, youth and adult.

The youth court would deal with young people between the ages of 16 and 18 or even 20, and would be given greater flexibility to transfer immature youths to the juvenile court, and unusually mature ones to the adult court. This would also recognize that some actions, such as truancy and staying out at night, are an offence for those under 16 but not for those over that age. Also, many young people in this age group resent being treated like children and might respond better to the new status. The youth court could be joined administratively to the juvenile court, using the same personnel and facilities, but sitting at different times, and with more formality. An exception might be made to have routine traffic offences heard in magistrates' court.

Under the present system some flexibility is provided in the power given the juvenile court to transfer a child over 14 who has committed an indictable offence to the adult court if that seems indicated. However, great variation exists in the application of this power.

Whether the individual's juvenile court record should be made available to the adult court if he is convicted there after he becomes an adult is also subject for debate. If the jury or magistrate is to assess the kind of treatment the individual needs he must have all pertinent information before him, and obviously the juvenile record is an important part of that information. On the other hand, the confidentiality of juvenile records is vigorously maintained for good reason, and even this much of an exception is considered by many people to be a dangerous precedent.

No service set up to solve a major social problem such as delinquency can hope to be effective unless it is staffed by fully qualified personnel. Such personnel are not now available in sufficient numbers.

Some of the required personnel must be university trained, and the federal government might consider making bursaries available for this purpose, along with supporting grants to the universities so they can expand their facilities. The government might also consider setting up a technical institute to train staff who do not require university training. Hopefully this would be available to all provinces, perhaps on some charge-for-service basis.

Canada has a rather good record in delinquency, compared to other countries. However, there is no room for complacency and we will maintain our record only if we constantly strive to better our services.

68. IF HANGINGS CONTINUE —
MAKE THEM PUBLIC*

Eric Nicol†

TORONTO (CP) — A record crowd of 28,000 last night watched Joseph Doaks die on the gallows in Varsity Stadium. The first person to be publicly hanged under floodlights — to accommodate those fans who work during the day — Doaks met death calmly.

    The event was televised by the CBC for out-of-town viewers, and in the ratings topped Ed Sullivan's show . . .

Facetious? Not at all.

I suggest that the public hanging is the logical desideratum for those who would retain capital punishment as a deterrent — still a majority of Canadian citizens, according to the most recent public-opinion polls.

It is true that lately the Governor-General-in-Council has commuted to life imprisonment about ninety percent of death sentences. But Mr. Justice A. M. Manson of B.C. has damned this practice as flouting the law of the land, which is firmly backed by the belief, virile both in parliament and among the public at large, that the death penalty must be kept on the books for its effect as a deterrent.

NO OTHER DEFENSE

No other argument for c.p. remains respectable. The eye-for-an-eye chestnut has been generally repudiated as an attempt to find divine sanction for an act of pure revenge. As chastisement the death penalty is even less defensible, being a corrective whose benefits to the offender are singularly short-lived.

In short, unless it is a deterrent the gallows — or the electric chair, or the gas chamber — is nothing. Nothing, that is, but a brutal vengeance, a killing whose agony of suspense far exceeds as torture anything the condemned person may have perpetrated.

Then should not the deterrent be as widely publicized as possible? If the state is to take a human life, should not this precious appropriation be exploited to the full measure of its value as a warning?

*From *Maclean's Magazine*, August 1, 1959.

†Mr. Nicol, newspaper columnist and free-lance writer, is the author of eleven books of humour, three of which won the Leacock Award for Humour. His home is in Vancouver.

Our medieval ancestors were more sensible about this, not only hanging their victims in public but also drawing and quartering them. Cutting down the hanged man while there was still the breath of life in him, disenboweling and dismembering him — who could ask for a more specific deterrent than this?

Yet, on evidence, these grisly exhibitions did nothing to discourage crimes of murder and theft among the rowdies, or treason in the mighty. As Arthur Koestler reminds us in his *Reflections on Hanging,* at that time when thieves were hanged for their crime, the crowd milling about the scaffold was thoroughly worked over by packs of pickpockets.

However, this is a departure from the point of my thesis. Merely as an aside I mention that some of us believe that capital punishment fails to justify itself as a deterrent, that most capital crimes are acts of blind passion or stupidity or bank robber's panic that never reckon the consequences. Just let it be footnoted that these crimes are controlled by social, psychotic and economic factors rather than the threat of the gibbet, as is easily demonstrable from the moderate crime records of countries (total: thirty-three) that have abandoned legalized killing.

End of digression. We'll assume now, for the sake of argument, that hanging *is* a deterrent, and I shall try to persuade you, if you are not already convinced, that the vulturous scaffold and its performance should be seen by as many potential murderers as possible.

I anticipate the objection that a public hanging would draw no audience, in this day and land of greater sensibility, and that the public *en masse* would turn a shuddering back on the terrible sight.

However, I believe I am correct in saying that the largest single crowd — well over 100,000 annually — to attend a sports event on this continent is the one that gathers to watch the five-hundred-mile motor race at Indianapolis. This eager multitude does not, one may safely presume, assemble for the exclusive pleasure of inhaling blue exhaust fumes. Isn't the titillating possibility of a spectacular smashup, with racing cars cartwheeling in flames into death and destruction, the main attraction?

Lest it be protested that Canadians do not share this ghoulish delight in violence, we need look no farther than the popularity in this country of professional wrestling, hockey, lacrosse, football and other pastimes in which the emphasis is never entirely off dismembering the opponent. Recently, too, the Ontario town of Lindsay introduced bullfighting to this country, a bloodless variety admittedly but indicative of a yearning for something less antiseptic. The public hanging would almost certainly catch the fancy of these hot-blooded people of southern Ontario.

Please understand: I am not suggesting that the public's behavior at a hanging should be in bad taste. Popcorn and soda-pop sellers could not be tolerated, difficult though it might be to keep them out of the grandstand. No admission could be charged for such an affair, and it might help to maintain a high tone by opening and closing with the massed singing of hymns. Those of the public who will balk at attending the public hanging, on grounds of indulging a base curiosity, will be able to find in the television broadcast the same comfortable privacy, without loss of dignity, presently enjoyed by our white-haired little old ladies who ogle the televised efforts of Whipper Billy Watson to disjoint Nature Boy.

A mere novelty, you say? People would soon tire of the public hanging as a spectacle? Here we can find assurance to the contrary, from witnesses of numerous hangings, that the possibility of the hangman's botching the job looms large, and that even those prisoners who refuse to struggle for life before the trap door is sprung will often do so at the end of the rope.

The public has never fully appreciated the significance of the trial judge's sentence: "to be hanged by the neck *until dead.*" As the two last words indicate, death is not necessarily instantaneous.

Those who have read Mr. Charles Duff's authoritative *A Handbook on Hanging* will remember that the clean breaking of the vertebrae is by no means routine in this type of execution. The probability of death by strangulation is a lively one, and even more completely bungled hangings are commonplace. In this regard Canada holds some kind of record, with the hanging of Antonio Sprecage, in 1919, which took one hour and eleven minutes "until dead."

The last public execution among the so-called civilized nations, aside from atrocities of war, was that in France in 1939 of a murderer named Weidmann. The press photographers were, of course, on hand for the event, and the subsequent editions of the Paris newspapers were so well documented with horror that the government was scandalized, accusing the papers of pandering to the public's lust for sadism, with the result that the guillotine was moved indoors. This instituting of private executions was a great help to the Nazi forces of occupation, who had a precedent for cloaking their disposal methods.

Perhaps you still are thinking that this plea for public hangings is a mere flight of gruesome fancy. If so I draw the reader's attention to an article ("Réflexions sur la Guillotine") written for *La Nouvelle Revue Francaise d'Outre-mer* by the distinguished French writer and philosopher

Albert Camus. Bitterly attacking the conspiracy of silence surrounding the state's killings, their exclusion as a topic of polite conversation, he says:

> "It is to the body politic what cancer is to the body of the individual, with this difference that hardly anybody has yet argued for the necessity of cancer."

The awful hush extends even to the identity of the hangman who feels required to assume an alias in his professional career, as though he were committing a crime rather than carrying out the law for which we, the state, are responsible. He is as guiltless as the rope. Yet we shrink from the hangman as well as from the service to the public that he performs. Very few of the eminent churchmen and other dignitaries who applaud capital punishment would think of having Mr. Ellis to tea. Is this his reward for carrying out a duty to the public welfare, a job that involves notoriously bad hours?

Moreover, as Mr. Duff has eloquently pointed out in his manual on hanging, now that hangings are becoming more and more occasional, the hangman has no opportunity to keep his hand in to practice his delicate technique.

Thus our public hangings bid fair to be enlivened by the kind of unexpected development that deserves to be witnessed, such as that occasion when the hanged gentleman's straining neck muscles proved so obstinate that several warders had to jump on his legs to add their weight to the peal of horror.

All witnesses agree that watching a hanging is an experience that cannot be duplicated or even approached by merely reading the press report of an execution. If the reporter who attends a hanging were to describe in detail everything that transpired, from the state of mind of the person who has weeks or months in which to contemplate the fact that he is about to have his neck wrung, to the final, desperate, contorted struggle that the will to live makes against unnatural death — such a report would never get past the editor's desk.

After all, it's a family newspaper.

No, the only way to get the full benefit of the killing as a deterrent is to pack the wife and kids into a car and get down to the stadium in good time to find a seat that isn't behind a pillar. Let's do away with the furtive midnight ritual that is observed only by a handful of men who can't particularly benefit from the spectacle — the warden, the chaplain, the doctor and the other professional witnesses.

Surely the condemned man deserves at least a rousing send-off, a chance to show that, if he couldn't live well, he can die well. Whether or not he feels sufficiently justified, like Sidney Carton, to say, "It is a far, far better thing that I do, than I have ever done," he deserves the right to earn that other tribute, that Malcolm pays to the traitorous Cawdor:

"Nothing in his life became him like the leaving it."

To rob even the most miserable rogue of this occasion for a last bit of glory — is this not too petty a larceny with which we are all charged?

Somebody must pay for our secret feeling of guilt, for our part in taking a God-given life, but it hardly seems sporting to make the hangee contribute.

Instead let's show the world that Canada believes in capital punishment with a conscience clear enough to make each and every hanging a public event.

Let's make sure once and for all that Canada's faith in hanging as a warning to potential murderers is not shaken one jot by our first-hand witnessing, every blessed mother's son of us, the dreadful drama of the gallows.

In his play *Strife*, in which striking workers and stubborn company management grind out a painful tragedy of obduracy, John Galsworthy has one of the company's directors cry out:

"I protest, I protest! I'm a humane man — we're all humane men!"

To which young Edgar Anthony replies scornfully:

"There's nothing wrong with our humanity. It's our imaginations, Mr. Scantlebury."

The public hanging, televised coast to coast at a peak viewing hour, will make it definite that Canada's support of the death penalty can in no measure be ascribed to lack of imagination.

The public hanging will make it possible for every Canadian to assess more accurately the need for legalized killing, both as a deterrent of which not a single case exists of its having deterred anybody, and as a quaint custom which in lieu of morris dancing links us with the picturesque past.

And when the CBC flashes the credits on our TV screens, supered over the shot of men cutting down the hanged body, I hope to see, in good big letters:

PRODUCED BY
YOU

SELECTED BIBLIOGRAPHY

Batten, J., "Vandalism, The Kids' Crime that No One Really Understands," *Maclean's Magazine*, September 22, 1962.

Becker, J., "Lottery in Our Courts," *Maclean's Magazine*, February 24, 1962.

Canadian Welfare, (Special Issue: Treatment of the Criminal in Canada,) Vol. 29, Nos. 3-4, September 15, 1953.

Cormier, B., "Divergent Views Between Law and Psychiatry on Problems of Sentencing," *Canadian Medical Association Journal*, Vol. 87, August 4, 1962.

Edwards, J. Le J., "Canadian Teaching and Research in Criminology," *University of Toronto Law Journal*, Vol. 5, No. 2, 1960.

Fulton, D., "A New Deal for Criminals," *Weekend Magazine*, Vol. 10, No. 49, 1960.

Jaffary, S., *Sentencing of Adults in Canada*, Toronto, University of Toronto Press, 1963.

Kirby, A. J., "The Ex-Prisoner's Second Sentence," *Saturday Night*, March 4, 1961.

Kirkpatrick, A. M., "Prisons and their Products," *The Canadian Journal of Corrections*, Vol. 4, No. 3, July, 1962.

McGeachy, J. B., "Is Our Judicial System Suited to the Ox-Cart Age?," *The Financial Post*, January 27, 1962.

McGrath, W. T., "Delinquency, Predicting It in the Bud," *Canadian Welfare*, Vol. 38, No. 1, January 15, 1953.

McGrath, W. T., *Should Canada Abolish the Gallows and the Lash?*, Winnipeg, Stovel-Advocate Press, Ltd., 1956.

McGrath, W. T., *Youth and the Law*, Toronto, W. T. Gage Ltd., 1964.

Murphy, E., "St. Vincent de Paul; The Way it is Now," *Maclean's Magazine*, September 21, 1963.

Parker, G. E., "Application of the 'New Penology' in the Prison System in British Columbia," *Canadian Public Administration*, Vol. 5, September, 1962.

Phillips, A., "Mafia in Canada," (Series), *Maclean's Magazine*, August-December, 1963.

Phillips, A., "The Criminal Society that Dominates the Chinese in Canada," *Maclean's Magazine*, April 7, 1962.

Sereisky, J. E., "Harvest of Apathy, Juvenile Delinquents," *The Atlantic Advocate*, Vol. 49, August, 1959.

Spencer, J., "Juvenile Delinquency and the City," *The Canadian Journal of Corrections*, Vol. 3, 1961.

Trent, Bill, "Canada Still Sends Children to Penitentiary", *Weekend Magazine*, No. 8, 1963.

Zay, N., "Gaps in Available Statistics on Crime and Delinquency in Canada," *The Canadian Journal of Economics and Political Science*, Vol. XXIX, No. 1, February, 1963.